AF478155

MAKING THE IMPERIAL NATION

**THE LEWIS WALPOLE SERIES
IN EIGHTEENTH-CENTURY CULTURE AND HISTORY**

The Lewis Walpole Series, published by Yale University Press with the aid of the Annie Burr Lewis Fund, is dedicated to the culture and history of the long eighteenth century (from the Glorious Revolution to the accession of Queen Victoria). It welcomes work in a variety of fields, including literature and history, the visual arts, political philosophy, music, legal history, and the history of science. In addition to original scholarly work, the series publishes new editions and translations of writing from the period, as well as reprints of major books that are currently unavailable. Though the majority of books in the series will probably concentrate on Great Britain and the Continent, the range of our geographical interests is as wide as Horace Walpole's.

GABRIEL GLICKMAN

Making the Imperial Nation

COLONIZATION, POLITICS, AND ENGLISH IDENTITY, 1660–1700

Yale
UNIVERSITY PRESS
NEW HAVEN & LONDON

Published with assistance from the Annie Burr Lewis Fund.

Yale University Press books may be purchased in quantity for
educational, business, or promotional use. For information, please e-mail
sales.press@yale.edu (U.S. office) or sales@yaleup.co.uk (U.K. office).

Set in Scala type by IDS Infotech Ltd., Chandigarh, India.
Printed in the United States of America.

Library of Congress Control Number: 2022940662
ISBN 978-0-300-25506-5 (hardcover : alk. paper)

A catalogue record for this book is available from the British Library.

This paper meets the requirements of ANSI/NISO Z39.48–1992
(Permanence of Paper).

10 9 8 7 6 5 4 3 2 1

CONTENTS

PART THREE: COLONIZATION AND THE DISCONTENTS OF

ENGLISH DOMESTIC POLITICS, 1667–1688

PART FOUR: BRITAIN, EUROPE, AND THE POST-REVOLUTIONARY

EMPIRE, 1689–C. 1700

MAKING THE IMPERIAL NATION

Minong

uessis

Upper Lake

English F.

Monsonis

Quebec

CANADA

Trois Rivieres

Mon.

Eko-
ros I.

Missilimakinac

villages

Huron
Lake

Front
as L.

Sautturs

Ouaouia
L.

Iroquois

Puants R.

Kikapous

Otentas

Ilinois

L.S.

Clan

Ma
I

Ihnese

Savage
vil.

Errie L.

Oubach R.

Jam

Ouenta R.

R.

Elinese

R. Wabache
& Iroui

VIRGI

Wany

vil.
lages

R. Vincenne

R. del Crose

R. Iroui

S. Senaco R.

Carolina

Charles
Town

F   L   O   R   I   D   A

R. Rouge

Alton

St. Math.

Florida

R. Maligne

S. Marie de
Palasy

S. Au
gustin

Gulf of
Florida

Ba

B

a. Iroui or

Bernard B.

Bayfoule

Gulf

GULF of MEXICO

Tortugos

Andros

Las Harras

CO

Panuco

C. Conducedo

C. St. Antonio

CUBA

Bay of

Catoche

Tupa

Campech
Bay

Camp.

Camanes

La Vera Cruz

St. Anco

G. of Honduras

Camarn

Jamaica

Xiopa

Andaluc.

NEW

P. Ri

Acapulco

St. Brux. ville

NO.

P. Escondido

SPAIN

C. C. Dios

St. Pe

P. Angeli

Villadol

Guatimala

Nicaragu.

S. Salvador

St. Michel

Euchea

Gulf of Amapella

St. Lucar

C. Blanco

Aranguez

Quibo

P. Mariato

Panama

ENGLISH AMERICA IN 1708

From Hermann Moll, *A New Map of North America*, in John Oldmixon,
The British Empire in America (1708).

Introduction: "This New Nature Come Among Us"

IN 1685, AN "ESSAY" EXPLORING THE "Interest of the Crown in American Plantations & Trade" was produced for the consumption of James II's Privy Council. Most plausibly the work of William Blathwayt, a longstanding colonial strategist and administrator, it surveyed the historic creation of the English dominions outside Europe and examined "the Influence those Colonies have on our People at home."[1] England, the author surmised, had been "infected by Trade and Navigation," with the kingdom undergoing its own sea change as it unleashed its energies on an uncharted world. Of the 200,000 English colonists dwelling in the New World, four in five had left their native shores within the previous fifty years. The newcomers represented such a broad slice of society that there were now "few of the middle Gentry of the Nation if not of the Nobility, but can reckon some younger branch of their family transplanted and thriving in those parts." The experience was all the more remarkable for the way in which it had been accomplished. Most European colonizing powers had relied on state administrations and centrally funded armed forces to build up their power bases overseas. The expansion of England, by contrast, had come out of a spillage of independent trade and travel: "a natural Emanation of the minds Freedom, every man being left to his own choice in a manner, from what part of the World to raise his Revenues by." It was "the industry of some few Private undertakers" that had pushed the realm across oceans and continents: the gambles taken by projectors and adventurers had enabled the

English to contend with the world's great potentates and become "not only their equals in Power & Strength, but able (would the King permit) to make ourselves their Masters."

Yet the "Essay" warned of perils as well as opportunities arising from this achievement. When the plantation of sovereign institutions had trailed in the wake of private initiatives, the extension of the royal domain had come with no proportionate increase in the power of the Crown. Without oversight from the mother kingdom, the English overseas world risked becoming a monument to all the disorders that attended on unchecked human liberty, with consequences refracting back into domestic society. It was the bustle of global traffic, novel tastes, and exotic encounters that gave vent to "that eternal noise and wild manner of talk" among merchants thronging together "in Citty Coffee houses"—many so transfigured by their exposures that "a stranger might believe there was not one Englishman in the room." Carried into the political domain, the consequences were even more dangerous. Ideas picked up overseas had served to feed those "Popular & Republican notions" that had encouraged "our discontented Demi-Politicians" to posture in and outside Parliament, with grave implications for England's stability. After a century of colonial activity, the author concluded, "the very genius of the people is alter'd." It was now in the "interest of the Crown" to revisit the way in which it governed its people, at home and overseas, and to "proportion its maxims to this new nature come among us."

The themes of the "Essay" characterized the hopes and anxieties that had inflected the political and social landscapes of the seventeenth century, as England's relationship with a wider world underwent lasting change. This book looks at how the ripple effects of colonial ventures entered into the political, moral, and religious debates of the domestic kingdom, arousing expectations for its future, sowing fears for its stability, and casting reflections back on the nature and identity of an expanding nation. In 1660, English interests beyond Europe were dispersed and underdeveloped, comprising chiefly scattered settlements, commercial outposts, and private fiefdoms. Over the coming four decades, however, governments endeavored to convert these dominions into a more coordinated base of territorial power. Frontiers were stretched north and south across the American Atlantic seaboard, from Maine to the borders of Spanish Florida. The creation of trading depots, forts, and settlements in India and the Gulf of Guinea showed further glimmerings of global ambition, while the vast resources poured into the city of Tangier presaged new plans for dominion and occupation along the Mediterranean shoreline. The colonial grip over these possessions was secured through an escalating movement of men, women, and children out of the British Isles. Proceeding in the background was the cultural and demographic transformation of great tracts of the West Indies, through African slave labor. Stuart monarchs ruled a political community that was expanding geographically and in numbers of subjects, with far-reaching implications for the religion, culture, society, and economy of the domestic realm.

Over three centuries later, the significance of "this new nature come among us" is still being disinterred. Moral questions concerning the origins of empire crashed back into British public life in the summer of 2020, amid vehement debate over the statues, memorials, museums, and other material remains linked to seventeenth-century magnates who had built imperial power on a foundation of territorial conquest and slave labor.[2] The vociferous nature of these exchanges would not have been surprising to those engaged in the public sphere of later Stuart England. Through the later seventeenth century, questions over the strategy and morality of overseas expansion filled books, pamphlets, theatrical productions, and parliamentary debates. But whereas the development of the English (later British) Empire is still retailed in many public forums as a near-invincible rise to global domination, seventeenth-century commentators saw fewer grounds for self-confidence. In 1660, English engagements outside Europe took place primarily in crowded shipping lanes and disputed borderlands, in regions plagued by skirmishes on land and piracy offshore. Colonization was punctuated by setbacks, reverses, and roads not taken. Regular defeats to native powers and European rivals exposed the gulf between the ambitions and the real capability of the Crown. Even in more settled domains, English governors had created an environment in which sovereignty was uneven, territorial limits contested, and royal authority stood entangled with the interests of landed proprietors and self-governing corporations. Domestic commentators described not a coherent, expansionist operation, but a more fluid and troubling arena of global encounter, one that all too commonly exposed the limits of English power in the world. This book suggests that if England's distant outposts stood on shaky foundations, their development had an equally unsettling effect on the mother kingdom.

The Meaning of Empire in Seventeenth-Century England

Modern scholarship has reasserted the international context to the history of the early modern British Isles. Influential essays and monographs have offered a picture of seventeenth-century English men and women mediating between their affinities toward compatriots, fellow Protestants, and Europeans.[3] Some of this focus has extended to the realm of plantation and colonization. We now possess a rich intellectual history of the early British Empire, and an increasingly comprehensive anatomy of the patterns of trade and migration that made up the Atlantic world.[4]

It is one of the principal intuitions of "Atlantic history" that early modern maritime ventures transformed adjoining regions of Europe, just as much as they altered the New World.[5] The challenge invited by this insight, however, has been taken up less assiduously by historians of the British Isles than by their counterparts focusing on North America. Colonial designs and colonial peoples have been featured only sparingly in the domestic political and religious histories of seventeenth-century England. The expansion of the realm is still commonly presented as having occurred above the cut and thrust of domestic affairs, with colonial policy itself portrayed as the preserve of governmental and diplomatic inner sanctums—that is, as a subject of marginal interest to most participants in the public domain. In many works of scholarship, the political impact of colonial expansion has been expressly downplayed, in favor of alternative ways of positioning early modern England within the wider world. Architects of the "new British history," sensitive to the importance of Scotland and Ireland in Stuart politics, have argued that the language of "empire" and "plantation" belonged to political experiments internal to the three kingdoms, with "greater Britain" possessing, at most, secondary salience.[6] For other scholars, the "empire" that held the gaze of more influential seventeenth-century commentators was the Habsburg Holy Roman dominion, reflecting the primacy of

Europe in English politics, over and above the pockets of territory emerging further afield.[7] A renewed focus on the British and European dimensions to the Civil War, the politics of the Restoration, and the 1688 Revolution has ironically set up blockades against the recognition of influences from outside Europe. In most British universities, the overseas dominions have been researched and taught in the separate sphere of early American colonial history.

Doubts over the political importance of the early English colonies have been reinforced by more rigorous attention paid to the early modern conception of "empire." The term is still deployed with near universality in studies of English overseas expansion—even by authors who have raised questions over its proper application.[8] It does, however, open up multiple problems of definition, as the progenitors of modern colonial historiography, Charles McLean Andrews and George Louis Beer, identified in the early twentieth century.[9] Modern imperial paradigms do not provide an easy framework for examining the loose agglomeration of overseas provinces claimed by the Stuart Crown, with each dominion legally and politically distinct from the others, and all outside the jurisdiction of the Westminster parliament. Neither did early colonization conform to the seventeenth-century idea of "imperium," which, in its origins, alluded rather to the possession of sovereign authority, or autonomy, than to control over an extended landmass. For the authors of the anti-papal tenet "this realm of England is an Empire," which powered the Henrician break from Rome, the political meaning of "empire" equated more closely to the modern notion of a sovereign *state*.[10] For some seventeenth-century commentators, the overseas dominions were emphatically *not* part of the "empire of the King of England," because they stood outside the integrated realm bound by uniform laws, governmental structures, and an established Church.[11] Of the 225 English works printed between 1660 and 1700 that carried the term "empire" in the title, only one alluded to the colonies and plantations belonging to the house of Stuart.[12] To write about the "politics of empire" or to discern an "imperial dimension" to later Stuart affairs, therefore, risks transposing a set of ideas that would have had limited meaning to contemporaneous authors. The problem of nomenclature has compounded a view of England's overseas dominions as out of sight and out of mind—remote from the political and ideological choices of the domestic setting, just as they stood outside its legal apparatus.

The difficulties posed by names and terms, can, however, be overstated. In the seventeenth century, no less than in the modern world, "empire" was "one of the most evocative words in the political vocabulary," as James Muldoon has put it, and a term capacious enough to cover "a wide range of political situations."[13] Looking back into antiquity, early modern commentators could find the concept of an "imperium Romanum" applied by Sallust to designate the geographical extent of territories brought under the city's control.[14] By the later seventeenth century, this variant of the term was being re-excavated by some commentators, as they sifted through their political vocabulary to diagnose the processes of territorial acquisition and competition taking place between states in and outside Europe. For Samuel von Pufendorf, an "empire" was a polity distinguished by its physical magnitude. This type of domain sat at odds with "those Communities" (duchies, republics, city-states) that had formed "when Mankind was divided into a prodigious Variety of distinct Governments," but which had now become vulnerable—"too little since the forming of mighty Empires."[15] For the political economist Nicholas Barbon, "the growth of Empire" meant the extension of a state's authority over new zones.[16] England, agreed his contemporary Charles Davenant, could be called "the seat of Empire" because it stood at the center of a nexus of dominions and plantations.[17] Following the same definition, William Penn saluted "so glorious an empire, as the Colonys of America make to the Crown."[18]

These asides, and many others like them, suggest that by 1700 the idea of "imperium" was undergoing a subtle conceptual shift. The "modern name of empire" was now applicable, according to the diplomat Sir William Temple, to "a nation extended over vast tracts of land and numbers of people."[19] The adaptation was fitful and untidy. There was no recognizable territorial unit called "the English Empire" as a term to unite all of the kingdom's scattered outposts and to distinguish them from the mother kingdom. Even if "empire" increasingly meant a polity that controlled spaces beyond its traditional borders, there was persistent doubt as to whether England actually merited that title, in view of the haphazard and decentralized nature of its own territorial enlargement. But the word was, nonetheless, being applied more consistently within a frame of reference created by English overseas colonization. Rhetorically and strategically, the expansion of the realm was being integrated into domestic politics—with the state of the overseas dominions becoming part of the way in which contemporaries assessed the character and interests of the kingdom, and judged its performance within a wider world.

If it did not meet the credentials of a conventional empire, the expanding community of Stuart England can be examined through other lenses and by alternative methodologies. Taking their cue from the works of Jack Greene and Bernard Bailyn, modern scholars of English America have highlighted the political, commercial, and religious bonds that connected subjects of the Stuart world in the absence of imperial power, thereby challenging by implication the exclusion of migrants and colonists from domestic historiographies.[20] Studies by Carla Pestana, Owen Stanwood, and Evan Haefeli—and, some decades earlier, David Lovejoy's analysis of America and the 1688 Revolution—have recast early colonists not as refugees, but as would-be participants in the upheavals of the kingdom, attentive to the politics of Old England and the "balance of Europe," as the perceived foundations of their territorial security, civic liberties, and religious inheritance.[21] These insights have played a part in invigorating broader new approaches to the history of the Americas. The rediscovery of a "vast early America," pioneered in the pages of the *William and Mary Quarterly,* has encouraged scholars to trace the imprint of the New World's "deep interior" on the colonizing kingdoms of Europe, and even on imperial operations taking place on other continents.[22] Yet attempts to connect study of the Old and New Worlds have emerged overwhelmingly from authors with a background in colonial American scholarship. While the English context has been imported more fully into study of the Americas, fewer historians of the Stuart realm have probed the logical implication that colonial and transatlantic influences could have exerted reciprocal influence over affairs in seventeenth-century Britain.

In recent years, some significant works attempting to address the imbalance have considered the political economy of the infant empire and focused attention on the inner divisions of the mother kingdom as formative influences over colonial development. Steve Pincus has argued that questions over the state interest in commerce, manufacturing, and wealth creation were as vital and divisive in later Stuart politics as were the conflicts over church and constitution, and that many of these frictions arose when contemporaries debated the management of the overseas territories.[23] A particularly rich line of inquiry concerns the politics behind the African slave trade, a source of profit and power that made possible many of England's fledgling imperial aspirations. Abigail Swingen, William Pettigrew, Holly Brewer, and Susan Amussen have shown how the turn toward unfree labor in the Caribbean was shaped by transatlantic debates over law, labor, and demography, which entered just as vividly into the party splits in Westminster as into the politics of the dominions.[24] Slavery has captured scholarly attention as the clearest and most shocking way in which colonization and the power of the domestic realm were intertwined. Indeed, its debilitating moral consequences supply one credible explanation for the peripheral place of empire within many older narratives of England's historic outgrowth as a "land of liberty." But it is less certain that seventeenth-century debates over the African trade gave voice to the full diversity of questions thrown up by English overseas expansion. The creation of slave-based societies in the West Indies was understood to be a *part* of the Stuarts' imperial vision, but only one line in a blueprint for empire that included political and economic experiments in non-slaveholding provinces, territorial designs in places far beyond America, and relations with a range of indigenous peoples, from subjects of the Mughal and Moroccan empires to unconquered Amerindians. Though it was emerging by 1700 as one of the commercial lifelines of the English empire, slavery was not the subject of fierce controversy that it would become by the reign of George III. For all its growing importance to colonial political economy, it contributed less conspicuously to intellectual or religious debate—if only, as Amussen has suggested, because its implications were shrouded with silence or evasion by most domestic authors.[25]

If some debates were circumvented, however, other moral and political ramifications of the pursuit of empire were more rigorously scrutinized. English subjects were sharply conscious that they belonged to a polity swelling in size and ambition. They evaluated, accommodated, and disputed the consequences of colonization, and ushered the overseas dominions into wider debates over the direction of domestic and foreign policy under the Crown. Yet commentators were equally aware of the limitations of the enterprise—the haziness of territorial boundaries, the elasticity in the nature and meaning of empire, the failure of the Crown to come up with any legal or institutional framework to bind its possessions together. To chart the politics of overseas expansion, it is vital to look beyond a recent scholarly emphasis on the reception and transmission of clearly defined ideologies of empire. Attitudes toward overseas expansion shifted subtly in later Stuart England, and often as the unintended result of other debates—religious, economic, moral, and cultural—as subjects searched for the language to judge the plantation process and understand the inscription it was making on their own society.

Continuity and Change in English Colonization

If the terminology around early English colonization remains contested, its chronology has been subject to equally sharp dispute. Particular contests have arisen among scholars seeking to trace the point at which scattered patterns of trade, travel, and migration gave way to centralized, supervisory policies coordinated by the state apparatus. A vigorous line in modern scholarship has stressed the salience of the 1660s and 1670s as a phase in this process. While a vital precedent had been set by the planning and funding of Oliver Cromwell's Western Design, no prince prior to Charles II had "presided over such a profound expansion of England's overseas empire," as Owen Stanwood has put it.[26] Under the restored monarchy, the English created settlements in Carolina, Tangier, and Bombay. Following the conquest of the Dutch New Netherlands in 1664, the court set about the formation of the "Middle Colonies"—New York, Pennsylvania, and East and West Jersey. Grants conferred upon the Hudson's Bay and Royal African Companies took English adventurers across other thinly charted frontiers. Geographical expansion was accompanied by more intrusive measures to control and exploit established settlements—the Navigation Acts, which threw a protective blanket over colonial trade; the development of the Royal Navy and the customs commission; and the creation of Crown councils that subjected the dominions to ever-closer scrutiny. From different perspectives, Alison Games and Stephen Saunders Webb have detected "imperial" tendencies toward centralization and militarization after 1660 that challenged the looser, commercially flavored structures created in the earlier half of the seventeenth century.[27]

Yet the notion of a Restoration shift or rupture in colonial development has been subject to trenchant criticism. Claims of imperial sovereignty over far-flung possessions were not new to Restoration politics. As Ken MacMillan has shown, an intellectual culture to sanction expansion and absolutism overseas, underwritten by sophisticated legal thinking, had been fully assembled during the reigns of James I and Charles I.[28] Conversely, the perilous state of the royal finances meant that the later Stuart Crown was scarcely better equipped than the governments of the previous half-century to make good its imperial pretensions. Expansion, L. H. Roper has argued, still rested overwhelmingly on legally privileged private initiative—partnerships of traders and creditors, cadres of aristocratic projectors, and communities of religious dissidents willing to undertake risky, long-distance investments in land and trade.[29] In the absence of an effective supervisory state, J. M. Sosin has contended, the overseas program of the Crown became inevitably reactive, opportunist, and short-termist. As Michael Braddick has suggested, English governments constructed "the shell of a developing fiscal-military empire," which concealed serious fragilities within.[30]

Any anatomy of the Restoration Empire certainly needs to accommodate the limits of royal control, the ill-defined institutional mosaic, and the elements of contradiction and incoherence that bedeviled many colonial designs. The early English empire was not constructed by a homogenous cadre of officials united in values and assumptions, or common administrative training. Adventurers like Anthony Briskett, the Irish-Italian projector who organized the original settlement of the Leeward Islands under Charles I, or Henry Gary, the Maltese-Venetian merchant made governor of Bombay in 1662, were more representative of the marginal, cosmopolitan figures who brought the colonial world into being.[31] English colonization was also geographically unstable. The coexistence of multiple projects was shown by the continuing hold of parts of Asia and Africa over the political imagination, as potential locales of conquest, commerce, and settlement that rivaled the Western Atlantic.[32] By 1685, Bombay and Madras constituted the largest metropolitan centers of the English overseas world, with populations of 60,000 and 100,000, respectively, and the East India Company ruled over greater numbers of indigenous peoples than all the colonial governments of English America put together.[33] In all of these environments, the power of the Crown rested on processes of negotiation with disparate interests, agencies, and authorities.

Yet if English interests moved across the world in a notably uneven way, the Stuart court remained the vital fomenting force behind most colonial enterprises. Moreover, after 1660, many contemporaries believed that the court of Charles II was developing an interest in its colonies that far outstripped the attentions of earlier rulers. While colonial schemes developed in many different continents and across various sea corridors, these dispersed operations were understood to be linked by a common strategic and ideological endeavor, reflected in the Crown's particular choices in foreign affairs. The perception was due in part to the influence of hundreds of "globe-trotting" individuals—soldiers, merchants, and administrators— who carried ideas and experiences from place to place. But it was also driven by genuine transoceanic challenges, from the connections between the Mediterranean and the Atlantic trade that inspired the acquisition of Tangier, to the problem of American-based networks of pirates who plagued the traffic of the Indian Ocean and bore their looted prizes back to New York and Philadelphia.[34]

The attitude of the Stuart Crown did not conform to Sir John Seeley's famous "absence of mind" descriptor of how the later, Victorian British Empire grew out of superior resources on the ground, rather than any underlying strategic vision.[35] Rather, the course of later Stuart colonial policy indicated exactly the opposite experience. The court and its associated projectors were alive to the possibility of English power outside Europe, and developed ambitious, coherent plans for overseas settlement, but lacked the tools to bring their grander hopes to fruition. Between 1660 and 1700, the fall of English rule over Surinam, the collapse of the Tangier experiment, and the calamitous outcome of the Scottish design on Darien brought the limits of imperial power into the domestic consciousness. Trevor Burnard has argued that even among the established settlements, only Barbados stood out by 1700 as a secure economic success, such was the challenge of fortifying productive, physically resilient societies at a great distance from British shores.[36]

Empire, therefore, appeared in the politics of later Stuart England as an aspiration, more than any state of self-evident reality. Yet the impact of the colonies was becoming more pronounced *within* the mother kingdom. During the half-century after the Restoration, the first Crown-sponsored missionary organizations appeared, in the form of the New England Company and the Society for the Propagation of the Gospel. As Bridget Orr and Karen O'Brien have shown, during the same period an interest in colonial experiences and non-European cultures grew perceptibly within the realms of poetry and theater.[37] Above all, it was between 1660 and 1700 that trade outside Europe became the furnace of the English economy: the galvanizing agent in the growth of customs revenue, and the incubator of lasting changes to the visual and material culture of domestic life. By 1700, the Atlantic Ocean accounted for 20 percent of the kingdom's total commerce. One-third of imports came from outside Europe, and 40 percent of exports represented either re-exports of non-European produce or the dispatch of goods to the Americas and the East Indies. While the capital was the principal beneficiary of these surges, the American trade gave equally visible stimulus to the Atlantic ports of Bristol, Liverpool, and Whitehaven.[38] The colonial world was advancing on the domestic kingdom: its influence registered in the inflow of exotic fashions and commodities, and the appearance of non-European peoples in English ports and cities. With port towns reconfiguring their interests, and citizens hungry for information likely to affect trade, these developments would start to intrude on the realm of opinion and discussion, just as they would stamp a mark on the architecture of state and economy.

The growing entanglement of the mother kingdom and its provinces took colonial affairs out of court confines and into new environments: the realms of print culture and manuscript circulation, scholarly discussion rooms, and public forums for the exchange of ideas and opinions. Pamphlets, polemics, reports on proceedings in colonial assemblies, and accounts of the history and geography of the dominions gained ready audiences in government, and in merchant and gentry households far beyond the capital. Debates about the overseas dominions began to contribute to the expansion of the "public sphere"—an environment distinguished, as Steve Pincus and Tony Claydon have argued, by heightened engagement with foreign affairs, and, increasingly, by an idea of the "the state" as an entity with concerns larger than the well-being of the individual monarch.[39] Many influential printed commentaries were themselves the product of colonial lobbies that were active at court and in parliament, when much of the legal spadework for upholding grants of land and office was undertaken in England. Conversely, as colonial polities matured and commerce intensified, printed works and manuscripts from the Old World began to move along the emergent maritime networks, inviting greater interaction between migrants and the kingdom from which they had emerged.[40] Yet these two-way flows did not necessarily elicit accurate and enlightening supplies of information. "Wee are here att the end of the world, & . . . when news comes we have itt by whole sale, very often much more than truth," lamented the Virginia landowner William Byrd in 1690.[41] The connections between Old England and its colonists were created as much by distortions, misrepresentations, and contested narratives as by clear communication of events. In coming to the attention of the domestic public sphere, colonists were inducted into a divisive, polemical world, and a political culture underlain by caricatures, conspiracy theories, and persistent invitations to partisanship.[42]

Between 1660 and 1700, a debate about empire was domesticated in English politics, shaped by exchanges between the mother kingdom, the colonial centers of administration, and the spaces in between. As a larger proportion of soldiers and statesmen, planters and laborers, merchants and mariners became caught up in overseas colonization, so a growing number of voices subjected it to interrogation. Colonial officeholders, in turn, became not simply local actors responding to regional circumstances, but also contributors to ideological debates played out across vast terrestrial and oceanic spaces. The empire that emerged in these decades was unsettled in its geography, ill-resourced, and at best brittle in the level of consensus that it could command. The conflicting visions for the dominions put forward in parliament and print, in councils and committee rooms, sit uneasily with Saunders Webb's image of a relentless, single-minded imperialism being the prevailing spirit in colonial policy. Yet the tone of domestic discussion conforms no more readily to the passivity and relative disengagement discerned by Sosin in government attitudes toward America. Instead the shifts and reverses in English colonial policy arose from intense domestic disagreements over the appropriate locales for empire, the most suitable methods of colonial governance, and even the rectitude of seeking out dominion overseas. When the maintenance of distant outposts strained every sinew of the Crown's financial capability, the creation of the overseas dominions became an intensely partisan endeavor: one that played into existing ideological fault lines in the Old World, and, increasingly, created new fractures in English politics and opinion.

Overseas Expansion and the Discontents of Later Stuart England

While the shape of the English overseas world had been established under earlier royal and republican rulers, it was the later seventeenth century that marked England's birth as an *imperial nation:* the beginnings of a process that would see the politics, religion, and culture of the country redefined by overseas expansion. Behind the immediate wrangling over colonial strategy, governance, and political economy, public questions ranged over the higher ends of territorial empire, including the enigma of what duties, if any, the English had concerning the non-European peoples who brushed against the boundaries of their domain. While overseas designs attracted vaulting millennial and philosophical hopes, champions of colonization were forced to confront misgivings within their own intellectual traditions. Domestic responses rested on old springs of intellectual anxiety, as authors sifted through the histories of other empires and contended with classical, scriptural, and Renaissance warnings against the dangers of territorial overreach. The influence of overseas expansion was evident not simply in wider and more intensive reflections on colonial affairs. Rather, the challenges of empire shaped the internal dynamics and many of the divisions of English politics. The colonies provided the terrain on which many domestic conflicts were played out, because their distance from the realm made them susceptible to political and ideological experiments not possible within England itself.

The pressures of an aspirant empire were made clearest when contemporaries considered how much England was being strengthened by the reserves of blood, treasure, and people expended outside Europe. Territorial expansion placed new financial strains on an already straitened Crown administration. Continued migration came into conflict with demographic anxieties, as the rapid growth in the domestic population through the sixteenth and early seventeenth centuries ground to a halt. These and other concerns over the state of the colonies became especially consequential because of the political vulnerabilities of the mother kingdom. By 1660, the politics of the English Atlantic world were conditioned by memories of Civil War and regicide, and dominated by the legacy of a failed eleven-year republic. The divisions thrown up by a century of upheaval gained wide scope for expression in America, where dissident communities could wield authority at arm's length from the Crown. English authors fretted over images of un-Christianized slaves, godless multitudes, and violent factionalism in Virginia and the West Indies. Conversely—with an eye to the New England provinces—they warned against the danger of colonial societies reaching sufficient levels of wealth, power, and sophistication to loosen their bonds with the kingdom that created them. Above all, they voiced anxiety over whether England itself could be safely insulated from disorderly politics and "fanatical" ideologies burgeoning in its outworks overseas.

If the actions of colonial settlers perturbed some domestic audiences, equally vigorous controversies arose over the way in which monarchs sought to regulate them. The courts of Charles II and James II used the royal prerogative overseas to a degree unfeasible in the domestic environment. In doing so, they clashed with critics in England, fearful of the implications for their own civil and constitutional freedoms. Through the 1670s and 1680s, English politics was destabilized by panics over the growth of "popery and arbitrary government"—fears of Catholic and absolutist tendencies believed to be slithering through the Stuart court, menacing both the Protestant Reformation and England's distinct foundation of constitutional liberties. In this context, the Crown's opponents anguished over separating the overseas dominions from parliamentary authority, attacked the promotion of Catholics through imperial office, and beat the drum against autocratic forms of colonial government as a potential laboratory for attacks on liberty at home. Empire could appear all too readily as "popery and arbitrary government" writ large. The discontents of the expanding realm provided explosive tinder to the tumults of the Popish Plot, the Exclusion

Crisis, and the 1688 Revolution. All of these controversies were made more sensitive by England's position as one component part of a multiple-kingdom monarchy. Parliamentary insistence that the colonies were legally and exclusively "English" conflicted with the reality of growing Scottish and Irish involvement, and with the claim to equal liberties and privileges within the overseas dominions, voiced by statesmen from both kingdoms. By 1700, the pressures of empire were shining a light on unresolved legal and constitutional tensions, and raising the prospect of decisive change within the state structures of the British Isles.

Beyond the immediate political frictions, the pursuit of empire cast reflections back on England's identity and obligations as a Protestant kingdom. Important works of scholarship, focused mainly on the imperial cultures of the eighteenth century, have seen overseas expansion as providing for the expression and ultimate fulfilment of an idea of English (or British) Protestant exceptionalism.[43] In earlier generations, however, the relationship between "empire" and the reformed religion was considerably less comfortable. The unease arose primarily because there was no single, unifying form of Protestantism dominant within the Stuarts' overseas world. In contrast to its Spanish rival, the kingdom of England had fragmented along confessional lines even as it expanded geographically, throwing colonial societies open to alternative flowerings of the reformed religion. While the Church of England struggled to cement its American footholds, rival Protestants—notably the Congregationalist establishment in Massachusetts—took the lead in organizing missionary work, and in building up an ecclesiastical machinery to regulate colonial societies. Domestic commentators fell into conflict over how far different churches and separate programs for the conversion of "pagans" could be incorporated into Crown colonial policies. Disputes over the religion of the dominions impinged relentlessly on church affairs at home. Colonial experiences stirred new debates over the management of religious variety, over the nature of Protestant orthodoxy, and over the legal and doctrinal parameters of the national church. For some authors close to the Stuart court, the organization of the colonies—with the Crown attempting to establish political absolutism *and* religious toleration—gestured toward an entirely different relationship between civil and spiritual authorities, in a kingdom riven by the claims of competing "tender consciences."

Protestant visions of the colonies sat within a wider field of ideas and allegiances, arising from England's historic affiliations on the continent closer to home. Through the reign of Charles II, the pursuit of empire was played out against a background of shifts in the "balance of Europe" induced by the military and economic decline in the power of Spain, and the new vulnerability of its colonies in Central and South America. "These Great Empires are not only Oppressive to the Race of Men while they are fixing . . . but their very Dissolution is attended with infinite Mischiefs," warned the political economist Charles Davenant in 1701. "When they come to their decrepid Age, they do not, like Natural Bodies . . . fall gently, and by insensible degrees," but "indure many Shocks, Disasters and Attempts" to the disturbance of the polities around them.[44] English approaches toward the New World were challenged by the international ramifications of this change, and by the emergence of new contenders for "universal monarchy" on other battlegrounds around the globe. Maritime conflicts against the United Provinces, gathering fears over the threat to European Protestants from the power of France, and alarm over Ottoman incursions into Central Europe gave rise to competing conceptions of the English national interest. Colonies were relentlessly interrogated over their capacity to protect true religion, uphold "the law of nations," and arrest the ambitions of would-be world tyrants. At the Elizabethan advent of English colonization, the power and wealth of the Spanish Empire provided grounds for seeing the New World as the essential theater for the Protestant battle against "popery." After 1660, when colonial wars were more likely to be fought against Calvinist Dutchmen, and when Protestant concerns were shifting toward a focus on Huguenot, Palatinate, and Vaudois minorities threatened by Louis XIV in Europe, that idea was no longer so readily received.

While commentators debated the strategy and value of territorial expansion, they also sought to dissect the great changes it imposed on their own society. Many of the conflicting images of empire became riveted onto discussions of the material commodities brought back from overseas—the fashions, fabrics, and unfamiliar delicacies that increased the visibility and physicality of the Crown's global aspirations, but also awakened ancient fears over exoticized "luxury" culture. In controversies over consumer fancies, as in political and religious debate, a gulf was being carved out between commentators who saw the kingdom improving and advancing through its overseas exertions, and opponents who fretted that colonization was making the *English* foreign and weakening, in turn, the civil and moral inheritance that supplied essential guards and bulwarks for the realm. Debates over colonization then, did not simply mirror existing fissures in the domestic realm. Instead, overseas expansion became an active agent in the formation of England's cultural and ideological divisions, as commentators strove to understand the "new nature come among us," and contemplated its implications for the identity and orientation of the realm. Many of these controversies were brought home in the Revolution of 1688, and in the repercussions of that event, as experienced on both sides of the Atlantic. The dethroning of James II, and the overturning of many imperial reforms devised at the Stuart court, left the future of English overseas expansion uncertain, and raised urgent calls for the moral and political redefinition of the colonial enterprise.

England in the later seventeenth century did not possess a powerful empire, but it was rapidly becoming an imperial *nation,* one in which colonial influences intruded not merely into state formation, but also into political, religious, material, and imaginative life. The reality of English colonization was determined by actions on contested marchlands at the edge of the known world; its moral and ideological meaning was shaped by the audiences that interpreted and disseminated those events before domestic opinion. This book argues that there was a crucial colonial dimension to many key moments of upheaval in post-Restoration politics, and that the importance of these settings was recognized and vigorously debated by contemporaries, as fragile overseas dominions came into contact with the politics of an equally fragile mother kingdom. Understanding this background obliges us not merely to look at England's settled plantations, but to incorporate the frayed edges of empire—the undeveloped outposts, defeated designs, and hybrid sovereign spaces—to consider the relationship between colonial ambitions and the ties binding England to the European continent, and to examine a political culture within its full global context. Probing the connections between these zones offers fresh insights into the origins of the British Empire. It also throws new light on the country that incubated the colonial experiment.

PART ONE

MAPPING THE RESTORATION EMPIRE,

1660–c. 1670

The Restoration and the Geography of English Overseas Expansion

IN 1659 AS THE ENGLISH REPUBLIC BEGAN its slow disintegration, the colonial projector Thomas Povey dispatched a flurry of letters from London to officials in the Caribbean. A year after the death of Oliver Cromwell, the attention paid to the colonial interest "hath extreamely suffered by our late Disorders of State," he warned the governor of Barbados.[1] Writing to his brother, Richard, in Jamaica, he fretted that no further English support could be promised, since "there is soe great a Confusion, and improbabilitie of a settlement in our Government . . . I am almost desperate of contributing any good or considerable advantage to your Island."[2] Povey viewed the colonial world through the prism of political and personal investments stretching across a decade. In 1654, he had been one of the moving spirits behind the creation of the Western Design: the Cromwellian scheme to shake the Spanish Empire in America by capturing the island of Hispaniola. By lobbying, contracting, and parting with considerable personal funds, he had helped to shape a landmark moment in English foreign policy and state development: the first time a transatlantic military expedition was funded by the central government, and the first time that English rulers had committed themselves to the conquest of a New World territory belonging to another kingdom.[3]

The seizure of Jamaica—a largely uncultivated Spanish provisioning base—was the unintended consequence of this expedition. By 1660, the island stood out as "our frontier plantation," in the words of William Morice, secretary of state to Charles II, and as a means to project English interests onto the threshold of enemy territory.[4] But the Western Design itself had been a crushing failure, and the eventual retreat from Hispaniola had struck a body blow to the credibility of the English Republic. The returning commanders, William Penn and Robert Venables, had been marched through Traitor's Gate into the Tower of London in 1655, while Cromwell himself spiraled into spiritual despair.[5] Four years later, Jamaica was beset by disease, malnutrition, and internal unrest and cut off from its supply lines while Spanish vessels swarmed in sight of the shoreline. Simultaneously, the hopes of the original projectors were running up against a political mood in England that, as Povey reported, damned the Caribbean venture as a monument to "ye Pride and privat Counsells, and sinister Designes of the Protector [Cromwell]," which "have all most ruined Trade, and lost allmost a thousand of our English ships."[6] After the Western Design, recorded John Scott, a scholar and adventurer living in Long Island, "many sober Gentlemen are of opinion, it had been better for England never to have planted Collonies abroad."[7]

Although Povey supported the return of the monarchy, the prospect afforded him few grounds for optimism as a colonial advocate. Under pressure from his Spanish allies, Charles II had pledged to surrender Jamaica, relinquish all other acquisitions made in the West Indies since 1630, and forbid his subjects from establishing another Caribbean colony. In this context, as Povey confided to Jamaica's governor, Edward D'Oyley, the best hope for the island was to "be honirably deserted" rather than "bee dishonourably neglected and bee left a Prey" to the waiting enemy.[8] Yet domestic and international expectations were to be confounded. Within months of the Restoration, the king had affirmed his "Royall Intention of supporting and encouraging Jamaica."[9] Far from dismantling the councils set up in Whitehall to attend to the colonies, Charles enlarged them, and wedded himself to a project of further expansion that far exceeded the aspirations of the fallen Protectorate. In June 1661, the statement of intent was made unequivocal when the king stunned European opinion-formers by announcing his marriage to the Portuguese princess Catherine of Braganza, and by taking as part of the bridal dowry the cities of Tangier and Bombay. Selling

Dunkirk—the other Cromwellian conquest from Spain—to the king of France, Charles shifted English foreign policy away from traditional European spheres of interest. Loyalists soon predicted that the power and security of the restored monarchy would be determined by ventures across continents and via seaways lying far from the center of the Stuart realm.

Through the decade after the Restoration, statesmen and commentators meditated on the historic processes that had brought about the creation of English overseas colonies, weighing up the value of alternative zones of commerce and settlement in a shifting diplomatic environment. For many commentators, the contours of England's overseas empire existed more in the abstract than in reality. The incapacity and ambivalence of successive governments meant that ideas of overseas expansion rested on the imaginative sediments laid down by a century of privately funded voyages and sporadic settlement schemes, undertaken by independent actors following wildly divergent personal motives. With the failure of all English expeditions mounted against Spanish territory in the New World, the Crown had been left with colonies of questionable value, situated far from the gold and silver mines that had supplied the original impetus toward conquests across the Atlantic. The acquisition of Jamaica, Tangier, and Bombay reawakened prospects of riches and glory overseas, but also heightened the strategic and financial dilemmas brought before the restored Crown. New commitments in the East and the Mediterranean shook English assumptions over the most effective way to pursue overseas dominion, provoking questions over where the Crown should commit its resources, how much territory to control, and in what form. The rise of Dutch power in Asia confronted Restoration commentators with an alternative model of empire, seemingly centered less on terrestrial expansion than on the protection of maritime spaces and commercial arenas. As they sifted through their overseas interests, rival readings of the world forced ministers to speculate over the merits of dispersed and semi-imagined zones of control, marked out only by fledgling networks of garrisons, settlements, and trading stations. The choices that they made electrified European rivalries, and steered a new generation of English soldiers and settlers into theaters of unrelenting international competition.

History, Geography, and the Imperial Consciousness

For over a decade into the reign of Charles II, the Restoration of the house of Stuart was presented, politically and artistically, as a moment freighted with imperial possibility. As he processed through the City of London to his coronation in April 1661, Charles II was serenaded by performers clad as camels and elephants, Indians and Moors. In festivities choreographed by the classicist and geographer John Ogilby and the colonial merchant Balthasar Gerbier, the king passed through triumphal arches embossed with images of Neptune and Mars, Atlas and Augustus. "Emblems, mottoes and inscriptions," modelled after Roman praise poetry, exhorted him to fulfill his personal and national destiny by attaining mastery over far-flung reaches of the world.[10] "His Majesty hath an Imperial name," declared one pamphleteer. "It was Charles that brought the Empire into France; Charles that brought it first into Spain: why should not Great Britain have his turn?"[11] By marshalling the prince and his people in a new "union of interest," predicted the natural philosopher Thomas Sprat, the expansion of the realm would create a thrilling future to banish the "unfortunate Divisions" that "are but of one or two Ages growth."[12]

The idea that the glory of the Restoration monarchy would be expressed through territorial expansion was built on historical and mythological foundations. Four centuries of scholarship adhering to the narrative set down by Geoffrey of Monmouth had identified the Emperor Constantine as an ancestor of the ancient British monarchy. Through this lineage, it was believed, the torch of world power had been ushered westward—having passed from Greece to Rome, the "imperial diadem" would finally be transferred to the princes of Britain, inviting them to exert dominion over uncharted lands lying beyond the Atlantic.[13] Embroidering the legend, a body of antiquarian writings positioned the Stuarts, through their Tudor forebears, as descendants of a line of prince-navigators who had stretched the boundaries of Britannia as a northern successor-state to Rome. This pedigree centered on Arthur, "who led his squadrons as far as Iceland, and brought the Northern people under his Flag," according to John Evelyn, "planting the confines of the British Ocean as far as the Russian Tracts."[14] Since the later sixteenth century, scholars had paid equal attention to certain "very auncient and auctenticall chronicles, written in the Welshe or Brittishe tongue," which, according to the geographer Richard Hakluyt, pinpointed Madoc, prince of Gwynedd, as "first discoverer" of the New World, in a voyage undertaken three centuries before the Spanish claimed rights of possession.[15] The claims of antiquity offered consolation for a more rueful recent history. The capture—or recapture—of lands farther west was presented as a way to redeem the humiliations that had caused Aquitaine, Normandy, and Brittany to slip through the fingers of distracted monarchs, and had led to millions of pounds being squandered by successors seeking to make good their flimsy claim over the throne of France.[16]

While England's territorial ambitions were being considered against an ancestral background, Restoration commentators agreed that more recent navigational developments had altered the complexion of European politics, and changed the way in which a kingdom would ascend to greatness over its competitors. Since the discovery of America, John Evelyn opined, all European nations had been "stimulated" by the impulse for "encounters and adventures . . . to visit strange and distant lands, to people, cultivate and civilize un-inhabited and barbarous regions."[17] Visions expressed through pageantry and panegyrics held up the history of English voyages and discoveries as demonstrations of national capability, and a way of honing the technical and intellectual mastery required for a kingdom to pursue territory overseas. In 1670, Charles II lent his own authority to the idea, commissioning a silver medal by the engraver Jan Roettiers in honor of *Diffusus in Orbe Britannus*: the dispersal of his subjects across the world.[18] The process leading up to this point had been haphazard and decentralized. By the later 1690s, the Scottish projector William Paterson would lament that "none of those wee Comonly Call the politicians" had imbibed the implications of the "new and violent . . . kind of destruction introduced into the rest of the world by these discoverys in the Indies."[19] The "dispersal of Britons" was due less to royal direction than to the actions of thousands of independent agents—traders, fishermen, clergymen, exiles, and mercenaries, who spanned the religious and geographic spectrum of the Stuarts' three kingdoms.[20] Yet, unregulated as most of these undertakings were, travel was part of the public business of the realm. Each individual venture required—nominally at least—a pass from the Crown, and governments issued affirmations of their authority through charters, proclamations, and company grants designed to regulate itinerant subjects.[21] Even when overseas settlements were transitory, therefore, the actions of wayfarers drew the Crown into potential diplomatic and military entanglements. Their seaborne journeys had, as the colonial projector Benjamin Worsley recorded in 1668, "increased the limitts of our dwelling," turning events in distant provinces into "an affayre of state."[22]

Personal testimonies from English travellers gained ideological significance in the hands of interpretative communities of scholars and statesmen in the Old World. The connection between travel and overseas expansion was framed through the medium of descriptive geography: learned treatises—threaded through with maps, sea charts, and hundreds of individual narratives—valorized English voyagers, anatomizing and exoticizing the worlds they had uncovered.[23] Many of these texts became vehicles for political exhortation. Richard Hakluyt's *Principal Navigations* (1589) retailed the history of one thousand years of sea ventures as the precedent for English voyagers needing encouragement to shake the Spanish hold on the Americas, plant settlements, and incorporate the Amerindians into the reformed Christian community. The Jacobean clergyman Samuel Purchas believed that the astounding feats of the kingdom's *Pilgrimes* (1625) provided evidence of providential intervention on behalf of English Protestants, foreshadowing the reclamation of the world for true religion.[24] By the 1670s, the leading works of travel literature were being incorporated into an archive in the Plantation Office, and had become staple fixtures in American governors' residences, merchant factories in the East Indies, and the libraries of provincial gentlemen.[25] Peter Heylin's *Cosmographie* (1652) circulated among settlers in Carolina fifty years after publication.[26]

The extent of actual knowledge that these works offered to the public domain was a matter of debate. Like the mermaids' tailfins, unicorn horns, and griffins' heads that appeared in coffeehouses and cabinets of curiosity, the literary culture of English travel notoriously blurred dividing lines between scholarship and fantasy.[27] *Purchas His Pilgrimes* spoke to the realm of masque and pageant, claiming to unfurl "an open Theatre" for "a shew of Discoveries on an English Stage, wherein the World is both the spectacle and the spectator, the Actors are the Authors themselves."[28] The Maryland planter

George Alsop warned that little of value could be taken from "Purchas in his Peregrination between London and Essex (which he calls the whole World)"; the Virginian scholar Robert Beverley concurred, proclaiming that "there are no Books, (the Legends of Saints always excepted,) so stuff'd with Poetical Stories, as Voyages; and the more distant the Countries lie . . . the greater License those priviledg'd Authors take, in imposing upon the World."[29]

Travel narratives certainly privileged the outlandish and the heroic. For John Ogilby, America opened up "a flourishing Hesperides, Regions where Sands were Gold, Earth Plate, and Rivers Silver . . . outshining all the Fables of Antiquity."[30] The most significant fiction, however, was political. Scholars like the author of a 1665 *Description of Guinney* wrote to enable the "Curiosity of the Subject" to "enlarge its self as far as the Empire of the Soveraign . . . that our pens should go as far as his Sword."[31] Their works supported the interests of private travellers by recasting them as agents of English royal power. The same texts corresponded with royal ambitions by using the actions of merchants, migrants, and mercenaries to lodge claims of "first discovery" on those territories prone to international contestation. In doing so, scholars imposed an imaginative *imperium* on uneven and contested sovereign spaces, transforming hostile frontiers and uncharted backcountries into stable and fruitful outworks of Old England. As the clergyman Thomas Fuller put it delicately in 1662, Richard Hakluyt had placed the writ of the Crown on "base and barren" landscapes that amounted to only a "bare name for the present," yet "may prove rich places for the future." When the need arose, "these Voyages will be produced and pleaded, as, good Evidence of their belonging to England."[32] Works of descriptive geography visualized an empire of aspiration rather than reality. They were no less influential for that.

Conquest, Conflict, and Chances Missed

New World colonization figured in the English imagination primarily as the product of ferocious international rivalries. For half a century, the convention of "no peace beyond the line" had confined European diplomatic accords to a space extending no farther west than the Azores, and only as far south as the Tropic of Cancer. This approach licensed piracy as a weapon of interstate rivalry in regions beyond, and unleashed a relentless competition for land and resources.[33] America, as Thomas Povey put it, was the key to "the mysticall and most curious strength of Spayne," and in 1660 the colonial environment was still defined for many English readers by the achievements of the conquistadors who had stormed across the Atlantic, demolished the Aztec and Inca empires, and prised open the hidden riches of Central and South America.[34] Strategically and economically, the continent provided a power base for the court of Madrid that "counterbalanceth all the old world were they cast into a pair of scales," as the royalist scholar James Howell observed.[35] A century and a half after the mines were forced open, the return of the treasure fleet from Mexico and Peru was still "a thing so solemne in this Country & of so general an influence over all others," reported the English ambassador to Madrid. The fleet carried, he estimated, "at least 40 millions of pieces of eight & Bars for the King," together with "silver, pearles & Emeralds" and cargo loads of logwood, sugar, tobacco, and drugs.[36] Since the 1580s, the riches borne in by the "galleones and flota" had sustained Spanish ambitions in Italy and the Low Countries, stirring visions of world dominion that shaped the self-presentation of the house of Habsburg.[37] At the festivities to mark the marriage of Carlos II to the princess Marie Louise of Orleans in 1679, the English ambassador saw fireworks fixed to the effigy of "an artificial Giant . . . upon a large scaffold of about 6 yards high in imitation of the Colossos of Rhodes with a Ship under saile between his leggs, a huge Globe on one hand, & the Sun in another."[38]

English strategists read, and feared, the prescriptions for Spanish, Catholic "universal monarchy" apparent in the works of Giovanni Botero and Tommaso Campanella.[39] Yet commentators were acutely aware that their own kingdom had squandered opportunities to offer a serious challenge for possession in the New World. Seventeenth-century authors vented their frustration over the decision by Henry VII to decline patronage to Christopher Columbus—"a most unaccountable stupidity & dullness in our ancestors," William Blathwayt would opine in 1685, "to suffer the Spaniards unmolested . . . to ransack every corner of that Golden World . . . shutting & locking up with Forts & Citadels all passages to those inexhaustible

Mines."[40] Henry's disregard was perceived to have set the tone for a century characterized by internal distractions, political myopia, and archaic obsessions with the reconquest of France. With four thousand men, Peter Heylin contended, Queen Elizabeth might have taken on the Spanish Empire and "broken it in pieces."[41] But no single royal vessel crossed the Atlantic under the queen or her two Stuart successors, and the Crown repeatedly opted, under pressure from Madrid, to curtail the course of plunder and exploration. The failure of larger maritime expeditions, from Walter Raleigh's plantation at Roanoke, to the privately funded Providence Island campaign of 1630, and, finally, to the Cromwellian Western Design, revealed the gulf that remained between England and its oldest colonial adversary in their ability to organize campaigns outside Europe.[42]

This narrative of thwarted possibilities conditioned the way in which English authors looked on those colonies that *had* been established across the Atlantic. The Stuart Crown marshalled a legal claim over the northern parts of America, grounded on the discoveries of Sebastian Cabot, who had sailed under warrant from Henry VII.[43] By the middle of the seventeenth century, migrant communities could be found well-established in the West Indies, and were scattered along the American seaboard, from the plantation world of Virginia and Maryland northward along a corridor east of the Appalachian range to the more densely populated New England provinces and, beyond them, the fishing stations of Newfoundland and Labrador. Together, these territories domiciled a population of approximately 200,000.[44] Sir William Berkeley, the longstanding governor of Virginia, believed that, by 1662, the Chesapeake tobacco markets were already accounting for 25 percent of English customs revenue, holding out the possibility that "this new western world" would generate "a wealth our fathers never knew."[45] But England's failure to extract precious metals from North American mountains had dented any chance of replicating the centrally steered, bullion-powered policies of the kings of Spain. Instead, the English exploitation of the New World had rested on chartered enterprise and self-funded private agents, with only limited institutional support and minimal evidence of a strategic plan. Consequently, royal councils possessed at most thin awareness of the congeries of scattered settlements, commercial outposts, and private fiefdoms that nominally pertained to the Stuart Crown.

In 1660, after five years of immersion in the archive at Whitehall, Thomas Povey reported that "scarce any Record, Testimonial, Letters or Papers of Consequence" existed in "any place, wch may informe and assist his Maty's Councels," let alone "justify ye original right and progress of many of our most considerable Colonies," and define their correct borders.[46]

By the later seventeenth century, many promoters fretted that the North American settlements were losing favor in the English imagination. The original images of "golden worlds" with limitless fecundity were running up against a stream of deeply negative accounts that had swept in from America—reports that chronicled the collapse of the Virginia Company in 1624, exposed the blight of disease and high mortality, and dramatized the terror of Indian onslaughts on isolated colonial settlements.[47] During the 1640s and 1650s the return to the Old World of thousands of colonists— some sailing back to fight in the Civil Wars, but others spurred by material necessity—intensified deep-seated doubts over the future of the English presence in the New World.[48] Ministerial reliance on private promoters to coax men and women into overseas adventures had met its limits, warned the Maryland planter John Hammond, because it was now "a received errour amongst the many slanders cast on these places, that we are sworn neither to Speak nor Write but glossingly of them."[49] In the absence of "publick encouragement" from Crown and government, William Berkeley complained, let alone "a publick store" to "enable us to procure men," the creation of an English empire in America had never risen out of the "imaginations or papers" of the Elizabethan cosmographers. Without political momentum, colonial investors risked becoming nothing more than "Architects, who can design excellent buildings" but had no space to "square their timber, or lay their bricks."[50]

Jamaica and the Renewal of English Colonization

Within months of the Restoration, debates over the state of the English overseas world were impinging on the court of Charles II, as it grappled with the legacy of Cromwellian imperialism. In Jamaica, conquest had been followed by incipient economic development. By 1661, approximately three thousand white settlers and five hundred African slaves were populating the island, under the aegis of a garrison and naval squadron.[51] But with its defense and protection taking a toll on government finances, Jamaica had nonetheless become a lightning rod for many longstanding objections toward expansion overseas. In London, a hostile lobby was formed out of merchants who had invested directly in the Spanish trade, or were concerned more broadly to secure a rapid peace in order to end disruptions caused by interstate provocations.[52] Other opponents blamed schemes for conquest in America on the Protectorate army's influence over English politics, and damned the colonies as an instrument to further the interests of officers who had usurped authority under Oliver Cromwell.[53] Among many court voices, greater excitement was aroused by the port of Dunkirk: the other recent conquest from the Spanish Crown, and the focus of an entirely different vision of territorial enlargement. Lord Chancellor Hyde posited Dunkirk as a "kind of staple for all Flanders and English commodityes," raising the possibility "(perhapps) of bringing the people & wholl Country . . . to a voluntarie surrender of themselves to His Maties Dominion, whereto there are more of them inclined than pleased with the Government of ye Kinge of Spaine."[54] Champions of Dunkirk could play to the old analysis, still persistent in royal circles, that "England was never considerable, since it wanted a footing on this side of ye water," as the diplomat George Downing put it, after the territorial losses of the fifteenth century and the evacuation of Calais in 1558.[55] The stakes of the debate were high because, as both sides acknowledged, the state of the royal finances rendered it unviable that *both* possessions could be maintained.

The decision to retain Jamaica sent a dramatic signal that the revival of the English colonies would stand at the center of Restoration foreign policy. In January 1661, the earl of Lauderdale discerned that while the court looked with dismay on the scattered and disorderly nature of the dominions, "I finde the King inclinable to draw them nearer together, & not disposed" to surrender Jamaica, "wch is lookt on as of vast importance, nor doe I see any scruple in keeping it."[56] By February 1661, the Privy Council had given de facto sanction to the occupation, funnelling gunpowder, ammunition, clothing, and provisions across the Atlantic.[57] The choice stemmed primarily from courtly enthusiasm. The king's brother, the duke of York, was especially susceptible to the case for keeping the colony as a token of national honor, and was untroubled by continuity with Cromwellian policy, boasting to the Dutch ambassador that "the English have ever united all this private differences to attend Forraigne."[58] But Jamaica was also the beneficiary of a lobbying force that connected London to the colonies—networks of merchants, planters, bankers, and military entrepreneurs who had emerged as creditors for republican governments, and as advisers on commercial and colonial policy. The key figures—Thomas Povey and Martin Noell, Thomas Kendall and Maurice Thompson—had enriched themselves via the Atlantic trade. Several members of this circle had cut their teeth in politics by agitating for the passing of the Navigation Ordinance in 1651, making the government, rather than privileged corporations, responsible for the regulation of colonial commerce.[59] Despite their association with emblematic Interregnum foreign policies, most of these men were not tarnished with republican or regicidal sympathies. Povey had been purged from his seat in parliament by the New Model Army in 1648.[60] Most of the projectors were, moreover, united with the court in a shared analysis of recent changes detected in world affairs. Ever-widening cracks could be glimpsed in the Spanish façade, it was argued, after the declaration of Portuguese independence in 1640, the buffeting effects of revolts in Naples and Catalonia, and the increasingly visible fiscal strains on the court of Madrid. Even if other Europeans had not fully realized it, these events, according to the English consul in Lisbon, "hath so altered the ballance that Spain must no more pretend to the universall monarchy."[61] Seen in this light, Jamaica became more than just the tattered remnant of an imperial protectorate. Even in its "suppressed and disabled condition," Povey argued, the island had "exceedingly disordered the Spanish Trade." Should it be "suffered to perishe," "the English Honour must suffer extreamly . . . whither wee shall think fit to keepe Spayne an Ennimie, or whither wee shall treate for a Peace."[62]

The logic of keeping Jamaica would strengthen the public positions of those veterans of Cromwellian foreign policy who could prove their loyalty to the throne, placing at the disposal of Charles II their business connections and knowledge of the colonies. The king fostered not merely the individuals, but also the institutional framework that had given life to the Western Design. The new Council of Trade, convened in June 1660, expanded on an experimental structure introduced by the commonwealth government, building on the idea of creating specialized agencies for trade and colonization that had emerged as part of a fuller prospectus for the renewal of England's civil domain.[63] After the Restoration, the number of council members rose to sixty-two, bringing together courtiers with a cross-section of the London merchant community. There was considerable crossover between this body and the new, forty-nine-strong Council for Foreign Plantations, conceived to handle the business of colonial governance. Although both entities were larger and more unwieldy than advocates such as Povey had recommended, the councils gave an institutional footing to the colonial interest, and went some way toward redressing the complaint that England lacked any supervisory institution comparable to the Spanish Council of the Indies.[64] In formalizing connections with private merchants and London interests, the Crown kept cash and credit in circulation, and widened the opportunities for transatlantic lobbying. Above all, the appointments brought into government a cadre of individuals who were ideologically and financially committed to colonization, and who sought to reorient the English state toward the purpose of expansion outside Europe. The rationale for a Council of Trade, Thomas Povey pronounced in 1660, was not merely to "regulate and improve" existing overseas interests, but also to awaken a "new Spiritt and genius to our Countrymen . . . rendering them active, and ingenious, and bold."[65]

The Braganza Match and the Empire of the East

The gamble that Jamaica could be maintained in English hands was influenced not merely by public lobbying in London, but also by diplomatic consultations that took place under strict secrecy. In June 1661, negotiations extending over almost a year bore fruit, when the king committed himself to an alliance with the newly independent kingdom of Portugal, sealed by his own marriage to the princess Catherine of Braganza. The key terms, hammered out by eight privy councillors, included the transference of Tangier and Bombay into English hands, and the promise of free trade for English merchants through the Portuguese colonies in West Africa, Brazil, and the East Indies.[66] In return, Charles would commit resources to the young Afonso VI, and vouchsafe never to return Jamaica or Dunkirk into the hands of Spain. The provocative implications registered immediately in European diplomatic opinion. Having maintained lordship over Portugal and its colonies since 1581, the Spanish Crown refused to recognize the secession, and in 1659, Philip IV was reported to be mobilizing for a new assault on his neighbor. Charles II offered a lifeline to the Portuguese, pledging to "give all fleets required and any other assistance," and backed up his resolve with a dispatch of three thousand troops from the British Isles into the Iberian Peninsula. Not surprisingly, news of the alliance was followed by seven days of public thanksgiving on the streets of Lisbon—and by furious opposition from Madrid.[67] Spanish diplomats in London threatened "everlasting war," made a last-ditch offer of one million crowns for the return of Jamaica and Dunkirk, and suggested that Charles would better please his subjects with marriage to the Lutheran princess of Denmark. It was gratifying to see the Habsburg court "so sollicitous for the advancement of the Protestant Religion," sneered Lord Chancellor Hyde.[68]

The Braganza match set the seal on the colonialist turn in English foreign policy. At court and in public, the alliance was presented as an opportunity to undermine the power of Spain by keeping a rival polity alive on its doorstep. After the failure of successive military expeditions into Spanish America, preserving "the vitall spirit" of the kingdom of Portugal was now seen by English diplomats as the superior way to "make more common those riches of the Indies which . . . the covetousness and averise of the Castillians have ingrossed to themselves."[69] Just as significantly, the marriage terms had created wholly new arenas for English colonial outreach, territories untarnished by the many frustrations clouding the settlement of the New World. Portuguese interests, as English diplomats noted, extended into "all the four partes of the world." In 1662, this reach was demonstrated when the queen's entourage arrived, accompanied by "such Indian Cabinets and large trunks of Laccar, as had never ben seene here," as John Evelyn recorded.[70] "I must tell you I do expect to find you marvellously learned in that whole trade of the East and West Indies, how to make both of more use to us," Edward Hyde instructed the new ambassador Richard Fanshaw, upon his departure for Lisbon.[71] English negotiators initially hoped to coax the Portuguese into granting Charles II a full protectorate over "the Governement of Goa."[72] But even in the absence of this prize, the two agreed acquisitions, Tangier and Bombay, held out "transcended advantages for the advancement of the trade and empire of this kingdom," argued Hyde, now earl of Clarendon, in 1662.[73] These assets offered the sweetener, he mused, "most like to dispose the whole Nation to a liking of this Allyance," against the "many objections which can be enough foreseen" to the idea of tying England in marital union to a Catholic dynasty.[74]

For all their optimism, Restoration privy councillors possessed limited knowledge of Bombay. With tensions running rife among the territory's multi-ethnic, multi-confessional population of over ten thousand, the new possession presented a daunting, divisive proposition among Englishmen already active on the Indian subcontinent.[75] The "Grand Nationall Intreague of Bombay" was "a designe of such high circumstances, & so little substance," warned the merchant Gerald Aungier—a future governor of the city—in 1662, that "those yt weigh it wth an experimentall & unbiased knowledge must needs looke (if Enemyes wth Scorn, if friends with Pitty) on ye manadgmt of our affaires in England."[76] But the notion of seeking an Eastern dominion was not new to English thought. Projectors could draw on a long pedigree of European writings about India, which came without the shock of novelty afforded by discoveries in the Western Atlantic.[77] In 1596, Richard Hakluyt had called on English travellers to unlock the "secret shores and hidden straits of China," and bring "new lands, very ample kingdoms, unknown peoples" under "the sceptre of our sacred highness Elizabeth."[78] Long into the seventeenth century, English ventures throughout the Atlantic were defined according to Asian objectives. For many commentators, America figured not so much as a prize in itself, but as an alternative sea route to the East, with a primacy placed on the search for "doorways," "keys," and "bridges" that would concatenate continents and ease the passage of fleets between them. In 1661, Edward Hyde adduced the importance of Bombay somewhat dubiously from its location at "a very little distance from Brazil."[79] The political economist Carew Reynell, otherwise a stern critic of territorial expansion, eyed the potential for conquests on the Isthmus of Panama, a possession that would connect the Atlantic and Pacific sea routes and enable England to conduct "the West and East-Indie Trade under one Voyage, carry what Silver we will from the West-Indies . . . and so come back hither with East-Indies Goods" as well as American riches.[80]

"The West with the East, and the remotest parts of the world are ioyned in one band of humanitie," proclaimed Samuel Purchas.[81] In a century when colonization was decentralized and experimental, English authors did not compartmentalize the world into two discrete units, allocating one place for plantation and one for trade. More commonly, they applied the same discourse to all zones of dispersed English activity, making the East Indies subject to many of the same debates over dominion and plantation that had arisen in relation to the New World.[82] The English had sustained an organized presence in India since 1600. Chartered with exclusive rights over every English vessel and subject venturing beyond the Cape of Good Hope, the East India Company (EIC) had built up a network of shipping routes, trading stations, and urban bases along the shorelines of the sub-continent and the Malayan Spice Islands, serviced by sea lanes and caravan routes, and supported by major settlements at Surat on the west coast of India and Madras in the east.[83] Under the writ of the Company, forty sail of ships shifted textiles, drugs, spices, lacquered ware, coffee husks, and other delicacies from across the region, charting routes through the Red Sea, and sketching out further explorations into China and Japan.[84] Honoring their mandate from the Crown, traders in Asia fortified their factories; framed a legal, civil, and religious order; and filled the bases with visual and material symbols of English authority.[85]

The relationship between the EIC and the Crown's colonial designs was enigmatic. Since the sixteenth century, companies had proved their value by raising fleets and soldiers at minimal cost to the royal treasury, and by driving national interests into zones beyond the reach of regular diplomacy. Many of these enterprises carried implicit, if largely unrealized, territorial impulses.[86] The first expedition of the Russia Company in 1557 came with royal license to "reare, plant, and fasten our banners" in any places, "which shall bee by them . . . newly discovered."[87] Yet while the Crown repeatedly endorsed the EIC to build "collonies or plantations within the Limits and Bounds of Trade," its merchants conducted most of their business within the legal and mercantile framework of the Mughal Empire. Forts, factories, and settlements claimed by the Company owed their existence to *firman* leaseholds issued at the plea-sure of regional princes. Since the reign of James I, EIC magnates had re-peatedly resisted attempts to confuse commerce with conquest.[88]

This stance created recurring tension between the Company and English governments of both royal and republican stripes. Between 1653 and 1657, the perception that the EIC served a private rather than a national interest had brought about a suspension of the charter, and a temporary experiment with free trade.[89] But the failure to find alternative ways of extending English authority in India preserved the essential rationale behind the monopoly grant. After the Restoration, moreover, the Company's concern to secure its privileges pushed it toward closer engagement with the colonial ambitions being rediscovered at court. In 1661, the directors funded the second triumphal arch for the coronation procession, and issued the first of a succession of gifts and loans to the court of Charles II, which by 1685 would run up to almost £325,000. The South Atlantic island of Saint Helena, acquired in 1659 as a stopping place for the Asian voyage, offered scope for experiments in agricultural production, and potential precedents for turning Indian holdings into full plantations. With the release of a new charter in 1661, the political orientation of the Company had shifted. The Company committee now bristled with merchants drawn from the Council of Trade, including many former investors in the Western Design. Its correspondence showed increased readiness for involvement and association with royal territorial plans.[90] This more visible alignment with the court of Charles II would benefit English traders in Asia, believed the investor Robert Ferguson, enabling them to command "that awe" necessary to secure favorable terms, and better "force" Indian rulers "to a performance of their Treaties and Agreements."[91]

If the interests of Crown and Company were not synonymous, they were forced into closer alignment by a shared threat, which appeared to strike at the power and security of the house of Stuart as elementally as had the Crown of Spain. Through the agency of the Vereenigde Oostindische Compagnie (VOC), the Dutch Republic had established an administrative stronghold at Batavia on the island of Java. This settlement served as the base for commercial and territorial operations that spanned increasingly wide sections of the East Indies and the Malay world.[92] Dutch soldiers had unseated Portuguese power in Ceylon by 1660. Advancing onto the subcontinent, they planted forts on the Malabar and Coromandel coasts, and established trading monopolies with local rulers. While English merchants fastidiously abided by their *firmans,* the VOC, according to the diplomat William Temple, had "raised a State in the Indies," one nourished by the banks of Amsterdam and a ready stockpile of thirty thousand soldiers. The English factories on Pulo Run and Amboina had fallen to violent assault by 1623, and within a decade, both islands had been walled, manned, and fortified by Dutch hands.[93] More alarmingly still, the riches of the East were seen to be furnishing the Dutch with resources to change the territorial balance in other parts of the world. The development of the New Netherlands, through a wave of American settlement in the 1650s, intruded "into his Maties rights in the very best part of all that Northerne Empire," as one Crown agent complained in 1664.[94] Across the New World, vessels from Amsterdam tilted at the old colonial order, capitalizing on the disorder of the Civil Wars to penetrate the commerce of Massachusetts, Barbados, and Virginia.[95] The same predatory behavior was visible even from the English North Sea shoreline, where Dutch fleets fished freely in the Crown's territorial waters and established, as one pamphleteer put it, "the very Fountain of their strength and happiness" upon the natural stock of the Stuart kingdom.[96]

For many commentators, the ascent of the United Provinces provided the most disturbing reflection on decades of English inertia toward the national interest outside Europe. Dutch actions shook the way in which the English mapped international politics. While the "Black Legend" of Spanish power was a well-established leitmotif, generations of English commentators had preferred to imagine the Dutch in a posture of homage, in recognition of the English blood and treasure expended in their service against Philip II of Spain.[97] Instead, as one Restoration author fumed, the "damn'd ingrate" had preyed on its preserver, and advanced its power in the New World and the East Indies by sapping strength from the very sinews that had brought about its deliverance.[98] Commercial and colonial frictions had already sparked one major Anglo-Dutch war, terminated by Cromwell in 1654. In the tense climate that followed the Restoration, when the streets of Amsterdam thronged with exiles, zealots, and other seething remnants of the English Republic, loyal authors read more sinister impulses into Dutch provocations.[99] English royalists professed that the actions of a state abroad could be determined by its internal ideological character. Accordingly, they identified the radical Calvinism of the Low Countries as a peril just as potent as the aging pretensions of Spanish "popery."[100]

These considerations heightened the political significance of the Braganza match and the colonial acquisitions that flowed from it, with the more militant sections of the EIC becoming particular champions of English rule over Bombay.[101] As a place held directly by the Crown, rather than at the grace of a Mughal *firman,* Bombay was presented as a potential springboard toward the kind of territorial authority in India that English merchants had been unable or unwilling to bring about. At court, and within the Company, bellicose voices hoped that the Crown would now be goaded by self-interest into addressing the long pattern of "strange and barbarous violences" that had been meted out by the Dutch, from the killings on Amboina to the capture of Pulo Run and the expulsion of English traders from the pepper-rich Malayan trading zones.[102] Portuguese authority in the East was itself depleted by the 1660s. Losses brought about by the Dutch and local powers had so winnowed down the once mighty viceroyalty that "they must suddainely loose all if his Maty do not relieve them," according to reports submitted by the EIC before the Privy Council. Seen in this light, the occupation of Bombay offered the opening stage of a larger design for English mastery on the subcontinent. Power in India would be cemented either by establishing a formal protectorate over Portuguese possessions, or by bringing the ailing *Estado* into effective dependence through free trade and the provision of convoys.[103] At the very least, as the EIC director William Ryder put it, "our nation may say in our dayes they have some considerable place in India," and "live there," in the city of Bombay, free of outside interference, "under their own commands."[104]

Tangier and the Empire of the Seas

For all the effusiveness of these arguments, any excitement raised in court circles over Bombay was dwarfed by the hopes that spiralled around the other acquisition from the Crown of Portugal.[105] Writing in 1699, fifteen years after its collapse and evacuation, Bishop Gilbert Burnet would recall Tangier as a place "spoken of in the court in the highest strains of flattery," marvelling that "such mighty things were said of it, as if it had been reserved for the King's reign, to make it as glorious abroad, as it was happy at home."[106] Burnet was correct that a remarkable stream of ambitions had flowed into a small city, in a region never previously subject to English colonizing designs. In the 1580s, Richard Hakluyt had staked the economic case for the New World on the projected decline of England's Mediterranean trade, which was now confronted by the rise of Ottoman power in the East, and by new Spanish and Portuguese religious laws, which hampered Protestant merchants seeking commerce with Iberian ports.[107] Yet despite these obstacles, English trade with the Mediterranean had proliferated through the seventeenth century, and many merchants active in the Western Atlantic had built their colonial experiments on the back of pre-existing Iberian or Levantine investments.[108] Under Charles II, the Levant fleet shipped out wool, cloth, tin, and colonial re-exports, with an annual value exceeding "one million pieces of eight," according to the English ambassador in Madrid.[109] The bounty of the Mediterranean returned in the form of Levantine silks and dyestuffs; Turkish cotton; and fruits, oil, and wine from Italy and Spain, all of which reaped "a very great income to his Majesty by Customes, and great advantages to ye Nation in Generall," as the consul in Tripoli affirmed.[110]

The importance of Tangier sprang from its position within this great thoroughfare. At the western edges of the seaway, where the Mediterranean met the Atlantic, the Straits of Gibraltar could be identified as the fountain of Spanish, and even ancient Roman, greatness.[111] Tangier, it was argued, could maximize its innate geographic advantages by developing as a safe haven for merchants venturing to and from the East Indies, and as a base to transmit American colonial commodities directly through to the Levant. The creation of a regional hub in the city was predicted at court to elicit a tenfold increase in English trade.[112] At the very least, the promise of a colony only two weeks' sailing time from England was a superior prospect, for many traders, to the two-month Atlantic crossing and the challenge of the American wastelands.[113]

The English interest in the Mediterranean, however, was more than purely commercial. Tangier, believed the earl of Sandwich, offered Charles II the chance to control the narrowest stretch of sea between Europe and North Africa, and so impose "what Conditions you Pleased upon all ye

World, that passe through."[114] A well-maintained naval harbor would "awe Spaine into a constant peace"; it would also strike a blow at other forces rife within the region, whose presence kindled equally vivid moral and confessional anxieties. Piracy was rampant in the Straits, a chokepoint for corsairs who plagued commercial traffic, and who, through the seventeenth century, would carry off over twenty thousand English subjects into North African prison cells to await ransom payments from the Crown.[115] Behind many of these pirates lurked the shadow of the Islamic world—represented by the governments of Morocco and the Ottoman regencies of Algiers, Tripoli, and Tunis, which intermittently sponsored sea-roving in order to boost their own revenues and deter European aggression. The perils of "Barbary captivity," publicized in Church charity briefs, and a genre of quasi-fictional printed accounts, heightened feelings of Christian fragility in England, at a time when Turkish armies were pushing over the ramparts of Central Europe, and preying on outlying territories of the Holy Roman Empire.[116] Presented in this context, the taking of Tangier took on heady implications. By placing a permanent guard there against corsairing activity, agreed the city's surveyor of works, Hugh Cholmley, Charles II would render "a considerable part of the Ottoman Empire . . . much more subjected to the English Power."[117] The consequence, for Sandwich, would be to raise up the king of England as "Arbitrator of the Interest of Europe" and a leader of the Christian world.[118]

In common with the debates over Jamaica and Bombay, Tangier unlocked wider questions, over not merely the geography of England's colonial interest, but also the nature and meaning of effective overseas dominion. By the middle of the seventeenth century, some English commentators had begun to suggest that control over seaways and shipping lanes was an equally potent, if not more certain, means to achieve international ascendancy than landed possessions.[119] The Dutch, it was argued, controlled comparatively little in the way of colonial terrain: even recent acquisitions in Ceylon had been largely confined to the territorial perimeters. Instead it was by establishing themselves as "Lords of the Sea-Coasts," in George Downing's words, with castles strategically stationed on rivers, islands, and estuaries, that they had been able to "stretch their power to the East and West Indies."[120] Dutch power was oceanic, agreed Sir William Temple, being maintained through a standing force of over thirty men-of-war, active "in the several Convoys of their Merchants Fleets."[121] By deploying these resources, the States-General had started to control much of the navigation of the Persian Gulf and the Spice Islands, and had similarly blocked many of its European rivals from access to the Baltic. In consequence, they had devoured many of the markets in world commodities, channelling Asian products into their own ports, and re-exporting them across Europe at a price of their own choosing, for returns of gold and silver.[122] The Dutch peril was especially pronounced because this type of power relied not on inherent economic abundance, but on political and commercial ingenuity. While the wealth and power of the Spanish princes rested idly on silver mines and sprawling provinces, believed the merchant Thomas Mun, the Republic had learned how to swell its supply of "ships, Arts and People," forging prosperity on the unlikely foundations of confined territories and arid soil.[123]

The example of the Dutch—and of the Venetians before them—cast doubt on the wisdom of looking to the territorial hegemons of the ancient or modern world as the template for durable overseas expansion. "Itt is The sea: that terefeies, & masters the land, & makes great Kinges . . . yet subjecte to you," insisted the marquis (later duke) of Newcastle, in a work of "Advice" delivered to Charles II a year before the Restoration.[124] For some authors, the vision of Charles II becoming master of the oceans increased ambivalence toward the American settlements that had already taken so much English labor. Had the Crown raised a sufficient fleet to command the North Sea fishery, the geographer John Scott suggested, Stuart kings might have "advanc'd ourselves to a high pitch of power and Riches," without "parting with such bodyes of people as we have done by Transportation to America."[125] Views of the primacy of sea over land delivered an equally pointed challenge to the Elizabethan case for upholding the territorial integrity of the Dutch Republic, as England's "counterscarp" against Catholic Europe.[126] Instead, the relationship had moved in exactly the opposite direction, reasoned Thomas Mun, whose treatise *England's Treasure by Forraign Trade* was published on the orders of the Privy Council in 1664. The Republic had exploited English protection to build up trade and shipping, and establish its own "outwork"—the sea—at the expense of its ally. While English thoughts "attend only upon the Spanish and French greatness," the

Dutch had been at liberty to "conquer in the Indies, and . . . reap the fruits of a rich traffique out of our own bosoms." Fattening themselves upon England's oceans, its trade and its fishing resources, they had robbed Stuart kings of a shield far more precious than flood-ridden fields and disused defenses north of Flanders.[127]

The question of exactly what constituted "empire" or "dominion" over the seas was more ambiguous. Most commentators agreed that the ocean was a space susceptible to legal regulation, agreement, and enforcement: it was more than simply the domain of freebooters and privateers.[128] Originally, however, English authorities had sought simply to sustain the freedom of the seas for all peaceful traffic. The oceans, their fish, and their trade were spaces held in common by all peoples, according to "the lawe of nature and of nations," Richard Hakluyt had argued.[129] Amid the clashes with the Spanish, Elizabethan commentators foreshadowed Hugo Grotius's *Mare Liberum* (1609), the famous defense of free traffic produced in support of Dutch merchants, which, as later Restoration authors saw it, had been flagrantly flouted by those same traders when they forced other nations out of commerce in Asia.[130]

As hostilities with the United Provinces rose, however, other very different ideas about how best to advance England's oceanic interests began to appear. If the Dutch had offended English worldviews by monopolizing commercial traffic in the Spice Islands, they had antagonized no less by claiming freedom of access to the waters around the British Isles and those parts of the West Indies that the Stuarts claimed as their own. "Thus you see these people do arrogate to themselves St Peter's power on the seas," George Downing informed Lord Chancellor Clarendon: "It is mare liberum in the Brittish Seas, but mare clausum [oceanic possession] on ye Coast of Africa & in ye East Indies."[131] English statesmen were not immune to the same inconsistency. In all parts of the world, stretches of sea impinged on state territories as creeks, straits, and sounds, Downing reminded his readers. In these settings, the sea was "no less capable of private dominion than the land," and polities were entitled to make limited claims of maritime dominion in the interests of their own territorial security.[132] Seen in this shade, the error of the United Provinces lay in the particular illegality of forcing other Europeans out of the Malayan seas, without force of statute or custom, but not in the *principle* of claiming jurisdiction over oceanic regions.

Building on this analysis, a more hard-edged vision of English maritime *imperium* had crept into domestic politics by the middle of the seventeenth century. Taking their cue from the writings of John Selden, a host of authors redesignated the "British Seas," and even many oceans beyond, as part of the "imperial diadem" of the Stuart Crown, expressly attacking the notion that "all Seas are common to the Universality of Mankind."[133] James Howell stretched the boundaries of the king's mare clausum "as far as the shoares of his Transmarin Neighbours, and as far North as the Arctic Circle." He identified the portcullis in the royal badge as the sign of the king's authority "to shut up, and open the sea when we thought fit." The "globe or ball" present in the royal scepter showed that this power tended toward "the Government of the world."[134]

In 1661, the language of an "empire of the seas" was grafted onto hopes voiced for English rule over Tangier, as an instrument to control the mouth of the Mediterranean and so take jurisdiction over the traffic that passed through it. The city was promoted with an appeal to the limitless possibilities of small, artfully managed coastal enclaves, rather than vast territorial conquests, as pathways to international mastery.[135] Yet if maritime dominion could appear as an alternative to the heavy artillery of territorial empire-building, it carried an equally rife potential to exacerbate international rivalries. In the Mediterranean, as in the East Indies, competing claims of sovereignty ramped up the pressure on crowded seaways, transposing onto them the same processes of competition and acquisition that had driven colonization on land. In an unstable legal environment, Thomas Mun predicted, the maritime titles brandished by contending states "would be sooner decided by swords, than with words," and this prospect was anticipated, if not openly relished, by the architects of English Tangier.[136] "The Spanyard will indeavour to gayne the place," anticipated one report from Lisbon, "knowing how pjudiciall it will be to have such a powerful Enimy to be so neare a neighbour. Nay, it doth vex the Turks, Hollanders and French."[137] The importance of the city, surmised Hugh Cholmley, would be proven by the diplomatic "commotions" certain to follow the establishment of English rule there.[138]

The Restoration Empire and the Reshaping
of European Politics

By 1660, when privy councillors, poets, and political economists were contemplating the expansion of English power, the lessons quarried out of Anglo-Dutch rivalry had disrupted received models of overseas empire. While the gold of the Spanish Main retained its glow, many of the public exhortations delivered to Charles II privileged different regions, alternative forms of territory, and other methods to enlarge the power of a kingdom. In the coronation revels hosted in London, overseas trade was presented as helping to achieve a form of dominion over the earth.[139] "Jewels, Spices, and Silks," scattered by performers among the crowd, were visualized as tokens of supplication from remote nations, while Charles II was duly anointed as lord over the treasures and "trade-winds" of Asia. "To you the Red Sea shall give precious shells, India her ivory, Panchaia perfumes, and China silk," promised the inscription on the EIC-funded arch at Cornhill.[140] In September 1662, the eastern sphere of interest figured ostentatiously in the revels laid on by London's livery companies in celebration of the royal marriage. The Drapers' pageant, devised by the poet John Tatham, bore in "a Banner of the Armes of *England* and *Portugall* impal'd," and a shield "in which is figured a *Portuges* with a Sword drawn, holding it over some *Indians* there, figured kneeling." On the river banks, the Merchant Tailors' display was fronted by "two camels" and "back'd with two *Indians,* bearing in one hand an Escutchion of the Arms of *England* and *Portugall* impal'd . . . betokening subjection."[141] The court and its ceremonial supporters were appropriating the imagery and glory of the Portuguese empire in Asia and Africa, and presenting England as inheritor and protector of its dominions outside Europe.

The colonial interest conditioned the financial priorities of the court and the agenda brought into Parliament, where MPs agreed in January 1662 to release an extra £100,000 in support of the new acquisitions.[142] The commitment ran potentially into perpetuity. Breaking from the prior pattern of English plantation, Charles announced that Jamaica, Tangier, and Bombay would be governed as Crown colonies, not under privately funded corporations or proprietaries, and rendered part of the "birthright" of future English monarchs. The scale of the enterprise was realized most visibly in Tangier, under a commission coordinated by the duke of York, which directed fleets into the Mediterranean, and worked with architects, engineers, contractors, and suppliers to lay the foundations for a substantial civil and military infrastructure. By February 1662, Tangier was heavily garrisoned, with 3,360 troops venturing into the Mediterranean alongside the earl of Peterborough as governor.[143] As they constructed courts, churches, and centers of administration, together with recreational spaces for a future settler population, the Crown's agents inscribed English power onto Tangier physically and imaginatively, naming streets, forts, and other public buildings in honor of court patrons and Crown governors. Soon the city was absorbing £75,000 every year: exceeding the sums spent by Charles II on all his other overseas outposts and home garrisons put together, and reflecting the court view of Tangier, recorded by Pepys, as "the most considerable place the king of England hath in the world."[144]

In all of these actions, the Crown supplied strategic impetus, and the growth of the Council of Trade enabled merchant petitions to travel more rapidly onto the royal agenda. But financial inhibitions, as well as deficiencies of local knowledge, meant that the colonial vision of the Stuart court was expressed just as vigorously in encouragement given to privately funded enterprises, which were underpinned by many of the older networks of merchants, adventurers, and military entrepreneurs who in previous generations had forged the English overseas world at their own expense. The Company of Royal Adventurers Trading to Africa, chartered in 1660, carried an especially overt stamp of approval, with the king investing £6,000, and with over half of the founding subscribers drawn from the royal household and the peerage. English merchants had maintained a low-level presence on the Guinea Coast and along the River Gambia for over seventy years, aiming to establish themselves in the lucrative markets in dyewood, hides, ivory, Guinea grain, and increasingly, slaves.[145] The interest of the Crown, however, was originally aroused by the connection between West Africa and the East Indies. The Portuguese, Dutch, and Danes had all used settlements in Guinea to support their Indian trade, building up forts as havens for vessels on the eastward road, drawing on local commodities to boost their stock, and acquiring African gold for Asian commercial exchanges. Clarendon saw the creation of "forts and castles in Guinny" as a by-product of the taking of Bombay, intended "for the more convenient navigation thither."[146] Meeting in Whitehall, and staffed by privy councillors, the new company was fashioned much more overtly as an instrument of royal power than were any of the overseas corporations endorsed by Charles II's kingly predecessors. With nineteen bases established between 1661 and 1665, it supplied the final component of an intended "empire of the seas" connecting England to the traffic of the Indian Ocean through a line of ports, "factories," and fortresses.[147]

More than the decision to retain Jamaica, the interests and acquisitions arising from the Braganza match altered the geography of English statecraft. The shift in focus now raised questions over the value of Dunkirk—a base seemingly at odds with the renewed set of objectives outside Europe. Dunkirk was a "place of noe strength," complained Sir Abraham Shipman, governor of Bombay; an "insupportable burden," agreed the earl of Teviot, commanding officer in Tangier, incurred for no more "than a supposed punctillio of honour."[148] For Hugh Cholmley, the opportunity of a merchant-led settlement in Tangier offered a complete corrective to "those neighbouring Conquests" in France and the Low Countries "in which our ancestors have so much delighted"; "all of which," he later added, "has since been lost, with more happiness, I think, to the interest of an Englishman, than was ever gained."[149] The hand of the Crown was forced, Clarendon recalled, when privy councillors confronted the reality of the "Charge and Expence" needed to the fulfil Crown's aspirations: "the Pay of the Land Forces and Garrisons; the great Fleets sent out . . . for the reduction of the Turkish Pirates of Algiers and Tunis," and "such supplies of horse & foote" necessitated "for the defence of Portugall."[150] In December 1662, these exigencies impelled Charles to decommission Dunkirk—selling the port for £320,000 to the king of France. In a symbolic statement of Crown priorities, coinage from the exchange was melted down, reminted, and channelled into Tangier.[151] While these actions raised murmurings at court—and, Pepys claimed, among "the generality"—it was not difficult to portray the choice as a diplomatic masterstroke, or at least the logical corollary to the colonial, anti-Spanish turn in Stuart foreign policy. The sale of Dunkirk promised to splinter the defensive agreement formed between Philip IV and Louis XIV in 1659, creating a "bone betwixt France & Spain," as James Howell put it, that was intended to divert their focus away from the decisions taken by Charles II and his Portuguese brother-in-law.[152] As late as 1665, Clarendon noted that the Spanish "are not willing that wee should keep ye Tanger and Jamica," yet "they dare not in any degree administer occasion of jealousie to France."[153]

The geographic changes sweeping into English foreign policy, however, meant that the court of Madrid was no longer the prime focus of national hostility. Instead, rising interest in the East and the Mediterranean was poised to bring all the unresolved frictions with the United Provinces into the open, setting the English and the Dutch on a collision course that would culminate in two more wars, in 1665–1667 and 1672–1674. It was now the Portuguese, not the Calvinists of the Low Countries, who represented England's territorial "Bulworke" against the court of Madrid, believed Richard Russell, chaplain to Queen Catherine.[154] Newly liberated from dependence on the Dutch, the Crown could at last untangle the "gold chains" of "that insulting nation," suggested the East India merchant William Ryder, which, he speculated darkly, had coiled themselves for too long around governments of a republican dispensation.[155] No equivalent to the EIC's catalogue of anti-Dutch grievances existed in West Africa, but the Royal Adventurers rapidly identified the Dutch West India Company as the main obstacle to their plan to make inroads into the trade of the region. According to the Council of Trade, the Republic had transplanted its "imagined" sovereign prerogative onto Guinea, and "since his Majtyes return played ye Devills & Pirats worse yn Algiers."[156] Over the following years, anti-Dutch feeling escalated in a long sequence of petitions and complaints issued by the Royal Adventurers and the East India Company, which often worked in concert to exploit the lobbying opportunities provided by the Council of Trade.[157] The sentiment was echoed among officers in Tangier, who assured Clarendon that a conflict "is much talked of and desired in these parts," as a chance for the city to prove its value to the Crown.[158]

In retrospect, Sir William Coventry, one of the more insistently "dovish" voices at court, blamed the institutional power of the new councils of trade and plantations for the outbreak of the second Dutch War. In his view, they had allowed private interests to direct government policy, and had encouraged gross overestimates of the actual commercial damage inflicted by the United Provinces.[159] But by 1664, the pressure to draw swords was supplied more vocally by a party of courtiers coalescing around the duke of York—who was "mad for a Dutch War," in the recollection of Samuel Pepys, and committed to an expansionist strategy to plant colonial power in Guinea and the East.[160] In poetry, theater, and street puppet shows, royalist authors dramatized the moral and ideological dimensions of Anglo-Dutch colonial rivalry with an intensity that fast overtook the real value of the contested regions.[161] Pulo Run, "a barren Sandy Soil, which yielded no Fruit, but only Nutmeg," made for an unworthy casus belli, in the judgment of the earl of Clarendon.[162] But such calculations of commercial benefit were being drowned out by the drumbeat of wounded national feeling, as loyal commentators demanded redress for the "affronts, injuries and violences, against his Majesty's honour," and subjected the republican States-General to all the moral high dudgeon that the royalist imagination could muster.[163] With Dutch authors responding in kind, both sides transposed onto zones in Asia and Africa the same language of territorial pretension that had underpinned Anglo-Spanish conflict in America.[164] By 1664, Clarendon recalled, courtiers aligned with the Royal Adventurers were claiming a right of "first discovery" in Guinea and Gambia on the basis of sporadic English trade since the 1580s: "a sufficient Foundation," it was professed, "to exclude all others, at least by the same Law that the Spaniard enjoys the West-Indies."[165]

The reshaping of Stuart foreign policy meant that, more than any of England's previous international conflicts, the Dutch wars of the 1660s and 1670s were fomented by a struggle for possession outside Europe. Valorized in Dryden's *Annus Mirabilis* (1667), the conflagration became an epic struggle between two nations "bewitch'd" by "Guinny Gold," "tempting fruits," and "spicy" shores, and poised to re-enact the drama of Carthage and Rome.[166] The need to support new colonial interests pushed the Crown toward a pattern of direct intervention outside Europe that flew in the face of warnings issued after the failure of the Western Design. English vessels launched the first preemptive strikes on Dutch fortresses off the Guinea Coast in June 1664. Confronted with obstruction by the Portuguese officials in charge of the Bombay handover, the duke of York mobilized a fleet to force the city into English hands, under threat of armed assault, by the end of 1665.[167] Simultaneously, the new Eastern and South Atlantic rivalries were beginning to change royal strategies in America itself. In March 1664, the king commanded four royal commissioners to cross the Atlantic: sent officially to settle complaints and appeals in the New England colonies, they also carried with them the terms of a new proprietary charter conferred on the duke of York.[168] Stretching over all the lands between Connecticut and the Delaware River, this new domain excised the sovereign integrity of the New Netherlands, and was recalled in 1670 as a mandate "to reduce under our obedience all those foreigners who had seated themselves between our Provinces of Maryland and New England in America."[169] On September 8, 1664, an English fleet arrived in the New World, breached Dutch defenses, and forced the city of New Amsterdam to surrender, preparing the ground for its remodeling as "New York." Nine years after the failure of the Western Design, a centrally funded military expedition had finally succeeded in capturing an American colony from a rival power.

Within a year of the Restoration, the house of Stuart had embarked on a colonialist project that developed, as Hugh Cholmley reflected, "agst ye disposition of ye rest of ye World."[170] By pouring resources into Tangier and Bombay, ministers laid down the skeletal framework for an empire that would reach across all parts of the known world. After the disappointments of early ventures into America, visions of English expansion and empowerment were given new substance by acquisitions in India, the Mediterranean, and the Gulf of Guinea, each of which was presented as a potential arena to determine the rise and fall of empires. In 1664, against this dramatic backdrop, a network of councils built up to protect Caribbean settlements against Spain took England to war with a different enemy—the United Provinces—a conflict sparked by confrontations in other zones of the world.

Yet no single "grand strategy" had triumphed in the competitive environment of councils and committee meetings. The concerns of Jamaica, Tangier, and Bombay were fronted by separate lobbies and interest groups contending for finite Crown resources and presenting alternative if not incompatible routes to glory and riches. The Crown had created fragile settlements, plunged inhabitants into the eye of an international storm, and raised new questions over how far the component parts of this overseas world could be united in a common institutional and commercial framework. The king's ambitions hinged on the chance that new possessions could become commercially robust enough to meet the pledge, made by the speaker of the Commons in 1661, that they would "repay this nation their principal with a good interest."[171] The royal strategy rested equally on the prospect of a new equilibrium in Europe. Privy councillors gambled that the resilience of the kingdom of Portugal, and the chance of permanent deadlock between France and Spain, would be sufficient to compensate for the final collapse of the old Dutch alliance, and the loss of England's traditional, protective "counterscarp" in the Low Countries. Through the following two decades, many of these assumptions would be tested to the limits.

2

The Moral Image of Empire in Restoration England

> She heard by her Imperial Majesty, how well and happily the World
> had been governed when she first came to be Empress thereof . . .
> that is, to have but one Soveraign, one Religion, one Law, and one
> Language, so that all the World might be but as one united Family,
> without divisions; nay, like God, and his Blessed Saints and Angels:
> Otherwise, said she, it may in time prove as unhappy, nay, as miser-
> able a World as that is from which I came, wherein are more
> Soveraigns then Worlds, and more pretended Governours then Gov-
> ernment . . . all which, said she, is a great misery, nay, a curse, which
> your blessed *Blazing-World* never knew.

SO MARGARET CAVENDISH, DUCHESS OF NEWCASTLE, brought *The Blazing World* before English readers in 1666.[1] Her narrative centers on a hidden continent reached through an icy passageway beyond the North Pole, revealed through communion with the soul of a lost seafarer who had ventured thither after her voyage had been blown off course in the winds and the snows. Cavendish describes the ascent of this unnamed heroine to preeminence over the uncharted world. Harnessing technological innovation to the arts of civic prudence, she forges a just and enduring polity, presiding over disputatious tribes of men blended with the forms of foxes, bears, birds, and other beasts. Her imperial city, constructed out of gold and decked with "diamonds of all colours," is aptly named "Paradise," for it brings a glimmer of perfection to earth. Willfully playful, elusive, and outlandish, Cavendish's contribution to English utopian fiction was nonetheless shot through with awareness of the pressures on the restored Stuart monarchy after the outbreak of the second Dutch War. While the empress stands impregnable over her new domain, the king of her native EFSI (unmistakably "England, France, Scotland, and Ireland") struggles against foreign enemies striking at the trade and tranquillity of his dominions.[2] Cavendish dreamed of a reprieve from wars, bloodshed, and division, and contemplated the possibility of empire as an instrument not merely for the glory of princes, but also for the social, moral, and intellectual advancement of their subjects. The power drawn from the heroine's extended dominion finally equips her to descend back into the old world, save her beleaguered king, and compel the tyrants and republics of the continent to bow before his sovereignty on the seas.

The Blazing World drew attention to the impulse in the English Renaissance imagination that had been set on fire by the possibilities of empire, and its concomitant forces, discovery and "improvement." For over a century, empires of the imagination had leapt out of the printing press, many bristling with utopian yearnings and thwarted political ambitions.[3] As Cavendish observed, "every human Creature can create an Immaterial World . . . of what fashion and Government he will . . . may make a World of Ideas, a World of Atoms, a World of Lights, or whatsoever his Fancy leads him to."[4] But after 1660, when the expansionist hopes of the court of Charles II broke into domestic politics, champions of the restored monarchy began to hint that the world of ideas could be translated into material reality. England, as the Royal Society fellow Thomas Sprat believed, was setting about the creation of a "mighty empire, the greatest that ever commanded the world." Its architecture could be glimpsed not only in "the Sugar-Works of Barbados, the Tobacco Plantations of Virginia . . . and the Vast Mole [naval harbor], which goes on at Tangier," but also in the mental and physical transmutations of the domestic realm. From the "shipwrights at work on the Banks of the Thames," to "the Cole-pits of Newcastle . . . the Clothworks of the West and the Plough-lands of Devon," English subjects were "busie upon their Natural Experiments . . . from whose labours mankind may expect prodigious Inventions."[5] These ideas echoed among the colonial lobbyists who began to appear in London, in centers of commercial, political, and scholarly exchange. The rhetoric in the petitions, pamphlets, and proposals of the age showed a consciousness that the 1660s could be a transformative moment in world history—a perception of the English empire unleashing radical possibilities, as Thomas Povey put it, for "the benefitt of mankind and the advantage of the Commonwealth of Learning."[6] Resettled in Tangier, Hugh Cholmley turned to "Nostradamus's prophecies" for the assurance that "the great Empire shall be with England, the envy of the world, above three hundred years."[7]

While the physical form of an English empire may have been embryonic, the imaginative apparatus was already being assembled. As strategic papers and cartographic studies introduced contested regions into English politics, so too was the enlargement of the realm being mapped ideologically, in a genre of commentaries meditating on the nature and meaning of empire in world history. English authors looked toward a panoply of imperial examples existing in many different forms and theaters—from fictional prototypes such as Cavendish's *Blazing World* to the lessons extracted from real colonizing ventures in ancient and contemporary settings. Restoration plays, polemics, sermons, and learned treatises annexed the precedents of the Chinese, Turkish, Mughal, and, above all, Roman and Spanish dominions, and converted their histories into materials for understanding the choices put before English governments. These discussions ranged widely, because not every author imagined territorial empire as the best template for wise, ever-improving princely rule. Seventeenth-century commentators wrestled with warnings drawn from scriptural and classical sources against the avarice, self-delusion, tyranny, and inevitable collapse that afflicted states seeking to expand beyond their divinely ordained boundaries.[8] Reflections on colonization were haunted by fears that, in jousting for new possessions, England risked being infected by the same spirit of tyranny that had engulfed its despotic, Catholic neighbors, and before them, the potentates of the ancient world.

In the debates of the 1660s, the revived colonial policies were therefore shadowed by older questions over how Christian, virtuous—and therefore durable—territorial expansion could become. Long into the later seventeenth century, colonial promoters such as the Quaker William Loddington still wrestled with the question of "what Title England has to America. And how can we *Salva Conscientia* undermine the Indians, taking Advantage of their Ignorance to get their Land?"[9] Authors discussed whether empires incarnated great civilizations, or whether "the commonwealth of learning" thrived better in small, self-governing polities attentive to the liberty of the subject. Repeatedly, they assessed colonization against a moral framework provided by the reformed religion. Many recent studies have de-emphasized the relationship between Protestantism and English colonizing ideologies, beyond the provision of a rhetoric of militant anti-Catholicism.[10] In the decade after the Restoration, however, Protestant concerns supplied a vital contribution to debates over English colonization. Churchmen bustled at the forefront of the colonial lobby. The plantation of America was posited in relation to the early Christian history of the British Isles. Lobbyists, statesmen, and natural philosophers envisaged a competition with Catholic empires over the "conscience of the heathen," in which the work of missionaries became as central to English authority as that of soldiers and governors. Yet English commentators reached no consensus over the policies necessary to make their dominions conform to Christian standards. Colonial discourse was streaked with unresolved uncertainties over the spiritual meaning of the New World, the Christian capacity of native peoples, and whether Protestant duty lay first in the propagation of the Gospel among "pagans," or in the cultivation of virtue *within* English settler communities.

In pamphlets and sermons, on the stage and in the correspondence networks that criss-crossed the empire, a growing body of English subjects was drawn into speculation over the consequences of overseas expansion, and its effect on public well-being. Through these exchanges, authors produced opposing verdicts over not merely the rectitude of overseas expansion, but also the type of overseas polity that the Crown ought to be constructing. Strategists fell into conflict especially over whether to emulate and purify the martial, missionizing model taken from Spanish America, or whether commercial and maritime resources made viable an entirely different route toward world ascendancy, one centered on lordship over the seas, with comparatively limited territorial pretensions and aspirations. All of these choices were seen to have repercussions for the political destiny of the domestic realm. If many observers agreed with Thomas Sprat that an expanding England was undergoing a sea change, they believed that the future shape of the kingdom—whether it was to advance or degenerate through its overseas exertions—remained dangerously unsettled.

Empire and the Cycles of Human History

Later seventeenth-century authors could agree that territorial expansion, conquest, and colonization represented universal forces in the drama of human history. Mankind, believed the jurist Edmund Bohun, was mobile, and its migrations, invasions, and resettlements provided "the great mutations that have happened in the World," through all the recorded centuries.[11] For most commentators, the original example was set by the sons of Noah, who had reclaimed the world for human habitation as the "great deluge" receded. George Scot, promoter of the emergent East Jersey settlements in 1682, saw the primordial development of human society as itself a process of colonization, "for what are new Families, but pettie Collonies," with each household requiring new land and resources to sustain life and health. As every family "removed further and further" from its place of origin, the resultant spillage of human activity would serve in time to "overspread the whole Earth."[12] It was political pressures, however, that turned virgin plantations into outworks of a territorial empire, and that accounted for much of the modern experience of colonization, which took place as the product of warfare and conquest. "It is the glory of every Nation to enlarge themselves," believed the Maryland planter John Hammond.[13] For the poet and playwright William Davenant, the search for dominion arose because "the Mindes of Men are more monstrous, and require more space for agitation . . . than the Bodies of Whales."[14] In the common estimation, James Howell believed, a prince who exceeded his counterparts "in multitude of People, in extent of Regions, in Wealth and Dominions," may be "considered most sublime and may claim superiority," just as "one Star exceeds another in glory."[15]

Yet if military and financial might would prove enough to conquer territories, commentators agreed that such resources were insufficient as means to preserve them. "Dominions," mused the Cheshire MP Roger Whitley, "are encreased or obtained sometimes with money, but never without valour or virtue."[16] Seen in this light, empire would arise not just from territorial enlargement, but also from a broader projection of a state's authority over others: *grandezza* attained in the cultural as well as the martial arena. For Sprat, an empire succeeded when its greatness invigorated an entire civilization, rendering other nations so "in awe" of a country's "morals, manners and fashions" as "to be ready to submit" to its command.[17] The Oxford orientalist George Lane believed that the primacy of the ancient "Arabian Empire" over its contemporaries stemmed not just from its "extent much larger," but also from its authors' ability to "reach the Glory of the Greeks and Romans both in Variety of Writings and Depth of argument."[18] Many writings appealed to an understanding of the world drawn out of Florentine humanist literature, in which temporal affairs were prone to "continual flux and vicissitude," as John Evelyn put it, and "princes that go not forward go backward," in the words of the Jamaica governor Sir Thomas Modyford.[19] The preternatural triumph of empire, according to Davenant, was to impose such total authority over the slippery forces of fortune that the world, in consequence, "stands still."[20]

English scholars jousted over the most compelling models to be curated from the ancient world. But approaches to empire took shape in the more immediate shadow of the Spanish colonizing enterprises that had defined the opening phase of European New World settlement. Much of what the English knew of America came from accounts provided by Spanish governors, explorers, and missionaries.[21] A strand in English discourse remained captivated by the vast temporal conquests underwritten by the court of Madrid, and the audacity of the professed mandate, taken from the 1493 Bulls of Donation, to bring the entire world under the fold of the Church of Rome.[22] "What a coyle do the Historians keep about the Achievements of *Alexander* the Great?" mused James Howell. "We well know that he subdued but part of *Asia;* but here a new world is conquerd about thrice as big as whole *Asia.*" The kings of Spain, he believed, had claimed the mantle of Gods: "if they are angry, they drive forth whole Nations . . . if they take Arms, they conquer not only whole Kingdoms, but new Worlds."[23] In the 1665 performance of Dryden's tragedy *The Indian Emperor,* all the pyrotechnic machinery of the London stage was deployed to capture the first appearance of the Spanish fleet on the shoreline of the New World: their galleons emerging as "Divine Monsters" breathing "fire and smoke" on startled

Amerindians.[24] Spain, however, was not the only contemporary rival to entrance the English imagination. After 1618, the ascent of the kingdom of Sweden gave rise to a genre of art and poetry that portrayed the house of Vasa as the true heir to Rome, and identified the reign of Gustavus Adolphus with the last of the Four Monarchies prefigured in the Book of Daniel.[25] In 1676, an enlarged edition of the works of the Jacobean geographer John Speed suggested that the contemporary Chinese empire had outstripped the rest of the world in "ample Cities, ingenious artificers and multitude of inhabitants."[26] From East to West, these examples acclaimed territorial expansion as an exhibition of supreme political capability, a practice legitimized by its scope to advance the universal interests of mankind.

Yet while a strain in English political culture encouraged and exhorted colonial expansion, historic experiences of empire awakened other images that were far less comforting. Most empires had arisen in "Blood, Slaughter . . . Riches and Spoyls," warned the Irish jurist Charles Molloy. However noble the intentions of their founders, expanding states left their "footsteps" in the form of "misery, devaluation and poverty."[27] For all the feats of her fictional empress, Margaret Cavendish acknowledged that the real effect of territorial ambitions was made balefully apparent in the Old World that her heroine had vacated:

> not any particular State, Kingdom or Common-wealth, was contented with their own shares, but endeavoured to encroach upon their Neighbours . . . their greatest glory was in Plunder and Slaughter, and yet their victory's less then their expences, and their losses more than their gains; but their being overcome, in a manner their utter ruine.[28]

The English counterhistory of empire was quarried out of a lineage of republican and humanist texts, taking inspiration from Livy and Tacitus, and developed latterly by the radical Calvinist tradition running from George Buchanan to John Milton.[29] It was no coincidence that Satan's venture from Hell to Earth in *Paradise Lost* was compared to that of a merchant-colonist voyaging beyond the Cape of Good Hope. Empire, in the Miltonian estimation, projected the hubris of the tyrant across the largest possible canvas: the symptom of fallen beings bidding to usurp an authority that could belong to God alone.[30] For these commentators, the essential narrative arc was provided by the trajectory of Rome, from republican liberty toward despotism, pride, and infantilized luxury, as virtue emptied from the public institutions. In the statues, altars, and limitless obeisance offered up to the emperors, the citizenry "degenerated into a fashion of deformed adulation," according to the scholar and diplomat Paul Rycaut, so that any meaningful Roman civilization had withered long before the eventual loss of colonial territories.[31] As the political economist Henry Martin, a proponent of colonization, conceded in 1701, "men are afraid of comparisons with the Romans, therefore later instances must be given."[32]

Critics of expansion extracted equally unappetizing material from the contemporary world. Through the later seventeenth century, as Ottoman armies encroached on Central Europe, and English merchants increased their familiarity with the Mughal and Persian polities, a ready genre of printed and dramatic productions brought the empires of the East before English opinion, and presented them as a synecdoche for moral and civic dissolution.[33] "Too truly *Tamerlain*'s Successors they," laments one witness in John Dryden's *Aureng-Zebe,* "each thinks a World too little for his sway."[34] While acknowledging some social virtues still persistent among the Turkish peoples, Paul Rycaut's 1667 *Present State of the Ottoman Empire* delineated an entire political order placed at the whim of a single individual "whose speeches may be irrational, and yet must be laws; whose actions irregular, and yet examples; whose sentence and judgement . . . are most commonly corrupt, and yet decrees irresistible." The workings of this "great Babylon" hinged on the labors of slaves, captives, and mercenaries "daily transported to nourish and feed the body." Methods of rule imposed over conquered provinces had been projected back to change the governance of the original territories, leaving Turks trapped in a system of uniformity that stifled minds and bodies. While "they thirst and haste to be rich," Rycaut suggested, it was the tragedy of the Turkish people that "their treasure is but their snare; what they labour for is but as slaves for their great Patron and Master." For all the magnificence of the palaces at Istanbul, private residences "are made slight, not durable"; travellers would "finde no delightful Orchards and pleasant Gardens" because a people uncertain of their future liberties had been granted no incentive to plant, sow, cultivate, or beautify. As the artistic life fell away, so the moral order was destabilized, with rewards and punishments dispensed only on the principle of an "entire and blind obedience."[35] From the earl of Orrery's *Mustapha* (1665) to Elkanah Settle's *Cambyses* (1667) and Dryden's *Aureng-Zebe* (1675), the London stage similarly depicted oriental and Asiatic households descending into unrestrained sensuality, fratricidal cruelty, and unhinged clashes over the royal succession.[36] Relationships became incestuous, and passions "unnatural," because—as English authors incessantly reminded their audiences—emperors themselves transgressed the laws of nature, by grasping at a power that was not theirs to possess.[37] In turn, the prize of *grandezza* became a false jewel: a mirage that tempted princes into the loss of their political sanity, their moral orientation, and invariably, their lives.

While these arguments indulged a particular set of orientalist motifs, English indictments of empire were not confined to the realm of Eastern "barbarism." In Europe, the reality of greed and lust for earthly power was registered in the form of "popery": a spirit many Protestants believed had been incarnated when Roman pontiffs began to engross the power and wealth of the city's fallen emperors, but which, by 1600, had gained expression in the Spanish bid for the "universal monarchy."[38] Through the seventeenth century, Protestant political and imaginative literature kept alive the "black legend" of Spanish atrocities against the native peoples of Central America. A new translation of Bartolomé de Las Casas's "Account of the Destruction of the Indies" appeared in 1656, followed by William Davenant's dramatization of *The Cruelty of the Spaniards in Peru*: both works intended to mobilize moral fervor for the Cromwellian assault on the Caribbean.[39] Such writings anathematized the basic foundations of the Spanish Empire, and delegitimized its rulers' claims "as Vicars of Christ to give power to dispose of ye kingdoms of ye world at their pleasure," in the words of the Scottish statesman John Clerk of Penicuik.[40] If there had been any providential sanction behind the Spanish taking of the New World, believed Peter Heylin, it rested on the duty of protecting and evangelizing the Amerindian population. This right had long since been nullified, after the conquerors instead "consumed the people in their Mines; and out of the thirst for Bloud . . . destroyed Millions of the Natives."[41] Beneath the patina of Catholic zeal, gold was "the God of the Christians" in Central

America, according to the Royal Society fellow John Davies, and in Dryden's account of the last *Indian Emperor,* the worship of precious metal proceeds inexorably toward the torture of the Aztec leader Montezuma, who is lifted on the rack at the exhortations of a fanatical priest after he refuses to disclose the location of the Mexican mines.[42] The Americas had become the playground for all the heats and lusts of popery, and the "tears of the Indians" functioned as a dreadful premonition of the fate awaiting Protestant Europe, if the universal monarchy fell into the hands of Madrid.

Yet English critics were adamant that the riches of America had opened up a poisoned well for Spanish princes. A growing chorus of commentators contended that in piling up "Crowns, Scepters and Titles one upon another," the Habsburgs had given rise to a wasteful and mismanaged dominion, one hollowed out by ceaseless wars and the fiscal needs of vast frontiers.[43] Dryden's *Indian Emperor* was shot through with portents of decline, culminating in the prophecy from one guilt-ridden conquistador that "into Spain wilt fatally be brought" the "price of Blood" occasioned by greed, enslavement, and expropriation of Indian lands.[44] From this perspective, colonial excesses became a providential cause of the run of Spanish defeats experienced at the hands of the Dutch, French, and Portuguese through the middle of the seventeenth century. The people of Spain had caught only fleeting glimpses of the riches that had "tantalised" their princes, reported the English ambassador, William Godolphin, in 1670, because the resources expended to maintain "Governours, Councils, & Soldiers," and secure "Guarisons, Audencias, Armadas," far outstripped any rewards delivered by distant provinces.[45] The Indies, as the Scottish projector William Paterson concluded in 1700, "hath rather conquered Spain than Spain hath conquered the Indies," and the anatomy of Spanish decline added the final component to the humanist and Protestant critique of empire—its insurmountable failure, degeneration, and collapse.[46] "The greatest monarchies of the world, the Babylonian, Persian, Grecian, Roman, have all had their periods, nothing remaining of them now but the name and memory," Peter Heylin reminded his readers. The reason was that when a polity "laboureth with nothing more than the weightiness of it self . . . it must in a manner needs decline." Too much "extent of empire doth sooner draw on a ruin, than either too little or a mediocrity," because endless grasping at territory followed not from reasoned strategy, but from pride and vice. From empty palaces to deserted pyramids, silent amphitheaters and crumbling temples, the stage of human history was littered with the debris of mighty potentates who had failed to overcome debilities created by their own "crying sins."[47]

The English imagination therefore split apart in response to the prospect of colonization. While one strand of opinion celebrated a chance to achieve greatness and restore virtue, a contending line of argument painted empire as a product of the tyrant's artillery of oppression: morally corrosive, intellectually sterile, and doomed to decline. Many authors, including John Dryden and James Howell, shifted uneasily between both perspectives. Far from setting up Eastern or Catholic empires as the cultural "other," narratives of world history impressed on their readers the potential parallels with the newly imperial Stuart kingdom, and came laced with thinly veiled warnings for the architects of English overseas expansion. Rycaut's history of the Ottoman Empire was interspersed with anxious praise for Charles II for protecting "the liberty of my own Country, where men . . . enjoy and eat of the fruit of their own labour." Rycaut adjured his compatriots to live peacefully "within our own borders" as a more abiding source of "glory and content" than "the honour of being slaves to the lusts of a Monarch, whose titles comprehend the greatest part of the World."[48] These arguments infused an idea—embedded in political commentary since the Elizabethan wars—of England as a commonwealth whose role in the world arose from *challenging* mighty empires, rather than from creating them. "If Neighbour states have provoked the World, we pity them," pronounced one survey of the state of Europe, in 1666, "if other Princes throw away their People with vain and ambitious Attempts, we are onely employed to secure our own Borders, to promote our own Interests and Honour."[49] The English "ancient constitution" was seen to prohibit large-scale conquest, by preventing monarchs from rising to the state of despotism necessary to attain it.[50] Even the island geography of the realm—a "little world" or "empire in itself"—militated against excessive outgrowth: "like a Tortoise in her shell," James Howell believed, "so prodigiously armd for her defence only."[51] The model of Rome, Spain, or Istanbul was not merely morally baleful, but politically unfeasible.

Protestantism and Overseas Expansion

English colonists crossed the seas sensitive to the anxieties made ambient in print, play, and sermon, and seeking ways to present their own undertakings as a break from the unappealing patterns of European history. Commentators agonized over whether it would be possible to create an alternative model of empire that universalized the laws, liberty, and religion of the English realm. Thomas Sprat insisted that his compatriots "indeavor, more than most other Nations, to preserve inviolable the freedom of mankind," so that "wherever the Bounds of our Empire have reach'd in ancient Times, there still remains on the minds of the people a Remembrance of the easiness of the English Government."[52] This conviction became amplified over half a century of military and ideological mobilization against the Crown of Spain. America appeared in the form of an Amazonian princess at the Grocer's Company procession through the City of London in 1672, exhorting Charles II for deliverance from "the haughty Spaniard," who "Ransack'd my riches, over-ran my land."[53] For one author, writing in the wake of the Restoration, "conquest can give ye Spanyard noe fayre pretence to ye Dominion of the Indyes." Conversely, it conferred rights upon the English, if the Indians—the "naturall proprietors" of America—called upon their protection, to unseat the "cruell usurpation" imposed from Europe.[54] Construed in this way, the Stuart dominion would develop as a force of *liberation* for souls and bodies trapped under tyranny, with Indian polities submitting, of their own volition, to the guardianship of the English realm. Another treatise in the possession of Thomas Povey invoked the defensive leagues formed between Christians against Turkish onslaughts in "Cyprus, Hungary &c" as a precedent for combined Anglo-Indian action against the power of Madrid.[55]

These ideas were presented with an overlay of Protestant fervor, and an intermittent mood of apocalypticism. As David Armitage has argued, English writings elicited no single identifiable or exclusively Protestant theology of colonization—instead many authors tended to impose the language of the reformed religion upon pre-existing classical or Thomistic justifications for overseas expansion.[56] Nonetheless, since the reign of Elizabeth, warfare, plunder, and piracy against Spain had been sanctioned by an understanding of the New World as the theater for destruction of the Roman-Iberian "Babylon."[57] Through the later seventeenth century, confessional narratives, scriptural injunctions, and millennial speculation still entered into Privy Council papers, pamphlets, and advertisements for settlement, introducing colonial activity to wide sections of the public domain."[58] For Peter Heylin, English colonization could be judged by its contribution toward a greater salvific purpose—first enshrined when Christopher Columbus cut a cross into the earth upon his landing on the American shoreline.[59] The claim of "Dominion by grace" had afforded in reality a moral rather than a legal sanction for Spanish colonization, modified through a century of political and theological debate.[60] But almost two hundred years after their dissemination, the Bulls of Donation were widely identified by English diplomats as the fountainhead of Iberian claims over the New World.[61] The precedent raised questions over whether the Protestant religion could supply a true and superior claim over the same "pagan" territory, as the foundation of a rival, redemptive form of empire.

Writing in 1584, Richard Hakluyt had been willing to endorse the Habsburg claim that divine workmanship opened up "the bottomless treasure of His riches" in America, in recognition of the piety of the "good Queene Isabella." He contended, however, that the Reformation, together with Spanish massacres of the Aztec and Inca populations, had brought about a providential supersession, passing to the princes of England the divine authority to command the conquest of the New World, for the conversion and reclamation of its peoples.[62] Later writers also saw viable intellectual material—however thinly acknowledged—in Spanish political theology. While the English Crown commonly invoked "first discovery" as the basis for claims over newfound lands, colonists including William Penn fretted that the principle risked appearing "slight and dangerous," without any clarification as to "how farr that Discovery goeth" beyond what "the Discoverers see with their own eyes."[63] The wording of many colonial charters subtly enlarged the claim, by placing "first discovery" on Christian underpinnings. In 1670, the grant conferred upon the Hudson's Bay Company extended across designated "Landes, Countryes and Territoryes which are not now actually possessed ... by the Subjectes of any other Christian Prince or State."[64] The Crown justified its right over Tangier, via purchase from the Portuguese, on the grounds that "no other Christians have ever had possession of it, in these late years at least."[65] More ambiguously, Penn suggested of Delaware "that a country wch is no body's is the Right of him that occupieth and enjoyeth it; for *there was no Christian Body* there at the time the Dutch seated it."[66] Implicitly, English authorities posited that lands unpopulated by Christians constituted a wilderness belonging to no one. America became open to Christian settlement because the expansion of the Church was the overriding reason why God had brought the New World before the gaze of Europeans.

For most, although not all, Restoration authors, the logic of this argument was the integration of Amerindians into the colonial moral and religious community, and, thenceforth, into the greater universe of Protestant Christianity. Many reflections came accompanied by reluctant admiration for the achievements of the global mission pioneered by Jesuits and Franciscans, despite its vitiation by the violence and error of Catholic empires. Authors spanning the confessional spectrum, from the Anglican royalist James Howell to the Presbyterian George Scot, were awed by the evangelical self-confidence emerging from the Spanish colonies, by the "Churches, Chappels, Monasteries and Convents" that threaded their way through "thousands of miles" of Central America, and the claim to have planted "the tree of life" through conversion of a heathen population.[67] English Protestants were acutely conscious of the command, emanating from the Book of Matthew, that "this gospel of the kingdom shall be preached in all the world," and fearful of the comparative paucity of Indian converts in their own colonial provinces.[68] Through the reign of Charles II, the New World appeared for a stream of commentators as a site of providential judgment on the kingdom.[69] The English, it was argued, would break the imperial cycle of tyranny and corruption only by nurturing a generation of Christian mariners, soldiers, merchants, and planters fit to bear the banners of the reformed religion into Indian communities and American wastelands.

Yet any notion that "true religion" could sanction territorial enlargement, and supply just claims for the Crown over American soil, failed to command visible consensus on either side of the English Atlantic. The theology of "dominion by Grace" jarred with the longstanding English boast to have occupied American lands only "by ye desire & voluntary consent of ye na-tives," as the royal commissioner in New York, Samuel Maverick, insisted in 1665.[70] A vigorous strand in Protestant thought recoiled from the notion of appropriating the intellectual weaponry of the Counter-Reformation. Writing in 1627, Bishop Joseph Hall had damned the practice of "planting religion by the sword" as an affront not merely to natural law, but also to the sacred truth that Christ's kingdom was not of this world. Since "dominion and propriety is not founded in Religion, but in a naturall, and civill right," Hall affirmed, errant belief could supply no just or rational grounds to take titles or territory from nonbelievers—to "debarre any man from a rightful claim and fruition of these earthly inheritances."[71] Hall, like many Protes-tant contemporaries, drew from the internal criticisms of Iberian methods issued by Francisco di Vitoria and other authors within the "School of Salamanca."[72] Advancing even further than these authorities, Hall urged churchmen to resist turning to the weaponry of empire, even if pagan princes forcibly and maliciously obstructed the movement of the Gospel. Barbaric and degenerate as heathen societies might appear, there could be no justification for having their peoples "cudgelled into Christianity" through conquest.[73]

The territorial realities of English colonization cleaved even more sharp-ly against the prospect of a missionary enterprise modelled after Spanish America. Unlike their Iberian rivals, English planters had failed to conquer or subjugate Amerindian societies, and the volatility of the frontier inclined most authorities rather to push native peoples away from the colonial bor-ders, erecting defensive walls between settler societies and the tribal dominions beyond. Through the century, the marriage of the Indian Poca-hontas to the Virginia frontiersman John Rolfe remained famous precisely because it was so rare.[74] The Puritan ideologues who had pioneered the settlement of Massachusetts had first defined their venture according to an evangelical vocation—signalled famously in the seal of the Bay Colony, with its depiction of an Indian issuing the scriptural exhortation to "Come over and helpe us." Yet the early development of colonial New England strengthened Calvinist doubts over the efficacy of conversion through hu-man agency. Protestant interests ran up against the sheer enormity of the pedagogic operation required to introduce speakers of uncodified languages to a religion centered on the written word. Protestantism lacked the visual and material translatability of its Catholic rival, and its missionaries were less at ease with seeking out local customs and beliefs as building blocks toward conversion.[75] With sentiments hardened by military and territorial clashes, a strong strand of New England Calvinist opinion came to envision the Indians more instinctively as "roaring Lyons and savage Bears" sent to scourge the sins of the faithful, than as human material for conversion.[76] Seating themselves far from the battlegrounds on the Spanish frontier, the New England settlers turned away from the Elizabethan blueprint for missionary-imperial expansion. They mapped America instead as a refuge against the "common corruptions of this world," in the words of the colonial leader John Winthrop, and as holy ground for the fortification of an enclosed Elect (Calvinist planters themselves).[77] For one later New York colonist, "the mysterious works of God"—the winnowing down of Indian numbers through Old World diseases—reinforced the identity of the New World as a site of renewal for existing believers, rather than as a place to capture new souls.[78]

In plantations up and down the American seaboard, English settlers reconceptualized great spaces of the New World not as mission stations or theaters of warfare against "popery," but as a *vacuum domicilum* awaiting the application of human labor. They extracted an alternative scriptural foundation from the "Grand Charter" of Genesis, which enjoined mankind "to increase and multiply and replenish the earth and subdue it," as John Winthrop proposed: imposing orderly cultivation on the wilderness, for the benefit of human habitation, and the moral life. From this proposition, colonists drew out the implication that "in a vacant soyle hee that taketh possession of it, and bestoweth culture and husbandry upon it, his Right it is."[79] This "agriculturalist argument" was popularized in images of America as a fertile goddess, or virgin bride ready to be claimed by a virtuous suitor—in John Hammond's pamphlet of 1656, Virginia and Maryland appeared as "two fruitful sisters."[80] Such ideas offered a justification for settlement that was biblical, but not specifically Protestant. Agriculturalist arguments were deployed in 1682 by the Catholic Lord Baltimore to stake his claim over disputed territories on the lower Delaware.[81] While this vision was not incompatible with missionary work, it de-emphasized Indian conversions as a commanding obligation—giving biblical sanction for settlers to confine their exertions to the occupation of "wastes, or *asperi montes,* which the Natives make no use of," in the words of Charles Molloy.[82] Englishmen, according to this analysis, could honor God as faithfully by clearing, planting, and harvesting the wilderness as by conquering pagan souls. By focusing on the creation of exemplary communities, they would draw any regenerate Indians toward them by providential motion.[83]

The Crown and the Renewal of the Protestant Mission

The Protestant imagination was therefore ruptured in response to America. Missionizing and agriculturalist arguments opened up rival theological approaches to colonization, and intimated radically different models for the development of planted territories. By 1660, however, circumstances both domestic and international favored those lobbyists who aimed to reintegrate evangelical work into English colonizing strategies. Anglo-Indian connections had increased steadily over half a century, driven by the settlers' need for territorial knowledge and military intelligence. Through the 1650s, the momentum had gathered especially in Puritan New England, after tribal conflicts devastated the territorial holdings of the Massachusetts Indians and flooded the neighboring Bay Colony with uprooted indigenous laborers. Magistrates in Connecticut sought to incorporate their Pocomtuc allies as "English Indians," on a foundation of mutual protection, and hoped to deepen the alliance through a union of souls and consciences.[84] In the "praying towns" established within Massachusetts at Natick, Roxbury, and Martha's Vineyard, the New England clergyman John Eliot constructed a platform for Christianization, and an interim model to ease the incorporation of proselytes into colonial society, with Indians, in practice, offered considerable agency over the terms of their own conversion.[85] These activities sat within wider global currents, as Protestant clergymen from across Europe began to compete more vigorously in the pursuit of "new lights" for the Christian faith on other continents. Calvinist consciences in North America were aroused by the translation of the Dutch Bible into Malayan in 1636. The subsequent harvest of conversions boasted by Dutch pastors in the East Indies offered evidence that the written Scripture was as effective as a tool for propagating the faith as were the imagistic "toys" deployed by Jesuits.[86]

The case for reviving missionary activities was sustained by a particular analysis of the origins and spiritual capability of the Indians themselves. However difficult the work of conversion might prove to be, most English authors did not see the gulf with indigenous peoples as unbridgeable—indeed, among the occupants of the New World, it was the Spanish who were more commonly perceived to stand beyond the reach of civilized humanity. The greater tendency in Restoration writings was to Europeanize the Indians: discovering monarchies, empires, and viceroyalties alongside analogous political and legal practices "as if the Sun had in his journies been imployed by God Almighty, the Author of all Wisdome *and* Goodness, to scatter and infuse it with his light into the minds and understandings of mankind," as the jurist Fabian Philipps suggested.[87] Racial identity—or any notion of biologically determined differences between peoples—was at most an inchoate element within European intellectual culture. Overwhelmingly, the shock of the unknown was contained by a monogenist theology that traced all human genealogies back to the colonizing sons of Noah.[88] Later seventeenth-century commentators were divided over whether the Indian pedigree pointed back to the Jews (William Penn and, with greater doubt, John Eliot), Phoenicians (John Ogilby), or Tartars (Peter Heylin and Increase Mather).[89] But their conclusions reduced differences of color or complexion to the surface product of climatic exposure, cosmetic practices—"dyings of Roots and Barks . . . to metamorphize their hydes into a dark Cinamon brown," according to the Maryland colonist George Alsop—or, simply, as Sir Thomas Browne had surmised, the unknowable "administration of angels."[90] Reports of indigenous beliefs offered fugitive glimpses of the consanguinity between Indians and Europeans—evinced in distorted recollections of the Flood, an understanding of the immortality of the Soul, and a conception, as Peter Heylin put it, "of some Ubi for the future reception of it beyond certain Hills, where those which lived honestly and justly . . . should find a place of everlasting peace and happiness."[91]

These claims militated against the rigid dichotomy between "self" and "other" that some modern scholars have read into early colonizing attitudes.[92]

For the New Englander Roger Williams and other close observers, the Amerindian character showed, to the contrary, that the boundaries between Christianity and heathenism were porous—and, indeed, shone a light on "heathen" traits detectable among settlers, and in unregulated corners of England and Wales.[93] In Massachusetts, these reflections were integrated into a long process of spiritual self-examination, as preachers interrogated the duties of godly societies, and agonized over how to approach those outside the Christian fold.[94] For many New Englanders, the adjustment in worldview was a discomforting experience. The Jewish genealogy ascribed to the Indians by some clergymen evinced anxious attempts to work evangelical processes into the familiar narrative of conversion and salvation gleaned from sacred history.[95] Yet, supporters argued, the history of the early church showed that even the most unyielding gentile nonbelievers could be coaxed into embracing the Gospel under proper stewardship. Since "we cannot expect the nations should be brought in by Angels from heaven," as the Puritan minister John Oxenbridge put it in 1670, the obligation logically fell to "the servants of Christ on earth." The duties of the faithful, he averred, could never be served by "retreating to any part of Europe," or in building colonies on vacant lands, "remote from the Indians" that "hath no immediate tendency to this service."[96] In this way, godly Protestants wove the Indians into a soteriological framework that implicated all humanity, and so invited the possibility of converting and reforming receptive individuals scattered throughout the darkest enclaves of the earth.

After 1660, the New England praying towns captured the imagination of the restored Crown as it sought to revive English territorial ambitions across the Atlantic. The Privy Council instructed the governor of Massachusetts that "improving the knowledge of Him and His Holy name in the correction of infidells & pagans . . . ought to be the cheife end of all Christian Plantations."[97] New charters dispensed to Rhode Island and Carolina outlined the promulgation of Christianity as a means to "enlarge our English Empire," and a baptism service for congregants "of riper years" was added to the 1662 Prayerbook, conceived for the use of "Natives in our Plantations."[98] In 1662, the Crown incorporated the praying towns within a charter granted to the New England Company to raise funds, print devotional literature, and integrate the "praying Indians" under English authority. Legally speaking, the Company grant was no innovation, and simply set the royal seal on pre-existing rights claimed by its antecedent body, the Society for the Propagation of the Gospel in New England, which had been founded during the Interregnum. Politically, however, the Company was transformed, and inducted into the colonialist strategy and ideology of the Stuart court, with eight privy councillors now seated on its committee, and the natural philosopher Robert Boyle appointed as governor. Under its aegis, John Eliot's translation of the Old and New Testaments into Algonquian emerged from the printing presses in 1663, as the first bible in any Indian language. Dedicated to Charles II, it was acclaimed by the Puritan divine Richard Baxter as such a "Work and Fruit of a Plantation as was never before presented to a King."[99] These initiatives pointed toward a transformation in the intended reach and ambition of the English Crown. "Change the education of men and you shall see that their nature will be greatly rectified and corrected," the Virginia clergyman Robert Gray had urged in 1604.[100] For exponents of the mission, no better precedent was offered to the English than the history of their own domain—once itself "rough and rugged . . . blind and barbarous as the Indians," as the Quaker William Loddington put it.[101] As the Long Islander John Scott recalled, the "improvement" of the "heathen Brittans" had rested on the agency of an occupying power—the Roman conquerors whose arrival opened the gateway for later Christian missionaries.[102] Just as the Romans had wrenched the Celts toward civilization, so too the possessors of English America now had a duty to replenish the spiritual as well as the physical wasteland, and to reframe the minds of the peoples they encountered.

The debate over Indian conversions was inherently bound up with political questions over the type of empire that the English were aspiring to create. Despite the "forward Protestant" language, patrons of missionary work were spelling out a vision that encroached ever more deeply on the intellectual resources of Catholic empires. John Eliot acknowledged that his apprehension of the Indian language as a system suited to reception of the Scriptures had been animated in conversation with a "French friar, sent Ambassador from Canada to our Massachusetts."[103] The fiercely Protestant Long Islander John Scott paid tribute to "the excellent Josephus D'Acosta": the Jesuit whose writings supplied an analytical rubric for understanding the "natural and moral" structure of Indian societies.[104] Pitched with appeals to the temporal needs and deficiencies of England's thinly populated overseas provinces, the American mission pushed equally toward the *practices* of the Spanish dominions. The charter to the New England Company endorsed the "educating, clothing, and civilising" of Indian converts, and encouraged "placing out the natives or their children . . . in English families and with English masters."[105] For the MP Roger Whitley, the logic of Christianization obliged English settlers to attempt a larger program of incorporation that would culminate finally with intermarriage: merging the tribes "as one People with us," as "our own Subjectes."[106]

By 1660, evangelical appeals that had dwindled through the early seventeenth century had been revitalized, as royal ambitions moved hand in hand with cultural changes within colonial Calvinism. Commentators repositioned Amerindians within the boundaries of God's domain, and identified their conversion as both an instrument of territorial outgrowth and an essential source of moral legitimation. As the planter gained nourishment from the fruits and corn of the earth, so the kingdom would profit from the harvesting of Indian souls: spiritual beings brought to fruition in newly fertile lands as subjects of the Crown, and as manifestations of divine blessing for its overseas exertions. These hopes possessed even greater logic in the emergent settlements of the East, where European migration had been minimal and English administrators ruled over large populations of non-Europeans. Through the 1670s, EIC governors extended legal rights in common with the English to the native inhabitants of Bombay, while Robert Boyle assembled a roll call of City of London and aristocratic subscribers in support of new projects for propagating the Gospel in the Indian and Malayan languages.[107] Yet many of these ideas sat uneasily with the original Protestant responses to Iberian conquests in the New World, and with the moral and theological commentaries through which past Calvinist authors had set up their window on the world. English commentators were enunciating a divine mandate for *imperium,* and lodging claims over peoples as well as terrain on behalf of Charles II. In doing so, they were moving closer to the very models of territorial expansion—Spanish, Catholic, and Roman—that they had hitherto deemed most liable to become oppressive, corrupt, and inimical to Christian teaching.

Natural Philosophy and Colonial Conquest

The creation of a Protestant mission was not the only way in which the English imagined their dominion both exceeding the achievements of the ancient states and being cleansed of the moral taints that had brought about their downfall. Through the decade after the Restoration, some of the strongest paeans to the possibilities of English overseas expansion arose among the self-proclaimed virtuosi who had established the Royal Society out of the correspondence networks around the Prussian émigré Samuel Hartlib.[108] In private exchanges and published literature, scholars hailed the intellectual novelty of the colonial experience, which they saw embodied in the torrent of exotic artifacts entering the port of London. There was "scarce a Ship come up the Thames," proclaimed Thomas Sprat, and "never yet any Land, discover'd," which had not given "us divers new sorts of Animals . . . Fruits, People of different Features, and shapes, and virtues from our own."[109] Sprat, Hartlib, and their associates pored over the routes of English voyagers, cultivating correspondents in colonial towns and trading factories, and coaxing their affiliates into carrying back physical traces of unfamiliar landscapes. "We have . . . taken to taske the whole Universe," the Society's secretary Henry Oldenburg informed John Winthrop, and "are obliged to do soe by the nature of our dessein."[110] By recording, preserving, and classifying "rarities" of art and nature, the virtuosi wished to impart a new set of attitudes, habits, and intellectual preferences: a receptiveness to the unknown, and a Baconian emphasis on utility and practicality, to prove, as John Evelyn put it, that "there is nothing meane in nature, nor has she produced anything in vaine."[111]

The aspirations of the Royal Society had not originally been conditioned by English territorial interests—the first contacts initiated by Henry Oldenburg included members of the Dutch VOC operating in Java, and Portuguese merchants sailing to Brazil.[112] But the search for patronage and publicity drew scholars to champion the "noble and inquisitive genius" of English colonists and merchants, and to link their own exertions to the goal of successful overseas expansion. Thomas Sprat even presented the Royal Society as the "twin sister" to the newly founded company of Royal Adventurers Trading to Africa, both institutions being created as instruments to achieve national greatness through overseas activity.[113] By 1668, East India House had become home to cabinets strewn with Asian curiosities—from which gifts were occasionally donated to the Royal Society.[114] Oldenburg ushered into the fellowship a cohort of supporters in Whitehall who aimed to call on the society's newly anatomized knowledge to enlarge the scope and ingenuity of the royal administration.[115] Thomas Povey, elected to the council of the Royal Society in 1663, urged the agents for Virginia that it would advance colonial interests to address queries submitted by those "Ingenious Persons" meeting "by his Maties Encouragement" in order to "raise by their Inquisition and Industrie some observations to the benefitt of mankind."[116] The collecting habits encouraged by Sprat and Evelyn were not immune to contemporary satire—in 1696, Mary Astell would pass a withering verdict on diletantes who "ransack all Parts both of *Earth* and *Sea*" to install "philosophicall toyshops" inside their studies.[117] But the fellows accentuated "curiosity" as a means toward measurable "improvements" in the public domain: converting "contemplations of Nature," as Oldenburg put it, "unto Use and Practise" to "render ym more serviceable for . . . ye Life of Man."[118] Sir Thomas Lynch, plunged as governor into the factional politics of Jamaica in 1671, sought to bolster his position by the creation of a gift-giving network, using a channel of intermediaries to introduce elements of Jamaican culture and experience to members of the Royal Society. Samples of vanilla, chocolate, and coconut crossed the Atlantic, accompanied by sketches produced by Lynch's wife and commentaries "upon the history and husbandry" of local crops.[119] These, the governor was bemused to find, had "occasioned my Matriculation among the Philosophers," with an account published in the Society's *Philosophical Transactions* in 1672, though "att best I shall be but able to talke like a Planter."[120]

The connections between political and scholarly networks meant that discourses on natural philosophy became a crucible for larger ideologies of overseas empire. With their cargoes of "curiosities," every returning vessel afforded resources to "render England ye Glory of ye Western World," Henry Oldenburg believed, "by making it ye Seat of ye best knowledge, as well as it may be ye Seat of ye greatest Trade."[121] Correspondingly, the language and imagery of scientific invention informed the rationale given for English colonizing practices. "I intend to throw away some money in making some experiments there," mused Anthony Ashley Cooper to Thomas Lynch, in writing of his Carolina proprietary.[122] Colonies became laboratories in themselves—with the planting of settlements considered akin to the plantation of new crops. Discoveries extracted from foreign soil were studied for ways to pioneer medicinal, dietary, or material improvements, and to inform calculations as to the value of overseas provinces. More elementally, the process of recording, anatomizing, and comprehending the world was seen to translate into a form of possession—the agriculturalist argument was appropriated for the practice of natural philosophy. "Wee can give man dominion over the Winds, Ayre, Water & Lands," promised the clergyman John Beale, "search the bowells of the Earth, & by our springs discover all her treasures."[123] Transferred into the fictional realm, natural philosophy provided the tools that enabled Margaret Cavendish's heroine to gain power and control over the Blazing World. The empress, she recorded, "spent most of her time in the study of Natural Causes and Effects," and "loved to discourse sometimes with the most Learned persons of that World," exhorting her *virtuosi* "to busie your selves with such Experiments as may be beneficial to the publick."[124] Mental mastery was perceived to pave the way for political and territorial supremacy—and an empire that would outstrip the tyrannies of the past, because it celebrated rather than suffocated intellectual inquiry.[125]

The link between scholarly and colonial enterprise was not new to the 1660s. Thomas Hariot, a veteran of the 1584 expedition to Roanoke, had appealed to the court of Queen Elizabeth to cultivate an intellectual fraternity for colonization, arguing that supremacy over the New World rested as much on "Mathematicall instruments, sea compasses . . . burning glasses," and "wildfire workes" as on militarized manpower.[126] Population surveys, statistical registers, and other tools of "political arithmetic" were all encouraged by Protestant "improvers" in Ireland as means to foment economic reforms, and to redeem the land and its people from social and spiritual malaise.[127] But through the later seventeenth century, reflections on overseas expansion contributed to a highly self-conscious scholarly battle of "ancients and moderns," as authors crossed swords over the extent to which classical authorities still provided the surest framework for intellectual life.[128] Sprat charged "the Method of the Schole-men" of Greece and Rome with "infecting" readers by "airy conceptions" that had "not much foundation in nature." By contrast, he believed, the principal blessing drawn out of eyewitness experimentation was to "make us live in England, and not in Athens or Sparta."[129] If contemporary scholars and statesmen still stood on the shoulders of the ancients, they could see farther and range more widely. The result promised unimaginable power for the kingdom that harnessed new knowledge and new technology to its own territorial advancement. Charles II's attraction toward this view of the world was attested by the earl of Clarendon, who saw in the king "so little Reverence or Esteem for Antiquity . . . that the Objections of Novelty rather advanced than obstructed any Proposition."[130] The possibilities were dramatized in the tumultuous climax to *The Blazing World,* where the empress returns to the Old World as a terrifying queen of sciences, marshalling engine-powered submarines, explosive fireballs, and floating platforms, in an expedition that worked "not onely" to "save her Native Country, but made it the Absolute Monarchy of all that World."[131]

These arguments carried moral and ideological implications. As they challenged classical understandings of the universe, so exponents of natural philosophy struck at assumptions taken from ancient writings over the profanity, obscurantism, and irresistible failure of temporal empires. Republican and humanist authors had seen only sinful self-delusion in the desire of mortal men to possess and control the far-flung world. By contrast, voices within the English virtuosi believed that an empire that made use of scholarly innovation would be steered by God's pleasure.[132] The conquest of the world by scholars and seamen represented, for the clergyman John Flavel, the opening of the divinely revealed book, of which "the Heavens, the Earth, the Waters are the three great Leaves," and "all the Creatures so many Lines in those Leaves," inscribed in "God's excellent Handwriting."[133] The discovery and utilization of the earth's treasures became a recapture of wisdom lost with the Fall—for the political economist William Petty, "hee who shall give the reason and use of what lyes in the 8,000 miles space between the 2 poles of the Earth" would "honour God more than by singing his *Te Deum* every day."[134] Where critics feared that an expanding empire violated "nature's law," champions of experimental science celebrated attempts to gain dominion over the world; to reveal, release, and improve on the blessings of the earth. In availing itself of "new learning," Petty believed, the enlarged English realm would become a vessel for the expansion of human capability, avoiding the fate of the "barbarous" empires because its triumph would arrest cultural decline altogether, enabling man "to advance from the bottome (where he now is) towards the top of the great scale."[135]

Scholarship, Commerce, and Rival Visions of Empire

The concept of a providentially supported "empire of knowledge" provided at least a rhetorical counterpoise to many of the objections to territorial expansion. More ambiguous was the question of precisely what kind of dominion best fulfilled the promises gifted by natural philosophy. Many enthusiasts within the Royal Society allied themselves to the court's plans for new plantations in America, and endorsed the propagation of the Gospel as an agent in the process. The link between natural philosophy and Protestant evangelism was exemplified in the career of Robert Boyle, governor and devoted helmsman of the New England Company. Boyle's writings described evidence of Indian conversions as the greatest of America's discovered "rarities" and an unfolding of God's plan for the resurrection of the human intellect.[136]

Yet while missionary projects in America took on key elements of the Spanish colonial model, the insights from natural philosophy became increasingly tied to the prospect of constructing an entirely different kind of empire, one that broke from unwelcome precedents in both the ancient and contemporary worlds. Henry Sheres, the Royal Society fellow appointed surveyor of works at Tangier, believed that Baconian methods of computation and calculation opened up the "untrodden path" toward world dominion, fostered through the study of winds, tides, and climatic variations that dictated oceanic navigation. This enhanced geographical consciousness, he argued, invited the English to eschew vast conquests and concentrate only on those parts of the globe that offered "knowledge and plenty," calibrated according to strict strategic and commercial tests.[137]

Whereas advocates for the praying towns imagined themselves cleansing America of "the drosse of Indian barbarism," in the words of one early Carolina tract, many voices within the virtuosi struck a cosmopolitan posture toward non-European societies.[138] In 1668, Henry Oldenburg wrote to

English Tangier's envoy to the Moroccan Empire, urging his correspondent to enter into the streets, markets, mosques, and synagogues of Barbary to track down "what Arts, Practises and studies they are particularly given to," and to investigate even Moroccan traditions of magic and fortune-telling for glimmerings of intellectual truths found "wanting in Christendom."[139] The projection of English power would rest on encouraging friendship and mutuality between peoples, argued Charles Molloy, capitalizing on the "wonderful" artistry of the divine power, which had endowed that "there is no Society Nation, Countrey or Kingdom but stands in need of each other," to "adorn the conveniences of humane life."[140] These arguments did not neglect the calls for a Christian undergirding to English global enterprise. It was through "civil traffic" and exchange, claimed John Flavel, that God dispensed "precious Gifts and Graces of his Spirit," binding the "Family of Christ" by common needs and mutual enticements.[141] But Sheres and Molloy envisaged advantageous trading patterns rather than territorial conquests, civil conversation over colonial imposition, as ways for Englishmen to spread the Gospel outside Europe and bring glory back into their own kingdom.

Ideas drawn out of natural philosophy therefore placed moral and intellectual authority on the notion of England pursuing an "empire of the seas" that maintained only the lightest territorial footprint outside its own borders. Taking possession solely of islands, isthmuses, and peninsulas necessary to attract commerce meant that the English could become lawgivers "to the World," according to the merchant James Whiston, without laboring "under the Toils of Alexander & the Cesars," and having to maintain "mighty Armies or charge of Numerous Garrisons."[142] Projecting power through control of trade and sea routes, Englishmen would garner all the fruits of foreign lands without incurring the burden of foreign occupation. "Ours is the harvest where the Indians mow," as the poet Edmund Waller suggested in a 1655 *Panegyrick* to Oliver Cromwell: "We plough the deep and reap whatever others sow."[143] The notion had a long pedigree in English commentary. Sir Philip Sidney—deeply skeptical of colonial entanglements— had believed that Elizabethan exertions in the New World would succeed only if they resisted emulating the Iberians, and focused on creating an "emporium for the confluence of all nations that love or profess any kinde of vertue or commerce."[144] The best precedent, for Paul Rycaut, came when "the mighty"—but inherently terrestrial—"force of the Ottoman Empire" was repeatedly "foiled and baffled" by the marine dexterity of "the small Republique of *Venice*."[145] Conventional empires stifled traffic, and so fore-closed human potential. By contrast, argued William Davenant, English maritime lordship would open up "all the Freights which ev'ry Country yields," so that "ships by trade each other still improve / More fruitfully than Sexes do by Love."[146] Defended by merchant fleets rather than stand-ing armies, such an empire rested on fostering liberty and industry in its own subjects. It promised vaulting levels of power at only a fraction of the cost, in blood and treasure, of terrestrial conquests.

These images gained political expression in the presentation of English objectives at Tangier, and in many of the strategies drawn up for the devel-opment of the city. For all the boasted might of the three-thousand-strong occupation force, the plan laid out by the city commission adhered to a political model grounded on visions of commerce and civility, rather than military might. In 1662, Charles II threw open Tangier as a "free port to all the world in amity with the Crowne of England," one made accessible to all seafaring peoples of the region—Christian, Muslim and Jewish—in an at-tempt to magnetize the trade of the Mediterranean.[147] The logic of this posi-tion inclined English strategists and officers toward an irenic approach to their new Moroccan neighbors, whom they viewed not as future subject peoples, nor even primarily as non-Christians, but as correspondents and partners in trade.[148] Hugh Cholmley predicted peace and commerce with the Arab and Berber powers because their princes knew "our King only desires Tangers for the Port whilst ye French they think would endeavour a Conquest of the Countrey."[149] Such propositions conferred a potency on events in the Mediterranean that transcended narrowly material hopes. Stuart rule over the Straits would not merely advance English power, but also fashion a completely different template for dominion. The empire of the seas had become a prize within reach, with consequences that would far outstrip the achievements of England's European competitors.

After 1660, the international ambitions of the English Crown galvanized a debate over the moral, cultural, and intellectual ramifications of overseas empire. These discussions ranged far beyond the immediate strategic and diplomatic dilemmas. Authors considered the political order best suited to upholding Christian rectitude, interrogated the power of human artistry over the constraints of "nature's laws," and probed the possibility of empires delivering social and cultural improvement over and against the relentless cycles of growth and decay. Most commentators agreed that the success of the English colonial enterprise hinged on constructing a new form of dominion that would banish the lurking shadows of ancient and contemporary tyrannies. Yet their responses revealed divisions deep-seated in the English imagination. One cohort of authors believed that the Roman-Iberian model of a "civilizing" territorial empire could be tamed and purified under the influence of "true religion" and political virtue. Rival voices argued that moving closer to the methods of fallen empires would only draw England into the same pathway of corruption and collapse. These critics championed the prospect of a commercial and maritime empire as a counterblast to the traditional template of colonization. In doing so, they created an ideology of empire that paradoxically retained and enlarged on many of the original republican and Protestant objections toward territorial expansion.

Through the 1660s, these alternative moral and political manifestos informed the contrasting presentations of English aims in Tangier, as a spatially limited emporium, and in North America, as the locale of territorial settlement and the intended epicenter of a Christian mission. But in defining themselves against so many historic and contemporary precedents, supporters of the Crown unveiled exalted promises for a future Stuart dominion that would prove intensely challenging to fulfill. In the debates of the following half-century, the same lexicon—of Protestantism, liberty, and commerce—that had legitimized the English pursuit of empire would serve just as readily to attack and oppose any colonial policies that fell short of the self-proclaimed ideal.

3

Conflict, Commerce, and Political Economies of Empire

THROUGH THE LATER SEVENTEENTH CENTURY, English commentators made a connection between the expansion of trade and the possibility of attaining a "mighty empire" overseas. It was the lure of profit, the London investor Samuel Lambe advanced in 1657, that had awakened in subjects the "boldness to venture to pass the maine Ocean," to "make new discoveryes," and to "enlarge our Nation with many new and large Plantations."[1] In past centuries, when "the greatest part of the World liv'd rudely, on their own Natural Productions," the natural philosopher Thomas Sprat recalled, "the seats of empire and trade [were] never the same. Tyre, and Sydon, and Cades, and Marseiles had more Trafic, but less command than Rome . . . or Macedon."[2] The modern magnification of world commerce, however, had changed the complexion of European states and kingdoms, drawing in medicines and foodstuff to increase life and health, commodities to delight, knowledge to expand minds, and weaponry to enlarge territories. When these "great wheels," as one pamphleteer put it, turned "into most kingdoms of the earth," mastery over "the magick of industry" became the hidden spring enabling even small republics to joust against the rulers of vast dominions.[3] By 1700, over one thousand merchants in London were engaging with American commerce, capitalizing on the proliferation of ships designed to hold heavier cargoes, the increased availability of warehouse storage, and the credit resources offered by the nascent private banking sector.[4] These individuals shaped the practical realities of English overseas expansion, calling on paid agents and pamphleteers to voice their interests within the domestic realm, and to raise debates over the growth and consolidation of emergent colonial territories.[5]

As recent studies by Abigail Swingen, Steve Pincus, and Leslie Theibert have detailed, contemporary discussions of English overseas expansion were flanked by rival models of political economy and political arithmetic, informing disputes over the most effective ways to mobilize the laboring population, increase agricultural and manufacturing productivity, and advance trade within and outside the kingdom.[6] Competitive trading lobbies worked to "domesticate" many of these principles by converting the language of learned treatises and statistical calculations into material fit for the realm of printed polemic.[7] Debates over the commerce of the overseas world were inextricably connected to the wider set of moral, ideological, and strategic reflections stimulated by colonization. In early modern England, the concept of a dominion being driven by commercial concerns struck no less pointedly than the pursuit of a traditional territorial empire against an "ill-deserved reproach," as John Evelyn put it, inherited from "the ancients."[8] A healthy *polis,* Aristotle had maintained, "cannot have its citizens living the life of mechanics or tradesmen."[9] Contemporary republican texts such as James Harrington's *Oceana* (1656) sketched a distinction between landed property, portrayed as the foundation of a virtuous commonwealth, and the transient, mobile, commercial goods that were deemed to foster only private ambition.[10] Among the first generation of colonial promoters, even advocates for the joint-stock companies had attempted to legitimize their endeavors by appealing, in public proclamations, to the heroic virtues of the active civil and military life.[11]

English authors meditated on the way in which merchant activities could be disciplined by civil and Christian virtue, and converted into service of the national interest.[12] Trade, insisted the Tangier administrator Henry Sheres, worked to "quicken our understanding and polish our manners," releasing moral and intellectual energies that would differentiate England from other empires, whose incipient heroism had collapsed into despotism, stagnation, and decline.[13] Commerce could be construed not merely as an agent of temporal empire, but also as a route toward its higher celestial ends, with earthly exchanges and the blessings of material prosperity supporting and vindicating godly enterprises.[14] For John Donne, in a 1622 sermon before the Virginia Company, seals, patents, and trading commissions represented wings that enabled the Holy Spirit to "flye the faster" across unconverted realms.[15] In any case, believed Benjamin Worsley, long-standing secretary to the commonwealth and Restoration councils of trade, the expansion of a kingdom's commerce had become "more conducing toward an universall monarchy (either for ye gaining or preventing of it) than eyther an Army or Territory though never so great." Booming trade raised money for both vessels and mariners. The customs from overseas imports, and the bullion reaped from exported goods, powered the military machine. While "universal monarchy" could terminate in a single battle or a dynastic crisis, attaining "universal trade" brought the appetites of foreign kingdoms and consumers into a dependence that would take generations to dislodge. With this secret now fully "understood by our neighbours," Worsley concluded, international realities threatened "to take away all choyce from us . . . eyther we must leade this great & general Affayre of State . . . or . . . be humbled under the power of them, that have the Ability best to Rule it & Governe it."[16]

Yet there was a tension between the celebration of merchant enterprise as a positive good in itself, and the understanding of commerce as an "affair of state," in the verdict of one 1665 Council paper, that should be conducted not "to the benefit of any profession," but to "the generall advantage of the people."[17] Printed debates were—into the 1680s at least—underpinned by the notion of commerce as a zero-sum game. The enrichment of one "trading kingdom" was considered to proceed at the expense of another, "like buckets, where one goes up the other goes downe," in the words of one merchant author.[18] This perception was made evident in the metaphors indulged in by later seventeenth-century writers—the presentation of commerce as the "golden ball," the "coy Mistress," the "lady"—or "the bird in a falconer's hands," as the Swedish envoy opined to Sir Edward Hyde in 1661, which "may be spoiled and lost either by letting it too free and loose, or by too much restrayning of ye wings."[19] Trade was identified as part of the prize in a fierce game of international competition, calling on governments to tether commerce toward a public end that was not strictly coterminous with the interests of individual merchants.[20] It was a mark of "the Prudence of our Country," Benjamin Worsley believed, that England possessed "few Commodities . . . but what are regulated by some statutes or other": contrived by "such of the Gentry of ye Nation whose interest it may be to be more concerned, in ye generalty of ye Trade of the Nation . . . then in the profit of this or that particular Trade."[21] The prospect of a heavily regulatory regime was threatened especially, believed the EIC director William Ryder, by the composition of the Cavalier Parliament, where there are "not above 20 or 30 merchants: which is a strange thing in an Island"—though a larger number of MPs maintained investments in the overseas trading companies.[22] But in reality many merchants proved equally assiduous in pressing the case for managed restriction. It was a peril to a kingdom, agreed the trader James Whiston, if its commercial outgrowth "happen to be of great Bulk & very unwieldy." When commerce had become the engine for international rivalries, the needs of the nation required mercantile activity to advance like a "well disciplind Army under able officers," rather than to sprawl across the world like "vast untrained Muscovitish multitudes."[23]

For most Restoration authors, the expansion of commerce hinged on the emergence of a strong Crown that would protect and control merchant activity, and receive the rewards from grateful subjects, in the form of revenue from customs, duties, taxes, and impositions. The creation of the Council of Trade institutionalized the idea that it was the duty of governments to stimulate commercial opportunities. This notion was visualized in London's Royal Exchange, where the piazza was lined with the effigies of monarchs past, with a statue of Charles II prominent at the center.[24] Within these parameters, however, any conception of how a mercantile dominion should be controlled in practice was less than clear-cut. The economic orthodoxies of later seventeenth-century England have, until relatively recently, been connected under the term "mercantilism": the unifying label for a set of beliefs that accentuated the finite nature of the world's stock of wealth, and the monarch's obligation to corral trade in such a way as to curtail the power of rival states and foreign merchants.[25] But scholarly discussions have increasingly questioned the validity of the term, or at least the idea that broad "mercantilist" tenets were sufficient to secure consensus over political economy. As Philip Stern and Carl Wennerlind have shown, the traditional conception of mercantilism presupposed a strong and coherent state apparatus, with the authority to define the national interest and the means to enforce it. This notion stumbles against modern understandings of seventeenth-century states as polycentric entities shaped by looser networks of agents and institutions, and capable, as a result, of developing competing political and material concerns. Decentralization increased when early modern polities expanded through plantation and colonization; so too did the scope for rival conceptions of the state interest to emerge in matters of commerce and production.[26] As Steve Pincus has argued, the particular problems encountered in the early English plantations militated against any unifying strategy for colonial development. By 1660, the failure to replicate the success of the Spanish Crown by unearthing gold and silver beneath North American soil had already opened up opposing prescriptions for how to manage colonial economies and generate profits.[27]

In exchanges across the English overseas world, merchants, statesmen, clergy, and strategists considered the commercial policies most conducive to the creation of virtuous colonies and a durable overseas dominion. In the process, they reached conflicting verdicts over the privileges suitable for English merchants, and crossed swords over the economic liberties necessary for colonial settlements. English commentators debated whether their outposts were best developed as springboards toward plunder and further conquests, as centers of intensive plantation, or as regional-commerce hubs that would allow merchants to break into the trade of rival empires. Should planters concentrate on extracting prized staple commodities to gain leverage over international markets, or should they set about creating a diverse economy that would maximize migrant industry and colonial self-sufficiency? Was the interest of the realm better served by creating free ports open to all traders, or by constructing exclusionary trading policies designed to safeguard domestic merchants and producers? These disputes impinged especially on the fragile new enclaves established in Jamaica and Tangier, as soldiers, merchants, and colonists began to flood the settlements in the face of international opposition.

The political economy of English colonization was determined in a changing global arena: one marked by the slow but widely registered decline of Spanish power, and by the appearance of other adversaries—the Dutch and the French—in war zones outside Europe. By 1670, the shifts in world affairs were disrupting the policies designed after the Restoration—challenging the acquisitive intentions that had justified the taking of Jamaica, and pushing the court of Charles II instead toward a modus vivendi with the Crown of Spain, and a vision of the Caribbean centered on peaceful plantation and commerce rather than on military adventure. Conversely, the growing volatility in the Mediterranean began to force authorities in Tangier away from the original blueprint of a free port trading in harmony with its Arab and Berber neighbors toward a more bellicose stance, in imitation of Elizabethan strategies in the Western Atlantic. A core consensus over the role of trade as the handmaiden of national greatness failed to cover up growing divides over the economic and diplomatic policies most appropriate for overseas expansion. Within and beyond the Crown administration, basic assumptions about the origins of national wealth and the means to maintain it would be tested to the limits.

The Economic Vision of English Overseas Expansion

The economic case for colonization had been embedded in English political literature since the early phases of Elizabethan activity in the New World. Beneath the gauze of militarized religion and anti-Spanish fervor, Richard Hakluyt's justification for overseas empire had played to the concerns of traders, manufacturers, and magistrates grappling with commercial stagnation, poverty, and social disorder.[28] Eighty years later, commentators still posited America in relation to the problem of the unemployed, able-bodied poor—the "thousands who live . . . not knowing how to dispose of their impoverished and beggared Families," as the Dorset manufacturer William Smith lamented, and the prisons "full of able Personages, who know no way to redeem themselves from that Captivity which buries them alive, and never have hopes of a Jubilee."[29] Colonial experiments were pitched, too, against the background of anxieties over domestic manufacturing productivity, and the call to revive an export economy, which, commentators feared, was becoming the casualty of changing patterns in world trade. Hakluyt had sounded the alarm over the religious frictions threatening English commerce in the Catholic Mediterranean states.[30] Fifty years later, the prolonged commercial depression triggered by civil and international warfare was similarly threatening the old footholds for the wool and cloth trade in northern and western Europe. By 1668, "the decay of our manufactures" had become "so extreame," Benjamin Worsley estimated, as to reduce English exports to a third of the level attained under Queen Elizabeth.[31]

For many commentators, this weakness registered most clearly in the relentless tide of foreign imports—silks, wine, salt, oils, and shipping materials—seen filtering in from rival states and kingdoms. English subjects had put themselves in thrall to foreign merchants "to supply our necessities . . . but more abundantly to satisfie our vanityes," as the Long Island projector John Scott lamented, and the "affectation of foreign modes and rattles" was inflicting both moral and economic harm on the commonwealth. By the 1660s, commentators were calculating that one million pounds was hemorrhaging annually into the kingdom of France alone.[32]

English voyages, trading excursions, and settlements outside Europe were therefore pinpointed as the lifeline to secure the prosperity and tranquillity of the Stuart kingdoms. Through most of the reign of Charles II, Crown policy still centered on encouraging "as many men as possible" to "remove themselves" to the New World as laborers, servants, and freeholders, by advertising the possibilities of America as a place where subjects could be "raised to a better condicon then if they had staid here," in the words of Benjamin Worsley.[33] Colonial opportunities, it was argued, would usher the surplus population into productive activity. The creation of flourishing overseas communities, too, would foment demand for manufactured goods from the Old World.[34] Meanwhile, new products grown, wrought, or extracted from the plantations could help to rectify the deficiencies of domestic production, and drive the demand for foreign luxuries out of consumer markets by offering equally enticing substitutes.[35] Finally, colonial development would enable the English to strike a blow at their competitors, by flooding Europe with American commodities and making rival states dependent on the Atlantic trade.[36] In connecting these centers of production and exchange, the merchant fleet would function as a "nursery of war," placing thousands of mariners at the disposal of the Crown.[37] Seen in this light, it was "manifest," for Benjamin Worsley, that the plantations "doe not more if soe much depend upon the interest of England, as the interest of England doth now depend upon them."[38]

By promoting and developing its American possessions, English authors believed, the Crown would reactivate the "great wheel" of national commerce. The colonies were perceived to outstrip other spheres of overseas trade because their influence did not, as Worsley averred, simply "swell one part of the Kingdome and make all the rest feeble," but "equally distributes itself into all parts," amplifying shipbuilding, woollen works, cloth manufacturing, and other productive activities across the entire realm.[39] It was, however, considered incumbent on governments to turn the "wheel" in fidelity to certain maxims laid down in the commercial literature of the early seventeenth century by influential and widely published authors such as Thomas Mun, Lewes Roberts, and Edward Misselden. For most Restoration commentators, the expansion of commerce served the public good only when it preserved the "balance of trade," so that "wee may in every part be more sellers then buyers" in relations with other countries—a strategy affirmed by the 1660 "Instructions" to the Council of Trade.[40] The purpose of the Atlantic commerce was defined as restitution of the public stock of gold and silver: to be attained either by reducing imports from other kingdoms, or by providing for an increase of exports into Europe.[41] On such an equilibrium hinged "the walls of our British Empire": the size of the merchant fleet put to sea and the superior virtues attendant on a self-sufficient society that fulfilled and constrained its material needs and wants.[42] For most of the century, these broad tenets commanded consensus among merchant and courtiers alike. Yet the rulebook was loose enough to offer up a sea of competing blueprints for the commercial policies best suited to an emerging territorial empire.

Plunder or Plantation?

Long into the seventeenth century, a powerful argument was made for replenishing the English coinage directly, by mining for gold and silver in conquered territories—following the example of Spanish enrichment in Mexico and Peru.[43] The Iberian precedent was explicit in continual injunctions issued from Whitehall; authorities were urged to chart the topography of colonies with a view to "what mynes they have of Gold, Silver, Gemms and pretious Stones," as the court instructed directors of the newly formed Hudson's Bay Company in 1670.[44] As the interests of the Crown swung south and east after Restoration, the economic template of the Spanish Empire was transposed onto other continents. The merchant Humphrey Giffard believed the seizure of "ye Golden Mines of Guiney" to be the ultimate endgame of the Royal Adventurers in West Africa, and through the 1660s, official encouragement to take "plantations," and clear the ground for mining operations, vied with the company's later focus as a fulcrum of the transatlantic slave trade.[45] In 1663, imported West African gold brought the Guinea coin into English commercial life: every piece was stamped with the arms of the Royal Adventurers (the elephant and castle), as a tangible reminder of the connection between precious metal and imperial aspiration.[46]

The repeated failure of England's New World territories to yield up a prize akin to Central America had not diminished the appeal of gold and silver. These frustrations did, however, invite the prospect of a different American strategy—forcibly wresting the existing treasures of the Indies out of Spanish hands. Following the intuitions of Sir Walter Raleigh, the original aim of English adventures in America had been to probe the chinks in the armor of the Spanish Indies, beginning with privateering raids but proceeding ultimately—it was imagined—to full conquests.[47] By the reign of Charles II, the MP Roger Whitley still judged the principal purpose of voyages across the Atlantic to lie in "taking from ye Spanyard those great & Rich Territoryes they possess in ye Indyes."[48] Governor William Berkeley adduced the significance of Virginia from its location "undoubtedly not 300 miles from the Spanish gold mines," close enough to strike upon the king of Spain "in the heart and navel of his dominions" and "have his bullion come home in our ships."[49]

The call to arms flourished, above all, in the Caribbean. Since its annexation in 1655, Jamaica had been militarized through ongoing conflict with Spanish privateers. Periods of martial law had been imposed, labor had been conscripted from the British Isles, and materials had been requisitioned from other plantations to improve forts and batteries.[50] Even if the intrinsic productivity of the island was questionable, its geographical significance could hardly be debated—situated as it was in such close proximity to Cuba and Hispaniola—nor its capacity to maintain troops and horses, and host squadrons to harry the king of Spain.[51] "It lies within his Bowels, and in the heart of his Trade," insisted the former naval chaplain Edmund Hickeringill in 1661, overseeing the main passage through which "the principall wealth of the Spanyard is drawn out of the South Sea."[52] Heroic visions of conquests in Panama, Chile, and Buenos Aires had swirled through the missives and manuscripts exchanged at Whitehall, which were suffused with calls for volunteers and promises to regenerate the "younge & idle Gentry of this Nation . . . who find encouragement and delighte in fforaigne action and Adventures."[53] For Hickeringill and like-minded commentators, the ultimate function of the island would be to lever English forces into the Spanish Main, enabling them to raise rebellions among the Amerindians, seize the mines, and "*immortalize* His Sacred Majesty one of the greatest *Emperours* of the World."[54]

Accepting the remote possibility of another centrally funded Western Design, advocates for Jamaica nonetheless urged the Crown to endorse armed action as a means of chiselling into the resources and morale of the Spanish viceroyalties. The principal tools at the disposal of the "war" party were over 1,500 "buccaneers": mercenaries of predominantly French, English, and Irish extraction who had turned to piracy after being driven by the Spanish from their island stronghold on Tortuga.[55] Edward D'Oyley, governor of Jamaica under the Protectorate, had invited these "Hunting Frenchmen" into the island in 1659. Under pressure from Spanish privateering in August 1662, his successor Lord Windsor unleashed a fleet of eleven vessels in a preemptive strike on Cuba, which was "considerable, or said to be so for his honour," in Samuel Pepys's barbed appraisal.[56] Subsequent assaults struck Campeche and Yucatán, and in 1664, the "forward" strategy for Jamaica was crowned with the promotion of the Barbados planter Thomas Modyford, one of the most vociferous ideologues behind the Western Design, to the governor's residence in Port Royal.[57]

The militant manifesto for Jamaica was not, however, the only vision to inform English actions in disputed New World territories. The idea of seeking glory through ceaseless struggles for gold and silver ran up against the growing anatomy of the ills of Spanish America, and a critique of the notion that Habsburg political economy afforded a viable precedent for overseas dominion. By the later seventeenth century, many European commentators were convinced that the conquistadors had already stripped the Mexican mountains bare, so that the power drawn by Spain out of its colonies had long passed saturation point. "Formerly there were also Emeraulds in America," intoned Samuel von Pufendorf, "and Pearls were found, but that Stock is long since, by the Avarice of the *Spaniards,* quite exhausted."[58] Moreover, even when Spanish exploits had left Europe awash with bullion, little of that prize was believed to have remained within the Iberian Peninsula, because relentless mining in distant provinces—and vast supplies of people dispatched to that purpose—had come at the cost of domestic production and innovation. Writing in 1676, Ambassador William Godolphin estimated that "scarce above an 8th part" of the treasures borne in by the "galones and flota" remained within Spain, the greater proportion being funnelled out in exchange for "manufactures" that could only be acquired from other parts of Europe.[59] The Spanish, in Godolphin's judgment, had been reduced to "ye packhorses of other nations, to carry their goods," and the "prodigious sloth" of the monarchy offered no match for the lean ingenuity of Dutch merchants who darted through Iberian ports, prising out gold and silver as they fed the wants of a kingdom hollowed out through lack of industry.[60] Which trader made the more lasting achievement, demanded Peter Heylin—the projector who amassed slaves to churn gold out of mountains, or the "sheep-master" who pocketed the proceeds at only a sliver of the "toil, charge and hazard" when the miners became dependent on his wares to stave off cold and starvation?[61] According to this diagnosis, English wool, more than "Indian gold," still held the key to forging sustainable power overseas. Art, craft, and industry outstripped the innate blessings of nature—even precious stones—as a fount of human flourishing and contentment.

Reactions against Spanish America pointed toward a different prescription for English settlement. For Heylin, Godolphin, and like-minded voices, the future for the colonies lay in long-term agricultural development, handicrafts, and manufactures, closer to the pattern of the New England farms and townships than the armored fleets of Walter Raleigh. English America could not in any case be compared to its Spanish competitor, because "wt began out Plantations it was ye effect not of conquest but of superfluous stock," as the merchant James Houblon recalled, with voluntary migrants seeking out material opportunities.[62] The "terrestriall greatness" of the "English empire," for the manufacturer William Smith, flowed from "the exuberance of these your over-peopled Kingdoms": the initiative of the migrants, and their conversion of an inhospitable wilderness into a place of productivity.[63] As Steve Pincus has shown, divisions in English approaches toward the colonial economy had been apparent as early as the reign of James I, in conflicting proposals raised over the future of the Chesapeake settlements.[64] Through the 1660s, however, the search for alternatives to conquest and plunder intensified on both sides of the Atlantic, amid anxiety on the Privy Council as to how far Crown resources permitted continual hostilities with Spain.[65] While the governors stocked their fleets and garrisons, discussions in London began to sketch out alternative pathways for Jamaica. Instead of a parasitic relationship with the Spanish viceroyalties, it was hoped that new attempts could be made to maximize the value of the island as an asset full of its own "merchantable commodities."[66] While Lord Windsor called the buccaneers to arms, Charles II commanded the demobilization of the old Cromwellian army in 1661, envisaging its ultimate replacement by a militia funded out of the revenues raised within the island. The decision was accompanied by a call for soldiers to turn toward plantation farming, with landholdings offered to the troops in place of payment of their full arrears. In addition, the island was freed from customs duties for seven years, with the intention of giving it time to reorder its economic life.[67]

The idea of an empire propelled by labor rather than conquest supplied an alternative moral as well as political economy for overseas expansion. Attentiveness to agricultural development would cast a stronger anchor for security and defense, the Council for Plantations contended in 1660, lifting Jamaica above the "debaucherie and idleness" rife among disbanded soldiers.[68] For Benjamin Worsley, the greatest problems the island faced stemmed from the penetration of piracy into "the very nature, interest and constitution of its Government," with many of the most notorious buccaneers, including the Welsh captain Henry Morgan, using their loot to amass land and power. A culture of militarism had crippled Jamaica, Worsley believed, eroding "its foundations, strength and increase in a way of Merchandise and planting," while allowing the tone of civic life to be set by "a crew of wild, dissolute and tattered fellows . . . who have hitherto been acquainted with nothing but Prey." Nothing, he concluded, was more likely "to invite our Neighbours to make a Warr upon us for it."[69] In mapping out an alternative course, councils in Jamaica and Barbados stipulated that "no one should beare Militarie Office without he were possesst of a certaine Quantitie of Land," carrying a consequent stake in the welfare of the civil domain, as a place of plantation.[70] The nod to humanist and Harringtonian principles was confirmed as Caribbean governors debated the most effective distribution of land, settling on grants of fifty acres as the prerequisite for independent and virtuous populations of freeholders.[71] The debates unleashed by the conquest of Jamaica had therefore set out the possibilities for English expansion as a choice between two mutually exclusive trajectories. Advocates for an aggressive anti-Spanish policy inclined, paradoxically, toward a model of empire strongly influenced by the conquistadors, and distinguished primarily by conquest and mining. Conversely, the appeal for peaceful relations with Madrid gratified those who feared bullion-powered territorialism as a conveyer toward greed, tyranny, and self-destruction.

Among many authors in England and America, the call for settlers to dedicate themselves to peaceful plantation ran alongside a broader critique of territorial expansion as a strategic good, and hints of skepticism over many of the ambitions indulged at court. "No forein Plantation should be undertaken," maintained the political economist Samuel Fortrey in 1673, but in "such countreys" that could be clearly calculated to "increase wealth and trade." Otherwise, the enterprise was better eschewed altogether, lest the charge become "greater than the profit," for a prince was "more powerfull that hath his strength and force united, then he is weakly scattered in many places."[72] Traces of this argument entered into directives issued from the Council of Virginia, which inveighed against profligate patterns of settlement that "have taken up as much land as all England," according to one administrator, despite "it being certain that all the Planters are not soe many as the Inhabitants of Stepney Parish."[73] In 1663, the ills of the "straggling, distracted" province were ascribed by the surveyor Anthony Langston to a careless stretching of the Virginian frontiers, which due to a lack of agricultural labor had led to vast estates lying fallow.[74] Particular concern was registered over the undersettled Northern Neck territory, which had been portioned out (by Charles II, then in exile) among a collection of absentee royalist aristocrats, including the earl of Arundel and the earl of Saint Albans. All resisted the jurisdiction of the governor and identified themselves as "proprietors" accountable to the Crown alone.[75] In 1669, after lobbying from the Council of Virginia, a reissued Northern Neck charter extended the rights of the proprietors for no longer than twenty-one years before their titles would be re-examined, and confined their landholdings to such tracts of territory that had been visibly "inhabited or planted."[76]

The "agriculturalist" argument, developed by Winthrop in Massachusetts and latterly by John Locke to justify the colonization of Carolina, has been seen by many modern scholars as a convenient rhetorical tool for divesting Indians and other indigenous peoples of their territorial possessions. The vision of precolonial America as *vacuum domicilum* certainly privileged the European model of agricultural settlement as providing the most verifiable claim of property rights.[77] Yet in the discussions of the 1660s and 1670s, agriculturalist ideas were invoked more commonly to "restrain" English settlements "to a lesser compass," as the Virginia deputy governor Herbert Jeffries put it, than to incite further expansion—to *discourage* unwarranted land grabs, and so minimize conflict with native peoples.[78] If the development of the soil—the mixing of labor into the land—was the basis for dominion, then any parcel of territory *not* demonstrably cultivated should be deemed unclaimed, and "wast to all comers," in Anthony Langston's words, no matter what titles might be brandished by settlers.[79] English landholders who had not subjected their estates to proper plantation had squandered legal proprietorship because they had failed to fulfill the public mandate on which the title had been granted. If planters stuck to these principles, the Crown's commissioners instructed the Council of Virginia in 1676, the Indians would "receive the same measure of justice from the English, as the English, by law expect from them."[80] The case for plantation over ceaseless conquest was held to honor the expansive potential of the New World. Here, as Locke's *Second Treatise of Government* would affirm, the assiduous planter "shall find that the possessions he could make himself" need not even "be very large," let alone "prejudice the rest of mankind," to raise up honor and prosperity.[81]

Staple Crops or Experimental Diversity?

Driven by ideological pressure and fiscal necessity, Crown policy concentrated increasingly on maximizing hands rather than lands, as the way to consolidate English rule in North America. But the tilt away from further conquests gave rise to new disputes over the best way to structure the embryonic plantation economies and determine their value to the mother kingdom. Many of the most vigorous exchanges centered on which "merchantable commodities" should be prioritized for cultivation. The readiest recourse for advocates of plantation over plunder lay in the cultivation of certain "staple crops" that offered large and guaranteed markets in the Old World. The prime examples—Caribbean sugar and Virginian tobacco—fulfilled the essential criteria sketched out for colonial imports, as commodities "vendible abroad," whose consumer appeal extended as far as Russia and Italy, and that carried the promise of garnering foreign bullion by exchange.[82] The flows of tobacco into England from the Chesapeake climbed steeply, from an annual supply of 500,000 pounds by 1634 to 36 million by the 1680s. By the end of the century, approximately two-thirds of the imported hogsheads were being re-exported into continental Europe.[83] In 1671, the London MP John Jones enumerated the value of the Chesapeake on the premise that every pair of exported two-shilling shoes brought returns of thirty pounds in tobacco. "Most part of the corporations of England do subsist by this trade of tobacco," he averred in the Commons. With £100,000 brought in annually from Virginia and Maryland, "the greatest part of the fleet depends upon it."[84]

By the middle of the 1650s, English Caribbean merchants were beginning to exercise similar domination over "the sweet negotiation of Sugar," as the Barbados planter Richard Ligon dubbed it, capitalizing on the collapse of Dutch Brazil to make inroads into European markets. Having driven the Portuguese out of the race "to furnish Spaine" and Italy, the islands were exporting annually over eight thousand tons of sugar into foreign markets, estimated the Jamaican governor Thomas Lynch in 1671—a vindication of the work of "10,000 English planters, which we humbly conceive could be no way employ'd in England more to the advantage of this nation."[85] Four hundred vessels, ten thousand mariners, and more than fifty refineries in England depended on the sugar trade, claimed the Council of Trade.[86] By 1700, the total import tonnage had touched twenty-five thousand, with the Caribbean "sugar islands" accounting for over 30 percent of the funds entering the exchequer from overseas trade.[87]

Calls to seize hold of the world markets in sugar and tobacco rekindled an aggressive vision for the projection of English power through military and economic means. On the Privy Council, these commodities were identified as the clearest alternative to an empire of mining, as the way to out-compete European rivals. The effect was to change the social as well as economic profile of the island colonies. The intensive, physically debilitating cultivation of a single crop pushed landowners toward reliance on slave labor, "the life of plantations," in the judgment of Edward D'Oyley; and "without whose hands," added the Guinea merchant Richard Ford, "they cannot be improved or usefull to his Matie or his subjects." The markets in bonded laborers were swelled by the West African turn in colonial policy— the slaves themselves were largely the product of links with local princes, whom the Crown sought to co-opt as allies against European rivals, and who capitalized by selling off captured peoples to English dealers.[88] Under these pressures, almost a quarter of a million individuals were forced across the Atlantic between 1676 and 1700.[89] The slave population in Jamaica rose from approximately five hundred in 1660 to over forty thousand by 1700.[90] Barbados by this point was maintaining more than fifty thousand coerced individuals—two-thirds of the total number of inhabitants.[91] Mainland tobacco farmers relied for a longer period on English indentured labor, but the African contingent in Virginia grew to approximately thirteen thousand—13 percent of the resident population—by 1700, after a surge in the final decade of the seventeenth century.[92]

The trend toward staple crops and slave labor assured the domination of the West Indian territories by large-scale planters, including many absentee landowners from within the English merchant community who could mobilize sufficient funds to sustain a force of unfree workers.[93] In recognition of the growing economic power of these magnates, the Crown offered "drawbacks" on sugar and tobacco import duties, when American goods were ferried out for re-export overseas.[94] The bans on tobacco production in England and Ireland, followed in 1664 by raids on suspected crops in the West Country, were other interventions that favored the Atlantic alliance of planters and traders.[95] But a dominion centered on staple commodities was nonetheless to be a royal empire, one as absolute and exclusionary in its economic rulebook as was Spanish oversight over the New World gold and silver mines. In 1664, the Crown bestowed monopoly rights on the Royal Adventurers for the transportation of slaves out of West Africa, aiming to wrench the plantations into dependence on a profiteering body stocked with princes and courtiers. Eight years later, the grouping was further fortified and empowered under a new appellation as the Royal African Company, with the duke of York, Prince Rupert, and leading ministerial personalities—the lords Shaftesbury, Arlington, Buckingham, and Clifford—all contributing as major shareholders. Under their authority, the bodies of slaves were liable to be branded with the initials "RAC"—the ugliest and most explicit demarcation of legitimate West African trade.[96]

Despite the rising profits, the grip of sugar and tobacco over the colonial economy caused serious concern to other interest groups active in the New and Old Worlds. The turn toward slavery and staple crops brought a rupture in English thinking over colonial development, which had focused hitherto as much on the creative usage of domestic migrant labor as on the value of American goods. "The more Comodities wee are able to Compass within our own plantations, ye more imployment wee are able to find for hands," Benjamin Worsley professed, and the greater the "multiplying of the English in those parts."[97] The Caribbean was perceived to abound in potential for other, undeveloped crops—cotton and indigo, cocoa and ginger, together with "drugs and wood fit for dying." A narrow focus on staple crops, Worsley warned, risked holding back knowledge of these resources, cramping innovation, and stifling the possibilities of an empire shifting from conquest toward plantation. On this premise, he urged the king to fix a price for sugar with the crown of Portugal, as a way to place checks on international competition.[98] Similar attitudes were voiced by governors and projectors in the southern mainland colonies. In 1661, the gift of a silk robe for the king's coronation was dispatched from Virginia. The sample was intended to reveal the hidden economic sinews of that colony if, as William Berkeley urged, its planters were given sufficient financial inducements, time, and a reprieve from their creditors at home.[99] Through the 1660s, the governor passed laws in the Virginia assembly to encourage production of flax, hemp, and potash, and to explore prospects for woollen and linen manufacturing—all were conceived as creative alternatives to reliance on the tobacco crop.[100]

The case for diversification corresponded with the wider scholarly ideologies stimulated by English colonization. Since the early seventeenth century, natural philosophers had popularized a conception of the earth as a storehouse of concealed riches: possessing "multiplicative virtue," in the words of one Hartlibian disciple, "as fire and the seeds of all things have."[101] The hidden possibilities for "improvement" pregnant within the forests, fens, and heathlands of the Old World were believed to magnify in the uncharted spaces of the globe. By the application of minds as well as bodies, suggested the Caribbean projector John Poyntz, planters could coax nature to "open her doors of treasure and inrich the industrious."[102] Through experimentation, and openness to new crops and commodities, Englishmen would unlock the providential promise of America, fulfill the divine command to be fruitful and multiply, and so attain an empire over the earth more complete than anything that military conquest could offer.

Supporters of commercial diversity jousted against the sugar and tobacco lobbies in representations before the Council of Trade.[103] The greatest incentive toward economic experiments was the possibility that American produce could displace the intruding foreign commodities that had so enraptured English consumers at the expense of domestic bullion. A long line of promotional literature located the English southern and island colonies within the same latitude as, in Berkeley's words, "all the best happiest & most fruitfull Countryes in the World." The fertility of the soil and similarity of climatic conditions invited planters to develop orchards and vineyards, and produce delicacies drawn hitherto out of the East and the Mediterranean.[104] Sketching out a vision for Catholic-run Maryland, the Jesuit Andrew White invoked the model of the grand duchy of Tuscany, envisaging fields of production for wine, oil, and fruits; intra-regional traffic (in this case, furs purchased from the Indians); and exports shipped across the Atlantic from free ports along the Chesapeake coastline.[105] In 1670, the Council of Trade endorsed proposals from the natural philosopher John Beale for transportation of "Nutmegs, Cinnamon, Cloves and Pepper from the East Indyes" to investigate whether they may "come to perfection in some of our Collonyes and Plantations" in America.[106] The call for diversity gained fullest expression in the promotion of the new settlements at Carolina. The "3 rich commodities of Wine, Sylk & Oyle" dominated the advertisements that circulated around mercantile networks in London, seeking out "skilfull men and fitt materials" for the "emprouvment of the countrey."[107] Anthony Ashley Cooper looked to the provincial crops as an incubator of new tastes and fashions, encouraging settlers to explore the production of "orange flower water and rose water" suitable for export.[108] Sugar and tobacco were implicitly repudiated in directives issued against replicating the produce of any existing colony.[109] The allure of bullion was treated with such suspicion that any gold and silver accidentally discovered in Carolina could be cited in correspondence only under coded names, lest the populace throw off industrious pursuits in search of treasure.[110]

Most advocates of economic diversity still adhered to a "zero sum" idea of global trade. The rationale for cultivating Asian flowers and seeds was defined by Worsley as to beat foreign spices out of English markets, and to strike at the powers of the Dutch East India Company.[111] But if the world's stock of wealth remained finite, its resources were perceived to stretch across a canvas wider than the human mind had hitherto comprehended, with secrets still to be quarried by invention and improvement. Proper management of the earth was deemed vital for the moral as well as economic fortification of new colonies. Where the production of staple crops hinged on African slave labor, mixed economies were seen to mobilize the free and industrious English population. Vineyards, orchards, and silk-works would raise up not merely flourishing commerce, but a "sociable" commonwealth, released from infantile dependency on the mother kingdom, and, as a declaration from six Carolina planters put it in 1666, "injoying a selfe sufficiency of all the principal necessaryes to life."[112] To make Virginia and Carolina flourish, believed the projector George Milner, governors would have to roll back sprawling agricultural landholdings, and usher carpenters and brick-layers, tanners and tailors into new urban settlements, backed up by an apparatus of banks, mints, and corporations.[113] Civil and economic possibilities were compromised, William Berkeley feared, when governments "laid the foundation of our wealth and industry on the vices of men," interposing "the vicious weed of Tobacco" over all other "accessions to happiness," and making populations vulnerable to seasonal vicissitudes and shifts in European patterns of consumption.[114]

Supporters of an empire of plantation over plunder shared certain assumptions: they viewed productive labor, more than land in itself, as the source of national empowerment, and concurred that the Crown should intervene to regulate the colonial economy. But behind this broad consensus, rival conceptions of the most effective forms of New World labor created incompatibly different blueprints for the dominions. Calls for economic diversification collided with the appeal of staple crops as the readiest source of customs revenue for the Crown. Virginian silk, hemp, and flax were a feature of the Royal Exchange by 1666, but the *London Gazette* hinted at the emerging clash of political economies in its rebuke of "the inhabitants of Maryland and Carolina," who, "encouraged by the probable advantages of their Neighbors Trade, begin to neglect their own in Tobacco's, and apply themselves to these new Manufactures."[115] The goal of colonies reaching "self-subsistence" may have promised to lower the burden on the mother kingdom, but the obverse effect—greater commercial independence—would be seen by many English commentators as a less than reassuring prospect. By proposing to transfer whole arenas of economic activity out of the Old World into the New, projectors raised the possibility of colonies acquiring material interests separate from those of the kingdom that had created them.

Free Ports or Navigation Acts?

The latent tensions created over the plantation economy broke through the political surface when Crown councils sought to determine the level of commercial freedom that should be allocated to the overseas dominions, as outworks of the realm in a competitive trading environment. The blueprint most attractive to many settlers centered on the creation of colonies as free ports, set at liberty to "trade with all nations in amity with the King," as Thomas Modyford urged the Crown in 1664, and made more responsible, as a result, for their own commercial development.[116] The idea was given forceful expression by Benjamin Worsley, who drew heavily on Dutch precedent in a treatise put before the council of the commonwealth in 1652, followed by a private paper produced nine years later for Edward Hyde.[117] Worsley argued that the rejuvenation of English trade would gather pace when the nation recast itself, and its colonies, as a "general magazine or store," to "buy and sell for the furnishing and provision of other Nations, as a man that keeps a Warehouse or Store-house."[118] This idea responded to the colonial experiences of the 1640s, when the Civil War had straitened the Atlantic supply lines, and settlers had become vitally dependent on open trade with Dutch merchants to sustain their links to European markets. It was through these connections, and especially the new contact with Dutch Brazil, Thomas Lynch recalled, that Caribbean planters had first learned the art of sugar production.[119] The case proved, for Benjamin Worsley, that access to world markets afforded "Cheaper & Surer Remedyes" to palliate the birth pangs of incipient settlements than any model of regulation imposed by the Crown. If the cost was to accept a certain supply of foreign imports into the marketplace, the reward would be brought home in the overall stimulus given to colonial productivity.[120]

The case for free ports gained political recognition in 1662 when Charles II conferred rights upon Tangier as an entrepôt, to be structured in imitation of the "marts of the world" in Livorno, Genoa, and Madeira.[121] Officers schemed to establish a "magazine" for Levantine goods, open up the "inland trade" into Africa, and break into "the riches from the Spanish Indies" by luring in traders from Cadiz and Seville.[122] Lowering the rent in 1665 for warehouses and private residences, Tangier's governor, Lord Belassis, promised fairs overflowing with "the fragrent perfumes off flowers, rare frutes and sallads."[123] For Hugh Cholmley, the attainment of free port status was a vital stepping stone in converting Tangier from a garrison to a full colony, one that could entice whole families to make the crossing out of England, on the assurance that their familiar economic liberties would be fully retained upon arrival.[124] In North Africa and the Chesapeake as in London or the West Country, "forein Nations trading into a Country make the people industrious," argued the merchant John Bland, who moved from Virginia to Morocco in 1663. If the aim of the Crown was to increase its stock of bullion, a flow of foreign gold and silver coinage was to be prized wherever it entered into English hands.[125] The outpost in the Straits emerged, accordingly, as a precedent for the economic freedoms sought within the Western Atlantic colonies. Lobbyists for Barbados and New York appealed to Whitehall for a grant of "ye same privilege in point of Trade as the Port of Tangier enjoyeth."[126] On the Council of Trade, the earl of Sandwich, Thomas Povey, and Secretary of State Sir William Coventry urged the king to sanction direct commercial links between Tangier and the American provinces.[127] A line of free ports, bound by the glue of commercial exchange, would serve, according to Worsley, to "improve and strengthen his Maties Dominions, & to unite them most by being increasingly assistant to, and mutually dependent on each other."[128] The implication was provocative. Creating a network of interdependent colonial hubs would decentralize the economic life of the emerging empire, and so challenge the status of London as the mercantile heart of the English overseas world.

These hopes, however, were to be confounded. The principle of free ports aroused controversy within and outside government, with opponents attacking the logic that England could appropriate Dutch or Italian examples to its own circumstances. In contrast to the trading cities encountered across the Channel, critics contended, the Stuart kingdom possessed its own natural resources, and, consequently, a manufacturing sector to nurture and protect. The wool and the draperies provided the spring of England's riches—"deservedly ye darling of our nation," according to the future secretary of state Henry Coventry.[129] To operate simply as "store-keepers of the goods of foreign nations," as the Whig statesman John Pollexfen later put it, and rely on a circular flow of imports and re-exports to keep the stock of bullion intact, risked exposing the domestic labor force to ruinous competition.[130]

By the 1660s, these counterarguments were entering into a legislative framework for the English overseas world that was utterly at odds with the vision of free or loosened trade. Through the early part of the century, the desire to regulate commerce in the interests of domestic production had justified placing considerable tracts of foreign trade in the hands of joint-stock companies, whose "orderly management" of merchants, mariners, and servants provided a far superior way to advance the national interest, according to Samuel Lambe, than a "confused trade" pursued to "privat advantage."[131] The greater part of the Western Atlantic stood out by contrast as a place unshackled by corporate privilege. But for most commentators, the implication was not that colonies should be opened up to unfettered commerce, but that governments should themselves intervene: maintaining the rights of all Englishmen to engage in trading operations, but narrowing the sphere of legitimate commercial activity. The idea entered the political agenda in 1651 with the passing of the Navigation Ordinance, which struck at Dutch practitioners of the "carrying trade" by decreeing that all foreign imports could enter the colonies only in direct transmission from their place of first shipment, on vessels pertaining either to the country of origin or to England itself. Only English-manned ships, too, could lawfully convey goods from the colonies back into the ports of the domestic realm. After the Restoration, the Crown enlarged the policy. A new Navigation Act of 1660 decreed that American commodities could leave the colonies only if the carrying ship sailed first to England to discharge customs duties before the cargo was re-exported to any other state. Three years later, the Staple Act decreed that only those goods springing from England itself, or that had travelled first through English ports, could be legitimately carried into the overseas dominions.[132]

Thus while the success of Tangier was staked on the benefits of an open trading regime, the political economy shaping the Western Atlantic settlements was shifting in the opposite direction.[133] The Navigation Acts carried constitutional as well as commercial implications—a concession of authority to parliament over the colonial economy, and, as I will explore in Chapter 9, a declaration that the dominions were exclusively the property of Charles II's *English* kingdom. Qualified privileges accrued to subjects of Ireland, as a country deemed subordinate to English rule, but Scottish merchants would be treated as foreigners.[134] The acts came pitched with appeals to English domestic opinion: the Crown commissioners of trade portrayed them as "recompence" for the "labour, blood, & vast expenses" that had been poured into the creation of colonies overseas, and recognition of the "loyall" and "liberall" posture of the realm in "contributing to ye King by theyre yearely Customes for maynteyning his Maty at Sea."[135] Blanketing the dominions against foreign competition, the Crown would enclose and protect the routes for transportation of goods—its laws serving as "the Highway wherein your subjects travel to their rest," as the manufacturer William Smith applauded.[136]

The acts described with unsparing clarity the status of the colonies as territories that would complement, not compete with, the mother kingdom, by providing markets for commodities native to England, and supplying raw materials unavailable in the domestic realm. In denying the colonies direct contact with foreign traders, the Crown smothered any incentive for planters to develop their own manufacturing industry, aiming to cement dependence on the kingdom that fed, clothed, and supplied them. Looking back in 1697, the Whig political economist Francis Brewster enthused that when "the disposition of those times seem'd to tend . . . for Pleasure more than Trade," the parliament had installed "a Centinel for the Traffick of the Nation," to counter consumer cravings and put English subjects "in mind of other things."[137] The Crown had wedded itself to an uncompromising vision of colonial development, and its laws and proclamations now issued a direct repudiation of the free port vision and its lobbying force across the overseas world. In December 1670, a renewed appeal from Barbados "to have trade as Tanger" was "read & discountenanced" by the Committee for Foreign Affairs as "unbecoming ye Petitioners."[138]

Criticism of the Navigation Acts was initially kept to a whisper amid the mood of resurgent Restoration loyalty. But the laws soon estranged merchants active in regions such as New England, where traders had relied on direct access to markets in Spain, Italy, and Portugal, because the local produce (boards, pipe staves, timber, and fish) "do better vend in other parts than here in England," as one complaint to the Privy Council put it.[139] Benjamin Worsley professed himself warmer toward the 1651 ordinance than its successors, and feared that blocking foreign merchants out of the Caribbean sugar markets offered provocation to rival powers, incentivizing the Dutch and French to create their own plantations instead.[140] Granting a monopoly of supplies to English traders threatened the equilibrium between the merchant and the planter, he added, in a paper put before Charles II, and risked that the one would "oppress the other."[141] The most outspoken discontent in the 1660s, however, came from Tangier. While the Navigation Acts licensed continued trade between the English plantations, this right was confined to the territories of the Western Atlantic, and so excluded the Mediterranean city from direct commercial relations with the Americas. "Yet all [are] knowing that Tanger can bee reputed no other but a Plantation," protested the merchant John Bland, and "in both places are relations of Brethren, Sonns, Fathers and Kindred": the threads that bound the overseas world.[142] Successive governors agreed that without the liberty of "general trade" extending into the Atlantic, Tangier could never fulfill its promised remit as a global entrepôt—in particular, it would be unable to serve effectively as a base for shipping English colonial produce into the Mediterranean. By 1672, Hugh Cholmley affirmed, all the American goods that Tangier received came from the Spanish or Portuguese colonies, "because the Charge of bringing and unladeing these in England, & shipping them againe from there is soe great that the Commodityes proceeding from the Growth of our own Colonyes cannot for this cause be sold so Cheape."[143] The creation of the Navigation Acts had exposed the many conflicting interests caught up in the web of English global enterprise. Soon the new arrangements would start to test the limits of unity over the Crown's colonial policies.

Dutch War, Spanish Peace, and English Political Economy

Throughout the 1660s, questions over plunder or plantation, bullion or raw materials, were posed and answered within an increasingly fissile theater of international relations. By the later years of that decade, English debates over political economy had been reframed by the unintended consequences of the Second Anglo-Dutch War. For all the strident optimism that had fuelled the conflict, the outcome brought baleful exposure to the limits of English power in the world. In West Africa, as Samuel Pepys recorded, the Royal Navy was "beaten to dirt . . . to the utter ruine of our Royall Company" [of Adventurers].[144] In Asia, attempts to regain the island of Pulo Run stumbled against superior Dutch firepower, prompting desperate calls from English merchants for the war to be "perioded" to prevent their complete ejection from the East Indies.[145] Dutch frigates sailed deep into Virginia, bombarding English merchant vessels along the James River.[146] Finally, in March 1667, the armies of the United Provinces descended on Surinam—Charles II's toehold of territory in South America—and wrenched the province out of English hands. Across the colonial world, weak fortifications, inadequate funds, and military inexperience had all been exposed to the attentions of hostile powers. "Whoever doth informe the king that wee are super abounding in men, Armes & Ammunition" should be "well enquired into," Governor Willoughby of Barbados fumed to William Coventry in July 1666.[147]

In revealing the extent of international opposition to English designs, the conflict had also ushered a deadly new interloper into the West Indies. As early as January 1664, George Downing had warned of intelligence that the young Louis XIV "holds very often councells . . . about rendring France considerable in plantacons & Colonies."[148] Two years later, the English islands reeled in the wake of a sudden intervention from the court of Versailles. French forces overran Antigua, despoiled Montserrat, and forced the evacuation of colonists from Saint Christopher. The fleet from Barbados, sent out to rebuff the assault, was lost to a hurricane, which claimed the life of Governor Francis Willoughby. Simultaneously, French land forces from Canada probed southward: their intention made evident in January 1667, when the coat of arms of the king France was found nailed to the wall of an outlying English fort in northwestern New York.[149] This was precisely the result that the sale of Dunkirk had been intended to prevent, with its goal of locking France and Spain into continental stalemate, and so giving the English Crown a free hand in places overseas. Instead, the might of the Bourbon monarchy was showing itself capable of simultaneous expression on two continents. In 1667, French forces surged into the Netherlands, devastated Spanish Flanders, and stretched the borders of their kingdom northward. "While other Princes slept," complained the author of *Europae Modernae Speculum,* "fortune hath turned her balance and rejected the Spaniard, so that the French king is absolutely the greatest Prince in the Continent of Europe, and now he aspires also to the Sea."[150]

These events exposed the inadequacy of a worldview that defined colonial adventures primarily in opposition to the threat of Spanish "universal monarchy," without regard to the consequences of a global reduction in Habsburg power. Over the following five years, the carnage in the Leeward Islands heralded an intensification of French activity. A fortification program proceeding on Martinique threatened to make the French "terrible to the English inhabitants in that part of the World," warned Thomas Lynch, and was prompting several planters to think of leaving permanently for

New England.[151] "Ere long," Worsley mused to Lynch, the court of Charles II would find it "as great an affair of state to balance power in the West Indies, as it is now amongst Princes in Christendom; and that, not only with reference to the Spaniard, French, Dutch, and the English; but also mutually amongst the French, Dutch, and Spaniard."[152] These conclusions were a gift to the fledgling peace lobby that had formed around different centers of the English world. The treasure fleet sent back from Central American mines dictated "the interest not of Spain only but of most other Nations in Europe," argued Ambassador Godolphin. Its safety, he insisted, was a vital means of preserving diplomatic equilibrium, and of keeping French power at bay.[153] Far from weakening the Crown of Madrid by plunder and piracy, it better served the English interest to preserve the stricken Spanish behemoth, and protect its treasures, lest the Habsburg dominions fall into the hands of a more dangerous conqueror, one better equipped to exploit the wealth within.

The goal of restoring the "balance" in Europe and the West Indies was driven forward by figures newly ascendant in Whitehall, after the 1667 impeachment of the earl of Clarendon—the main political casualty of a war about which he had never been more than ambivalent. Under the influence of Sir Henry Bennett, now Lord Arlington, the peace agenda dominated the concerns of a new, streamlined Council of Trade.[154] Prolonged consultations in The Hague linked England and the United Provinces in the Triple Alliance with Sweden. In 1667, a new Anglo-Spanish agreement sealed in Madrid brought formal cessation to the war that had commenced with the Western Design. Three years later, after relentless lobbying by Godolphin, its terms were extended across the Atlantic—bringing the landmark recognition by the Habsburg Crown of the English right to "Empire, Territory and Dominion" in the New World.[155] "You have obtained that from Spaine which none of your predecessors ever could," Arlington saluted Godolphin's efforts: "a Peace beyond ye Line," and an end to fifty years of struggle for the essential survival of the English colonies.[156] On the back of these accords, the Council of Trade sketched out the political economy of Anglo-Spanish rapprochement, and looked to extinguish the old Caribbean humor of plunder and privateering.[157] The obligation on England and Spain to suppress piracy by "joint and united forces" became more urgent,

Benjamin Worsley averred, because so many of the buccaneers were themselves of French origin, while others were part of an Irish Catholic diaspora with historic ties to the kingdom of France.[158] Peace was seen to offer alternative ways to release the treasures of the Spanish Indies. Although the treaty of 1670 had offered the English nothing in the way of Caribbean commerce, its terms permitted English and Spanish vessels to use each other's ports in emergencies. "If wee can once demonstrate to the Spaniards our capacity of Living like good Neighbours," Godolphin predicted to Charles II, the English could attain "further Libertyes in those Indyes," with "such great and advantageous concessions and priviledges" as to cast the Crown of Spain "into a great dependence upon us."[159] The long-term consequence, he hoped, would be to establish English merchants as principal suppliers of the Spanish viceroyalties, and so capitalize on the decrepitude of Iberian domestic industry to vent English manufactured goods directly into colonial ports. The ultimate prize—not attained until 1713—was identified as the capture of the *asiento* contract, which conferred the exclusive right to ship West African slaves into Mexico and Peru.[160]

The dispatches sent between Jamaica, London, and Madrid began to inform policy across other English frontier colonies. Developing his blueprint for Carolina, Anthony Ashley Cooper called for an end to southward raiding parties, and linked the survival of the colony to its leaders' willingness to "bind the people's mind wholy to planting and trade," suppressing any instinct "to molest either the Spaniards . . . or any of our neighbour Indians in their quiet possessions." Laying "a way open . . . to gett all the Spaniards riches in that country with their consent" would, he believed, afford a surer basis for prosperity than "to have our people live by rapin and plunder."[161] In setting out the implications of the peace, statesmen and privy councillors grafted onto outlying parts of English America a manifesto strikingly akin to the original irenic and commercial blueprint that had informed the development of Tangier. As "the greatest Seat of Trade of any in the West Indies," in Worsley's projection, Jamaica would function both as a "magazine" for regional commodities and a springboard to launch English commerce across wider reaches of the New World.[162] After his appointment as governor in 1671, Thomas Lynch's policy proposals would echo aspects of the Tangier strategy, advocating invitations to Jewish traders to operate in Jamaica, as agents to unlock the markets of other empires and assist the planters by breaking down the stranglehold of the big London merchant houses.[163] Casting off fading dreams of conquest in Panama and Hispaniola, the subjects of Charles II would aim to compass an empire of commerce, getting as close as "the laws of the Nations will permitt," as Lynch urged, to the tottering Spanish rival.[164] Should these goals be accomplished, peace advocates promised, the English would lay their hands on a surer supply of the metals flowing out of Spanish mines than could ever be attained by methods of war.

Yet the turn toward peace and plantation nonetheless gave rise to a torrent of strategic and political questions, and rested on a settlement that, its champions feared, was far from robust. The vision of reformulating the Caribbean through Anglo-Spanish trade ran up against the new bars designed to privilege English merchants: "our act of Navigation being no lesse Repugnant to a free Trade there then the Spanish constitution of that Government," Godolphin complained, by preventing the sale of colonial goods to foreigners without prior passage through the mother kingdom.[165] Through the early 1670s, Anglo-Spanish tranquillity in the Caribbean would rest on a knife-edge, while two thousand buccaneers swarmed the seas, and every local altercation threatened to reignite old hostilities.[166] By this time, moreover, the vision of *imperium* through emporium had come under severe pressure in the very location that had given rise to the idea. Isolated from the trade of the Atlantic by the Navigation Acts, Tangier struggled to fulfill its vaunted free port potential. With merchant vessels harried by corsairs, essential funds, victuals, and medical resources frequently failed to arrive.[167] Belying expectations stemming from the Spanish peace, English merchants were continually obstructed from access to the Andalusian ports, with a succession of traders imprisoned on suspicion of carrying off materials to assist the building project in Tangier.[168] To the south, the magnates of the Barbary Coast refused to believe English assurances that the settlers sought only "good correspondency and commerce." Their reaction soon confounded confident predictions that the "effeminate Moors" had become too raddled by vice and luxury to pose a serious military threat.[169] In 1664, the death of Tangier's second governor—Andrew Rutherford, earl of Teviot—alongside four hundred comrades in a Moorish ambush, brought home the depth of regional hostility to the English enterprise.[170] With the dream of bringing together the fruits of four continents failing to materialize, Tangier risked emerging less as a burgeoning entrepôt than, as Hugh Cholmley came to fear, "a little camp trading in drink."[171]

Beneath the cosmopolitan tone struck by the Crown, certain confrontational impulses had run through even the earliest stages of planning for Tangier. In 1661, the merchant James Wilson had impressed the duke of York with a florid manifesto for "the conquest of Barbary," comprising a Protestant mission and a full program of Anglo-Scottish settlement modelled after the plantations in Ireland and America. Following the caravan routes inland to make themselves "Masters of the Rivers," Wilson anticipated that colonists could stretch their dominion far enough to link Tangier to the Guinea trading factories established by the Royal Adventurers.[172] Over the following decade, the failure to establish secure regional relations ushered elements of these harder-edged visions closer to the political mainstream. The earl of Sandwich agreed that if Tangier struggled to attract maritime commerce, the "distracted condition" of the Barbary Coast, under its competing warlords, offered opportunities to advance into the interior, assume mastery over the many Moorish towns that "will naturally fall into our hands," and turn at last toward the Atlas Mountains: the "richest Mines of Silver in ye world."[173] By October 1670, Hugh Cholmley—once the advocate of an irenic emporium—had also begun to shift his attentions from sea to land. It was only by establishing a "considerable collony" to command the wider environs, he concluded, that Tangier might "stand upon its own legs"—given that "peace to any purpose is impossible with Men absolutely Barbarous."[174]

The strategic turn was cemented when commentators in England began to graft onto North Africa the most aggressive interpretation of the agriculturalist argument for colonial occupation, by reimagining the Arabs and Berbers as unsettled, unruly, and more akin to the Amerindians than to the organized Islamic empires of the East.[175] For Charles Molloy, the "vacancy, which gives us a right to plant," persisted wherever a territory is "not absolutely incorporated, as among the roving Arabians and Moores in Barbary, and other Affricans and Americans, who possess one place to day, and another tomorrow."[176] These shifts in thought illustrated the fragility of the economic models, visions, and blueprints plotted for the creation of an English empire. While officers in the Caribbean distanced themselves from their privateering inheritance, the plan for Tangier was moving in the opposite direction. An international marketplace was being recast as a seat of conquest, powered by silver, slavery, and militant religion.

"Trade, like Religion, is what every Body talks of, but few understand," Daniel Defoe would complain in 1727.[77] In the decade following the Restoration, the maxims of political economy became more fully a part of English discourse, and commercial concerns were increasingly at the forefront of judgments concerning foreign and colonial policy. But the question of how to organize the trade of an emerging empire generated little consensus, because English attitudes toward the creation and control of wealth were themselves bitterly contested. Visions of shaping "the emporium of the universe" within overseas territories collided with anxieties over the balance of trade, and the appeal of a more rigidly integrated domestic and colonial economy. Hopes for an empire to enlarge English territorial holdings sat in tension with the idea that the purpose of expansion was to advance English *manufacturing*. Notions of an unending struggle for gold, silver, and further portions of the earth were countered by the appeal to human artistry and industry, as tools to release the secrets of nature without the risk and burden of further conquests. If England's mercantile interests were disputed, or, as Defoe would suspect, not truly understood, this was because commerce never was evaluated purely on its own terms, but was viewed as a means to the higher end of national *grandezza* and civil virtue. Disputes over trade were absorbed into wider debates over the moral framing of empire and over the negotiation of a shifting diplomatic landscape to England's advantage. As a result, different colonial and commercial interests could fall into conflict—with rival trading rulebooks seen to possess radically different implications for the strength and authority of the state abroad.

PART TWO

THE IMAGE AND THE GOVERNANCE OF THE ENGLISH COLONISTS, 1660–1688

4

"People of Another World": Colonial Subjects, Colonial Liberties, and English Domestic Opinion

AFTER THE RESTORATION, STATESMEN AIMED NOT MERELY to extend the territorial possessions of the Stuart Crown, but also, in the words of the 1660 Council of Trade, "to regulate and improve what is already ours."[1] Royal charters, instructions, and proclamations reminded colonial authorities of their duty to "enlarge our English empire" by imposing order on provinces seen to have slipped from the grasp of the mother kingdom amid the tumults of the 1640s.[2] Laying down a mandate for the councils of trade and plantations in 1660, Martin Noell and Thomas Povey urged the Crown to reduce the dominions into "a more civill and uniforme waie of Government," aiming for the creation of "one embodyed Commonwealth" with colonies contributing "to ye service of ye whole . . . whose head and Centre is here."[3] This language harked back to an older conception of imperium, as denoting not merely geographical expansion, but also the unfettered exercise of sovereignty *within* a given territory. Following Roman and Spanish precedent, the creation of an empire was seen to rest on a concentration of power under one supreme authority.[4] From this fountain would flow one common jurisdiction, imposed over all territorial communities, with overarching structures of government created to bind them to the mother kingdom. Unless English monarchs could demonstrate this capability, it was doubtful—in the eyes of many observers—that the agglomeration of dominions outside Europe could merit the name "empire" at all.[5]

Yet the management of the overseas dominions created a ratchet of challenges for the royal administration. As contemporaries frequently observed, English colonization began not as a result of closely controlled military and territorial projects, but rather because waves of subjects had travelled independently across the Atlantic—enticed into America by a variety of economic, ideological, and personal motivations. Through the seventeenth century, statesmen appealed to the same voluntaristic material interests, pitching the colonies' "large room for industry and reception," in Clarendon's words, as the prime incentive for settlement.[6] In time, this approach would prove a source of strength for the plantations. Peter Moogk has argued that the absence of equivalent forms of promotional literature in the kingdom of France accounted at least partially for the comparative demographic weaknesses of seventeenth-century Canada.[7] But the decentralized nature of English colonial development also meant that settlers, operating under the thinnest layer of royal authority, had wide latitude to establish their own social, legal, and institutional structures. Of the two conceptions of the term "colony" current in later Stuart England, the American settlements conformed to the definition offered by the New England author John Josselyn: a locale for "people that come to inhabit a place before not inhabited, or *Colonus quasi,* because they should be Tillers of the Earth."[8] They did not visibly cohere with the other meaning of "colony" as a subdued and subordinate province, dependent on the central power that erected its civil order.[9]

English America grew through the seventeenth century not as a single cultural province, let alone an organized unit of government, but as an uneven and disconnected nexus of territories steered by disparate political authorities. The distribution of power between the Crown and its overseas officeholders was fluid: "negotiated" as Jack Greene has put it, according to shifting political, military, and economic circumstances.[10] This reality was reflected at the institutional level in the corporate and proprietary land grants that abridged—in practice if not in theory—the power of a distant monarch in many colonial domains. But even in Crown-ruled colonies, the exercise of royal power required collaboration between the Council of Trade and its appointed governors on the one hand, and, on the other, uncodified webs of supporters drawn out of local interest groups. Private networks of individuals able to master the mechanics of long-distance trade, investment, and credit continued to provide the essential lineaments of English expansion long into the later seventeenth century.[11] Moreover, when the risk and expense of the Atlantic crossing acted as a deterrent to the king's more prosperous subjects, colonial opportunities invariably carried greatest appeal to groups whose place within the Old World had become politically or socially uncomfortable. Through the century, overseas settlement relied disproportionately on individuals with ideological or religious identities that were uncertain, if not explicitly divergent from the orthodoxies favored by the law of England.

These conditions were amplified in the two decades prior to the Restoration, when the English Atlantic world was refigured by the consequences of civil war. Colonial populations surged, according to some estimates, from fifty thousand to approximately two hundred thousand.[12] The pressures of conflict pushed preachers, radicals, and transported prisoners, as well as tens of thousands of economic migrants, through oceans and across continents. In theory, the political inheritance left by commonwealth and Protectorate governments, from the passing of the Navigation Ordinance to the creation of the Council of Trade and the launching of the Western Design, had given Charles II precedents for the projection of state power. In reality, the spillage of people had made the English Crown's grip over the New World more tenuous. For three decades after the Restoration, these changes were compounded by further extensions of English territory, together with the spiralling cultural and demographic changes unleashed as the Caribbean plantations shifted toward slave labor. The acquisition of Tangier and Bombay imposed English sovereignty over other unfamiliar peoples: indigenous inhabitants jostling alongside the Portuguese, French, Jewish, and Italian communities created by prior patterns of commerce and colonial rule. The conquest of the New Netherlands brought Dutch, Swedish, Finnish, and Sephardi Jewish settlers under the rule of Charles II.[13] In the West Indies, the principal wellspring of white migration between 1660 and 1700 was the overwhelmingly Catholic kingdom of Ireland, which had supplied a community of approximately fifty thousand Caribbean subjects by the conclusion of the century.[14] The embryonic English empire was multilingual, multiconfessional, multicultural, and multiracial. The Crown was only one actor within a transoceanic world mapped out by planters, pirates, merchants, mercenaries, and a host of other competing interest groups.

As they deepened their engagement with colonial policy, commentators, statesmen, and parliamentarians scrutinized the political, social, and moral conditions of the overseas territories, and considered the most effective governance of an enlarged dominion. The diversity of colonial life invigorated widely varying challenges for authorities in the Old World. The staple-crop-producing Chesapeake and Caribbean colonies—considered in this chapter—were viewed increasingly as the kernel of English overseas riches, but were tainted by growing associations with immorality, irreligiosity, and civil disorder. In other parts of America, as Chapter 5 will show, the danger for the Crown stemmed from vibrant forms of religious life that diverged from the orthodoxies of the domestic realm, creating ideological rifts that were dramatized especially by the politics of the Massachusetts Bay Colony. Contests over the image and reputation of English settler societies stemmed in part from constitutional uncertainties, from unresolved doubts over how far migrants carried the liberties of the "ancient constitution" with them into their new environments, and from emerging conflicts of economic interest. Behind these frictions lay a wider genre of moral anxieties, voiced in English commentary since the later sixteenth century, over the effects of overseas ventures on the minds, behavior, and allegiances of mobile subjects. These fears rose to a height in the mid-1670s, when civil discord in Virginia, Anglo-Indian conflict in Massachusetts, and slave revolts in the Caribbean posed urgent questions over the robustness of the worlds created on the outer rim of Christendom.

English understandings of the colonies were often inchoate and impressionistic. The erratic passage of transatlantic information brought distorted narratives, blurred depictions, and a continual disjuncture between image and reality, a gulf made apparent when colonial stock characters broke into the realm of verse and theater.[15] But Restoration views of the value and virtue of English overseas expansion were increasingly informed by judgments made on the colonists themselves. Pamphlets, plays, and parliamentary exchanges probed the extent to which the domestic realm benefited from the activities of overseas migrants. Commentators wrestled with the conundrum of whether distant territories constituted a part of England itself, and questioned how far colonial peoples could still be considered "English," in blood, manners, and customs, when their domains appeared to be drifting far apart from the cultural moorings of the mother kingdom. These debates increasingly inflected English attitudes toward the non-Europeans encountered through the colonizing process, and guided views of what were appropriate forms of association between peoples of different cultures and ethnicities. Anxieties over the state of the colonists similarly dictated the early evasive and conflicted responses in England to the growth and intensification of plantation slavery in the king's Caribbean territories.

Government, Law, and the Idea of an English Empire

The reality of how far royal power could penetrate through England's overseas outworks rested partly on the political and administrative machinery created in the court of Whitehall. Accordingly, the flux and impermanence of the bureaucratic structure has been cited by many scholars to support the view that English colonization was frustrated by limited attention spans within the court of Charles II.[16] The councils of trade and plantations created in 1660 lacked independent decision-making powers, and were so large as to be unwieldy. Their proceedings, Clarendon recalled, generated notably greater levels of discussion than resolution.[17] The Crown administration was filled with anomalies: the business of Tangier, and, until 1668, New England, was set outside the aegis of both councils, and allocated to smaller court committees.[18] After the Second Dutch War, Benjamin Worsley could still complain of "the want of such an authority to whome all plantations should report . . . for the benefit of the whole and of His Majesties Government."[19] In 1667–1668, the two councils were dissolved, and a single overseeing body, with a reduced merchant composition, created in their place. In 1670, a separate council for plantations was re-established, and in 1672 the two groupings merged again under a common secretariat. A further act of remodeling in 1675 wrested colonial affairs into the hands of a small committee of the Privy Council. Yet for all of these inconsistencies, the groupings themselves possessed energy and ambition. Under the influence of the earl of Sandwich and Anthony Ashley Cooper, the refashioned councils of 1668 and 1672 met on average twice a week for all parts of the year that the Privy Council was in regular session, and marshalled an annual budget of more than £7,000.[20] Inducted in 1671, John Evelyn stepped into "a very large room furnished with atlases, maps, charts, globes."[21] His task was to gather statistical charts, diplomatic intelligence, and volumes of reports from colonial councils, solicited with "such instructions, charges, & particulars to be layd upon them as they dare not to forfeite theire duty therein to his Maty and to this Nation," as Benjamin Worsley bluntly prescribed.[22]

The link between empire and political centralization was backed up in many of the justifications given to assert the basic right of English settlers over parts of the New World. By the "*Jus Gentium,* or Law of Nations," acknowledged William Penn, the possession of any "waste or uncultivated Country" fell to "the prince who was at the charge" of its discovery—not to the individual discoverers.[23] "'Tis a Fundamentall Point consented unto by all Christian Nations," the New York jurist John Palmer would agree in 1690, "that the First Discovery of a Countrey inhabited by Infidells, gives a Right and Dominion of that Countrey to the Prince in whose Service and Employment the Discoverers were sent."[24] The political theology of "first discovery" was supplemented by the right of conquest.[25] After 1664, the authority of the Crown to divide up the Middle Colonies as it pleased was supported by the Council of Trade because those territories had been taken by force from the Dutch, thus overriding any older patents claimed by English planters.[26] The case was sanctioned further by appropriation of an Iberian political economy. By "the law of nations," believed the New England royalist John Josselyn, "no person can pretend interest in Gold, Silver, or Copper . . . but the Soveraign Prince." Just as the Spanish Crown imposed its *quinto* tax to claim one-fifth of the value of gold and silver prised out of Central America, so any operations that unearthed "pretious stones" on English terrain constituted "Mynes Royall," as the Council of Trade reminded the Hudson's Bay Company and the Bahamas proprietors, which meant that an equivalent portion of profits would pertain to the king.[27]

The constitutional status of the dominions was ambiguous. Nominally and legally, the dominions existed not as the public property of the kingdom, but as private possessions of the individual monarch. The earl of Sandwich defined overseas territories as "regalities," while the duke of

Albemarle described the king as private "proprietor" of Barbados. Both terms identified the colonies as zones outside the realm of England, and therefore as set apart from the laws passed to govern it.[28] While the Iberian New World had been fully incorporated into the state of Castile, and made subject to the same system of law, English monarchs had entered into separate and often complex relations with individual colonial provinces, keeping their internal affairs insulated from parliamentary legislation. For many advocates of a more overweening central authority, these conditions presented a frustrating obstacle. Samuel Maverick, one of four royal commissioners posted to New England in 1664, urged that Massachusetts, as "the considerablest of all his Maties Colonies in America," be "annexed to the Crowne of England" by an act of parliament, in order to secure its allegiance.[29] Yet, viewed from a different perspective, the legal fluidities of colonization enabled the Crown to claim powers far more absolute in its overseas outposts than could be safely professed in the Old World. John Palmer saw the colonies as subject to "the Dominion of the Crowne of England," but "not to the Empire of the King of England." By "Empire" he meant the integrated polity whose laws passed through parliament before receiving royal sanction. In separate dominions, by contrast, "the Crowne of England" operated outside this historic apparatus, and so "may Rule and Governe ... in such a manner as it shall thinke most fit," following the precedent of lordship over medieval Wales, before its incorporation under Henry VIII.[30] In this environment, royal proclamations carried force unchecked by any need for approval from Westminster—and, as a result, became far harder for colonists to resist on constitutional grounds.[31]

It was unclear, then, how far the colonists had borne with them into their new settlements the latticework of laws, customs, and liberties seen to stem from England's "ancient constitution." Through the later seventeenth century, influential colonial voices maintained that physical distance carried no implications for the rights of Englishmen—and that since migrants had sacrificed blood and treasure to plant in "an uncultivated parte of the world," as the agents for Virginia put it in 1675, they "ought by Lawe to enjoy in such plantation the same Liberties and priviledges of Englishmen in England."[32] Virginia, contended the assemblyman William Fitzhugh in 1683, was unlike the older locales of Crown conquest, such as medieval Ireland, in that it possessed no framework of "antient municipal laws" prior to the arrival of English settlers. Migrants logically fell back on the "Customs & Laws of England" to provide the civil spine of the province: the foundation on which courts and assemblies were erected, justice was dispensed, and subjects were assured that they remained "freemen and not slaves."[33] Seen in this light, the common law and the parliamentary statute book provided colonists with a canopy of liberties to protect them at once from despotic governors and from undue overreach by Old World authorities.[34]

The court of Charles II was not impervious to these arguments—indeed, the claim to be defending subjects' liberties served frequently as a political weapon for the court as it sought to clamp down on vested interests or hostile ruling cliques within colonial councils and assemblies. In 1668, the royal bequest of Bombay to the East India Company enjoined the publication of all laws, to provide evidence that the inhabitants "enjoy [the] Liberties ... Capacities and abilities of ffree Citizens and naturall Subjects within any of our Dominions to all intents and purposes as if they had been abiding and borne within this our Kingdom of England."[35] The creation of a mayoralty in Tangier in 1669, backed by aldermen and a common council, introduced a governing structure designed to mirror that of the City of London, an attempt to honor the commitment of the earl of Peterborough, the first governor, to uphold "the good and wholesome Lawes by this Nation already established."[36] In most colonies, the Crown endorsed a tripartite structure of governor, council, and assembly, as the political order most consistent with the governing arrangements of Old England. Yet the court and its agents were equally conscious of the judicial ruling issued by Sir Edward Coke in 1608, that although the powers of the supreme authority transferred into a newly settled province, the common law of the mother kingdom did not automatically follow—so that English court rulings could be applied only at the discretion of the Crown.[37] "You are under a great mistake if your think our Statute booke be law in Bombay," the directors of the East India Company informed their factors in 1686, noting that "none of our Statutes or Acts of Parliament" extended "further than the Kingdom of England" or "the Dominion of Wales."[38] Many settlers, moreover, proved just as selective in their approach toward laws passed in Westminster. For the leaders of provinces governed by Congregationalists (much of New

England), Quakers (Pennsylvania and West Jersey), and Catholics (Maryland), an appeal to the "laws of England" was a double-edged sword, since their own authority rested on the premise that legislation passed in Westminster to bolster the established church did not apply overseas.

The sensitivities of the Restoration court and most of the ruling colonial interests converged in a more nebulous consensus that the dominions should be governed in a manner "agreeable" or "not repugnant" to the laws of England—aiming, as the Council of Virginia professed in 1662, to "adhere" as far as "our capacity and constitution of this Country will admit."[39] In reality, justifications for the organization of overseas provinces came strewn with appeals to Roman law, Christian precepts, or, as the Carolina proprietors outlined, the "strict rules of Equity and Justice" that would establish statutes "consonant to reason" and make subjects "live together as honestly and hapyly as it is Possible."[40] While recognizable legal forms were approved as providing stable social foundations, most parties could accept that colonial conditions allowed for multiple exceptions to the rulebook that governed Old England. Even many moderate-minded Crown officials tended to look on local law-making institutions as negotiable gifts of the princes who had annexed the overseas territories and licensed settlement there by their own subjects.

Corporations, Proprietaries, and Colonial Identity

The legal and political authority of the councils of trade was complicated less by any inherent limits of ambition than by pre-existing obstacles of the Crown's own making. Since the inception of the colonizing process, governments had placed large portions of the overseas dominions in the hands of self-funded proprietors or joint-stock corporations, which were furnished with civil, judicial, confessional, and military authority to carry out their responsibilities. By 1660, this model for managing the risk and expense of overseas ventures commanded such consensus that Virginia stood out as the sole dominion governed directly by the Crown, after the dissolution of the founding company in 1624.[41] There was nothing necessarily inimical to royal authority about these intermediary agencies—nor did the practice constitute a radical departure from governance in the domestic realm. The proprietary charter granted to the Lords Baltimore for rule over Maryland was modelled on the powers allocated to the medieval prince-bishops of the Durham Palatinate.[42] Concurrently, 181 English urban boroughs possessed corporate status, akin to Massachusetts and Bermuda, by 1641. Through the seventeenth century, the "relentless waves of civil society," as Phil Withington has put it, were directed by a burgeoning host of local assemblies, councils, and committees, operating under terms struck with the Privy Council.[43] The Crown never saw its grants as an attenuation of sovereign powers—not least because it reserved the right to issue writs of *quo warranto,* and call back charters for examination and amendment. Yet the apparatus nonetheless paved the way for a proliferation of local interest groups that were at once politically assertive and legally self-conscious, and created uncertainty as to where the dividing lines had been drawn between the powers of separate authorities. Being "something at a loss in the practise of Palatinates out of England and Wales," the Carolina councillor Joseph Dalton informed Anthony Ashley Cooper in 1671, "some questions have arisen in whose name Originall and Judiciall Writts and Indictments of Treason and Felony should be made."[44] In order to stabilize and dignify the civil authorities, the political cultures formed within the colonies rested on a view of the Crown charters as representing more than just flimsy documents that could be revised or recalled at royal pleasure.

The authority of royal proclamations, more absolute in theory in the colonies than in the domestic realm, could therefore appear more precarious in reality, not least in the eyes of many English commentators who fretted that the excesses of corporate power posed a severe threat to a stable kingdom.[45] "The Truth is, that Every Corporation is a petty free state, Againest monarkey, & they have Done your Majestie more mischeefe, In these late disorders . . . then anything else hath done," advised the marquis of Newcastle in 1659, sharing the antipathies of his household tutor Thomas Hobbes.[46] The same connection between corporate pretension and political sedition was made by some voices within the councils of Oliver Cromwell, and many historians have seen traces of Hobbesian conviction in the acts of those colonial advisers whose careers straddled the regime changes of 1658–1660.[47] The English interest, insisted one of these men, Sir Martin

Noell, required that such "Collonies as are ye Proprietie of particular persons, or of Corporations may bee reduced as neare as can bee to the same methods and propositions wth ye rest."[48] The Navigation Acts were devised without reference to the "privat interests and mysteries" of corporate privilege, as Thomas Povey put it; instead they laid down the rights of *all* Englishmen to trade in the Atlantic under state regulation.[49] In 1660–1661, Jamaica and Tangier were both placed under direct Crown control, after Charles II brushed aside offers from groups of merchants, aristocrats, and military entrepreneurs to take the reins under a corporate or proprietary rulebook.[50] Simultaneously, the death without heirs of the second earl of Carlisle enabled the Crown to take control of the family proprietorship that had covered Barbados and the Leeward Islands since 1627.[51]

Yet in spite of these actions, the Crown was still constrained, through most of the reign of Charles II, by the same political and financial limitations that had first incentivized the use of "private" authorities overseas. Just as Cromwell had restored the powers of the East India Company in 1657, and confirmed the proprietary rights of the Catholic Lord Baltimore over Maryland, so the court of Charles II showed itself unwilling to abandon the old levers of self-funded colonial government. The earl of Clarendon did "not think it a seasonable Time, when the Nation was so active and industrious in foreign Plantations, that they should see a Charter or Patent questioned and avoided, after it hath been so many Years allowed and countenanced."[52] As English territories expanded through the following fifteen years, the centralizing zeal of 1660–1661 proved to be the exception rather than the rule. The corporate model was endorsed in 1667–1668, as growing debts compelled the Crown to discharge Bombay into the hands of the East India Company. A year later, this resilient legal traditionalism was confirmed in the sole obligation imposed on the newly created Hudson's Bay Company—an annual tribute of two elks and two black beavers submitted as a gesture of fealty.[53] The proprietary method was revived in the 1663 grant to Carolina, and members of the same aristocratic landholding circle collaborated to establish a government over the Bahamas in 1672.[54] The Middle Colonies, supervised after 1664 by the duke of York, were further subdivided over the following twenty years, with governing authority allocated to proprietary rulers in Pennsylvania and the East and West Jersey colonies.

Between 1660 and 1675, any change in the shape of colonial administration lay not in the structures and models favored by the Restoration councils, but in the selection of individuals given a stake within the overseas world. Where many of the original corporate entities had been accused since the 1630s of amassing an interest contrary to Crown authority, the new agencies were tightly intertwined with patronal networks within the royal household. While the king's brother took on the proprietorship of New York, his cousin Prince Rupert was one of the most active directors on the committee of the Hudson's Bay Company. Both men participated energetically as committee members of the Royal African Company. In the overlapping membership of the Hudson's Bay Company, the Carolina proprietorship, and the Jersey lordships, a nexus of personalities within the court administration—including John, Lord Berkeley; Sir George Carteret; Anthony Ashley Cooper; and the earl of Craven—were able to build up expertise and public identification with colonial policy.[55] The effect was to bind new territorial experiments more closely to the Crown, but without a significant rupture in the internal regulation of the provinces. The most durable centralizing measures taken after 1660—the Navigation Acts, the development of a professionalized customs apparatus, and the expansion of the navy—pushed England toward a more integrated *oceanic* sphere of influence, but were not initially conceived as interventions in internal colonial governance. In civil affairs, the Privy Council still encouraged the development of stable, and financially self-sustaining, local elites. In the absence of any major political overhaul, the limits on Crown agency were visible within the regular course of colonial affairs. Between 1660 and 1682, only twenty-five of the sixty-nine governors promoted to office in the New World owed their positions to royal appointment.[56]

The lack of overarching Crown authority was a defining feature of the accounts of the New World—both laudatory and pejorative—that emerged in Restoration print, enlarging the sense of possibility invested in colonial designs. As they plotted ways to build commonwealths from the ground up, colonial leaders presented themselves as experimental philosophers inscribing civil order onto the tabula rasa provided by a vacant wilderness, with husbandry over minds and manners accompanying cultivation of the physical environment. The discourse of proprietors and projectors was shot through with images of colonies as "embryos" or newly seeded gardens; Thomas Woodward, surveyor-general to Albemarle County, Carolina, admitted to Anthony Ashley Cooper that "my Zeale for this Place . . . transports me to this kinde of building Castles in the Aire."[57] For the Boston preacher Cotton Mather, any readers who "mistook Sir Thomas Mores Utopia, for a Country really Existent," and sought to "undertake a Voyage thither, might now have certainly found a Truth in their Mistake," for "New-England was a true Utopia."[58] As part of the plantation of English "civility," familiar household structures, forms of urban planning, architectural designs, and systems of land tenure were all exported—where possible—into territories overseas.[59] Yet the available freedoms still afforded opportunities for divergence—or at least the chance to "re-create" an idealized England that departed substantially from the realities of the Old World.

Corporate and proprietary provinces competed ideologically to attract settlers, contending over which social and political models would best promote civil and material flourishing. The organizing principles behind the Carolina colony carried shades of aristocratic republicanism, introducing hereditary noble titles—landgraves and cassiques—for substantial property holders, whose power would be balanced, according to Harringtonian principles, by the allocation of 60 percent of colonial land to freeholders.[60] This foundation, however, was admonished by many of the projectors who developed the new Middle Colonies after 1675. "Nothing can be more discouraging to a . . . rational man," complained the East Jersey promoter George Scot of Pitlochie, nor impose a more stifling block on settlers rising to "Eminence and honour," than enlarged hereditary powers.[61] Sketching out schemes for West Jersey and Pennsylvania, William Penn and his Quaker associates looked to the Dutch and Italian republics and the canonical texts of civic humanism. Proposals for secret ballots, proscriptions on gambling, and publicly funded education in "trades and skills" for every adolescent male were outlined as ways to secure "the preservation of Right to all, the suppression of Vice, and encouragement of Vertue and Arts."[62] The leitmotif deployed by all projectors was the prospect of *regeneration,* social and personal, in the expansive moral hinterland of a New World. George Scot saw colonization as a means to restore men and women to virtue, by returning them to the seedbed of society and civility, when survival hinged on the practice of "Labour, frugality, simplicity and justice, having neither Leisure nor occasion to decline to Idleness, Ryots, Wantonness, Fraud or Violence."[63] At its most ambitious, this idea centered on the rehabilitation of "fallen" individuals—the vagrants, prisoners, and discontented consciences transported beyond the Atlantic, often under duress. All conquering empires owed much of their original manpower to "those of the meanest quality and corruptible lives," William Berkeley believed. But anyone prepared to "experimentally and morally weight the nature and Conditions of Men, shall find naturally a Change will follow the alteration of our conditions." If English governors emulated the "severity and discipline" of Romulus, then "those who stood idle in the Markett place" could be made "industrious and vigilant" in a New World.[64]

"Utopian" manifestos were rarely pitched as ideological rebukes to the Crown. It was not until six years after the publication of the 1669 Fundamental Constitutions of Carolina that Ashley Cooper (then earl of Shaftesbury) and his circle began to associate themselves with opposition to the court—and most of the other proprietors remained avowed supporters of Charles II. Rather, the aim of published rulebooks and constitutions was to provide the social, legal, and economic balance to keep a colony stable, self-sufficient, and limited in the burden it imposed on Old England. Precepts drafted in the mother kingdom could, moreover, run aground all too readily in colonial conditions. In the absence of the creators themselves, the high-flown constitutional orders imagined for Carolina and Pennsylvania were never properly enacted.[65] But the cacophony of rival visions for America showed how the ideological foundations of England's overseas world remained contested, with many colonial leaders repudiating the Roman image of an imperial authority projecting itself with absolute power over subordinate peripheries. Possession of the soil alone, without the civil and political rights of self-government, offered no more than "the Ring without the Stone," in the judgment of William Penn: in other words, a pledge of insufficient value to coax men into undertaking the trials of the transatlantic passage.[66]

Economic Interests and the Question of Colonial Liberty

Even as they asserted their privileges, most planters were at pains to spell out that they were not seeking greater separation from the mother kingdom. Authorities remained acutely sensitive to shifts in Old World opinion, and recognized the exigency of domestic support for preserving commerce, manpower, and defenses.[67] England constituted the vital "magazine of people" as Francis, Lord Willoughby remarked in 1664, and the overseas territories depended on "a constant supply every year."[68] After the Restoration, colonial leaders labored to gain more visible representation in English politics. The Council of Virginia had developed an organized agency in London by 1662; in 1668, the "Gentleman Planters" of Barbados convened for lobbying purposes in the capital.[69] Settler dynasties such as the Byrds of Virginia and the Bromleys in Barbados expended considerable effort to have their sons reared in English schools or universities, and individual family strategies were intimately bound to wider designs for colonial development.[70] The New Englander John Pynchon settled his physician son on a recently purchased estate in Buckinghamshire in 1672, and eyed the investment as a means toward supplying servants for his Connecticut landholdings.[71] Pitching their case into the public domain, colonial leaders argued that their enterprises worked to the benefit of Old England. As much as they strengthened its outlying frontiers, they also replenished the realm internally, when virtues as well as material goods sown in overseas societies returned to support and enhance the mother kingdom. By the 1660s, believed the manufacturer William Smith, this promise was already being made visible, as growing numbers of colonists returned home, "so improved in Wealth and Judgement as have rendered them capable of Worthy Offices in the Magistracy of their Country."[72]

Yet closer familiarity did not necessarily breed unity of outlook. After 1660, the quickening stream of rules and directives from Whitehall began to expose latent conflicts that wedged settlers apart from some of the interest groups claiming to speak for them in the Old World. Colonial agents concentrated on cultivating English merchant interests, represented especially by MPs for the port towns and cities connected to the Atlantic exchange. Traders and planters, retailers and manufacturers could find common cause in campaigns to lower the duties levied at the customs house on American goods, and to challenge the 4.5 percent levy on exports from Barbados.[73] Yet the merchants, tobacconists, and sugar bakers of the domestic realm were also unbending supporters of the Navigation Acts, and committed to upholding that legislation as the way to drive out foreign competition from the colonial markets. Adhering to the "Maxim of Production abroad and Manufacture at home," many of these groups went further than the Crown in seeking to tighten the colonial economy, advocating prohibitive rates of customs to deter the growth of any plantation industries that threatened to compete with Old World labor.[74] Through the later seventeenth century, vigorous animosities would arise over the shipbuilding industry started by colonists in Massachusetts, and attempts by the East India Company to recruit English "throwsters, weavers and Dyers" to train Asian laborers in European methods of silk production.[75] Domestic interest groups urged the Crown to confine colonial activities, by law, to the production of primary, unwrought goods, to be embellished, manufactured, and marketed in England itself.[76] In March 1671, conflicts over the Caribbean economy hurtled into parliament when the Commons defied the Crown and the House of Lords by voting in favor of prohibitive duties on "refined" white sugar imported from the colonies, which MPs saw as a threat to the profits of the fifty refineries situated in England.[77]

These contests revealed starkly contrasting images of the constitutional as well as economic status of the English colonies. Support for unconstrained manufacturing within America appealed to a conception of colonists retaining their domestic liberties wherever they were planted.[78] The division of labor between the Old World and the New should be determined, believed the Long Island scholar John Scott, purely on the grounds of where it was likely to be most "improving" for the kingdom as a whole.[79] The Navigation Acts of 1660 and 1663 had already committed an act of self-harm by blocking planters from selling sugar directly to European merchants, and provoking the French to develop their own plantations instead, professed one pamphlet produced by the Barbados agents in 1670. The products of French Martinique and the conquered half of Saint Christopher were now flooding "the markets of Flanders and Holland" at a cheaper price, and any further impositions would only deepen England's international vulnerability.[80] Some of these arguments mustered qualified support from the Privy Council, where colonial productivity was judged according to its potential to lever the nation above foreign rivals.[81] If even domestic sugar bakers were perturbed by the arrival of white sugar from Barbados, suggested the earl of Anglesey in 1671, it sent a signal as to the damage that could be inflicted on European competitors.[82] By contrast, the planters' critics deemed it perverse to allow colonies that had been created to serve the national interest to "lessen the imployment of our people here," threaten domestic manufacturers with new competition, and attenuate the industrious workforce that kept Old England productive.[83]

In the conflict over colonial manufacturing liberties, the legal and economic tensions of colonization began to play out across an increasingly interconnected English world. More troubling for some observers, the disruptive activities of the colonial lobbyists threatened to place equally severe *constitutional* pressures on the mother kingdom. The debate over West Indian white sugar created acrimony in Westminster, with the king in April 1671 forced to prorogue the session in response to deadlock between the two houses.[84] By intervening against the Commons in defense of the Caribbean refiners, the Lords had breached the privileges of the lower house over financial legislation, complained the MP Richard Hampden, and violated the precious convention that the peerage "keep their hands out of our purses."[85] Just as menacing, for other parliamentarians, was the linkage between colonial debates and the growing practice of popular petitioning.[86] The "Gentleman Planters" of Barbados flooded the chamber with printed appeals and complaints, backed up by lists of supporting signatures. Virginia tobacco barons clustered "at the door" of the Commons when potential enlargements of the Navigation Acts were debated in March 1671, provoking discord among MPs over the right of colonial agents to be heard before the house.[87] The danger of these proceedings, feared Lord Treasurer Thomas Clifford, was to unbalance the delicate workings of the law, in the interests of demagogues and well-organized vested interests, for "small innovations have too often been earthquakes to shake the government," and "there is but one degree betwixt petitioning and commanding."[88] Unresolved political problems had travelled with the two-way flows of goods and peoples along the Atlantic sea roads, with implications that ranged far beyond the original sources of economic disagreement.

Colonial Disorder and English Domestic Opinion

The argument in favor of colonies being entrusted to manufacture and, if necessary, compete with Old World producers presupposed the basic robustness of English migrant societies: their successful adaptation to the cultural and environmental challenges of overseas settlement. This defense, however, became an increasingly challenging task for lobbyists after the later 1660s, when a series of well-publicized disorders drew attention to ills that had crept into the infrastructure of the dominions. In 1666–1667, as has been seen, colonial fragilities were forced into the open when the assault by French and Dutch forces led to the near collapse of much of the English Caribbean. Behind the defensive weaknesses unmasked in Saint Christopher, Barbados, and Surinam, Crown agents pinpointed gaping social and economic problems: high mortality rates, fragile supply lines, and struggles to attain sufficient supplies of migrants. "Aboundance Remove dayly from Barbadoes and other Islands thither," reported the governor of Maryland in 1673, describing the beginnings of a demographic slide that would result in the European population of Barbados dropping by nearly half over the fifty years after the Restoration.[89] This diagnosis was hardened by a crop of narratives attributing the defeats to failings in the civil order, which had reputedly sapped the capability of colonists to mount an effective self-defense. Some circulated papers attacked the demoralizing "oppressions" perpetrated on the planters by rulers such as Governor Willoughby of Barbados. But rival accounts, issued by colonial authorities, fixed the spotlight firmly on the conduct of the settlers themselves.[90] The fall of Surinam to the Dutch had been hastened, believed Lieutenant Governor William Byam, by the traits of a people "runn retrograd": the "backwardness of many, the Infedellity of more" creating a "confluence . . . wch our Sinns had ripened, all concurring to subject us under the yoak of our Enemies."[91] For Byam and other like-minded complainants, autocratic government in the colonies was justified by a crisis of public morality that threatened grave consequences for English power overseas.

Murmurings over colonial behavior reached a crescendo in the middle of the following decade, after an eruption of disorder in two of the most consequential regions of English America. In June 1675, the outbreak of King Philip's War engulfed the New England colonies in the worst Anglo-Indian conflict experienced for almost forty years, bringing the loss of over three thousand indigenous people, as well as six hundred colonists, and the ransacking of outlying English settlements in Massachusetts, Connecticut, and Rhode Island.[92] Tensions between settlers and natives played an equally convulsive role in the Virginia rebellion mobilized by Nathaniel Bacon in 1676, which was provoked by the inadequate state of defenses on the frontiers, by restrictions on the Indian fur trade, and by alleged corrupt practices of the ruling council. The insurgents torched and looted their way through Jamestown, drove the governor's household into flight, and brought a crushing end to the regime built up for over thirty years by Sir William Berkeley.[93] All of these episodes gained exposure in English public debate, heightened by a keen appreciation of the likely effect on the mother kingdom.[94] The rebellion in Virginia was so disruptive to the tobacco plantations that in parliament it was calculated to have cost the Crown £100,000 in customs revenue.[95] Reports of invasions and rebellions increased domestic engagement with the endemic colonial problems of piracy and lawlessness—amplified further between 1675 and 1678 when a spate of slave revolts sent waves of turbulence through Jamaica and Barbados.[96] These incidents shone light on the reality behind the arcadian images offered up by colonial projectors, and gave rise to a cultural dissection of migrant societies that proved notably unflattering to the colonists themselves.

Concerns over the character of colonial peoples fell within a longer panoply of misgivings, voiced since the sixteenth century, over the transoceanic movements of English subjects, and the enclaves they were constructing beyond the reach of king and parliament. The adulation of English global enterprise by authors such as Hakluyt and Purchas had generated a vigorous counter-literature that interrogated the impact on minds and behavior of ventures outside familiar national and confessional boundaries.[97] Too many travellers, Benjamin Worsley conceded, so subsume themselves within "uncouth, strange or disagreeable" customs that "they forthwith become aliens to their owne Countrey & by degrees contract an Interest & affection that is forreigne."[98] For over half a century, images of renegades "lost forever . . . to their King, their Countrey, and their Religion," in the words of one Scottish projector, had shadowed the movement of settlers and seafarers into Ireland, India, Africa, and the Levant.[99]

Set against the dangers of the East, America did not stand out as a zone of particular cultural vulnerability. With the plantations coated in English laws and governed through the English language, Worsley insisted, "noe other change attends those that soe remove but that of ye Clymatt."[100] Yet other commentators were more alert to the possibility of New World settlers undergoing an inward transformation in their new environments.[101] The concept of the "creole" was in linguistic currency by the end of the century, and migrants such as the Surinam author Robert Sanford professed self-consciousness over their own deviations in speech and writing from "the elegancy . . . of our Eastern English," having "been absent from my native Europe," and "lost" in "places unrefined from their aboriginal Barbarisme."[102] In 1672, within a year of his appointment as governor of Jamaica, Thomas Lynch could only conclude that "this Ayre, I think, disposes People more to knavery and covetousness yn yt of Europe."[103]

Many of the prevailing problems were linked to wrong turns taken in the course of colonial development. Thomas Lynch feared that the domination of Jamaica by large-scale slaveowners and absentee landlords was holding back the transition toward plantation farming, with poorer freeholders straitened further by the high prices that the Royal African Company had fixed on the slaves it sold.[104] These pressures explained an unremitting temptation to engage in privateering rather than the cultivation of crops, Lynch believed, and accounted for the great tracts of Jamaica that remained undeveloped.[105] Critics of the Chesapeake plantations believed that destabilizing influences had intruded even on the infancy of English settlement, when control over Virginia had been attained through straggling and isolated fifty-acre farm holdings, under colonists living, according to the projector George Milner, in "a perpetuall state of Warr & mutuall feare."[106] Considering that by 1700 even Boston mustered only six thousand inhabitants compared to the hundred thousand people dwelling then in Mexico City, English America was certainly ill-endowed with urban settlements—a serious danger, Milner averred, when towns provided the associative framework to "civilise men yt otherwise . . . would insensibly laps & degenerate to barberisme."[107] For other voices, cultural fears wound back further, to the besetting sin of English colonization—the appeal to material betterment rather than higher Christian duties as the prime incentive to emigrate, and the conception that vagrants, rebels, and prisoners offered material for a secure body politic. Looking back in 1715, the Scottish clergyman Francis Borland concluded that the failings of the Stuart colonies had arisen by providential rebuke, when "our Land hath spued out its Scum, and no spot of God's Earth can entertain or receive, but as a burden to it."[108] In presenting America as a place to draw the bedraggled and the unvirtuous back into service of the realm, colonial promoters had relied on the motif of plantation as a pathway toward personal reinvention. But if the theme of rehabilitation was central to the case for colonial settlement, so it became especially liable to hostile scrutiny, when the real weaknesses of the dominions were brought before the domestic gaze.

The contested vision of America as a site of personal redemption presented an irresistible target for the satirists and entertainers of the London stage. "We are Ruled by a Councill," attests one Virginia settler in Aphra Behn's 1678 play *Widdow Ranter,* "some of which have been perhaps transported Criminals, who having Acquired great Estates are now become 'Your Honour,' and 'Right Worshipfull,' and Possess all Places of Authority."[109] For Behn—who claimed to have personally witnessed the crumbling Surinam colony—the plantations became places of masquerade, where social, gender, and moral dividing lines were blurred and confused. In her fictionalized narrative of Bacon's Rebellion, bankrupt forgers ministered as parsons, pickpockets became magistrates, and the alumni of "Newgate and Bridewell" wielded authority from taverns and brothels. The distemper is epitomized in the character of Behn's eponymous widow, the cross-dressing, sword-wielding, hard-drinking "Ranter"—her name itself redolent of the sectarian license that had turned the Old World upside down in the 1650s.[110] The corrosion of settler societies caused all the more alarm because of its apparent foreshadowing in the ancient history of the Americas. The Indians had themselves emerged from the Old World, the Jersey promoter George Scot reminded his readers—for Christian teaching offered them no provenance other than as the offspring of Noah—and had since collapsed into barbarism, leaving only a distorted afterglow of their ancestry present in tribal laws, customs, and beliefs. Following the primeval pattern, "the very first Planters doe soon degenerate in their habits, customs, and Religions, as a little wine poured into a great vessel loseth it self."[111] Striking at the same theme, Henry Neville's fictional *Isle of Pines* (1668) dramatized the moral descents of a party of Elizabethan adventurers, marooned in the Indian Ocean and drifting into polygamy, violence, and lawlessness. While the Dutch navigators who discover them enthuse over the prospects for the island, if "manured by agriculture and gardening," the lives of the English planters ridicule the possibility of such improvement. "UnEnglished" and de-Christianized, the people of the isle had stripped themselves not merely of their European garments, but of "the sence of sin" that kept the "hedge of government" intact.[112]

Indians, Slaves, and Degenerate Englishmen

For many commentators, the frailties of the colonial order were made most glaringly apparent in English encounters with the indigenous, non-Christian peoples of America. The trauma of King Philip's War broadcast the failure of generations of settlers to fulfill the original hopes for the conversion and incorporation of America's native peoples. Indeed, contingents of "praying Indians" were reported to have been among the most adept and severe antagonists in their attacks on the colonists: their exposures had given them fatal insights into English military tactics and defensive weaknesses. After the conflict, the number of New England praying towns fell from fourteen to four; in other parts of English America, as was widely bewailed, evangelical work had failed to get off the ground altogether.[113] For many critics, the deficiencies of the Protestant mission could be linked back to the same maladies that had undermined the moral order *within* settler societies. From New England to Virginia, professed the preacher Increase Mather, unschooled and unregulated Englishmen had proved themselves "too ready to run wild into the woods again." People who "lived themselves too like unto the Heathen" had failed to set examples of good conduct that might have enticed the Indians toward English authority.[114] Far from weaving native peoples into membership of a Christian commonwealth, English settlers had only debased them further, when relations on the frontier were pockmarked with violence, and periods of truce yielded up little more than sales of guns and alcohol. Simultaneously, colonists had left their own societies exposed to the habits and customs of their unregenerate pagan neighbors.[115]

These discussions were complicated, however, by divisions growing within English opinion over the proper role of indigenous peoples within the colonial experiment. For Mather, and clerical counterparts elsewhere in America, the remedy lay in reconstituting the old Elizabethan mandate of an imperial Christian mission. If the rulers of Spanish America had imposed the faith through persecution, lamented the clergyman Morgan Godwyn—a veteran of the Virginia and Barbados missions—the English had cleaved to the other extreme, choosing "trade before religion" and depriving colonists not merely of industrious convert-subjects, but also of moral purpose and spiritual vindication. Because Christianity was nothing if not a proselytizing creed, he warned, inattentiveness to evangelical duties would end by corrupting colonial societies and hastening the downfall of the entire expansionist venture.[116] But a rival, emerging diagnosis cast doubt on the intrinsic value and efficacy of missionary ventures, and admonished colonial authorities, conversely, for their *failure* to set up proper segregating walls between settlers and pagans. As early as 1639, the council of Catholic Maryland had sought—in a direct affront to the colony's Jesuit mission—to close off connections with the Yaocomico peoples, imposing stricter regulations on trade, and banning the withdrawal of any settlers "out of an English plantation to inhabit or reside among any Indians."[117] For Benjamin Worsley, the first New Englanders were to be "honoured" precisely for their resistance to the conversion and incorporation of native peoples, for by "preserving their marriages free from mixture with Indians . . . Their is noe Creolian seed."[118] The salutary warning, wrote the Leeward Islands governor Sir Nathaniel Johnson in 1686, was provided by the mutation of Spanish Americans "into such a dastardly and mongrell breed of mullatoes . . . that they are now certainly become the very scum and off scowringe of all mankind."[119] Racial assumptions were still only sporadic in colonial discourse, lacking the pseudo-scientific overlay that would develop in later imperial cultures. Yet an early willingness to speculate over differences between peoples arose, paradoxically, out of anxieties over the *settler* populations, and attempts to explain their startling moral deterioration.[120]

It was no coincidence that the worst of the anarchy in Neville's *Isle of Pines* is perpetrated by the offspring of the founding governor and a "negro woman." Published in 1668, the story echoed reports of disorders fomented in the Leeward Islands by the mixed-race, illegitimate son of Governor Thomas Warner.[121]

It was against the background of changing attitudes toward Indians and colonists that the West Indian slave plantations flickered before domestic opinion, and English authors made their first—limited and hesitant—attempts to engage with the social transformations wrought by the adoption of unfree labor. Through the 1660s, slavery became embedded within the legal framework of the Caribbean, differentiating Africans from the waves of indentured servants, transported felons, and political prisoners who had made up the original island labor force. The 1661 Barbados Slave Code, which provided for hereditary chattel slavery with unfree status passed through the maternal bloodline, was exported in near-identical form to Jamaica three years later. The same principles were endorsed across the embryonic outposts of coerced labor on the American continent, with formal codification imposed in most slaveholding provinces by the end of the century.[122] But the existence of unfree labor dramatized the legal ambiguities and moral equivocations implicit in the relationship between settler colonies and the mother kingdom. The 1677 Treasury case *Butts v. Penny* recognized slaves taken through the African exchange as "goods" brought legitimately across the Atlantic, subject to the monopoly rights of the Royal African Company. Three further adjudications between 1697 and 1706, however, affirmed that the common law recognized no bonded status extending further than villenage. The implication was that a slave became free as soon as he or she stepped onto the soil of the English kingdom. The legitimation of coerced labor in America therefore rested on a conception of the colonies as no longer comprising parts of the realm that had created them.[123]

Questions over the ideological foundations of the slave system have aroused sharp contestation in English scholarship. A long skein of historical writing, renewed by recent, fashionable reappraisals of the origins of western liberalism, identified slavery as the natural evolution of a "possessive individualism" that gained fullest expression in the colonial environment. For scholars following C. B. Macpherson, enslavement was the product of a rapacious capitalism that moved inexorably from making claims over Indian land toward making claims over African people—all sanctioned by ideas of "liberty" that did not extend conspicuously beyond white Europeans.[124] An alternative perspective, voiced most recently by Holly Brewer, ascribes responsibility to the centralizing imperial ideology nourished within the Stuart court—the power that stimulated the trade to Africa, protected it with fleets of war, and used the Royal African Company as an instrument to achieve an orderly empire, with wealth created and controlled under the guiding hands of the Crown. The "headright" principle, which parceled out colonial land on the basis of a settler's possession of bound laborers, is seen to have moved in step with the hereditary status of slavery—with both policies enshrining the vision of a rigidly stratified society, one that echoed back to the older legal doctrines underpinning feudalism and villenage.[125]

Colonial slavery was certainly more of a political choice than an organic outgrowth of Western Atlantic commerce—a transmutation reliant on the power of navies, Crown officials, local militias, and altered laws. Yet just as visible was the breadth of consensus that it commanded, embracing figures of disparate ideological identities. Despite the rare public qualms expressed by the Quaker George Fox, his co-religionist William Penn unsuccessfully sought a slave labor force for Pennsylvania, "for then," he professed, a man has them always while they live" (a drafted comment revealingly excised from Penn's missive to Friends in London).[126] It is striking just how muted in contemporary discussion were questions over the essential legitimacy of the practice. Slavery was not concealed from public scrutiny. By the 1680s, discussions of the appropriate regulation, treatment, and utility of the African labor force had become a recurrent fixture in domestic verdicts on the dominions. But if slavery was recognized as increasingly important to the colonial economy, its moral ramifications were entangled within pre-existing colonial anxieties, focused as much on the state of settler societies as on the treatment of non-Europeans. Responses to slave labor heightened fears over the frailty of Christian and civilizing influences in the American "wilderness." But for all the transformations it drove through colonial societies, the practice of slavery did not fundamentally change the terms of seventeenth-century debate over English overseas expansion.

Flashes of dissent against economies driven by human traffic entered, sometimes obliquely, into some appraisals of English America. By 1688, Aphra Behn's prose romance *Oroonoko,* perhaps the most evocative early denunciation of the slavers' cruelty, could annex the vocabulary of a small but persistent stream of critical treatises, pamphlets, and poems to inform its narrative of a "royal slave" kidnapped by traders to Surinam. Trade with the plantations had left the Stuart kingdom teeming with morally dubious goods, forged through "the Sweat of *Negroes,* Blood of *Moores,*" complained one anonymous verse critic in 1662.[127] "To advance our carnal interest / We parallel the Practice of the Beast / in merchandizing souls," thundered the radical poet George Wither, "yea more then so / Have set to sale, both Souls and Bodies too."[128] His meaning, however, was elusive, in view of the louder concerns expressed in parliament since the 1650s over the "spiriting away" of kidnapped youths and political prisoners from within the English domestic population. Among many audiences, complaints over the plight of these "Christian slaves" tended not to foster humanitarian sentiment, but rather to harden the sense of distinctions between peoples—the iniquity of the practice lying, according to one MP, in the reduction of Englishmen to a bonded status associated otherwise with Africans.[129] More overt anxiety was registered over the *treatment* of enslaved populations, and in particular, the lack of Christianization—a provocative protest, in view of widespread English Protestant unease as to whether Christian teaching permitted a believer to be kept in a state of bondage. The call to undertake missionary work among Africans in the Caribbean entered into a succession of bills drafted, but not in the end put before the Westminster Parliament, by circles connected to the New England Company.[130] Shared critiques of nonbaptism, as a "murdering of the soul" that violated humane obligations, united the Anglican clergyman Morgan Godwyn and the Catholic duke of York with the Protestant Dissenters Thomas Tryon and Richard Baxter, and the case for conversion was put into practice by a vigorous Quaker mission in Barbados.[131]

An alternative criticism, leavened by moral and religious feeling, developed against the political economy of slavery and staple crops. Reliance on African slaves clashed against the original strategies and ideologies of English colonization, with their focus on the creation of virtuous settlers, artful "improvers," and industrious consumers able to stimulate the wheels of the Atlantic trade through their own productive activities. For commentators still attached to this vision, slavery tended rather to exaggerate than alleviate the vulnerabilities of colonial societies, by displacing more improving forms of industry, and setting up dangerous demographic imbalances. With black Africans now the dominant population in many parts of the Caribbean, any revolt would be sufficient "to devour many such places as Nevis," according to the governor of Barbados.[132] At best, believed the merchant-scholar Thomas Tryon, slave labor could be sanctioned only within the confines of a Christian moral economy, which would prioritize "innocent" enjoyment of the earth's "Fruits, Grains and Seeds" over the "violent and cruel Art of making such large quantitys of Sugar."[133] The London trader Edmund White called for the schooling, baptism, and induction of Africans into skilled manufacturing arts, in imitation of East India Company governance over Asian weavers and silk workers. This approach, he believed, would prove their potential as "capable of learning" and "when they are kindly used . . . the truest servants."[134]

Yet, for Tryon and White, as for the overwhelming majority of critical authors, the use of captive Africans as bonded labor was still an unavoidable feature of colonial expansion—a mystery of the Divine will, as some Anglican missionaries perceived it; anticipated if not entirely absolved by the practices of rival European empires.[135] If slavery was one of the factors making empire a morally precarious enterprise, it was a danger that should be negotiated or disciplined by Christian principles, rather than averted in its entirety. The self-censorship of many critics helped to spare the slave system from any comprehensive ethical scrutiny. For Aphra Behn, the significance of Oroonoko's plight resided in his regal, rather than his bonded, status. The traders of Surinam had revealed their political turpitude by putting an African prince in chains, and by breaking the oaths they had made to restore him to his liberty. In the absence of Charles II's governor, the ills of the colony are encapsulated by the paradox of an enslaved African standing as the only visible figure of royal authority.[136] Confessional scholars were pushed toward awkward formulations as most strove to balance belief in the spiritual volition of Africans with acceptance of their corporeal bondage. The stance made for a marked departure from the tenets of the

Amerindian mission, with its presumption that proselytes, including the smattering of Indian slaves in Virginia, could be incorporated into the Protestant civil and moral community.[137] By concentrating on the denial of the Gospel as the cardinal evil rather than unfree labor in itself, domestic critics ironically helped to accommodate a system that mocked England's boasted self-image as a land of liberty.[138] Behind these equivocations lay hard economic realities—the rewards to be reaped from staple crops, and the struggle to attract sustainable, alternative streams of English migrants. By agitating against the Royal African Company, Caribbean lobbyists were able to divert the terms of public discussion, ensuring that more pamphlet ink was spilt before 1700 debating the freedom of Englishmen to trade, unfettered by monopolies, than over hazier notions of the rights belonging to non-Christians.[139]

On both sides of the Atlantic, the defense and acceptance of slavery, and of the non-conversion of slaves, carried echoes of the pessimism that had entered into English attitudes toward the Amerindians—doubts over the capacity of "heathens" to accept "civilizing" influences, together with a willingness to believe that some peoples were unequipped for "Christian" liberty and independence.[140] The clergyman Morgan Godwyn accused planters of a self-serving adoption of Iberian-Aristotelian beliefs in the existence of "nature's slaves." Under this influence, he suggested, "Negro and Christian, Englishman and Heathen, are by the like Custom and Partiality made Opposites." Godwyn added that "another no less disingenuous and unmanly Position hath been . . . privately (and as it were in the dark) handed to . . . That the Negros, though in their Figure they carry some resemblances of Manhood, yet are indeed no Men."[141] These inchoate ethnographies flitted—sometimes inadvertently—through Behn's *Oroonoko*. The nobility of the "royal slave" is held up against a fashionable notion that "all wit is confined to the white men." Yet Behn gestured to the same prejudice by sketching a crude physical differentiation between Oroonoko and his compatriots—his "polished" skin and Roman nose denoting a princely pedigree that rendered him conspicuously (and, for contemporary readers, reassuringly) less African in appearance and demeanor.[142] Such evolutions in thought muffled the clarity and coherence of any critiques of West Indian labor practices.

Early Caribbean slavery did not create, but hastened, a surreptitious change in English approaches to the wider world: a declining engagement with ideas of conversion or "improvement" as colonial goals, and a more rigid enunciation of the differences between peoples, often in the interest of protecting migrant societies. Strikingly, this perspective was voiced even by some critics, as well as proponents, of the use of bonded labor. *The Selling of Joseph* (1700) by the New Englander Samuel Sewall opposed the introduction of slaves into Massachusetts, not merely out of humane feeling, but because they presented an apparent threat to the moral and biological purity of the godly commonwealth. Imported Africans, he warned, "can never grow up into orderly families," could never be nurtured as godly Protestants, and would "remain in our Body Politick as a kind of extravasat Blood": with disorder threatened by the likely sexual intermingling.[143] Whereas early commentaries on the Amerindians had de-emphasized physical appearance, Sewall now saw the evident "disparity in . . . Conditions, Colour & Hair" as denoting deeper incompatibilities between Englishmen and Africans—warranting not inhumanity toward another race, but walls of separation nonetheless.[144] Defenses and critiques of slavery, therefore, spoke alike to a narrowing of England's imperial hopes and pretensions. Earlier assumptions as to the mutability and malleability of non-Europeans were being superseded by the use of "white" or "black" as terms to denote insurmountably different forms of humanity, embedded into legal structures as well as political discourse. The "civilizing" mandate of English colonization was being challenged—not least because of doubts over the colonists' capacity to fulfill it.

Slavery was much less of a preoccupation of early modern commentators than it has been to modern scholars concerned with excavating the longer and deeper legacy of empire. Most contemporary ruminations focused more extensively on the civil, moral, and spiritual state of English slaveholding settlers than on the captive Africans in their midst. The result was that unfree labor was entrenched as an economic reality long before it was made subject to full moral interrogation. Yet even authors who did not question the principle of slavery could invoke it to raise uncomfortable questions over developments within the dark corners and hidden peripheries of the English world. The West Indian and Chesapeake settlements appeared to be drifting into an alien civil and moral dispensation, even when, as colonial agents regularly declared, the mother kingdom was one of the prime beneficiaries of their emerging economic orders. If slavery was acquiesced as a force for profit and productivity, the cost was to cast doubt over how much the plantations could any longer be considered parts of England and Christendom—and whether the colonists had remained English at all.

At the very time that the centrality of the overseas world was increasing in English trade, warfare, and diplomacy, the colonies appeared to be evolving into a shape less familiar and increasingly disturbing to the mother kingdom. "Shame," "sin," and "scandal" were the watchwords with which hostile commentators dissected the environments created in Virginia and the West Indies. These writings turned back against projectors many of the arguments that had originally advertised the possibilities of settlement. Far from providing for personal regeneration, territorial expansion was seen to have allowed prisoners and vagabonds to bring whole societies down to their own depths. The planned regeneration of the Amerindians had given way to the degradation of the English, with migrants shedding the skin of civility and Christianity as they habituated themselves to a heathen landscape. Such broadsides provoked furious responses from colonial promoters. Englishmen, the Maryland settler John Hammond complained, had chosen to "vilifie, scandalize and cry down" their overseas compatriots, as if "because removed from us, we either account them people of another world or enemies." These insults curtailed the power and growth of the realm, he claimed, and stifled human flourishing by "perswading many souls, rather to follow desparate and miserable courses in England, then to ingage in so honorable an undertaking as to travile and inhabite there."[145]

The American lobby labored to change the image of the English New World. By the 1670s, promotional literature was conspicuously retreating from the old defense of colonies as places of rehabilitation, accentuating instead the pre-existing social virtues of those coaxed into migration. While the Crown still sought to reconstitute overseas outposts with supplies of "malefactors" and "poor debtors who are in Gaole," the assemblies for Virginia and Maryland passed laws against the migration of felons in 1670 and

1676.[146] The Carolina proprietors pitched their advertisements toward "men of estates" who could demonstrate moral and economic credit sufficient to construct a stable civil order.[147] "Forbear to invite the poorer sort yet for a while," Anthony Ashley Cooper instructed one agent in 1671, "it being substantiall men and theire Familyes, that must make the Plantation."[148] The problem for the planters was that their own preferred remedies were liable only to inflame controversies over the management of overseas domains. Most colonial authorities agreed that the answer to the ills that caused scandal in England lay in greater self-sufficiency and civil responsibility. Critiques of the Navigation Acts, attacks on the monopoly granted to the Royal African Company, and concerns over the unbalancing of colonial agriculture by staple crops all linked local infirmities to the absence of the economic liberties afforded to those living in England. These complaints, however, ran up against political barriers and vested interests entrenched within the domestic realm. Reports of poverty and disorder provided the clearest provocation to anti-colonial sentiment. But the arguments raised in parliament showed that English opinion could be equally agitated by the opposite possibility—of a rise in prosperity that risked setting up the colonies as competitors with the mother kingdom.

Concerns that the dominions were struggling to fulfill their original promise carried domestic political consequences. By the early 1670s, as we will see in Chapter 6, negative depictions of the settlers were stimulating opponents of the court, who began to question how far the pursuit of empire cohered with the greater national interest. Conversely, the response of the court was to seek a fuller insertion of "imperial" authority, with the Council of Trade empowered after 1668 to monitor and, if necessary, veto legislation in the colonial assemblies.[149] Closer royal involvement with the colonies did not, however, lead to greater stability. By bringing the Crown into a more direct relationship with its dominions, royal councils dragged provincial discontents into the domestic realm, giving them new opportunities for expression in parliament and the pamphlet press. Observing the mood at court in 1672, Thomas Povey advised the governor of Barbados to keep "2 or 3 particular Friends about Court, and as many in the Cittie." It would be especially wise, he added, to disclose the identities of "the most popular and troublesome" assemblymen, lest "any complaints shall be made here against or relating to the Government."[150] The colonies had become at once more foreign and more visible to the politics of the mother kingdom. By the later 1670s, these exchanges had prepared the ground for a confrontation that would ignite when the Crown began to examine the religious and ideological principles, as well as economic interests, prevailing in councils and assemblies overseas.

5

Protestantism, Pluralism, and the Politics of Allegiance in the Restoration Empire

BY THE 1670S, THE WORLD CREATED THROUGH English overseas expansion was appearing in many domestic judgments as a disturbing palimpsest, with the promised utopias and arcadias blotted out by confusing, disorderly realities. Many of these critiques had confessional overtones because the state of religious life provided one of the starkest illustrations of the disjuncture between imperial visions and colonial outcomes. In the Chesapeake and the Caribbean, civil maladies were perceived to stem from *irreligiosity*—a dissipation created in the people when "many of them never saw England & know not what ye nature & dignity of ye Clergy is," according to one Barbados minister.[1] But in other parts of the overseas world, the confessional challenge was very different. In New England, clergymen had established fledgling Indian missions, schools for settlers, and structures for social and moral discipline. But the organizing congregations stood at a self-conscious remove from the Church of England. Advertising their animosity toward the king's bishops, they imposed a rival set of doctrinal orthodoxies and envisaged the New World as the cradle for a radically different Protestant Reformation. For supporters of the Crown, therefore, the problem of the northern provinces was not spiritual emptiness, but rampant fanaticism, with the posture of the Massachusetts Bay Colony seen to carry especially dangerous consequences for royal authority on both sides of the Atlantic.

While playwrights and satirists amused their audiences with narratives of "creolean" degeneracy, more serious political misgivings focused on the ideological prehistory of the colonies. Providing space for gathered churches and dissentient congregations, the New World magnified the confessional divisions of Stuart England: a polity characterized in one recent scholarly verdict as "a religiously pluralistic society that found it difficult to accept pluralism."[2] Since the 1620s, rival religious communities had planned, funded, and justified the migratory movements that had become central to the creation of English America. In the 1640s and 1650s, newly arriving Protestant congregations planted seeds of the theological radicalism that had been unleashed amid the commotions of the Civil War. By the time of the Restoration, the English colonies yielded up a competitive spiritual environment, with a diversity of views powered by the medley of corporate and proprietary structures that had further pared down the power of the Crown. The wider the web of empire extended, the larger the space it created for communities, creeds, and individuals whose place within the domestic realm had become uncomfortably confined.

The relationship between religion and the regulation of a territorial empire, comprising disparate regions, peoples, and governing structures, posed questions at once political and theological. In drafting a blueprint for the colonies, English churchmen were forced to define the soul and the substance of the Protestant religion, and fix the boundaries of their domain in such a way as to uphold Christian orthodoxy, minister across fragmented sovereign spaces, and propagate the gospel among "pagans." The politics of the 1660s created challenges of a more temporal nature. Royalist fears over the state of the overseas world gathered in the wake of "our late unhappy troubles," as Governor Francis Willoughby put it, when religious dissent was seen to have fueled radical and republican sentiment, and colonial assemblies echoed with the "troublesome spirit of Englishmen who I find to bee in all parts of the world tainted with that designe of usurping a power to themselves beyond the boundaryes of the sett rule."[3] Through the decade after the Restoration, Crown concerns focused less on the "otherness" of godly settlers than on their continuing affinities with discontented brethren and remnants of radical Puritanism across the Atlantic. Questions over the religion of the dominions were umbilically bound to controversies impinging on the mother kingdom, as privy councillors considered rival options for the reconstruction of the Church and for taming the cacophonous pluralism stirred up through the Civil Wars. Solutions pursued in America carried the potential to disturb English politics, by opening up new possibilities and alternative visions for how the Crown should perform its duty as "nursing father" of a Christian realm.

After the Restoration, the court of Charles II initially resisted the call to apply uniform or coercive church policies overseas, and sought instead to establish bonds of amity with the Puritan rulers of the Massachusetts Bay Colony, envisaging the Indian mission as a tool of political reconciliation. This position was promoted in England by circles of "Presbyterian royalists" seeking to reconstitute the established Church as a broad, "comprehensively" Protestant institution, and so keep a public foothold for the godly in the Stuart kingdom. Irenic hopes for the colonies collided, however, with the domestic settlement forced through parliament in 1662, when the Act of Uniformity drove a splinter between the Church and the Puritan tradition, and threatened, by implication, to delegitimize many forms of Protestant worship in America. Across the following two decades, more visible assertions of sovereign primacy in commercial and legal affairs made inescapable the question of how far the Crown should extend Church privileges into its dominions overseas. In the 1670s, when loyalist anxiety rose again over Dissenting activities, Church leaders lobbied the Crown to make good its imperial claims, and to establish more absolute authority over religious life in the English colonies.

The centralizing turn in royal policy reached a climax between 1683 and 1688, in the program of reforms that brought about the abolition of the Massachusetts Bay charter, and the creation of the Dominion of New England, on a model inspired by imperial Spain. For all the controversy caused by these reforms, however, the Crown's blueprint disappointed Anglican hardliners, and diverged both in practice and principle from the uncompromising Church policies pursued in the domestic realm. English statesmen rejected the imposition of a single church on the colonies, even while they abolished assemblies and clamped down on *political* opposition in America. Instead, they posited religious toleration as the superior foundation for stability, prosperity, and obedience in overseas settlements. The contrast between policies enacted on different sides of the Atlantic did not escape political attention. As English commentators considered the civil and religious framework that best satisfied the needs of an expanding empire, so their thoughts contained repercussions for the way in which "allegiance" was defined at home. For Catholics, Quakers, and many voices at court, the English plantations became the locale for experiments in confessional plurality, conceived to renegotiate the terms of civil loyalty by distinguishing between temporal obedience and the dictates of the private religious conscience. After 1685, the colonial combination of toleration *and* absolutism informed the explosive project, devised by James II, for dismantling the powers of the established church and introducing sweeping religious liberties into the three kingdoms, on a condition of obedience to the throne.

Rival Churches and the Challenge to Royal Authority

As early as 1662, the Stuart court was incorporating moral and religious regulation into its plans for the English overseas world. Instructions submitted to Sir William Berkeley commanded the "suppressing of all vice and debauchery" in Virginia, as lapses were especially "abominable" in places "exposed to so many dangers . . . in daily hazard of perishing," and needful of "protection and assistance from God Almighty."[4] These injunctions responded to clerical appeals sent in from the New World, in print and petitionary form. For the Virginia minister Roger Greene, the welfare of the English colonies rested on equipping the "orthodox Protestant Church" with "beauty, wealth and ornament" sufficient to "nurse up children of her own" and create morally armed communities of worshippers that could counter the "herds of Heathen" beyond their frontiers.[5] Directed back across the Atlantic, these arguments supplied a provocation to pious and philanthropic campaigns within the domestic kingdom. Through the later seventeenth century, calls for moral reform among English subjects were framed with reference to the challenges accompanying an expanding realm. Campaigns were especially targeted at the seafaring populations of ports and cities, who, without proper spiritual fortification, warned the merchant James Houblon, risked acting to "ye Great Scandall of our religion & Government" overseas.[6] Roger Greene called for the endowment of "Virginia Fellowships" at Oxford and Cambridge, supported by regular parish collections, to sustain the colonial ministry.[7] Later, recommending Lenten sermons by returning missionaries in London, Morgan Godwyn hoped that a raised awareness of colonial conditions would turn England into a "nursery" of charitable devotion, sensitive to the importance of education, catechizing, and "Christian living" in the preservation of the civil order.[8]

In time, the evangelical springs unleashed within the Restoration Church would produce a stronger ethos of Anglican voluntarism, and give life to independent, associative activity among congregants who sought to plant the Gospel in neglected corners of English society.[9] In the 1660s and 1670s, however, champions of orthodox worship in the New World, as in the Old, believed overwhelmingly that spiritual virtue relied on strengthening the institutional apparatus of the Church, and mobilizing royal authority to protect it. Colonial clergymen and their supporters appealed as much to temporal self-interest as to the pastoral conscience of the Stuart Crown. The role of ministers, opined the Privy Council, was not merely to "prevaile with men to live better," but to "increase the zeale and allegiance of many to his Majtie's service, and unite them in the better defence when any danger should happen."[10] Most governors in the Crown colonies threw their weight behind the strengthening of the ministry on similar terms, as an obligation demanded by "the policy if not the religion of the state," in the words of Thomas Lynch.[11]

Such sentiments fell in line with the thoughts of the first generation of colonial promoters. In the writings of Elizabethan and Jacobean clergymen, the original case for colonization had presupposed the export of one overarching form of Protestantism into the New World: a single Church bounded by the authority of the royal supreme governor, and structured by the familiar ecclesiastical machinery of dioceses, deaconries, parishes, and schools.[12] Through the seventeenth century, however, these ambitions ran up against the weaknesses of the colonial Church of England, which had been wrested from the historic and institutional buttresses that supported the clergy at home. The challenge of transferring the paraphernalia of worship across the Atlantic—building churches, schools, and libraries, and installing legal and financial safeguards to protect them—tested the capabilities of the English episcopate. Without a resident bishop in America, the process of training, recruiting, and dispatching colonial ministers was impeded by the rigidity of the diocesan structures—in particular, the need for prior ordination in the Old World and an episcopal license before any venture across the seas.[13] By the 1670s, even the Crown colony of Virginia supported only ten Church of England clergymen among a geographically dispersed population of thirty thousand Europeans, with a resident minister seated in only one out of every five parishes.[14] Without any diocesan office, the planting of an ecclesiastical order remained dependent on the partiality of individual governors, and a whole matrix of lay officials— magistrates, assemblymen, vestrymen, and colonial agents—whose support could not be guaranteed.[15]

The danger perceived by many observers was that the colonial Church of England lacked institutional features to distinguish itself from pervasive and well-staffed Protestant rivals. "Very few" orthodox ministers would venture thither, bemoaned the Maryland promoter John Hammond, "thinking it a place wherein surely the fear of God was not." Into the void had stepped pretenders to spiritual authority, "such as wore Black Coats, and could babble in a Pulpet, roare in a Tavern."[16] Through the 1640s and 1650s, while ecclesiastical discipline collapsed in the Old World, Presbyterian chapels were established in Port Royal, Jamaica; communities of Independents entrenched themselves in Bermuda, Surinam, and the Bahamas; and Quaker and Baptist preachers swarmed into the northern dominions, thriving in environments that privileged voluntarist initiative, portable forms of worship, and decentralized congregational structures.[17] Only in Massachusetts did a strong and monopolistic church establishment prevail, and it did so through a conception of "true religion" that diverged dramatically from the orthodoxies of the mother kingdom. Since the 1630s, the Puritan migrants coalescing under John Winthrop and his associates had forged a self-enclosed, Calvinist moral community centered on networks of congregations run by local lay and clerical authorities, with public office confined to individuals considered worthy of full church membership.[18] Most of the ministers settled in Massachusetts before 1640 never formally severed themselves from the Church of England, and congregants regularly protested, in the words of Samuel Sewall, that no worshippers "did more fully concur with the Doctrine of the Church of England contained in the 39 Articles." Yet the Congregationalist ecclesiology, the rejection of the authority of English bishops, and above all, the proscription of the Book of Common Prayer laid down a transatlantic splinter that aroused intense mutual suspicion.[19] After the Restoration, it was unsurprising to the Crown commissioner George Cartwright that the Bay Colony was, of all provinces, "the last and hardlyest persuaded, to use his Maties name in their forms of Justice." The Boston General Court resisted until 1663 the obligation to issue its writs in the name of Charles II.[20]

For admirers on both sides of the Atlantic, the Bay Colony provided the clearest template for the potential flourishing of England's American provinces. The mixed agricultural and fishing economy, and the interlinked networks of urban settlements, made Massachusetts a model of political economy for the Carolina proprietors, in contrast with the sprawling, unprofitable estates of Virginia. Winthrop's rejection of transported felons and vagabonds enabled Massachusetts to stand out as an immediate counterblast to the moral fragility detected in the Chesapeake and the West Indies.[21] Yet the civil and material growth of the province caused no less anxiety than its spiritual evolution. With its shiploads of beef, pork, timber, corn, and fish, the Bay Colony was already making inroads by 1660 into the market for provisioning the Caribbean: threatening, some voices feared, to inch out merchants from Old England.[22] On the back of this success, the province's traders flexed commercial muscles outside America. Ships were seen in Boston "daily arrived from Spaine, France, Holland & Canaryes," while Massachusetts men filled the markets of Jamaica with French brandy, and sent their own fish and timber into the Mediterranean. Such breaches of the Navigation Acts were calculated to be costing the Crown over £100,000 a year.[23] Massachusetts coined its own currency, levied taxes, and imposed an "oath of fidelity" to its ruling General Court.[24] Its ability to posture "in affectation of a republican forme of government," as councillors in Virginia put it, was enhanced by the absence of any copy of the original 1629 charter in Whitehall. Having carried all documentation with them across the Atlantic, the founders of the Bay Colony had left no institutional footprint in the Old World, narrowing the prospects for outside legal interference.[25]

Soon after the Restoration, the Crown fixed its political attention on the Massachusetts settlers, "a numerous and thriving people," in the words of the earl of Sandwich, who "in twenty years are more likely . . . to be mighty rich and powerful and not at all careful of their dependence upon old England."[26] New England, in turn, became central to the larger cultural and political fears expressed in English print over the effects of overseas expansion. While there were few overt similarities between "fanatical" Massachusetts and "heathen" Virginia, Congregationalism was seen by its critics to encourage the same subversion of civil and social hierarchies. The connection between civil privileges and full church membership had created a looking-glass world, one pamphleteer believed, where "poor Coblers and pitiful Mechanicks" reigned ascendant, and "the richest Merchants and wealthiest People stand by as insignificant Cyphers."[27] Just as concerning was the influence of Massachusetts over other parts of English America, through commercial and confessional networks, as well as unlicensed territorial outgrowth. By 1660, Boston's authority had been extended over Maine and New Hampshire—claimed respectively by the absentee royalists Ferdinando Gorges and Robert Mason.[28] As intracolonial trade accelerated the spread of books and ideas, Boston Congregationalism extended its sphere of interest, and fomented small breakaway movements among ministers who rejected episcopal ordination in Virginia and Bermuda.[29] Massachusetts, seen through royalist eyes, had become a "free state," or "little Rome," offering not just a rival church establishment but also an alternative moral and political center for the English empire in America.[30] Even Benjamin Worsley—whose Puritan past made him instinctively sympathetic to the province—agreed by 1668 that the Crown would soon have to contend with the Bay Colony by enticing its settlers toward the underpopulated West Indies.[31]

Within Crown circles, the stakes in any confrontation with Massachusetts were raised higher by the fragilities identified in English domestic politics, and the possibility that influences sown in America could all too easily slip back across the Atlantic. A host of prominent Puritans and radicals had relatives exiled and resettled in New World provinces, from where they kept up a regular correspondence with the mother kingdom. In 1661, Robert Sanford claimed to see "Olivers policies . . . daily practised" in Surinam, where families such as the Harleys and the Martens held plantations. "The same planet," Sanford feared, "still retains some vigour of its Malignancy, especially at so great a distance from the Royal beams."[32] The offer of protected space for dissidents in the overseas territories was justified by some authors as a means of managing domestic tensions: purging the body politic of ill humors, and, as the Carolina proprietors put in 1665, keeping those "that either cannot or will not submit to the Government of the Church of England" in a place where their productive activities would serve "the good of the Kinges Dominions."[33] But the security fears that accompanied the Restoration in England cast doubt on the notion that problems could be simply exported onto another continent.

As the training ground of the radical statesman Sir Henry Vane and the New Model Army chaplain Hugh Peter, Massachusetts had already "furnished Cromwell with many instruments," commented George Cartwright.[34] The abiding danger was brought to the doorstep of the Crown in January 1661, with the failed London uprising against Charles II led by the Boston-born cooper and Fifth Monarchist Thomas Venner.[35] By the end of the year, the Privy Council had been apprised that two missing regicides, William Goffe and Edward Whalley, had found refuge in Massachusetts and Connecticut, where they had been "entertained . . . with great solemnities and feasted in every place," as one Crown agent reported.[36] The royalist scholar Fabian Philipps captured the radicals of New England as "birds of prey," "pearching" on the Atlantic seaboard in readiness for another descent on the mother kingdom.[37] Massachusetts disturbed courtly minds less for its alleged lunge toward autonomy than for its continual proximity to the troubles of the three kingdoms. While the Crown remained on high alert against religious and political sedition, the peril of colonization seemed to lie in the sanctuary it offered for the debauched and the disaffected, enabling them to manufacture new worlds, and menace the one they had vacated.

Colonial Missions, "Comprehension," and Protestant Reunion

After 1660, loyalist commentators pressured the Crown to intervene in English America and address signs of political and religious insubordination, as a matter of domestic as well as colonial security. Although the Massachusetts Bay Company was not regulated by parliament, the Corporation

Act of 1661 set a precedent for closer surveillance over local governing elites, linking political sedition explicitly to deviant religious opinions.[38] In America, too, early Restoration policy set the stage for a potential confrontation with New England, as the Crown was drawn closer to the affairs of the north in grappling with the problem of the Dutch New Netherlands. After the successful conquest in 1664, the mission to "curb Boston" was made central to the agenda of the Crown commissioners tasked with restoring the king's name to assembly legislation and enforcing compliance with the Navigation Acts across the Northern and Middle colonies.[39]

This program of self-assertion was not, however, replicated in the Crown's instructions and directives for colonial religion. At court, opinions over ecclesiastical policy were divided. Contending against the bishops, rival lobbyists challenged the notion that an episcopal church centered on the pre–Civil War Prayerbook would provide a stabilizing influence in geographically distant regions threaded through with religious diversity.[40] Even many advocates for a colonial religious establishment urged the Crown to construct a looser, all-encompassing ecclesiastical framework to better reintegrate Puritan settlers. The Carolina councillor William Owen argued in favor of a broadly Protestant ministry for his province: "not strickt episcopalle nor yet licentious nor rigid presbiterian nor yet hypocriticall but swayeing in an even Ballance betweene all opinions."[41] The belief that colonial policy should give legal latitude to alternative forms of Protestantism was heightened in the context of encounters with non-Christians. In Ireland, the MP Vincent Gookin, whose nephew Daniel supervised the Massachusetts praying towns, fretted that enmities between Protestants stifled the prospect of new conversions, when "the Papist sees not where to fix if he should come to us . . . sees not what friends or security he could partake if he *should* fix."[42] When no single church was materially equipped for mastery over colonial terrain, the challenge of missionary work strengthened calls for collaboration between different congregations, and inclusiveness in the definition of Protestant orthodoxy.

The Crown showed itself to be receptive to the language and logic of these appeals. Distancing itself from more hardline loyalists, the court aimed to enlarge royal power in Massachusetts and its neighboring colonies within the framework of existing charters, and sought to establish a mutually agreeable modus vivendi with Puritan populations in New England and other parts of America. The new 1662 grant issued to Rhode Island and Providence offered exemptions to the Independent congregations from "the liturgy, ceremonies, and articles of the Church of England," in the hope that the colonists' "serious intentions of godly edifying themselves in the holy Christian faith . . . may win the Indians to the knowledge of the only true God and Saviour of mankind."[43] Liberty of conscience was also attached to an evangelical end in the rules devised for the Carolina proprietary, and embedded into the Fundamental Constitutions of the colony in 1669.[44] Toleration, protected by the absence of an established church (but denied, revealingly, to Catholics and atheists), was defined not as a morally neutral position, but as one of the "Methods of Gentleness and Meekness" necessary to coax "Jews, Heathens and other Dissenters" into the Christian fold.[45] The direction of royal policy was made clear with the grant bestowed on the New England Company in 1662, endorsing it to raise funds from English parishes to support the Indian "praying towns" created by Massachusetts Congregationalists.[46] The aim enunciated by the governor, Robert Boyle, was to bind Puritan settlers back into the royal domain through spiritual partnership—marshalling Boston as an assistant in the process of making the empire Christian, and winning new indigenous subjects for Charles II. Shared involvement in the mission, Boyle believed, would correct the "easily evitable want of understanding" between the Crown and the Bay Colony, and strengthen New England liberties against any hostile attentions from the Old World.[47]

The New England Company was a product of domestic as much as colonial politics. It was no coincidence that the corporation was steered in England by advocates of a church settlement based on "comprehension": the idea of accommodating different strands of the Protestant religion within a single establishment, with provision, if necessary, for alternative forms of worship. The company's strongest Privy Council patrons, the earls of Manchester and Anglesey, were exemplars of the Presbyterian royalist persuasion that had retained a place at court, and had campaigned to place Charles II at the helm of a Church that was broadly Protestant in its liturgy, structure, and theology, resisting any return to the narrower orthodoxies of the reign of Charles I.[48] While comprehension in the domestic context focused on reuniting Presbyterians and Episcopalians, the language and theology of the campaign could be applied equally to legitimize correspondence between the Church in England and the Congregationalist establishment in Massachusetts. The Puritan divine Richard Baxter, who advocated for "reformed" or "reduced" episcopacy as a platform for reunion, believed that Bay Colonists had discerned "the Inconveniencies of Separations" after the excesses of "souldiers and Schismaticks" across England and America through the 1650s.[49] The receptiveness of some New England clergymen was evidenced in a stream of spiritual works dedicated to Charles II, culminating in 1663 with the Algonquian Bible itself.[50] Later in the decade, the same irenic instincts informed the creation of the Halfway Covenant by members of the Boston Third Church, as a means to widen the eligibility standards for baptism, reconnect Massachusetts to fellow Protestants overseas, and extend Christian ministry among the unconverted.[51]

The missions formulated in the early 1660s were accompanied, therefore, by calls for the unpeeling of those "things indifferent" that had created fault lines between Protestant congregations. The writings of Boyle and Baxter, and New England Company associates such as the Scottish Presbyterian John Dury and the Somerset rector John Beale, caught the echo of a larger movement for Protestant reunion, formed among scholars and preachers amid the fires of the Thirty Years' War, when divided European reformers had reeled in the face of sweeping Catholic advances.[52] This ethos was carried by members of the same circles into the missionary programs devised for Wales, Ireland, Lithuania, and the East Indies.[53] All of these enterprises aimed to mobilize spiritual labor from different churches for the creation of a universal community of professing Christians, one built up through scriptural translation, dissemination, and conversion. It was not viable, Baxter argued, for Protestants to maintain denominational exclusivity if they wished to advance true religion, for "merchandizing, travaile," and a "want of Pastors" repeatedly took individuals beyond their familiar congregations, leading them to depend on the greater fellowship of reformed Christians.[54] The Anglican Morgan Godwyn agreed that the reclamation of Indians and Africans rested on reconstituting an ideal of Christian unity. To "neglect or hinder this Work," due to rivalry between different congregations, would be "a manifest betraying" of a shared "Protestant

Interest," and "no less an advancing of Popery: which they that do, can be no other than open Enemies to the King and Kingdom."[55] In many nominally Anglican colonies, there was strategic as well as theological force behind these ideas, when the paucity of qualified clergymen made comprehension a de facto reality. Two Swiss ministers, together with a Scotsman of Presbyterian background, accounted for three-quarters of the active livings in Jamaica in 1671. Ten years later, the governor of the Leeward Islands identified "French and Dutch Calvinists and Lutherans" staffing the parishes under his authority.[56]

Yet in the New World, as in the Old, ecumenical initiatives ran up against the polarizing reality of the Restoration politics of religion. By the summer of 1662, conferences between Presbyterians and Episcopalians had failed to secure spiritual or political understanding, and plans for a "comprehensive" church collapsed, as Anglican royalists gained the upper hand on the Privy Council and in the Cavalier Parliament. The new Act of Uniformity placed on a legal footing the antagonism between the revived, episcopal Church and its Dissenters, and so prepared the ground for an exodus of "godly" Puritan ministers from parish livings. In the fluid context of Restoration politics, these measures were not entirely peremptory. The foundations of the Church remained unsettled for over a decade, with pressure for comprehension or at least toleration for non-Anglicans renewed periodically within court and parliament.[57] But the bishops had set about "unchurching" the Puritan tradition, and in purging Presbyterian and Congregationalist ministers from the parishes, they hastened the decline of Calvinism within the established Church.[58] The result was to cut off the ideological bridges between established congregations in England and Massachusetts. The legal fracture between Church and Dissent cast thousands of American settlers toward the political margins: pushed, in the royalist imagination, into an ideological netherworld populated by sectaries, regicides, and fanatics. For their part, Richard Baxter recorded, agents for Massachusetts recoiled when they "came over and saw how things went" in England, and "began to remember again, that there is something beside Schism to be feared, and that there lyeth as perilous an Extreme on the other side."[59]

The Restoration church settlement struck a fatal blow at the idea of assembling a unifying and collaborative Protestant coalition to attempt the conversion of non-Christians and take on the spiritual governance of English America. Hostility to Dissent, Richard Baxter lamented, stifled any prospect of collections raised in Old World parishes for the New England missions.[60] John Eliot insisted that his Indian proselytes had "submitted ymselves to ye English government"—a claim that the Long Island geographer John Scott delicately changed to "his Majesty's Government" when bringing it before a court audience.[61] But antagonists such as the New England Crown commissioner George Cartwright were opposed to any royal involvement with the missionary project, considering it unclear that political authority over Indian converts extended any further than the Massachusetts Bay Company.[62] Feuds between Anglican and Dissenting chaplains inhibited the growth of missions in the Eastern as well as Atlantic theaters of the English overseas world. The EIC governor of Fort Saint George bemoaned in 1678 that the consequence was to "give advantage to the Romish churches" on the subcontinent, who "draw away many who would have been bred up by the English." The splits, however, were at their most vehement in the West Indies, where Anglican clergy and civil officeholders attacked the incipient Quaker mission among unfree Africans as a source of social subversion, and as an alleged contributing factor in the slave revolts of the later 1670s.[63] For Richard Baxter, the discontents of the English dominions—the godlessness of the island colonies, the unabated animosities between churches—all spoke to a universal crisis that threatened the long-term future of the reformed religion. "We are not of such large and publick Minds," he lamented; "every one looks to his own Concernment . . . all seek their own things."[64] These divisions increased the impediments to establishing an English mission among "pagans" in the New World.[65] When they were required to choose, colonial clergymen of all stripes privileged upholding Christian orthodoxy among settlers, and beating back the power of other Protestant congregations, over propagating the Gospel anew.

Toleration and the Politics of Colonization, 1662–1675

Through the 1660s, the effects of the Act of Uniformity threatened to isolate Massachusetts not merely from the established Church, but also from many of its natural supporters in the Old World. For the pro-Dissenting privy councillors still active at court, and striving to reclaim royal favor for the godly, republican tendencies within the Bay Colony were a severe embarrassment. William Morice, the secretary of state whose Presbyterian background had prompted expectations of sympathy within New England, chastised Boston for its want of "duty and cheerful obedience" and urged replacement of the governor, John Endecott: "not a person well affected to his Majesty's person or his Government."[66] Outside Whitehall, New England Company networks supplied the Bay Colony with a solid bloc of Presbyterian and Independent supporters on the London common council.[67] But correspondence with the Old World was complicated after 1662, as the "godly" fragmented into discrete congregational streams. Their numbers were now split between Presbyterians, Independents, Quakers, and General and Particular Baptists outside the Church, and another strand that remained, discontentedly, inside the fold of the establishment.[68] None of these groupings strictly cohered in theology or ecclesiology with the Congregationalist model of the godly commonwealth crafted in Boston, and the differences made transatlantic affinities more fragile than many New Englanders had hoped.

For many English and Scottish Presbyterians, the theological radicalism of the Bay Colony, and its comparatively thin dividing lines between lay and clerical church members, strained the bonds of spiritual kinship. Conservative-minded Puritans such as Thomas Edwards observed the "fanatick" zeal of New England émigrés returning to enter into the Civil Wars in the 1640s, and concluded that Bay colonists had set up insufficient safeguards for true doctrine.[69] From a different perspective, the authorities in Massachusetts were interrogated for their approach toward individuals *outside* the church. In England after 1662, support for liberty of conscience among Protestants had sprinkled through many of the godly communities, with Independents, irenicists within the established Church, and many Presbyterians inveighing against laws and animosities that tended to divide the faithful. In this context, the intolerance in Boston, advertised by the execution of three Quakers in 1659, together with the bar against Anglican worship, created grounds for alarm. Lobbying in London in 1689, the Boston preacher Increase Mather would be confronted by Independent pastors levelling accusations that "we had persecuting Lawes amongst us."[70] As governor of the New England Company, the moderate churchman Robert Boyle fretted that violations of religious conscience were "the more strange & the less defensible in those who . . . crossd the vast Ocean to settle in a wilderness that they may there enjoy the liberty of worshipping God." Such measures, he warned, were likely to be of "very bad consequence" for Dissenters in England.[71]

The political isolation of the Bay Colony emboldened episcopalian hardliners around the king. Between 1670 and 1672, plans were drafted at the Privy Council for creating bishoprics in Virginia and the Caribbean, and constructing a cathedral in Jamestown: all were conceived to bring settlers and Amerindians into "the same doctrine in sacred things, the same manner of offering their prayers up to almighty God, and finally an uniform discipline in things ecclesiastical."[72] An accompanying proposal to extend the jurisdiction of the archbishop of Canterbury over all current and future dominions held out the prospect of conflict with New England.[73] Yet these projects failed to gather momentum. After the death in 1672 of the first intended Virginia bishop, Alexander Murray, and the political disruptions of the Third Anglo-Dutch War, the plans fell permanently into abeyance. The Crown drew back from confronting Massachusetts with claims of Episcopal authority, and even in securely loyal colonies sent mixed messages to the ecclesiastical establishment.[74] Directives from Whitehall obliged governors in the Leeward Islands toward "profession of the Protestant Religion as it is practised in England," enjoined "due reverence & exercise" of the Church in Jamaica, and demanded "special encouragement" for its ministers across New England.[75] But the court stopped conspicuously short of granting Anglican clergymen the hegemony they had requested over religious worship.[76]

Until 1675, these reservations reflected the influence of cadres of pro-Dissenting and crypto-Catholic privy councillors who bristled at the terms of the Act of Uniformity and provided internal court resistance to the claims of the Anglican episcopate. The fall of Lord Chancellor Clarendon in 1667 had ushered many of these individuals—including Anthony Ashley Cooper, the duke of Buckingham, and the earl of Arlington—to the forefront of the administration, and their imprint was detectable over abortive bills for comprehension drafted in 1667 and 1668, and the Declaration of Indulgence offered to Dissenters and Catholics in 1672.[77] The passing of the sternly pro-Anglican Test Act in 1673 highlighted the weakness of this position, set against the majority sentiment in court and parliament. But obstacles to the colonial Church of England arose equally from many local civil authorities, who considered the economic and demographic needs of English settlements to be incompatible with religious policies of monopoly and exclusion. Governor Modyford of Jamaica, a professed ultra-royalist in civil affairs, believed that religious liberties supplied "needful and prevalent baits" to "increase the number of his Majesty's subjects," and offered inducements to Quaker merchants, including the missionary-preacher John Perrot, to settle and trade on the island.[78] At the other end of the Stuarts' overseas world, the administration in Bombay asked few confessional questions of the "French, English, Jermans, Danes or other Christians" whom it encouraged to settle. In this region, the distinguishing feature of personal identity was not religion, but nationality.[79]

These approaches swayed Crown policy. Addressing the governor of Jamaica in 1674, the Council of Trade invoked the disparity between the "poverty and emptiness of Spain and the vast riches and number of people in the United Provinces," as evidence that liberty of conscience was the stratagem most "agreeable with modern policy."[80] The duke of York, highly resistant to establishing a law-making assembly in his New York proprietary, was conspicuously more welcoming of *religious* liberties, proclaiming that "no individual" was to be "molested" or "disquieted" as long as they own "the substance of Christian Religion, and entertain no tenets prejudicial to the ends of Government and Society."[81] In practice, the Crown's early confrontations with Massachusetts and the other New England colonies centered not on attempts to impose a new Church order, but on calls to widen the franchise and extend toleration beyond the Congregationalist fold especially, but not exclusively, to Anglicans. Such stipulations upheld a principle closer to the 1660 Declaration of Breda, with its promise of "liberty to tender consciences," than either the uniformity endorsed by the Cavalier Parliament or the broadly defined, but still resolutely Protestant, "comprehension" policy defeated in 1662.[82] At home, the constraints on the royal prerogative obliged Charles II to accept intolerant ecclesiastical policies demanded in parliament. The absence of these inhibitions across the Atlantic enabled the court—paradoxically—to enlarge the space for freedom of worship, in an environment far from the dictates of the penal laws. This approach revealed opposing interpretations of the religious privileges extended to settlers in the chartered colonies. For the clergy and magistrates of the Puritan provinces, "Christian liberty" had been granted to ruling corporate authorities to establish church foundations within their own domains, and to determine for themselves the extent of legitimate worship. For the Crown, colonial religious liberty meant freedom of worship for a wider range of politically compliant individuals, but under watchful royal supervision.

In its political and patronal choices, the court further complicated the confessional ecology of the English overseas world. The Council of Trade upheld the liberties of Sephardic traders in the Caribbean, and supported unfulfilled plans for a Jewish-run colony bordering Surinam in 1664.[83] The Tangier commission advised authorities to support and protect "a Synagogue for the Jewes in case they desire it," and—with implications that would prove more controversial—resolved to "connive at the Roman Catholique Worshipp, for ye Satisfaction of those that shall be of the profession."[84] The Catholic penetration of the Stuart empire exemplified a permissive atmosphere within the Crown administration, which allowed many individuals to maintain ambiguous confessional identities. Richard Nicolls, first governor of New York, furnished Philip Calvert, Catholic governor of Maryland, with a communion chalice and devotional books in 1668— pleasing evidence, for Calvert, that "you may be as greate a practiser of the Religion as you are a master of the honor of Ancient Rome."[85] In Tangier and Bombay, merchants from English and Irish recusant communities were encouraged originally in deference to the Crown of Portugal, which had demanded that the "first people to be employed ... be Catholics," so that the switch of sovereignty "may be effected without any stir or danger."[86] But the Crown also sought to avail itself of Catholic expertise in trade involving the Mediterranean and the Iberian Peninsula, where religious émigrés had maintained clerical institutions, private residences, and financial investments since the later sixteenth century.[87] The extension of trading opportunities, together with land and office in the colonies, offered ways for the Crown to manage the numerically significant Irish Catholic population, believed Ambassador Godolphin in Madrid, and turn "to the use of our National Interests . . . those whose abilities might have entitled them to much more profitable employments, if their Religion were not a barre to them at home."[88]

The same pattern was apparent in the English Caribbean, where Irish Catholics possessed a foothold stretching back to the original settlements of 1627. By the 1670s, they accounted for a purported 65 percent of all the adult Europeans in the Leeward Islands, as well as approximately 10 percent of all property holders in Jamaica.[89] An older historiography linked the growth in the Irish colonial population to prisoner transportations and forced labor. In reality, the Irish inflow mirrored the patterns of English colonization, mixing together coerced or indentured servants with cohorts of free and voluntary individuals—part of a larger Irish diaspora that encompassed settler communities created in many Spanish and Portuguese colonies.[90] There were obvious grounds for disharmony between these free-flowing migrants and English colonial authorities, which were heightened after 1667, when Irish Catholic planters were alleged to have aided the French invasion and devastation of Saint Christopher Island.[91] But the transnational Catholic connections that aroused such suspicion could also be exploited for English political and commercial advantage. Irish Catholics' familiarity with the Iberian world made them natural brokers in the attempt to crack into the trade of the Spanish empire, after the peace of 1667.[92] By the reign of Charles II, the ports of Galway and Waterford had become equally essential to the provisioning trade of the English Caribbean. The economic development of Montserrat in particular was steered by a close-knit cadre of Galway families—the "fourteen tribes" that had dominated the city's corporation since the later fifteenth century and used the wealth from Caribbean trade to sustain priests, chapels, and underground Catholic agencies across their own corner of Ireland.[93]

Catholic influences moved from the realm of commerce into the colonial civil and military infrastructure. Sir Hugh Cholmley—himself a Protestant—sought to fashion Tangier as a recruiting ground for Catholic kinsmen and associates, drawing back into English service cohorts of royalist veterans who had entered into the French or Spanish armies rather than return to the three kingdoms after 1660.[94] Four Crown-appointed governors of English Tangier were professed or suspected Catholics; so too were half of the city's military officers, according to one report produced in 1666.[95] In the Leeward Islands after 1670, public life came to reflect the demographic density of the Irish Catholic interest, under the governance of the Tipperary soldier Sir William Stapleton. The roll call of councillors and assemblymen in Montserrat, Nevis, Saint Christopher, and Antigua bristled with Gaelic and "Old English" surnames, while grants of high office were handed out to the governor's kinsmen and military associates.[96] Though the evidence of Catholic worship is opaque, the weakness of the Protestant ministry meant that in practice, limited attempts were made to wean migrants away from prior allegiances. As Jenny Shaw and Kristen Block have suggested, Irish and Catholic integration was quickened by the "racialisation" of the West Indies, as governors' reports foregrounded categories of "white" and "black" over distinctions within the free population.[97] Settlers took equal advantage of constitutional ambiguities. "In ye busyness" of taking the anti-papal oath of allegiance, "ye are not concerned untill you come into Engld," believed the recusant lawyer Richard Langhorne. For all individuals "upon or beyond ye Seas," there was "no authority to administer ye Oaths wch can only be given by ye Kings Bench . . . or Quarter Sessions of a County."[98] Under these conditions, Catholic governors were able discreetly to expand the liberties of their co-religionists. In the Leeward Islands, William Stapleton devised alternative oaths for officeholders, which offered pledges of fidelity to the Crown, free of commitments to the reformed religion. In 1672, power in Montserrat was transferred to civil magistrates for the performance of marriage ceremonies.[99]

By the later 1670s, English colonial rule was raising provocative questions about the appropriate governance of a kingdom divided along religious lines, and about the relationship between the temporal and confessional obligations of princes and subjects. As recent scholarship has established, policies of toleration or persecution were not perceived as intellectual opposites in later seventeenth-century England, but tended to be judged on relative terms, by their capacity to advance civil and moral tranquillity. This turn, as Alexandra Walsham has argued, was not synonymous with "secularization." Toleration was viewed more commonly as a posture of Christian forbearance assumed by authorities than as a positive good in itself.[100] Religious variety could, however, be warranted where the Crown lacked the resources for "rough or peremptory" measures, as the earl of Sandwich put it, and where it would "endanger insurrections or a general dispeopling," as the Catholic

Lord Baltimore insisted of his Maryland proprietary, if subjects were obliged to "maintain Ministers of a contrary persuasion to themselves."[101] Backing up this approach, the 1649 "Act concerning Religion" in Maryland famously outlawed use of the words "papist," "Puritan," "heretic," and "idolater" among a litany of other insults liable to breed intolerance and disharmony.[102] The law was shadowed in the Leeward Islands, where William Stapleton sought to smother national, religious, and political disputes under a ban on terms such as "English dog," "Irish dog," "Roundhead," and "Cavalier."[103]

Yet if toleration could be justified as a means to an end, there were visible differences between commentators over the greater objective that it was designed to serve. The qualified liberty of conscience made available in Carolina, and promoted for the entire English empire by Robert Boyle and Richard Baxter, was devised with evangelical intentions, because it was considered as a route toward Protestant reunion. But the form of toleration encouraged elsewhere by the Crown carried a less obviously spiritual rationale. For many colonial authorities, demonstrations of temporal or economic utility were frankly privileged above Anglican or even Protestant identities as credentials for entering the public domain. In Tangier, Hugh Cholmley believed it sufficient for an individual to be "Protestant in interest," and doubted why the act of "building a Citty in Affrica" should be made subject to confessional scruples.[104] Crediting Jewish traders for dealing more fairly with Jamaica planters than the commercial barons of London and Bristol, Thomas Lynch concluded that "if wee did not think them better Xns [Christians], wee should judge them better neighbours and Merchants."[105] Outlined in this way, colonial toleration served in practice the more minimalistic end of preserving civil peace and commercial outgrowth rather than aiding a Christian mission. In 1675, the Irish Catholic commentator Charles Molloy would adduce that "Trade and Commerce are now become the only Object and Care of all Princes" interested in the expansion and empowerment of their domains.[106]

Religion and the Remodeling of Empire, 1675–1688

For most of the reign of Charles II, the combination of irenic religious instincts and political caution meant that evasive or recalcitrant colonial authorities had the space they needed to resist full submission to royal authority. Restive voices on the Council of Trade continually pressed ministers to send out "a few of his Majesty's first-rate frigates" into the port of Boston, to intimidate the New England magistrates and force them into compliance with royal commands. But as late as 1672, the Crown resolved that its opening gambit could "be only a conciliating paper at first, or civil letter, till we had better information of the present face of things."[107] Regal patience had its limits, nonetheless, and a new direction entered into colonial politics in March 1675, when the Crown dissolved the commission granted to the combined Council of Trade and Plantations, and annexed all colonial affairs to the jurisdiction of a smaller committee, drawn exclusively from a cadre of Lords on the Privy Council.[108] The reforming sentiments of this new body were animated by calls for greater efficiency in the face of rising French and Dutch colonial competition.[109] But equally formative were fears over the domestic discontents that had surfaced in England after the Third Anglo-Dutch War of 1672–1674, the political attacks on Catholic tendencies within the Stuart court, and the drift of Dissenting congregations and dissident statesmen such as Anthony Ashley Cooper (now earl of Shaftesbury) into organized opposition.[110] Privy councillors were on high alert for signs of deviant ideologies snaking in either direction across the Atlantic, and were agitated by perceived slights against royal authority in councils and assemblies. The mood in Whitehall was made explicit in June 1676 when the Lords of Trade urged Charles II to proscribe the anniversary thanksgiving offered in Jamaica for the conquest of 1656, as a moment that risked valorizing the island's Cromwellian inheritance.[111]

The change in court strategy was made irreversible after the year of colonial violence experienced in 1675–1676, and confirmed with the dispatch of one thousand troops to Virginia to put an end to Bacon's Rebellion and "induce the people unto their due allegiance."[112] For the Lords of Trade, the disorder in the Chesapeake, together with King Philip's War in New England, vindicated a perception that England's outworks were in crisis: reinforcing, as the customs commissioner Edward Randolph put it, "the necessity of a Reformation, by a superior hand."[113] The conflicts that blazed around the dominions had also created an opportunity to look into the affairs of the old Puritan provinces, and uncover the truth behind an impression that "all things stand not soe faire . . . to many of his Maties good and loyal subjects there."[114] The initial phase of reforms materialized between 1677 and 1681, and began with a resolution to bring Virginia under the sway of Poynings' Law—the 1494 ruling that commanded prior royal consent for all measures proposed in the Irish parliament.[115] Subsequently, the Lords declared their intent to impose the same convention on Jamaica, convinced that "commonwealth spirits" lurked within the assembly and among the plantocracy.[116]

The first strike on Massachusetts was declared in 1677, when the Crown set about wresting New Hampshire apart from Boston's jurisdiction and securing it under direct royal control. When negotiating the rights of corporate colonies, the committee conceded, the Crown was constrained "in matters of law" (by judicial verdicts) as to the liberties endowed within foundational royal charters. But colonial governance was also inflected by "matters of state"—into which category fell the Bay Colony's violation of the Navigation Acts, the protection of "the King's Murtherers" (Goffe and Whalley), and the possibility that Boston magistrates had "formed themselves into a Commonwealth" with unremitting slights on the dignity of English monarchs.[117] Here, they maintained, the Crown was under no such legal limitation. In May 1678, dissatisfied with the responses from Boston, a packed committee meeting concluded that the problem of New England could be resolved only by a writ of *quo warranto*, and the recall of the Massachusetts Bay charter.[118]

The Crown in reality lacked the resources or even inclination to impose a military autocracy on America. Most of the one thousand troops sent to Virginia were returned within nine months. William Blathwayt, when managing the revenues of the Committee of Trade, prioritized rigorous enforcement of the Navigation Acts as a method "much more effectuall" than soldierly dictates in bringing intransigent authorities to heel.[119] The intention, nonetheless, was a new rulebook for empire, and a challenge to the notion that charters or assemblies constituted permanent buffers against royal power. The initial centralizing momentum was stalled only by the descent of the domestic realm into political instability, with the outbreak of the Exclusion Crisis in 1679, and the beginning of the Whig attempt to force the Catholic duke of York out of the line of royal succession. In this context, plans for Poynings' Law were quietly dropped in favor of new financial settlements with Virginia and Jamaica, while the strike on New England fell into temporary abeyance, "until a fitter season shall present to re-assume this whole business."[120] But by 1683, after the king had bludgeoned his way to victory over his domestic opponents, the impetus for reform had returned. The legal case against the Massachusetts Bay Colony was accelerated by the successful use of *quo warranto* proceedings to recall the charters of the City of London and other Whig-supporting corporations in England. The direction of colonial policy was made clear in 1683 when the Lords of Trade rejected offers from the Whig lords Monmouth and Shaftesbury to migrate to America, in order to restore domestic tranquillity without recrimination. Declining Monmouth's proposal to fund a settlement in southern Carolina, the Committee of Trade pronounced it "not convenient . . . to constitute any new propriety, nor to grant any further powers that may render the plantations less dependent on the Crown."[121] A year later, the Lords served notice to Boston that its charter had been expunged.

The reign of James II marked the climax of the loyalist program that aimed to change the legal and political underpinnings of the overseas dominions. In 1685, all provinces north of New York were pulled into a single territorial unit: a Dominion of New England, to be overseen by a governor-general (Sir Edmund Andros) based in Boston, with a council selected by the Lords of Trade. A year later, New York was brought under the same jurisdiction, together with East and West Jersey, which were stripped of proprietary status. The law courts of the Bay Colony were remodeled, to provide for closer compliance with English legislation; all grants of land were declared to rest on the will and pleasure of the Crown; and the king made clear that there would be no future for the old assemblies, general courts, and other representative institutions that had constrained the regal power in these parts of America.[122] Reform was conceived to extend across the English overseas world. The governor of Virginia, Lord Howard of Effingham, lobbied for a dominion that would incorporate his own province together with Maryland and Carolina.[123] More advanced plans gathered pace for the creation of a Dominion of the West Indies, with royal ambition signalled by the selection of a governor of Jamaica—the duke of Albemarle—from the highest rank of the peerage.[124] In New York, Crown officials endorsed Governor Thomas Dongan's attempts to establish a military protectorate over the League of Iroquois Nations: incorporating the tribes as

"His Maty of Great Brittains subjects" to attain a monopoly over the fur trade, and a military bloc against encroachments from French Canada.[125] The idea of reorganizing territories under governors-general was not original to James II. Benjamin Worsley had advocated in 1668 that one individual should be made "generall of all the Plantations in the West Indies," following the French colonial model.[126] But the policy amounted to a triumph nonetheless for that persuasion in English politics that looked to the Catholic dominions and viceroyalties as templates for colonial planning. The seal of the Dominion of New England, with its depiction of an Indian and a colonist kneeling together in submission before the throne, was distinctly redolent of the Habsburg idea of an absolute regal empire.[127]

The political and ideological shockwaves sent across English America as a result of royal measures have been considered extensively in modern historiography.[128] Less well studied is the way in which the new colonial policy diverged from the parallel Tory ascendancy being established in England. Between 1675 and 1678, the domestic policies devised by Lord Treasurer Danby had centered on fortifying Church power: enforcing Anglican monopoly privileges through the 1673 Test Act and cracking down on Protestant Dissenting worship.[129] The Tory reaction that followed the Exclusion Crisis brought an even more aggressive reassertion of Church authority in England, after the pledge to protect and support Anglican institutions had sealed the bishops' backing for the succession of the Catholic duke of York against the apparently greater peril of Protestant Nonconformity.[130] As Whigs were purged from the public realm, chapels were closed, and hundreds of Quakers were thrown into prison, the Anglican keynotes of "passive obedience" and "non-resistance" set down an uncompromising legal and ideological orthodoxy. The ripple effect was felt within the New World, where the rumor of bishops being sent across the Atlantic was reported in Massachusetts as "a thing more dreaded than the Indian war."[131] Henry Compton, bishop of London, had been admitted as a Lord of Trade in December 1675, and campaigned from this vantage point to impose diocesan jurisdiction over all "forreine plantations."[132] After 1681, the political headwinds of the Exclusion Crisis further energized the Anglican interest, and Compton ferried forty-five new clergymen across the Atlantic over the following eight years.[133] It was "high time," agreed Richard Dutton, the Tory governor of Barbados, "to let the people know that there are religious as well as civil duties to be required of them."[134]

The more fervent clerical hopes, however, were to be confounded. Despite its encouragement of an increased Anglican *presence* in the colonies, the Committee of Trade still held back from the pursuit of religious uniformity, or even the creation of a formal ecclesiastical establishment. Instead, the Crown continued with tolerationist policies, and even increased the colonial leverage available to congregations that were being simultaneously put under pressure within the British Isles. The Quakers were encouraged to build up a base in underpopulated territories, a policy famously enshrined in the proprietary grant conferred in 1680 on William Penn, but involving an even wider tract of the Middle Colonies.[135] Two London Friends secured proprietary rights over West Jersey in 1678, while a larger Anglo-Scottish Quaker cohort featured among the twenty-four landholders who were allocated control over neighboring East Jersey.[136] The result was to pave the way for the most demographically significant colonial venture since the Puritan Great Migration, with eighteen thousand settlers venturing into Pennsylvania alone by 1700.[137] The acquiescence of the Crown stemmed partly from political expediency: by offering up new colonial opportunities, privy councillors hoped to head off opposition from Dissenting merchant networks in London.[138] But royal backing for the Quakers in America continued even after the resolution of the Exclusion Crisis, when the court was at its most self-confident. As one of the proprietors of East Jersey, the high Tory earl of Perth endorsed promotional literature that offered religious liberty to Scottish Friends and Presbyterians in 1682, a time when "the distractions of this Kingdom . . . are come to that hight that a reconciliation of the differences among our Churchmen appears improbable in the highest degree."[139] In Pennsylvania, congregations of over twenty Anglican worshippers gained the right to petition for an ordained clergyman. Yet beyond this concession to the churchmen, the committee obliged William Penn simply to provide for the settling of the "Protestant religion"—an injunction open to widely varying interpretations.[140]

The practice of religious liberty survived the remodeling of English America under James II. Pennsylvania itself remained untouched after 1685 and avoided absorption into the Dominion of New England. While the

Crown eroded political and constitutional privileges in Massachusetts, the retention of "libertyes . . . in ecclesiasticall concernes" was presented by loyalists such as the Boston merchant Richard Wharton as the readiest way to coax settlers toward "obedience & subjection to his Maties commission & flagg."[141] Though Anglican churches sprang up across New England, and clergymen preached in Boston, the heart of the old Puritan power base, the Crown disappointed Tories who had expected public privileges to accrue to followers of the Book of Common Prayer.[142] Instead, the court of James II committed itself to a "Magna Carta for liberty of conscience" in the Dominion of New England as part of an attempt to win over constituencies of "moderate" settlers and drum up local support for the new government. Congregationalist chapels and schools were to be left unmolested, the Crown enjoined, where they did not foment civil disobedience.[143] This approach was designed not to temper, but to enlarge, royal power. Crown officials predicted that liberty of conscience would reveal a hidden continent of non-Congregationalist opinion. It would also probe the most significant chink in the armor of the Bay Colony: after new waves of migration in the 1650s, there was now a considerable proportion of inhabitants of diverse religious allegiances (over 70 percent in major centers such as Salem) who lived without the privileges of full church membership.[144] Toleration offered the opportunity to usher these figures into the public domain, and shape an entirely new civil order in Massachusetts and its surrounding territories.

The separation between political absolutism and ecclesiastical policy was confirmed in the stance taken by colonial authorities toward the Amerindians, whose conversion had once been outlined as a prerequisite for secure relations. The Irish Catholic soldier Thomas Dongan, governor of New York between 1683 and 1688, lent discreet support to an English Jesuit mission at Saratoga, in the northern reaches of his territory. But in correspondence with royal and French officials, he actively downplayed the extension of Christianity as part of the planned protectorate over the Iroquois, and was adamant that he would permit "noe Christians" of any congregation "to converse with them," except in certain designated locations, and "not without my License." As the "awe and dread" of the tribes across America, the "Five Nations" were "a better defence to us than if they were so many

Christians," Dongan explained to the Committee of Trade. Missionizing risked compromising that relationship. Worse, he believed, it genuflected toward false notions that the propagation of the Gospel afforded a "just title to the government of a country"—conceding the ground on which Louis XIV had staked many of his territorial claims within North America.[145] Dongan's gifts to tribal leaders consisted more commonly of guns than bibles or crucifixes, and he rebuffed as "a little hard and very Turkish" the pressure from French Jesuits and New England Puritans to curtail the trade in rum.[146] His jurisdiction over the Indians was to be settled on *politique* principles of civil allegiance, commercial bonds, and military service—following the precedent of rule over mixed European populations within New York, where "all being tolerated . . . the people seem not concerned what religion their neighbour is, or whither hee hath any or none," reported one Virginian observer.[147] Under James II, the public presentation of English overseas expansion still affirmed a Christian duty to the New World. But the real program tended to de-confessionalize the dominions, neutralizing the dangers of religious division by driving congregational allegiances into the private domain. Rather than allying itself to any single church, the Crown was deploying "indulgences" and "dispensations" to break down the power of local confessional oligarchies and elevate loyal individuals of any confessional stripe and strand.

Colonial Policy, Religious Liberty, and the Reframing of the Mother Kingdom

By the middle of the 1680s, the Crown had endorsed a disjuncture between throne and altar in the overseas plantations—political absolutism would make no claims over individual religious consciences. This approach was conditioned originally by the commercial and demographic needs of the colonies. Increasingly, however, it was intensified by domestic circumstances, and by the contradictions inherent in the loyalist movement that had emerged in support of Charles and James during the Exclusion Crisis. For all its reliance on the power of the pulpit, the anti-Exclusionist endgame was to preserve the place of a Catholic prince in the line of royal succession. Between 1679 and 1685, the political theology of Anglican Royalism was mobilized for an objective that would blur the religious identity of the kingdom and render the future of the Church uncertain. Through the reign of Charles II, the court's conflicting ecclesiastical policies—uniformity in the domestic realm; toleration in "foreign plantations"—coexisted because they took shape on opposite sides of the Atlantic Ocean. But after 1685, and the coronation of James II, the two strategies collided. In Britain and Ireland, the king shocked political opinion by unraveling the Tory Anglican ascendancy and beginning a programmatic campaign to weaken the monopoly powers of the established Church, in the interest of his Catholic co-religionists. More surprising still was the breadth of the king's tolerationist strategy. Through a new Declaration of Indulgence, and planned revocation of the Test Act, James also pledged to rehabilitate Dissenting Protestants, and he mobilized Nonconformist leaders such as William Penn in the search for a new coalition in favor of liberty of conscience.

The colonial policies of James II developed in close correspondence with this planned overhaul of the domestic realm. As the Boston preacher Increase Mather conceded—to his bemusement—the strongest court advocates for a policy of religious liberty in New England were the Catholic statesmen now promoted to the Privy Council and responsible for developing many key features of the royal agenda.[148] Under their influence, moreover, the moral and civil argument set out for liberty of conscience in the colonies began to impinge on political debate *within* the domestic three kingdoms. England's international ambitions were made central to an ideology of "sceptical Toryism," conceived originally during the Exclusion Crisis by scholars who sought to prepare the intellectual ground for a Catholic king ruling over subjects of the reformed religion.[149] One of Mather's court correspondents, the Catholic author and former Jamaica merchant Henry Neville Payne, used a pamphlet defense of the king's policies to recall that "the Roman Empire was ever August when it Tolerated all sorts of Religions . . . and introduced all sorts of Gods of all Nations into its dominions."[150] William Petty, a Protestant scholar in particular favor with James II, judged that only "a well grounded liberty of Religion" could provide "the tooles for making the Crowne and State of England more powerfull than any other now in Europe." Petty invoked the pressures of colonial expansion to make a case for the Crown becoming an absolute authority in the temporal estate, while preserving space for free worship in the private realm. Echoing the bans imposed on political and religious insults by Catholic governors like Baltimore and Stapleton, he concluded that "no monarch" tasked with filling up "so great a share of the unpeopled Earth" as English America could viably ground his policy on "those gibberish denominacons and uncertain phrases . . . Papist, Protestant . . . Annabaptist, fanatic."[151]

These ideas were a cause for suspicion in English politics. The common accusation, endemic since the early 1670s, was that calls for toleration under strong royal authority provided cover for creeping Catholic advances over the realm. A subtler line of attack came from the Whig scholar and critic of colonization William Petyt, who raised the alarm in 1678 over a breed of "New Polititians, the Hobbists," whom he believed to be indifferent to the Protestant foundations of the kingdom, on grounds of disregard for religion in general, and wedded to a non-confessional form of "absoluteness" as the "virtue" behind successful governments.[152] The "Hobbist" allegation was not without substance. Some notables at the court of Charles II, including the earl of Arlington, the duke of Buckingham, and Joseph Williamson, had indeed given protective patronage to scholars accused of Hobbesian heresies. Thomas Hobbes himself had dedicated *De Principiis* to Arlington in 1666. These tenets of *Leviathan* were believed by some critics to have guided Crown domestic policies during the early 1670s— experiments with schemes for religious toleration, and attempts to emasculate the authority of Church and parliament alike so that the Crown could rule with equal "absoluteness" over subjects of all persuasions.[153] Toleration and absolutism went hand-in-hand, the MP Sir John Denham had warned in 1672, because it was impossible to wield authority over multiple churches without recourse to standing armies "to keep them under and in obedience to the government."[154] Frustrated in England in the 1670s, these ideas found more opportunity for expression—and greater political logic—in the New World, where the Crown was called on to preside over multiconfessional populations, and garner obedience in exchange for protection, without the mediating authority of a powerful church.

While questions over the purpose of James II's tolerationist absolutism have created fierce divisions among historians, the king's colonial interests have been portrayed largely as a by-product of the royal agenda rather than an especially potent influence over it.[155] Yet after 1685, the ideas of the "Hobbists" informed a body of treatises and addresses that appropriated colonialist political economy in order to defend the push for liberty of conscience at home. First, the pursuit of overseas empire was identified as its own reason for thrusting back the monopoly powers of the Church of England. Toleration in England was the prerequisite for empire, believed the former secretary of state Leoline Jenkins, because it encouraged immigration, and therefore filled the kingdom with sufficient numbers of new subjects to compensate for movements into overseas colonies.[156] Second, supporters of the Crown applied to England itself the colonial arguments made in favor of liberty of conscience as a cause of commercial and demographic prosperity. Echoing Governors Modyford, Lynch, and Dongan, the 1687 Declaration of Indulgence damned persecution as "contrary . . . to the interest of government, which it destroys by spoiling trade, depopulating countries, and discouraging strangers."[157] England's religious penal laws had always, in reality, been passed on grounds of temporal peace and obedience rather than Christian obligation, averred the lawyer and naval administrator Peter Pett. A new conception of the "civill interest"—centered on population growth, commerce, and colonial expansion—meant that, logically, the laws should shift. Changing circumstances required new tests for the magistrate in determining the worth and loyalty of English subjects.[158] Colonial toleration, therefore, did not merely survive the "absolutist" turn of the Stuart court; it provided rhetorical and intellectual precedents to justify the intended reconstruction of England itself. Having acted to "relieve his distressed subjects," William Penn believed, the king could now establish for "himself a new & larger Empire, in adding their affections to their duty."[159]

The expansion of the Stuart realm laid the foundations for a distinctively post-Reformation empire, but not, as earlier promotional voices had imagined, a polity glued together by a cohesive Protestant ethos. Decentralized patterns of migration, confessional variety, and resilient corporate and proprietary structures all spoke to an absence of the religious as well as political uniformities considered characteristic of most contemporary empires. Far from providing an exhibition of English Protestant *grandezza,* the plantation of America was creating a world in which the scars of Civil War split open, casting light on divisions that, for many clergymen, threatened the future survival of the Reformation.[160] The colonial policy sketched out at court did little to allay these anxieties. After 1660, the Crown retreated from the role of spiritual guardian and repositioned itself as the (occasionally reluctant) sponsor of confessional pluralism, striving to temper confessional hostilities by neutralizing the power of *all* colonial congregations. Whereas royal power in the three kingdoms drew on the moral and legal resources of the Church, the centralization of the colonies was underpinned by a philosophy of tolerationist absolutism, which privileged administrative reforms and commercial statutes over confessional allegiance, as means to keep territories loyal and stable.

As these developments registered inside the mother kingdom, the colonies became a screen on which many contemporaries began to project anxieties closer to home. Judgments regarding colonization were colored by doubts over how far a kingdom riven by recent conflict could expand safely outside its own borders, and whether the layer of domestic tranquillity was thick enough to withstand the power delivered to dissidents overseas. For critics, misgivings over "fanaticism" in the dominions were matched, paradoxically, by fears over godlessness and by admonitions against the Crown, which had allowed missions to lapse and had developed its dominions with little more than lip service to Christian duty. These oversights, it was feared, contained perilous implications for the mother kingdom. In a 1678 Commons sermon, the clergyman Edward Stillingfleet fretted over the tension between Protestant virtue and the ways in which "great and mighty empires" were maintained. While he did not fear that "the Church of Rome should prevail among us by strength of Reason," the danger endured that "if men be loose in their principles, and unconcerned about *Religion* in general, there will not be courage and constancy enough to keep it out."[161]

The influence of the colonies did indeed grow over the management of religious affairs within the three kingdoms. By the early 1680s, the plantations had emerged as the training ground for an alternative conception of temporal allegiance, stripped of the confessional divisions forged by oaths, tests, and bars. Under James II and his supporters, political stratagems pursued in the New World would be ferried back across the Atlantic—not in the form of "popery," but, nonetheless, in defense of a blueprint that would render England less recognizably Protestant, with royal authority now deployed *against* the established church. These actions intensified domestic scrutiny of England's overseas dominions. The possibility that colonies might, in time, alter their own mother kingdom had been anticipated—and feared—since the beginning of the seventeenth century. By the 1680s, this anxiety was running rife.

PART THREE

COLONIZATION AND THE DISCONTENTS OF ENGLISH

DOMESTIC POLITICS, 1667–1688

6

Warfare, Luxury, and the Domestic Critique of English Overseas Expansion

BY THE 1670S, EVENTS IN AMERICA, Tangier, and the East Indies had entered into the cut and thrust of English domestic debate. The pursuit of overseas empire was becoming a part of England's commercial economy, political consciousness, and national imagination. While commentators discoursed over the regulation of settler societies and the character of colonial peoples, the consequences of plantation were not believed to lie confined to the overseas dominions. Contemporaries began to remark on unfamiliar influences—visual, material, dietary, and demographic—coursing through parts of the domestic kingdom. Asian garments, Amerindian headdresses, and dramatic narratives focusing on events outside Europe bedecked the London stage—evidence, as Dryden put it, that "Our Poets trade to ev'ry Foreign Shore," and that "the Product of Virginian Ground" was now "to the Port of Covent-Garden bound."[1] The growing ubiquity of African "servants" attending on noble households registered in commonplace observations, as well as in family portraiture and account books.[2] Above all, overseas expansion was made tangible in the stream of commodities and curiosities imported into auctions, shops, and private households: exotic "rarities" converted into items of mass-produced luxury.[3] The kingdom had been inhabited by whispers of worlds unknown, and for many authors, the shifts in modes and fashions spoke to deeper alterations in English lives and mentalities. Surveying the crossings of migrants, merchants, and fleets of war through the Atlantic and the Mediterranean, a rising number of commentators concluded that England itself was being refigured, with unsettling consequences for the social, civil, and economic scaffolding of the realm.

Through the latter half of the reign of Charles II, the domestic implications of colonial ventures were held up to increasingly searching evaluation. Nominally and legally, the dominions were private possessions of the monarch, and stood outside parliamentary purview, whether they had been placed in the hands of companies or proprietors or were ruled directly under royal fiat. Yet the passing of the Navigation Acts had set a precedent for closer monitoring of colonial affairs, and the interests of MPs, together with a growing body of public commentators, moved rapidly beyond questions of trade. The resulting debates did not always run in a comfortable direction for the court of Charles II. After 1667, and the disappointments of the Second Anglo-Dutch War, a chorus of critics subjected the outgrowth of the realm to wide-ranging interrogation. Voicing animosity toward the wars, plantations, and patterns of trade developing outside Europe, they made overseas expansion central to the political divisions forming within and outside parliament. Many of the anxieties voiced over empire were not new to the decades after the Restoration. Yet critiques of English overseas ventures were made salient by a changing climate in domestic politics, dramatically confirmed in 1672 after the outbreak of a third war between England and the United Provinces. Disquiet over the Crown's overseas priorities fueled the rhetoric of an embryonic "Country Party," whose activities offered the first sign of organized political dissent against the Restoration court.[4] Country concerns, expressed in parliamentary speeches, pamphlets, and treatises, incubated a spate of alternative manifestos for the improvement of the kingdom—its prosperity at home, its power abroad, and the most effective use of its laboring population—many of which evinced pronounced skepticism toward the wisdom of colonial expansion.

Country authors weaponized ancient philippics against empire, and grafted onto them the language of modern political economy, sharpened by growing fears over courtly corruption and misrule. Agitated by the fiscal and military pressures on the colonies, they struck at the old consensus that the national interest rested on coaxing underemployed subjects into fragile settlements across the Atlantic and lavishing Crown resources on attempts to defend them. Casting eyes over the clothing, furnishings, and delicacies ushered in from outside Europe, they fixed equally hostile scrutiny on English activities in the East Indies, and assailed the court's idea of command over the Asian trade as a means of national empowerment. The growth of concerns over "luxury" in seventeenth-century England has been well sketched by Paul Slack and Christopher Berry.[5] These debates have not, however, been located within the competing models of empire present within English political discussion. In the 1670s, as we will see, anxieties over luxury proved especially potent because they challenged the notion that an Eastern "empire of the seas"—comprising control over international markets and fashionable commodities—represented a benign alternative to the traditional, territorial model of colonial expansion.

The effect of these controversies was to shatter any public unity over the expansion of the English realm. Reactions against colonization contributed to a broader groundswell of discontent over the stances of the Stuart court, while the pursuit of overseas empire became, in itself, a major new source of cultural as well as political division. Contesting the claims of the opposition, defenders of court policy brought a moral, economic, and intellectual defense of overseas expansion into the public domain. The result was to leave the political nation split between two incompatibly different visions of how England could be made to flourish in the world.

Colonial Rivalry and Financial Strains, 1667–1672

Domestic doubts over territorial ventures arose most immediately from the fissile realities of the colonial environment, and a rising perception that English fiscal and military resources were becoming dangerously overstretched. As discussed in Chapter 3, the diplomatic realignments of 1667–1668, which brought England into peaceful relations with Spain and the United Provinces, denoted a war-weariness common in European capitals. Yet the agreements left significant territorial disputes unresolved, and failed to put an end to acquisitive impulses emanating at once from colonial officials on the ground and their paymasters in the Old World. Over the following five years, the idea that English settlers should dedicate themselves solely to trade and agricultural improvement was continually tested by relations with each of the major European powers.

In many disputed regions of the New World, the most urgent anxieties arose over the designs of France, which had "aped us all along ever since they sett up to be great at sea," as the merchant James Houblon warned the Board of Admiralty.[6] After the Caribbean invasions of 1667, Saint Christopher was subject to an uneasy partition and French frigates were regularly reported "hovering about the Leeward Islands," challenging the undermanned defenses in Montserrat, Nevis, and Antigua.[7] The French monarchy was also militarizing its Canadian provinces, sponsoring expeditions south past the Great Lakes, and fortifying a settlement on Newfoundland to probe the limits of English authority. In 1669, Charles II's presentation of "Ruperts Land" to the Hudson's Bay Company as "one of our Plantacions or Colonyes in America" denoted an attempt to wrest back the initiative from Louis XIV, projecting English territorial claims onto the threshold of Canadian territory.[8]

Yet in America as in Europe, attempts to pinpoint England's principal adversary were highly contested. While officers in the Leeward Islands agitated over the threat from France, the peace with Spain was undermined in the seaways around Jamaica by the failure of the buccaneers to lay down their arms, and by the rumored complicity of authorities on both sides in acts of piracy.[9] Furious envoys from Madrid regaled the court of Charles II with claims of ransacked Spanish vessels steered triumphantly by English mariners through the Thames.[10] Reports from Yucatán raised equally vitriolic clashes over English log-cutting incursions into Central America that were intended to lay hold of the prized resource of Campeche wood, which commanded an extensive market in Europe.[11] Thomas Modyford, governor of Jamaica between 1664 and 1671, was a particular target of the court of Madrid and the peace lobby in English politics: both audiences were provoked especially by his promotion of the privateering admiral Henry Morgan onto the governing council of the island.[12]

Modyford certainly maximized the opportunities for English governors to use their discretion in "extraordinary Cases," for which "rules and directions" could not be rapidly prescribed from London. The use of military force against even low-level Spanish harassment was justified through powers granted by James I to the East India Company: the right "to

Revenge any Injury which they should . . . receave from the Subjects of any Prince or State . . . well knowing that the tedious chargeable and unsuccessfull processes in Forraine Courts would much impoverish his Subjects."[13] Morgan's fleet stormed Portobello in July 1668, defending their actions as a preemptive strike to "prevent the invasions of the Spaniards"; liberate captured Englishmen from "dark, noisome, stinking prisons"; and loot the "magazines" apparently stocked with pilfered English goods.[14] Three years later, the "Jamaicaneers" raised a thousand men for a devastating raid on the Isthmus of Panama, sacking the principal centers of Spanish occupation in a bid to seize hold of what Morgan called "the greatest mart for silver & gold in the whole world."[15] The effect was to reduce the Queen Regent in Madrid to "a distemper and excess of weeping and violent passion." She was convinced, in the words of Ambassador Godolphin, that "private directions" from Whitehall must account for the scale of the assault, for she "could not forbear to wonder how . . . so powerfull a Prince could be so long disobeyed by his owne people."[16]

The court of Charles II was sufficiently rattled to sentence Governor Modyford to a spell of detention in the Tower, and it soothed the peace lobby by promoting Sir Thomas Lynch to supreme command over Jamaica. But the presence of Morgan's allies in the council and assembly rendered the new governor scarcely more effective in stifling the roots of violence. By October 1672, piracy was disrupting the Spanish economic year, delaying by four months the return of the galleons from Lima and Panama.[17] Fears of dismissal, even of assassination, punctuated Lynch's correspondence, as he struggled to retain his grip over the contending island factions.[18] On the back of privateering exploits, blueprints for conquest circulated among English officeholders in the terrestrial and maritime borderlands of the Atlantic world. "We are here settled in the very chaps of the Spaniard, whose clandestine actions both domesticke and forraigne" could not "be so blotted out of the memoryes of the West India planters," the Carolina councillor Joseph Dalton reminded Lord Ashley in September 1670.[19] His fellow planter William Owen argued that the growth of the English population created scope for an expeditionary force to assail the Florida garrisons, raise an Indian uprising against Spanish authority, and create a colony that would "make us in som measure capable to stand upon our owne Leggs."[20]

The call for another Western Design endured in mainland America and the Caribbean because colonists sensed the receptivity of privy councillors grappling with strategic dilemmas from a remote distance. The Privy Council had issued covert instructions to Modyford in October 1669 "not to part wth the Privateers," but "if he sees they would run to the French . . . rather to connive" to keep them in English service.[21]

While relations with the Crowns of Spain and France remained unstable, most of the old commercial and territorial disputes between England and the United Provinces lingered, unresolved, into the 1670s. Fears ran unchecked on both sides over the safety of Surinam and New York, after both colonies changed hands in the war of 1664–1667.[22] In the East, the Dutch still invoked their own territorial rights, or the terms of alliances with local princes, to justify clampdowns on rival commercial activity, which robbed the EIC of access to Ceylon and the Spice Islands—and left the English so "besieged" and "blocked up," according to one merchant representative, as to make "us and the whole world pay three or foure times more" for regional goods "than we did formerly."[23] These confrontations, together with the festering grievance of English claims over Pulo Run, drew the court of Charles II into closer involvement with the Company, and to champion its territorial claims.[24] The line between regal and corporate interests was blurred even more persistently in West Africa, where governors of the castles held by the Royal Adventurers succeeded in convincing the duke of York of "ye great want they are in," and secured a pledge of funds from the royal treasury in January 1672 to underwrite a program of fortification, together with new supplies of ammunition.[25] The release of the new charter in the same year, remodeling the Adventurers as the Royal African Company, with an enlarged stock and an invitation to develop a standing army, intimated a new push for supremacy over the markets, coasts, and riverways of Guinea. The directors and their pamphleteering supporters echoed the language of the militant party in Tangier: seeking out funds and weaponry on the assumption that "heathen" rulers in Africa "cannot be obliged by Treaties without being awed by a continuing and permanent Force."[26]

Across the English overseas world, military and diplomatic strains were putting royal strategies and blueprints for empire into a state of flux. After the fallout from the raid on Panama in 1671, anti-Spanish voices on the

Council of Trade raised defiant comparisons between Henry Morgan and "the famous Drake." Lord Berkeley—an active investor in Carolina and the Hudson Bay—was especially receptive to Modyford's claim that an army of ten thousand would be sufficient to wrest the entire Spanish Indies into English hands.[27] Less than a year into his posting, Governor Lynch professed himself "horribly troubled" by whispers of a creeping turn in the court agenda.[28] With little affirmation forthcoming from Whitehall, he was reduced to ordering copies of the *London Gazette* to try and discern the thinking of his political masters.[29] Lynch's fears were well founded. At the Stuart court, a bellicose faction fronted by the duke of York and the Lord Treasurer, Thomas Clifford, still nourished the old enmities with the United Provinces and the court of Spain, and doubted that France supplied the long-term threat to English interests in the colonies, in view of its more visible preoccupations with territory in the Low Countries. While they accepted the need for checks on Bourbon power, York and Clifford's circle rejected the idea that French actions obliged the Stuarts to maintain complicated diplomatic ties with the Spanish and Dutch, their traditional rivals in the colonial field. In May 1670, their political priorities shaped the secret terms of the Treaty of Dover and a new alliance that pledged Crown support for French strikes on the Dutch in Europe in return for acceptance of any new territories taken by the English "from the places and countries in America now belonging to the Spaniard."[30] In November 1671, the order was issued for the release of Thomas Modyford from the Tower of London, with frigates dispatched to stand guard over Barbados and the Leeward Islands in readiness for war.[31] Six months later, the terms forged at Dover finally ruptured the peace settlements of five years' standing, and subsumed the kingdoms of Charles II in a new conflict against the United Provinces.

Demands for mobilization and fortification in the dominions, followed by calls for fitting out fleets and raising armies in the Old World, enlarged the fiscal burden on the already straitened Crown administration. The impediment provided by financial weaknesses can be exaggerated—in 1676, the dispatch of fourteen royal vessels to Virginia, carrying over a thousand troops to restore order after Nathaniel Bacon's short-lived rebellion, demonstrated an expansion in the reach and capability of English governments that would have been unthinkable to privy councillors in the first half of the century.[32] Nonetheless the disparity between the grand designs formulated for English colonization and the real resources at the disposal of the Crown strained political confidence, and renewed the concern stated by Clarendon in 1663 that the king's overseas commitments had "brought a greater charge upon himselfe, then was consistent with his own afaires in the straights he was then in."[33] These frictions were amplified by the continual appeals and complaints from colonial governors—many of whom were forced to resort to their own private means or raise personal loans from the City of London to support their domains.[34] One of the few areas of consensus between the planting and privateering factions in Jamaica lay in shared trepidation over the condition of "a vast country to be kept by a few men," in the judgment of Thomas Lynch: "a port to be defended with no ships," and "ammunition, guns, carriages, fire ships, platforms, &c. to be had and made without money."[35]

The problems of maintaining a foothold on distant continents provoked continual pressure from the councils of trade for reform of the domestic administration. Convinced that the king could never be "considerable either at home or abroad" if he was reduced to "begging of his Parliaments," George Downing looked to Dutch precedents to press the case for a national bank that would mobilize long-term, funded loans to the Crown from private financial sources.[36] Yet this and other, similar schemes crumbled against opposition from fiscal traditionalists on the Privy Council, and without new springs of revenue, the prospect of fresh military exertions created continual apprehension in domestic political circles.[37] Venturing to London to lobby for the interests of Tangier in April 1670, Hugh Cholmley was dismayed to find that many of his audiences "shew so little kindness for the place, as scarce to be civill unto good manners."[38]

These conditions threatened to create a crisis of confidence—domestic and international—in the power of the court of Charles II. The discharge of Bombay to the East India Company in 1667–1668 spared the Crown an annual cost of £20,000, but offered only temporary palliation to address the misgivings voiced around English bases and settlements.[39] Only two years after the capture of New Netherlands, the New York governor, Richard Nicolls, was counselling retreat from outlying northwestern territories, lest "in grasping at too much in ye first settling, the whole will bee lost."[40] Cholmley feared that the scale of the investment needed at Tangier was suited only to more "plentifull & larger monarkys and not to those whose business it is in the first place to narrow their expenses."[41] The strains on the Crown were brought home in January 1672 with the Stop of the Exchequer: an official suspension on the repayment of royal debts, which dealt a shattering blow not merely to the king's private bankers, but also to the "multitudes who had put their money in their hands," as Bishop Gilbert Burnet later recalled.[42] Four months later, William Godolphin warned that "intelligence," crackling along the diplomatic networks between Brussels, Paris, and Madrid, had magnified the "idle talk of Coffee Houses" to raise up "horrid representations of the discontents in England [and] necessities of the Crowne."[43] These canards, he feared, were emboldening rivals to probe the limits of English defenses, and draw the royal administration into engagements to which stronger monarchies would have been immune.

Country Politics and the Cost of Colonization

Concerns over the rising burden on the royal coffers provided the readiest impetus for dissent against colonial designs. Serious opposition had begun to register in public debate in 1667, when defeats to the Dutch, followed by the plague and fire that struck the City of London, unleashed waves of despondency tinged with apocalyptic speculation. "Our Native Countrey is full of wasts, sadness and murmurings," reported the East India merchant Thomas Blackerby.[44] Samuel Pepys advanced that "it will cost blood to answer for these miscarriages" and feared that the fallout from the war would focus on the choices in foreign, colonial, and dynastic policy that had hastened international conflict. His prediction appeared cruelly vindicated when a mob attack on the residence of Lord Chancellor Clarendon brought the erection of a gibbet outside the gates, emblazoned with the verse "Three sights to be seen. Dunkirke, Tangier and a barren Queene."[45] In Parliament, the articles of impeachment delivered against Clarendon came freighted with grievances over the way in which the Crown had attended to its overseas possessions. Claims of arbitrary arrests and abuses of power under the Willoughby regime in Barbados were accompanied by a denunciation of the sale of Dunkirk to France—"disliked and condemned by all" who spoke in Parliament, recorded the MP John Milward—and allegations that the decommissioning of the port had been swayed by gifts and bribes from colonial lobbyists to privilege their interest in courtly proceedings.[46]

These attacks went beyond the vilification of the Lord Chancellor himself, to elicit larger reflections over the pressures placed on English politics by relentless colonization. "Let us for bear to vaunt, as we have done, of Conquests," demanded the poet George Wither, or "overween as if we thought none were our equals." For the Calvinist Wither, the errors of a failed war threw light on deeper ills stemming from the pursuit of territorial empire: a "carnal interest" that corrupted rulers into neglecting their proper duties, and which had broken the Anglo-Dutch unity that sustained the Protestant Reformation in northern Europe.[47] Just as concerning, for the loyalist William Godolphin, was a belief increasingly stated in the Commons that overseas adventures sat at odds with England's traditional material interests. Foreign powers, Godolphin warned the court, were well aware that nothing was more likely to "breed clamours in London . . . then ye apprehension of loosing our trade."[48] Over the following five years, many of the complaints stemming from the Second Dutch War were enlarged by a loose-knit collection of MPs who began to appropriate the old label of the "Country Party" to express broad-based critiques of the court's choices in domestic and foreign policy. Country politics in the early 1670s represented a polycentric phenomenon, with no seamless continuity of leaders. Yet the unifying preoccupations behind the "party"—a defense of the liberty of Protestant subjects, anxiety over trends toward arbitrary government at home, and militant opposition to the growth of Francophile "popery" at home and abroad—created bonds between parliamentarians and a body of London activists, some with roots in the old traditions of Puritan politics and radical agitation against Cromwell's Protectorate.[49]

Country skepticism toward the overseas dominions was revealed in a body of political treatises centered on the defense of English manufacturing interests, the regeneration of the civil order, and the clarification of the kingdom's proper role within the world. These works posed questions not merely over the immediate financial strains, but also about the deeper social and economic consequences stemming from far-flung territorial designs. Voicing his thoughts in a succession of pamphlets between 1668 and 1680, the radical city alderman Slingsby Bethel professed it "an unprofitable charge" to "maintain Foreign Colonies," where "the Seas must be perpetually crossed for supplying of them with Men, Money, and necessaries."[50] The particular folly of an island kingdom seeking out a territorial empire had been evinced in the fruitless labors of medieval monarchs to sustain the conquest of France, suggested the MP Richard Temple in a manuscript treatise of 1669. Separated from its outlying enclaves by oceanic space, England possessed no "naturall ligaments" to "render the union easy cheape & safe."[51] The political economist Roger Coke agreed that relentless acquisitions transgressed certain verities of statecraft that remained as meaningful in the modern as in the ancient world. Bringing together the moral and economic content of Country Party arguments in a printed broadside of 1675, he insisted that "the Glory, Majesty, and Grandeur of every Prince, consists not in the greatness of their Territories, but in the number of their Subjects, and good government of them." Colonies, on this estimation, offered nothing without the benefit of a bustling, productive labor force. More commonly, they threatened it, by robbing princes of their subjects and hollowing out the realm from which they had sprung.[52]

These claims shed light on a change in English economic thinking, which threatened to strike at one of the principal justifications, used since the sixteenth century, to sanction ventures into America. Through the 1660s, most colonialist commentators still endorsed the Hakluytian diagnosis that England's population had outgrown the opportunities available within the domestic realm.[53] As late as 1681, William Penn would voice the old orthodoxy that "A Plantation seems a fit place for those Ingenious Spirits" that "are much clog'd and oppressed about a Lively-hood."[54] But these arguments, framed originally in a climate of Elizabethan anxiety over poverty, disorder, and underemployment, were being rapidly overtaken by new concerns over the dent in the population and birth rates caused by the Civil Wars, the trade depressions of the 1640s and 1650s, and the plague of 1665–1666. Benjamin Worsley calculated that by 1668, the population of England stood at 250,000 lower than "the usuall course of mortality" would have allowed: modern estimates affirm a drop of over 400,000 between

1656 and 1686, when emigration was no longer countered by a favorable balance of births over deaths.[55]

As Abigail Swingen and Mark Goldie have shown, these developments were given growing attention in the political literature of the 1670s, with implications for the way in which colonization was appraised.[56] With too many communities already "devoured" by conflict and contagion, warned the former secretary of state Sir William Coventry, "the diverting of the young and prolifick People to the Plantations" was wearing away at resources precious to the mother kingdom.[57] Since the beginning of England's fixation with the Americas, agreed Roger Coke, the kingdom had "lost the trade to Muscovy" and Greenland, while the fishing coasts, "which should be the Glory, Strength and Ornament of an Island . . . became decaid." Should projectors succeed in "the Project of Peopling *Carolina* from the Residue of the men we have left in *England*," the country would be "enfeebled" beyond hope of rehabilitation.[58] For the barrister and pamphleteer Carew Reynell, the shrivelling of "sea-towns and inland corporations," the proliferation of "decayed Gentry," and the "many Forests [that] lie unimproved" all revealed the baleful effects of a policy that had seen thousands of English subjects "decoy'd away to New-England and Virginia."[59]

Most Country authors were not hostile to all forms of expansion, and were prepared to entertain the prospect of a limited trading empire, regulated according to domestic manufacturing needs. Slingsby Bethel approved the Newfoundland fishery as a model for involvement in the Western Atlantic; Carew Reynell suggested that the "Barbary Trade would be good if Tangier might have a free entercourse to them."[60] Reynell and Temple both acknowledged the attraction of the diverse plantation economy espoused by Ashley Cooper for Carolina, as a way to produce goods, including silk, wine, and oils, "wch wd otherwise be purchased from strangers" in Europe.[61] All of these commentators, however, were on high alert against any form of territorial self-aggrandizement beyond the acquisition of "forts and islands in profitable places."[62] By the early 1670s, they were signalling alarm that the prescription for peace, commerce, and experimental plantation had been vacated in favor of the expensive militarization of colonial settlements and an excessive concentration on staple crops.[63] In practice, Country treatises imposed unviable scenarios and politically impossible conditions on the colonies to justify their place as part of the realm. For Reynell, the occupation of America would benefit the mother kingdom only if the New England provinces could be scaled down through a combination of repatriation and resettlement in Jamaica and Barbados. The "insignificant" Leeward Islands should be abandoned entirely, he suggested, and their populations "removed southwards" in search of a location better equipped to pursue the Spanish trade.[64] With the cost of colonial occupation rising, averred the scholarly pamphleteer William Petyt, Englishmen chased only "the shadows of trade," while other nations "ran away with the substance."[65] It was Dutch voyages through "to *Muscovy,* into the *Baltick,* up the *Elb,* to *Turky* and *Italy,*" concurred Roger Coke, that really pointed the way toward attaining "universall commerce."[66]

Country authors appropriated many of the moral and philosophical arguments that had previously been adopted by the Council of Trade, to defend a spatially limited model of empire centered on commerce and plantation. With the king's ministers apparently departing from that vision, and now encouraging further expansion, critical commentators turned those ideas against the court, and used the same language to question the need for *any* extensive territorial possessions. English natural philosophers had proposed that true "empire" over the earth would be gained by productive and "improving" labor. For Samuel Hartlib and Benjamin Worsley, the implication was that the Crown would strengthen its dominions by attracting a larger number of subjects to existing colonies, rather than engrossing further territory. But Country commentators believed that this line of thought threw open the potential for wastes and heathlands lying untouched within England itself, as resources that could transform the kingdom without *any* burden of occupation over distant lands. Carew Reynell and William Coventry proposed experiments in domestic tobacco production—proscribed by the Crown in 1661—and pushed for planters in England to gain fiscal privileges over the Virginia crop should their efforts prove successful.[67] The problem of England's underemployed labor force could be addressed, both believed, not by sending droves of disorderly subjects overseas, but by more creative management of the able-bodied poor as an economic resource.[68] The "multitude" could be reformed and redeemed by the creation of storehouses "for the publick work . . . in dead times of trade," by systems of poor relief that incentivized marriage and procreation, and by trebling the customs duties on foreign commodities to encourage exploitation of the hidden properties beneath the soil.[69]

Seen from this perspective, all the remedies for England's discontents lay, neglected, within the Old World. Promises of enrichment through overseas empire were damned as a fallacy drawn out of the Catholic kingdoms, whose self-defeating invasions and acquisitions had failed to address the real grounds for their decline. "The severity of the Spanish, and their Plantations, have ruined them, and will us, if we look not to it," warned the MP Charles Harbord in the parliamentary chamber in 1672.[70] The "accidental discovery of the Indies," William Petyt agreed, could never compensate for the absence of economic ingenuity in the Iberian Peninsula, and the closing of the human mind through oppression and superstition. The danger was that England was sliding toward the same state of impoverishment that beset Spain—a husk of a kingdom pockmarked with deserted villages and forsaken towns, stalked by "Priests and beggars," with its "ordinary people . . . gone to America."[71] To save themselves from ruin, Country authors concluded, the English must cease perverse imitation of the "popish" powers, and look northward: summoning up the industry and energy that had powered the United Provinces and the Hanseatic League, and calling colonists back to their benighted homeland.

The "Country" and the Colonists

Admonitions against the economic consequences of colonization connected to a wider palette of Country concerns, many of which echoed back to ancient anxieties over the preservation of virtue in an expanding realm. The colonial lobby was attacked for elevating private mercenary interests, which had "left us intricated and fettered," William Petyt believed, "in destructive constitutions of Trade" inimical to the "common good."[72] In the same civic humanist language, Slingsby Bethel argued that conquests, acquisitions, and dispersals of subjects enlarged the greatness of kings only on the back of "burthens and oppressions" that disabled their people.[73] The truth of the maxim, he believed, could be gleaned by peering back into English history, when Charles I and Archbishop Laud "gave us the first wound in our trading stock," by "forcing multitudes of people" into New England on grounds of conscience, from "which, when we shall recover God knows."[74] Although these complaints focused on the ills in courtly thinking, opposition authors were also clashing inescapably with the interests of settlers invested in the success of colonization. Commentators gave short shrift to the common defense that colonies raised new markets for English manufactures. At best, explained William Petyt, exported commodities went only to dispersed populations who "would have taken off a far greater Quantity" had they remained at home.[75] At worst, the hemorrhaging of subjects into overseas colonies was engendering rivals for trade, wealth, and people. Country pamphleteers endorsed the argument, pushed by domestic silk workers and sugar refiners, that colonists should confine their economic activities to the production of primary, unwrought goods, lest they threaten trade and employment in Old England. But whereas the manufacturers believed that stricter regulation could make the plantations work to the benefit of the domestic kingdom, Country commentators were skeptical that such a spillage of people could ever be effectively controlled.

By singling out Massachusetts as the prime competitor, these writers exposed a cultural as well as economic rupture within the expanding realm. Leaders of the Bay Colony were eagerly attentive to reports of parliamentary discontent. Conscious of the common Puritan lineage connecting them to many domestic critics of royal policy, they anticipated support from the Commons in defending the liberties of New England against a centralizing Crown.[76] But, as has been seen, the church establishment in Boston was struggling to retain its connections to the English "godly." Congregationalism in Massachusetts was at once too loose in its ecclesiology for Presbyterian tastes, and too prone, in the eyes of many Independents and Anglican irenicists, to persecute other Protestants. Despite their pro-Dissenting instincts, domestic Country authors were sensitive to any associations with the "republican" spirit in New England. Many proved receptive to the view that worldly self-aggrandizement had debased the primitive virtues of John Winthrop's émigré community, and corrupted "the spirit that carried you into the wilderness," in the words of the Presbyterian earl of Anglesey.[77] John Blackwell, the former treasurer to the Protectorate army who served later as deputy governor of Pennsylvania, discerned an "idolatry" toward money in Boston, which was alien to the virtues of "the good old Puritans of England."[78] This position paralleled the way in which some Nonconformists had accommodated themselves to anti-Dutch foreign policies of the mid-1660s: viewing the United Provinces as a state corrupted away from Calvinist rigor by acquisitive materialism.[79] Unconvinced by the providential calling of American settlement, Country Protestants began to assess Massachusetts through a similarly worldly lens, as a polity that damaged England because it had been "suffered," in Temple's words, to "produce the same product & commodity with us, and to be a magazine to the other plantations."[80] Slingsby Bethel, whose works were read and admired in Massachusetts, was more generous in appraising the "good Laws and Discipline" that had enabled New Englanders to overcome "the barrenness of that Country" and attain self-sufficiency. But he remained adamant that godly communities would find a more fitting outlet for their virtue by returning home across the Atlantic. The societies now "imprisoned by the sea" represented nothing but a monument to Laudian misrule, from which no benefits to the mother kingdom could ever viably flow.[81]

The burgeoning critique of English overseas expansion broke into the open in April 1672, amid the confrontation in parliament that followed the outbreak of the Third Anglo-Dutch War. The conflict was legitimized by the court in speeches and polemics that placed the overseas dominions, the "sovereignty of the seas," and the East Indian "spice islands" at the center of the national interest.[82] "If you will give no money, and so have no fleet; which way will you secure the Plantations and Tangier?" the new secretary of state Henry Coventry demanded of the Commons, adding that the collapse of colonial defenses would amount to the "most fatal blow you can give the nation."[83] Yet a clarion call that had successfully mobilized consensus in 1665 managed only to rouse bitter contention in the altered climate seven years later, not least after a series of military catastrophes demolished the buoyant predictions offered up by the war party. Dutch forces burned the Virginia tobacco fleet in July 1672, temporarily recaptured New York, and transported the governor, Francis Lovelace, via a merchant ship to Cadiz, to the visible delight of the Spanish port authorities.[84] By the spring of 1673, John Evelyn recorded, the hospitals of the Medway towns were filled with "divers wounded & languishing poore men," ferried in from English naval vessels, while the Stop of the Exchequer had left a multitude of "Widdows & Orphans" ruined across the kingdom.[85] The reaction to the Third Dutch War crystallized the Country view of England's exertions outside Europe as a product of princely vainglory and private interests, which were dragging the kingdom into entanglements at odds with the national interest. In the Commons, opposition voices mobilized a majority to reject the king's appeal for a supply of extraordinary revenue. Observing the wider mood across the City of London, Henry Coventry bewailed, "I never saw the skye so over cast."[86]

The consequences of anti-colonial sentiment were felt on the other side of the Atlantic. By the middle of the 1670s, projectors spoke increasingly of political obstacles to their recruitment of servants and laborers for the American voyage.[87] The growth of domestic disquiet was made apparent in a surge of legal cases brought in London and Bristol against colonial merchants accused of "spiriting away" youths to the plantations—apprentices breaking contracts with their masters, or children kidnapped against the will of their families.[88] Claims of nefarious conduct by recruiters for America enlivened a crop of anti-colonial productions on the stage: the damning view of settler lives and morals was given lurid expression in plays such as *Bellamira* (1687) by the Country and Whig MP Charles Sedley.[89] The economic impact of these critiques is difficult to gauge. Ventures to the New World still attracted approximately 1,800 English souls annually, according to Charles Davenant's calculations in the 1690s. But the rate of migration had dropped markedly from the torrent of 1630–1660, when over two hundred thousand individuals had crossed into the dominions.[90] The difficulties of sustaining a regular supply of English migrants sealed the dependence of the West Indian colonies on an enslaved population—with planters forced now to look to Africa, as Thomas Lynch envisaged, for an "encrease of many Thousand Subjects."[91] Just as consequentially, reports of domestic ill-feeling heightened the political strains in English America, intensifying settlers' consciousness of their own vulnerability, and denting confidence in the protective authority of the Crown. By 1689, the New York projector Richard Daniel could conclude that "a vulgar error has too much prevailed with some of our great men to the prejudice of these Plantations, vizt that Colonies . . . drain us of our people . . . and consequently we should be richer and greater without them."[92]

The "Empire of the Seas" and the Problem of Luxury

Country antagonism toward empire may have been triggered by the economic strains of overseas expansion, but increasingly, authors began to probe deeper into the moral and cultural consequences arising from overseas ventures. By the middle of the 1670s, critics were fixing attention on the rising tide of imported "luxury" commodities funneled into domestic markets and households from America, the East Indies, and other centers of English global enterprise. Since the early 1660s, apologists for English maritime outreach had placed imported goods at the center of a popular vision of national empowerment. Scholars and statesmen encouraged the exhibition of the "rare" and the "wonderful" in parks and gardens to excite public sentiment and mobilize support for colonial ventures.[93] Sir William Berkeley aimed to raise the profile of his colony by stimulating fashions for Virginia silk and wine in England, and by ferrying planks of native walnut trees into gentry households, as wainscot for rooms "which I beseech . . . may be called the Virginia Chambers."[94]

The transmission of rarities from beyond Europe shaped the associational culture of overseas expansion, driving the growth of the transatlantic patronal networks that secured promotion and preferment. William Byrd, appointed auditor-general of Virginia in 1686, constructed a web of Old World affiliations with gifts sent to fellows of the Royal Society, including precious crystals, live rattlesnakes, and "an Indian habitt for your boy," given to the geologist John Clayton in an "Indian baskett" containing "allso some shells to put about his necke" and "a bow & arrows tyed to itt."[95] The ascent of William Blathwayt—the recipient of many such offerings—in the colonial administration was reflected in the changing appearance of his Gloucestershire country house. By 1689, Virginian walnut trees and Bermudan cedar stood along the walkways at Dyrham Park. The interior was embellished with blue calico furnishings, "caffa" cushions, and Japanese lacquers, alongside ornamental sculptures of African slaves.[96] Under these influences, the component parts of the Royal Society's "philosophicall toyshop" shifted into drawing rooms, hallways, parks, and gardens, with exchanges willfully blurring the distinction between scholarly and sensory excitement. From intellectual fascination to technological utility, comfort, or display, these items were rapidly gathering a variety of meanings and associations.

Through the 1660s and 1670s, the ornamental interior landscape became less rarefied. Unfamiliar commodities and curiosities burst out of private collections and into the markets, fairs, coffeehouses, and public auctions that made up the urban commercial arena.[97] "They say, you English people are the most given to staring, and throw away your money upon strange Sights, of any people in the world," jibed one pamphlet author, and the evidence was unmissable, as Eastern bathhouses were built onto the back of taverns, monkeys performed before the crowds at Bartholomew Fair, and, by 1678, the craze for exotic animals had prompted an investigation into the unlicensed keeping of crocodiles in the City of London.[98] The changing visual and material landscape was denoted above all in quotidian consumer habits.[99] While the sugar and tobacco markets stood at the center of the overseas inflows, the appeal of the New World was reflected in escalating supplies of ginger, indigo, and cocoa beans. The luxury potential was evidenced in the "beaver hat" fashions that stimulated the Hudson Bay trade in furs and skins, and the Campeche logwood brought in through privateering actions in Central America—with the Campeche tree releasing a rich, orange-red dye that excited surging interest among consumers and clothiers.[100] Luxury tastes simultaneously took products of the Guinea trade across the kingdom, with the York Cutlers incorporating elephants' teeth into their manufacturing processes, while the Somerset Clothiers used imported dyewood to brighten up their garments.[101]

Increasingly, however, these supplies were dwarfed in consumer demand by the offerings of the East. By the 1670s, "the great Mart for silke and Taffities" was being driven by the EIC, as India merchants adapted to counteract Dutch control over the spice trade, and enticed local weavers into Company settlements at Madras and Bombay to speed up supplies.[102] By the mid-1680s, encouraged by a ready market among London drapers, approximately 1.5 million pieces of calico were being shipped annually into England, accounting for over 70 percent of the entire Company stock.[103] Submitting instructions to the Eastern factories in 1687, the Company declared its intent to triple its supply of blue calico, the brilliant color and intricate designs having captured attention among the buyers at trading centers like the Royal Exchange.[104] "From the greatest Gallants to the meanest Cook-Maids," the political economist John Pollexfen later reflected, "nothing was thought so fit, to adorn their persons, as the Fabricks of India."[105] A demotic world of luxury consumption had been created that mirrored the lifestyles of patrician connoisseurs and conscripted the same cultural associations, with retailers co-opting the language of natural philosophy—"curiosity" and "discovery"—to increase the allure of exotic wares.[106]

Restoration commentators agreed that changes in material culture tended to alter the mental fabric of a kingdom. In *An Evening's Love,* Dryden's playful reflection on the Anglo-Spanish peace of 1667, the expansionist identity of the Iberian realm is exemplified in diets and fashions drawn into Spain from places far beyond Europe. "I found I was chawing a limb of Cinamon," recalls one English emissary, "then I went to cut a piece of Kid, and no sooner it had touch'd my lips, but it turn'd to red Pepper." His companion rejoins that "I imagin'd his Catholick Majesty had invited us to eat his Indies."[107] The exoticism of the royal table speaks to a deeper process of mixing and mingling—the Moorish descent of the play's heroine embodies the conquests that had altered Spanish culture and bled into the nature of the population itself. Dizzying as these changes might appear, they could be presented as an exhibition of a kingdom's strength. For the Royal Society scholar Edward Chamberlayne, novel imports represented "the materialest part" of "the Glory," which "has of late rendered the Brittish Empire famous throughout the known World."[108] Writing in praise of the East India trade, the political economist Henry Martin would recall in 1701 that when the Romans "conquer'd great Nations, they injoin'd the conquer'd People to send them Tributes of their Manufactures."[109] As anxieties over depopulation rose, and the mobilization of the able-bodied poor dwindled as a theme in colonial promotion, the public presentation of overseas ventures centered increasingly on the *goods* drawn out of English voyages, and their command over international consumer taste. Commercial exchanges became manifestations of English mastery over the markets and sea roads of the East. The genius lay in the ability to achieve dominion over so many theaters of activity without the burden of territorial occupation.

Yet not all English commentators relished the vision of a kingdom bathed in novel material pleasures. Within the correspondence networks of the

Royal Society, the clergyman John Beale voiced growing anguish to Robert Boyle and Henry Oldenburg that the excitement of engaging with public tastes was pulling the fellowship away from its proper scholarly rigor. While the overseas markets offered opportunities to pioneer improvements to English diet and livestock, the society's members had instead encouraged merchants to spin "cobwebs of phansy," sending in "baboones, & all sorts of Monsters" to "defraud the simple gazers of their purses," and laboring "with more care to please the eye, or phantsy, or to delight the palate . . . than to susteine humane life."[110] Such careless vulgarity, he believed, came with unregistered moral dangers. It was, Beale warned Robert Boyle in 1683, a matter "in which the Royall Society is nearly concern'd," should the reputation take hold that "the Virtuosi doe now publiquely . . . commend Prodigallity, Pride, Vanity, and luxury, to bee for the good of the Nation."[111]

Beale's critique marshalled a well-developed inheritance of moral and theological commentary. Powerful strains in Christian, classical, and humanist thought viewed luxury as the concomitant to all the errors and corruptions of an expanding state: at once the handmaiden of imperial despotism and the herald of civic decline.[112] Trinkets and tributes from conquered provinces had been "fed" to the Roman citizens by Nero and Caligula, recounted the Scottish jurist George Mackenzie, to distract the people from the attenuation of their liberties, so that a city that had once "by Wit, and Courage subdued the World," was eventually "drowned in the inundation of Riches, which these brought upon it."[113] Now the same deluge appeared to be running through Stuart England, and the growing moral concern became a polemical weapon in the hands of authors hostile to the court of Charles II. Luxury softened and effeminized a people, Slingsby Bethel and Carew Reynell contended, leaving subjects too intoxicated by material gain to contemplate a higher framework of values.[114] For Richard Temple, the departure from England's old frugal, patriotic virtues had become coldly apparent in the domain of knights, squires, and the nobility. "The very furniture of our houses, are chang'd," he lamented, "our Beds now all silk . . . under foot, carpitts of India . . . our very Cabinets, Chests and Drawers all forreigne with the lyning of our Coaches."[115] Charity, hospitality, and provincial pride—all the springs of civic virtue were creaking, William Coventry agreed, while the gentry gravitated toward London, the center of exotic consumption, and the shires languished, without due attention or improvement.[116]

The traditional territorial and centralized model of empire was a well-established target of republican and humanist jeremiads. The perceived connection between material abundance and civic decline, however, raised equally disturbing questions over the commercial "empire of the seas" promoted by some court supporters as an alternative means of strengthening the kingdom. Merchant-scholars such as Thomas Mun had long accepted that overseas trade could prove a double-edged sword if its industry collapsed into the service of "Piping, Potting, Feasting, Fashions."[117] Now Country authors voiced equal alarm that attempts to turn England into "the storehouse of the western world" were allowing foreign traders to undercut the profits of domestic labor with cheaply produced imported goods.[118] By 1675, these concerns had infused a stream of petitions mobilized by certain manufacturing industries—the weavers of London, Canterbury, and Worcester; the clothiers of Coventry; and the yarn-makers of Cambridgeshire and Suffolk—whose call to rescue "a hundred thousand" threatened day laborers was presented as a struggle against the sins of the age.[119] In previous decades, the target of this invective had been trade with France and Italy, which was seen by hostile Elizabethans to be drinking up the wealth of England and fomenting a dangerous ardor for novel fashions.[120] By the reign of Charles II, critics imputed an even greater peril to the East, where the threat to the national interest appeared to gain worrying acquiescence, if not outright encouragement, from a Crown bewitched by prospects of maritime empire.[121] For Petyt, Reynell, and other like-minded authors, East and West offered parallel threats to the manufacturing productivity and civil decency of the kingdom.[122] India, no less than the mines of Spanish America, appeared to be beckoning England toward the worst temptations of empire—a channel for misplaced cravings and corruptions rather than an arena for virtuous exertion and national improvement.

Country authors challenged the conception that national power was being projected in any meaningful form through the Asian exchange.[123] "We are losers by most of our Trading," Carew Reynell concluded, and the guilty men were the merchants who "tempt us with all sorts of Indy and Japan trifles."[124] Richard Temple considered the Crown equally culpable, in providing inducements to foreign commodities as a means to swell the customs revenue, "whereby the Consumption thereof is much incourag'd and Countenanc'd . . . in point of Interest."[125] The litmus test, most authors agreed, was whether sufficient quantities of this material gained re-export to produce a net gain in the quantity of bullion flowing through English ports. To this end, applause was offered up for the fabled Dutch practice of cladding public hangmen in silk garments, to dampen consumer enthusiasm, and increase the quantity of Asian produce taken out of the United Provinces into other parts of Europe.[126] But in England, Country commentators lamented, all the fabrics of the Indies remained trapped in domestic shops and households, swamping the market and sating the people, while sending the vital stock of gold and silver bullion into the clutches of Asian dealers. Accordingly, there could be scant grounds for seeing the Indian trade as providing for any meaningful form of English dominion. Looking back in the later 1690s, the Whig statesman John Pollexfen would conclude that "the vaults of the Great Mogul and his Nabobs" had become "the Gamesters Box" that reaped the endless profits arising from European profligacy.[127]

This restatement of old economic orthodoxies was streaked with darker social and cultural fears. In scholarly surveys of the world, costumes, furnishings, and forms of diet were frequently dramatized as markers of national, religious, and moral identity, with the degenerate traits of Eastern civilizations seen to be encapsulated in their own extravagant material culture. One East India merchant reported on Hindu worshippers bearing in "their Gods of State, garnished with the Riches of the Orient, cut in horrid shapes"; the "priests" surrounded by "their dancing Wenches . . . with Ephods of Silk and Gold upon their Breasts."[128] The goods of the New World could be damned by association not merely with "pagan" natives, but also with the original European colonists. In 1662, the commercial physician Henry Stubbe bemoaned that his efforts to promote chocolate through the London markets were being hampered by its reputation as a drink beloved of the Spanish conquistadors, and a stimulus to their own "carnal lusts and desires."[129]

Behind the response to unfamiliar commodities was therefore an urgent process of moral and cultural examination—how far could the natural and material produce of a landscape be deemed innocent of the manners and morals indulged by its people?[130] The 1676 preface to an edition of works by the cartographer John Speed insisted that "though the nations of Asia suffer for their monstrous irreligion," yet "the Earth, which did not offend, reserves her place," with commodities that "surpasseth all other countreys" in their potential to improve "the common life."[131] Other commentators, however, were not so sanguine. The brittle character of moral life among colonial settlers was, as Chapter 4 has shown, a well-established theme in English discourse, shot through with fears over the threat of penetration by pagan influence. Through the stream of newly arriving commodities, critics feared that the people of England were themselves being dragged toward the porous cultural frontier. As Rycaut's *Present State of the Ottoman Empire* reminded readers, the popularity of Turkish garb was an outward sign of the collapse of Eastern Christianity—with conquered peoples beginning to "delight themselves" in the "Language and Habit" of their conquerors.[132] Now the same fatal mimicry was perceived to be engulfing England, with its coffeehouses, calico sales, and exotic menageries offering at best a grotesque parody of foreign realms, and at worst an imitation so complete it would corrupt a whole country.[133] "Like Apes, the English imitate all other people in their ridiculous Fashions," damned one author of 1661, "with the barbarous Indian he smoaks tobacco," while "as Slaves they submit to the Customes even of Turky and India."[134] Power over the realm was perceived to be passing into the hands of distant potentates—emptying England of its people and its bullion, wearing down civic life, and unsettling the identity of the nation itself.

By the middle of the 1670s, the luxury debate was providing a formidable counterweight to the economic case for commercial and maritime expansion. Attacks on exotic inflows played to broader cultural misgivings over the growth of the towns and cities that were seen to be benefiting disproportionately from long-distance trade.[135] In Bristol, where "all men that are dealers . . . launch into adventures, chiefly to the West Indies plantations," the Tory jurist Roger North saw "pride and ostentation . . . publicly professed. Christenings and burials pompous beyond imagination."[136] In London, privy councillor Robert Southwell feared that "emulation to Luxury" was serving to "melt down the order of Superiors . . . and bring us all towards Levelling," while the city absorbed such a concentration of the kingdom's wealth as to create "a tumour . . . and too much matter for mutiny and Terrour to the Government if it should Burst."[137] The American trade had once been envisaged as a way of redressing concerns over foreign imports. Some lobbyists still tried to differentiate the political economy of the "western plantations," which "receive only what we carry, or that is produced of our own innate growth and making," as John Scott insisted, from the bullion-consuming "toyes and baubles" borne in from the East Indies.[138] But New World produce was interrogated just as fiercely over whether it was an appropriate focus for English labor and consumption. Hostile anatomies of Virginian tobacco, well rehearsed in Jacobean sermons and treatises, would return in the 1670s, as the price plummeted to less than a shilling a pound, and the product shed any lingering courtly or patrician associations.[139] Concurrently, Thomas Lynch fretted that the reputation of Jamaica was being undermined by "the great Anti Virtuosos," who valued the island only as a storehouse of things eye-catching and the beautiful, and so exposed it to a moral counterblast in England.[140] In 1685, the Crown accepted a parliamentary increase in duties on calicoes, sugar, and tobacco in spite of considerable reservations among the king's ministers. The Tory earl of Ailesbury feared that English global expansion was being threatened by an emerging consensus that "forrein Trade was the Ruin of the Nation," and that it needed urgently to be rolled back.[141]

The Court Defense of Overseas Expansion

The attacks on luxury, overseas commerce, and the English interest in India sparked a vigorous response from the Crown. Quantifying the annual re-export value of Asian commodities at £100,000, the Council of Trade backed the traders carrying wrought material in from the East Indies, just as it supported the import of refined sugar from the Caribbean, against parliamentary opposition.[142] In both cases, the council pushed domestic manufacturers to rise to the challenge of foreign competition—for if they failed, English laborers were just as "capable of using their industries in other trades as useful to the Kingdom," the earl of Anglesey maintained.[143] "It truly seems strange to mee," William Godolphin opined to the earl of

Arlington, that parliament should "lay impositions" on the very materials "by which in time we shall destroy the trade of other nations."[144] Backed by supportive political economists, defenders of the court presented an entirely different reading of England's commercial strength, distinguishing between an outflow of specie and a want of wealth, and insisting that the one did not meaningfully denote the other, since prosperity could not be measured simply by possession of coins. In an international trading arena, averred the Tory merchant Dudley North, money will never naturally "superabound," for any that have "great sums" will "thrust it . . . into trade . . . purchases, or cashiers, where the melting pot carries it off, if no use," so that "better profit, can be made of it."[145] The "trade of the world cannot be forced," the Council of Trade contended in 1674, but increases in commercial exchanges worked to the benefit of the kingdom, for "mony and Bullion is like a River wch overflowing in its passage doth always leave so much behind, as the neighbouring meddows for a long time after feele the benefitt thereof."[146] To hoard gold and silver as an end in itself would be to take the same pathway as Spain: prioritizing the products of mines over outlets for trade and industry.[147]

Court supporters assailed the moral as well as the political economy that informed Country literature. While alert to the dangers stemming from "wanton-nesse and luxury," Benjamin Worsley diagnosed material appetites as an unbreakable sinew among a people at liberty, who "never use much to deny themselves anything that they like or that they have gott the habit or Custome of." The interest of the Crown, he believed, lay in attempting to steer this impulse toward the common good: manipulating public tastes with fiscal privileges for new American commodities like chocolate, which were likely to boost trade and encourage colonial diversification.[148] Leading natural philosophers issued defiant defenses of the consumer marketplace as an agent not merely of national strength, but also cultural advancement.[149] "Knowledge and plenty vie together," asserted Thomas Sprat—exotic imports stimulated intellectual inventiveness, even if the motivating force was the desire for pleasure.[150] If Spain had indeed been "lessened by its Acquisition of the West Indies," believed the Tory apothecary and pamphleteer John Houghton, the decline happened not because of the colonies per se, but due to an absence of the commercial genius necessary to maximize them as assets—the very spirit most threatened in England by authors who decried against "prodigality, pride, vanity & luxury."[151] In any case, a taste for high living, once inflamed, could not be easily extinguished, and new restrictions on the Indian trade would only tempt consumers into the arms of foreign merchants, at a price of their own choosing. "He that frames his Politie upon what Mankind *should* be," mused another Tory, Charles Davenant, "will find himself almost ever in the wrong."[152]

In upholding its preferred model of political economy, the court was provoked toward a more robust defense of overseas expansion, to push back against the emerging tide of moral and cultural criticism. The case that "Plantations do not depopulate, but rather increase or improve our People" was one of the declared purposes of John Houghton's *Collection of Letters for the Improvement of Husbandry and Trade* (1681–1683). Just as re-export sales outweighed the initial loss of bullion on Asian goods, he argued, so the immediate effects of migration were eclipsed when colonial demand gave stimulus to domestic production—resulting in a busier, wealthier, and, ultimately, larger population in England.[153] Meetings of the Privy Council Committee of Trade, put in charge of colonial affairs in 1675, elicited lively expressions of the benefits springing from overseas expansion, and alarm over the public doubt cast on these advances.[154] In February 1675, the committee proposed the collation of material from maps, voyage narratives, sea captains' journals, and governors' reports for a "continuation of [Samuel] Purchas his History," conceived to reinvigorate the heroic ethos behind English colonization.[155] Materializing in 1685 as *The English Empire* by Nathaniel Crouch, the intention was to inspire subjects to emulate "those Gallant Achievements of our [Elizabethan] English Heros," and so restore the greatness of "this land of Wonders."[156] In the 1660s, such appeals had been a regular feature of loyalist rhetoric, which portrayed the expansion of the realm as a unifying banner, beneath which many different voices could declare their commitment to the restored Crown. Twenty years later, the political ground had shifted, and the promotion of empire no longer commanded such obvious public approval. Overseas adventures instead cast a mirror on domestic divisions and anxieties that the court had proved unable to suppress.

After 1667, critics of the court of Charles II began to suggest that the resources lavished on overseas interests represented "far more already then

Consistes with policy or proffit for the nation."[157] Whatever short-term wealth accrued to the Crown, Carew Reynell argued, "it were better to supply his Majesty some other way than by prejudicing the common good."[158] As empire encroached more tangibly on English subjects, concerns that had first centered on the lives of settlers and migrants refracted back to raise fears over the state of the kingdom and the changing habits of its people. Questions over expansionist policies unlocked wider controversies over the direction of the consumer economy, the appropriate management of the laboring population, and the means of national empowerment. In all of these exchanges, the king's opponents put forward a consistent proposition—that royal ambitions outside Europe were enticing England out of its correct orientation in the world, and placing at risk the liberty, prosperity, and virtue of the Stuart domain.

Behind the immediate antagonisms over warfare, expense, and the "balance of trade," the debate over colonial ventures showed a political imagination splintered in response to the changes overtaking the English realm, and torn between competing understandings of "improvement." The Crown and its supporters welcomed encounters with new lands, new tastes, and new commodities as signs that the kingdom was fulfilling its oceanic destiny, elevating its subjects, and erasing the residue of its recent Civil Wars with glory and riches anew.[159] Country literature, by contrast, was shot through with fears over hubristic designs abroad, and the effects of "fantastical and voluptuous" follies at home.[160] For all the "insatiable gains" occasioned by "Discoveries and Plantations," Englishmen could boast of few feats to rival ancient Rome, the diplomat William Temple reflected. Knowledge of the world had magnified little beyond familiarity with "the customs and manners of so many original Nations, which we call Barbarous, and I am sure have treated them as if we hardly esteem them to be a part of Mankind." Instead, the "great Increase of Wealth and Luxury" had raised the spirit of "avarice . . . of all Passions the most sordid, the most clogged and covered with dirt and with dross."[161] For the critics of empire, none of the novelties of the age could challenge the ancient insight that human flourishing depended on the renovation of the existing body politic and the recovery of spurned wisdom—in other words, on the restitution of moral and cultural goods that had been promiscuously cast aside.

7

"Popery," Europe, and the Crisis of English Overseas Expansion, 1675–1688

BY THE MIDDLE OF THE 1670s, any lingering domestic consensus in favor of colonization was cracking apart. The infrastructural strains on the overseas provinces, the wars they provoked and the wounds they received, made the expansion of the realm appear, for many observers, less a projection of national strength than an exposure of painful political and military deficiencies. In the wake of the Third Anglo-Dutch War, concerns over the fiscal burden of colonial ventures began to escalate toward a more urgent call for a change of course to prevent permanent national and moral decline. These tensions reached a crescendo between 1675 and 1683 in a chain of controversies, playing out simultaneously across different precincts of the Stuart domain. As shown in Chapter 5, rebellion in the Chesapeake and the Anglo-Indian conflict across New England cast light on the vulnerabilities of American settler colonies and pushed the Crown toward a program of self-assertion and centralization that was freighted with political risk. In the Mediterranean, the advance of the Moroccan Alaouite Empire started to exert an irreversible toll in blood and treasure on the troubled settlement at Tangier and provoked a bitter debate over the wisdom and rectitude of Charles II's intended North African empire. All of these developments collided with a domestic cataclysm that was threatening to bring the kingdoms of Charles II to the brink of civil war. After 1675, loose Country networks began to converge into an organized opposition to the court, with critics tearing into Francophile, Catholic, or autocratic tendencies detected in the conduct of domestic and foreign policy. The unrest intensified in 1678, when the exposure of an apparent "popish plot" provoked a parliamentary bid to exclude the duke of York from the royal succession. The resultant confrontation splintered the realm into two rival parties—"exclusionist" Whigs and loyalist Tories—with clashing manifestos for the redemption of the kingdom, and the banishment of its traitors and fanatics.

The relationship between domestic and colonial developments in the later 1670s, long neglected in modern scholarship, is now being recovered. Recent studies have shown how discontent with the Crown in English America was stimulated not merely by colonial grievances, but also by greater international fears over the safety of liberty and true religion. News of distempers in Westminster crackled along sea roads and shipping lanes, while boatloads of Huguenot refugees decamped across different parts of English America, and anxieties over the resurgence of militant international Catholicism spread out through the arteries of the Stuart empire.[1] Yet if colonial turbulence is increasingly studied in the context of frictions within the mother kingdom, the role of the overseas dominions in the crisis of English domestic politics has yet to be explored. The link between the two theaters has been sketched overwhelmingly in a way that asserts the primacy of the Old World, and the ripple effect of its divisions on affairs beyond the Atlantic. Here I offer a more reciprocal analysis of the relationship and suggest that tensions originating in overseas territories became a dynamic cause in the destabilization of English politics in the later 1670s. Shared fears over "popery and arbitrary government" created meeting points between dissidents in England and opponents of imperial centralization in the kingdom's overseas world. Conflicting attitudes toward the court's project of colonization helped to draw party dividing lines in Westminster, and transformed the Exclusion Crisis into a clash between starkly opposed conceptions of England's place within the world.

After 1675, opponents of the court began to assimilate the grievances of overseas colonists into their political lexicon, and sounded the alarm over alleged methods of misrule in distant settlements, as ominous portents for the future governance of England. Discontent over the management of the empire exploded back into English politics in 1678, when the Crown put before MPs an appeal to save the city of Tangier from its Moroccan besiegers. The effect was to cast the parliamentary spotlight over the growth of Catholic civil and military power, in Tangier and many other parts of the colonial domain, and over the motivations of the courtiers who managed these promotions and preferments. This controversy burgeoned when critics began to examine colonial policy in the context of England's older web of strategic interests and international obligations. As recent scholarship has emphasized, the political tremors that produced the Popish Plot and the Exclusion Crisis were quickened by fears arising in Europe, when the relentless growth in French power, together with renewed anxieties for the survival of continental Protestant communities, shifted the tectonic plates of international politics.[2] Here, it will be seen that these events deepened dissent over the colonialist focus of Stuart foreign policy, and threw doubt on the old link made between English overseas expansion and the advancement of the Protestant interest. A growing cohort of Whigs concluded that expensive commitments to the plantations, the perpetuation of Anglo-Dutch rivalry, and the neglect of French designs closer to home were all creating a wrong turn in the conduct of foreign affairs, wrenching England apart from its historic duties toward the "balance of Europe."

Whig arguments did not, however, go uncontested. Through the Exclusion Crisis, loyalist supporters of Charles II presented his critics with an alternative calculus to inform the conduct of foreign policy, asserting at once the strategic primacy of the colonial interest and the necessity of upholding royal authority to guide and direct it.[3] For many loyalists, the "Christian" battle against Islamic empires in Tangier and the Mediterranean became a higher and more urgent calling on the realm than the Whigs' cherished commitment toward fellow Protestants in Europe. The eventual triumph of the court and the Tories in 1681 refigured the politics of colonization. It has been shown how the resurgent court used its victory to impose a program of reform on its principal American possessions. As will be seen, the Crown tried simultaneously to change the way in which colonization was managed from within the domestic setting—aiming to use royal monopolies to strip parliament of authority over the commerce and politics of the overseas dominions, while reinstating the expansion of the realm as the central tenet of English foreign policy. The Stuart vision of empire culminated under James II, with a confrontational attempt to construct an English dominion in Asia, pursued by the Crown in concert with the militantly loyalist faction at the helm of the East India Company.

English Colonies and "Arbitrary Government"

The politics of the colonies and the domestic realm were brought together primarily by loyalist anxieties. The streamlined Committee of Trade, created in 1675, was the product of changes that had shaken the political nation after the outbreak of the Third Dutch War. The ejection of the earl of Shaftesbury from the Crown administration was followed by an attempt to break the Ashley Cooper patronage network and pare down its influence over Carolina and the West Indies, with the dismissal of Locke and Worsley, among other members of the old Council of Trade.[4] Under the stewardship of Lord Treasurer Danby, the centralization program rolled out in America moved hand-in-hand with the enlargement of the standing army in England, and a raised level of scrutiny over regional politics and opposition networks.[5] Supporters of the Crown played on rumors of transatlantic links and bonds connecting seditious actions across different parts of the English overseas world.[6] It was the "popular Harangue" against the Dutch War, stirred up by MPs "jealous of theire own Interests, and [just] as careful not to promote those of the King," that accounted for the growth of faction and insubordination in the Caribbean assemblies, believed Sir Thomas Lynch.[7] Other loyalists sensed the spider's touch of the Massachusetts Bay Company behind the rise in English domestic distempers. It was "correspondence between the factious parties" on different sides of the Atlantic, Edward Randolph maintained, that had made New Englanders so "daringly presume" of the king's enfeeblement.[8] Concurrently, he believed, the very existence of enclaves like Massachusetts as a "good retreat" emboldened domestic dissidents to joust against the Crown within the mother kingdom.[9]

Until the later 1670s at least, fears outstripped reality. The Massachusetts Bay Colony did possess a cadre of Dissenting supporters in London, knitted together through the New England Company and spearheaded by the Whig MPs Henry Ashurst, Robert Clayton, William Thompson, and Thomas Papillon.[10] Henry Cornish, one of the Whig radicals who would be executed after the Exclusionist Crisis, had kinsfolk in Boston, while the London

Whig printers Richard Chiswell and Benjamin Harris (who later emigrated to Massachusetts) both capitalized on news-gathering networks within the Bay Colony.[11] As has been seen, however, much of the original Country opposition had been notably disengaged from colonists' interests, and suspicious of Massachusetts in particular as a potential commercial rival to Old England. It was indicative that Roger Coke's printed critique of the Navigation Acts, published in 1675, focused entirely on their restrictive impact on European trade, without acknowledging the parallel grievances voiced by settlers across the Atlantic.[12]

Yet if they were ambivalent toward the liberties claimed by settlers, critics of the court were sensitive nonetheless to the older Tacitean and civic humanist maxim that acts of despotism in colonial dominions set ominous precedents for subjects living at the center of an empire. The perceived connection between overseas expansion and a creeping threat to English freedoms had been invigorated in the 1650s, in royalist and republican attacks on the Cromwellian Protectorate, after its administrators fixed on a new use for the Caribbean: the destination for over five thousand political prisoners.[13] Latterly, Thomas Povey identified the greatest obstacle facing Atlantic projectors with the view of plantations as little more than prison camps, and the belief that colonial leaders plotted to possess "the Bodies of Englishmen against their Wills and carry them from their native Country, and dispose and keep them as Servants."[14] Through the following two decades, retrospective attacks on Cromwellian colonial policy became a vehicle for thinly veiled commentary upon the court of Charles II, and its apparent predilection to follow "in the steps of Oliver" overseas, as the Whig MP John Darrell reflected.[15] Opposition voices drew particular attention to the constitutional ambiguities of the overseas dominions, which were set outside the protective safeguards of parliamentary scrutiny and common-law precedent. In the colonies, as the MP Thomas Lee complained of Tangier, a man falling foul of the authorities need "never know what his crimes are, and no Habeas Corpus can reach him."[16] For some parliamentarians, the claim that overseas territories had diverged from the laws of England created a case for statutory annexation, so that the dominions and their peoples could be properly regulated from Westminster. "If we have value for our liberties," the MP Richard Temple declared, "we would secure them by Law."[17]

These concerns, expressed sporadically through the first half of the reign of Charles II, gathered force after 1675, when purges within the Crown administration enlarged the ranks of critics rallying against the court, and extended the opposition beyond its original Country base. The gravitation of the Shaftesbury circle into opposition brought the Crown into conflict with a growing number of voices more attentive than the old Country pamphleteers had been to the liberties of settlers, and less hostile to the colonies themselves than to the particular maladies detected in colonial governance. As the epicenter of the Shaftesbury nexus, the Carolina Coffeehouse in London became a repeated source of concern to Crown agents.[18] Sir Peter Colleton, another Carolina proprietor and Barbados landowner, lobbied the Lords of Trade with forthright opposition to the Navigation Acts, secured election to the Commons in 1681, and broke with the royalist background of his own family to back the Whig Bill of Exclusion.[19] The West Indian planters' lobby, and its links to adversarial elements in the Jamaican assembly, caused persistent anxiety for the court, as a group considered capable of raising dissent in Westminster.[20] As William Pettigrew has shown, hostility to the monopolistic Royal African Company provided a particular lightning rod to align dissidents in the West Indies with Whig-sympathizing merchant "interlopers" in London.[21] After 1675, the transatlantic circulation of news and information stimulated reactions in different provinces against the centralizing designs of the Committee of Trade. Jonathan Ashurst, brother to the New England Company director Henry Ashurst, was one of the leaders of the Jamaica faction that led the charge against the imposition of Poynings' Law on the island.[22]

If they maintained a spectrum of attitudes toward colonization, opposition voices agreed that autocratic practices in the dominions threatened to become a laboratory for political trends pernicious to domestic constitutional liberties. By the later 1670s, views of the Crown's colonial agenda were becoming inextricably connected with the reputation of the Catholic duke of York—one of the dominant influences over policy toward the dominions in his roles as proprietor of New York, former Lord High Admiral, chair of the Tangier commission, and an active governor of the Royal African Company. James had made his attitude toward political dissent in the colonies clear in his firm resistance to the creation of a New York assembly.

Reporting on opinion in London in 1680, William Penn warned that observers took the "modell of government in New York to be the schem & draught" for the duke of York's rule over Old England, "if the Crown should ever divolve upon his head."[23] While opposition commentators still doubted the capacity of the Crown to fulfill its grander territorial ambitions, they began to express equal trepidation over the consequences were it to succeed and attain fiscal autonomy through the colonial revenues. Traditionally, a House of Commons dominated by the squirearchy had welcomed the surges in the customs induced by overseas trade, as an alternative to taxation on landed property. But by the middle of the 1670s, the sentiment was increasingly countered by a fear that "if the king wants no money, we shall have no parliaments," as the loyalist author John Houghton recorded.[24] Reading the temper of the house in 1675, Sir Hugh Cholmley expressed his pessimism over the future of English colonial ventures "when I consider how fearfull they are of his Majtie's growing rich."[25]

Popery, Tangier, and the Exclusion Crisis

As these misgivings mounted, the disruptions in the colonies became central to the rise in parliamentary tensions over wider disputes of domestic and foreign policy. The recall of the legislature in 1678 was the consequence of Bacon's Rebellion, believed the MP William Harbord: the collapse of the tobacco markets having "abate[d] the customs" so "extremely . . . that notwithstanding all the shifts the Treasurer can make this Parliament or another must sitt."[26] Events within the Mediterranean played an equally decisive role in bringing the king face-to-face with his domestic opponents, and fomenting the campaign themes of an organized Whig opposition. By the middle of the 1670s, a swirling tide of regional threats had exposed the "tricks and frauds . . . chimeras & promises" that, one Whig author believed, had drawn the English into Tangier.[27] Inland, the Moroccan emperor Moulay Ismail Ibn Sharif had regained a grip over the territorial holdings of the Alaouite dynasty. He had established himself, according to one report, as "absolute master of all Barbary and therefore the harder to be drawn to any termes," as his forces began to turn hostile attentions toward the English settlement.[28] In 1677, the provocation of corsairing activity unleashed a five-year war between Charles II and the Regency of Algiers, which would divest English vessels of goods worth over £800,000, and stifle the supply lines so severely as to bring Tangier close to its breaking point.[29] With regular funding for the city severely straitened, the king turned to the House of Commons. If the call to rescue Tangier was not, despite the claims of supporters, the principal reason for the return of MPs in October 1678, the appeal for extra funds was nonetheless integral to the royal program conceived to seize control of the parliamentary agenda and rally MPs to their duty.[30] The city *did* feature in the calculations of the court's adversaries, but not in the way that Charles II had hoped.

The misfortunes in the Mediterranean had become a leitmotif in opposition commentary as early as 1667, when a sarcastic eulogy to the earl of Clarendon by the poet George Wither recalled the "thousands brave English" sent "without remorse or fear" to their destinies in "that Grave, Tangier."[31] By this point, the reputation of the city had fallen into sufficient disrepute that customs officials in the Devon ports were assailed by rumors that "we are papists, and trapanners of poor people for Tangiers."[32] Hostile commentaries heaped attention on the moral transgressions of settlers, and the casual brutalities inflicted by the soldiery—blamed in part for cohorts of English "renegades" reported melting away into service of the Alaouite Empire.[33] By the later 1670s, many commentaries were linking the ills of Tangier with the corruption detected within court politics. The political attack was mobilized by a circle of disenchanted settlers and a "factious" party in the Levant Company whose voyages brought familiarity with the problems in the region.[34] At the forefront of the settler opposition was John Bland, a Virginia landowner and one-time mayor of Tangier, whose disaffection increased after his son was executed for involvement in Bacon's Rebellion.[35] Closely observing the temper of parliament, the complainants began to draw attention to the influence amassed by Catholics within the city, under governors such as the earl of Teviot, Lord Belassis, and Sir Thomas Dongan. Bland outlined the management of Tangier as the symptom of a gathering "popish" conspiracy against church and kingdom, writing to the earl of Shaftesbury with evidence of authorities who had "made it their business to ruine the Protestant Interest," to "the dishonour of the Church of England in the eyes of the Nations round about."[36] In 1678, he turned to the pamphlet press to spell out "the true grounds of the people's aversion for Tangier," and recalled the ancient verity that "there was never yet a Citie or a Nation that ever prosper'd since the beginning of the World that slighted the Religion of its Countrie."[37] These reports entered into the bloodstream of opposition politics. It was during a brief sojourn in Tangier that Titus Oates claimed to have picked up the first whispers of a popish plot against the life of the king.[38]

Colonial pressures broke into the open as parliament turned its attention in November 1678 to the king's appeal for extra funds for Tangier. Lacerating the city as a "nursery for popish solders" and "seminary for popish priests" full of "the duke's creatures," the king's opponents presented Tangier as a touchstone for all the perils of popery and arbitrary government: "one result also," a Whig resolution of March 1679 declared, "of the same Counsels and Designs which have brought Your Majesties . . . Kingdoms into those great and imminent Dangers."[39] At the very least, Whig MPs argued, a supply of funds could proceed only on the prior condition of the duke of York's exclusion from the royal succession. Otherwise, if the strategic significance of the city was questionable, and its governance positively malevolent, as the MP and diplomat Sir William Temple believed, the only safe resolution was to have Tangier "blown into the air, or otherwise reduced to its first chaos."[40] In a political climate engulfed by Oates's allegations, the prospect of parliamentary support for Tangier collapsed. Instead, the exposure of English miseries in Barbary provoked MPs toward a fuller interrogation of the powers bestowed on Catholics in cities, garrisons, and governors' households across the colonial domain. Whig protests secured the dismissal of Ambassador Godolphin, alleged patron of Catholic émigrés in the Mediterranean, and brought the arrest of Secretary of State Sir Joseph Williamson, who was accused of providing the promotional avenues for former recusants to move around the empire.[41] In 1679, Governor Stapleton was put under investigation as the sponsor of the Irish "popish interest" that had "interloped" into the Leeward Islands.[42] Seen through the lens of Protestant anxieties, the overseas colonies were subverting the civil order of the English realm, dragging subjects into zones governed by alien laws and by men who, John Bland claimed, confessed themselves "better lovers of France than [of] their own king."[43]

The growing breadth of the Whig coalition diluted some of the anti-colonial animosities expressed by earlier Country authors. Opposition concerns now focused less on disorderly settler populations than on the disposition of the Crown officials sent in to regulate them. John Bland was adamant that Tangier could be virtuously reformed, calling for the recovery of commercial relations with Moroccan and Spanish neighbors, the empowerment of the city's merchant aldermen, and new Protestant missions among Arabs and Berbers.[44] Shaftesbury and Locke maintained their commitment to the Carolina project, and studied ways to reconstitute the province as a locale for Whiggish enterprises and ideas.[45] Printed advertisements and campaigns wooed Scottish Presbyterians, together with Quakers—a "people" for whom Shaftesbury harbored "a great regard . . . and am obliged to take care of"—with a view toward a new transplantation of "Protestant families."[46] Literature targeted at the Huguenot diaspora in London and the Low Countries referred suggestively to the Fundamental Constitutions as providing for a "Republique en forme de Palatinat"—albeit "par la permission de la Majeste Britannique."[47]

Rising support for the colonists in Westminster was seen in April 1679, when the incarceration of Danby and the departure from the capital of James, duke of York, cleared the way for the return of Whig notables to the Privy Council, and levered several of their number—including the lords Shaftesbury, Russell, and Essex—onto the Committee of Trade.[48] Radicalized by their experience in opposition, the reinstated members proved more vocal as champions of the liberties of planters, who as "Englishmen," Shaftesbury insisted, could not simply be "governed as the Irish."[49] Though the rapprochement failed to last a year, the Whigs succeeded in briefly stalling the course of centralization in New England, and putting paid to the plans for imposing Poynings' Law on Jamaica and Virginia. Anxious to calm the transatlantic tempers, the duke of York acceded in 1682 to the creation of a New York assembly, though its initial incarnation would not outlast the province's integration into the Dominion of New England.[50]

Yet if their political arguments were not straightforwardly anti-colonial, Whig interventions fanned wider critiques of the particular kind of imperial dominion that had evolved under Stuart monarchs, drawing from an ancient reservoir of moral and cultural fears over territorial expansion. The author of one anonymous manuscript, produced purportedly by an English Hamburg merchant, captured misrule in Tangier as the climax of a colonial project that had wasted the treasure of the kingdom, estranged allies, and sacrificed commerce while producing only two settlements (Jamaica and Barbados) of more than dubious value.[51] Warning that Irish soldiers in the West Indies "may be brought hither," the MP William Harbord vowed that he would part with "my Blood and my Money" to support the Crown, "but not with my Birthright."[52] By 1682, the Quaker William Loddington—a supporter of colonial enterprises—lamented that the main premise on which critics "ignorantly Brow-beat or Tongue-Beat the American Plantations" arose "from Fears, that these Plantations do strengthen Popery," by drawing loyal Protestants out of England and putting malign officers in command of them. This impression, Loddington lamented, was exacerbated by the Quaker penetration of the Middle Colonies, in view of the suspicion among some Protestants that the Society of Friends was composed of "papists" or Jesuits in disguise.[53] At the center of all these complaints, the ills of Tangier supplied a unifying banner, bringing together disparate cohorts of opposition statesmen and commentators who began to advocate evacuation of the embattled city as a lesser evil than allowing it to continue in such a state of misrule. As the city's "popish" condition gained exposure, Whigs came to agree that even when a colony proved "a place of great moment," in the words of the former attorney general Sir William Jones, "the preservation of religion" was a "far greater" national priority; the moral needs of the domestic kingdom outweighed the benefits of any beleaguered distant outpost.[54] The management of empire had become the supreme expression of the depredations entering into English politics: an exhibition of arbitrary government writ large, presaging terrible civil and moral consequences for the mother kingdom.

Empire, Europe, and the "Protestant Interest"

Whig interrogations targeted the European as well as domestic ramifications of English colonial designs. As has been seen, the formation of the original Country Party had been spurred by questions over the expense and exigency of the Second and Third Anglo-Dutch Wars. Through the 1670s, these doubts developed into a deeper critique of how central colonization had become to Stuart foreign policy, an argument shot through with apprehension over the growth of "popery" and the perception of an impending, international struggle for the survival of true religion. Charles II's critics fixed their attentions especially on the threat of France—whose predatory impulses had been revealed not merely by assaults on its neighbors, but also by the aggressive regime of commercial protectionism imposed by Louis XIV's ministry of finance, and by the militant Catholicism professed from the court of Versailles. These developments provoked critics of the Stuart court to re-evaluate certain assumptions deeply embedded in English diplomatic thinking. From the reign of Elizabeth to the Cromwellian Protectorate, generations of strategists had supported an Anglo-French alliance, with even many militant Protestants conceiving of the Bourbon kingdom as more a *politique* than a popish power, and as a legitimate instrument for preserving the balance of Europe against Spanish universal monarchy.[55] But by the later 1660s, France was beginning to appear less a counterweight to Spain than a force that could usurp it as the hegemonic power in Europe: making it potentially the principal threat to the security of the English state and—as the steady erosion of Huguenot freedoms appeared to show—the liberties of continental Protestants. By 1670, a fear had begun to crackle in English commentaries that Charles II was too dazzled by the magnificence of his Bourbon cousin to comprehend the scale of the alteration in world affairs.[56] With the outbreak of the Third Dutch War, the appearance of courtiers seemingly dancing to the tune of Louis XIV exposed the inner sanctum of the court to aggressive public questioning, and—in view of the Catholic sympathies seemingly rife among the king's ministers—conspiratorial suspicions.[57]

There was nothing necessarily anti-colonial about the foreign-policy blueprints of the opposition. Many of the critiques of the French alliance fell into line with sentiments voiced more discreetly among governors such as Thomas Lynch, who pushed for the preservation of the Anglo-Spanish peace. But the broad debate growing over foreign affairs forced a reappraisal of the court's emphasis on interests outside Europe, when examined against other views of how the kingdom should perform overseas. Domestic scrutiny focused most immediately on the geography of the French advance. Long into the later seventeenth century, a strong strand of European opinion held that the kingdom of Louis XIV was "not so much addicted to Sea" as its neighbors, in the words of Samuel von Pufendorf, with the result that "Navigation does not flourish so much in *France* as it might."[58] Louis XIV had made his colonial interests known in the Caribbean interventions of 1666–1667, but his attentions had subsequently shifted to the contested territories in the Low Countries and the Rhenish Palatinate. By 1675, the Sun King had added the duchy of Burgundy to his litany of European conquests, and French forces had crossed the Rhine, casting eyes on the outlying cities and provinces of the Holy Roman Empire, and wearing down Austrian, Dutch, and Spanish opponents through a succession of battles and sieges, until the peace of Nijmegen in 1678. These developments suggested that the French attacks on English America represented an alarming but exceptional moment in a campaign of expansion that was concentrated overwhelmingly on territories less far-flung.

By the later 1670s, most strands of English opinion could unite around the proposition that France was primarily a European, rather than a colonial, power. They fractured, however, over how the English should respond. For supporters of the Crown, a view of the English interest as primarily *colonial* diminished the dangers of French expansion in Europe, set against challenges posed by other rivals more clearly focused on maritime affairs. This position, characterized in 1671 by the envoy to Lisbon, held that "the French by enlarging themselves within land" in the Low Countries "would not be a jott more formidable" to England, in contrast to encroachments by the "Hollanders" in Asia and America, which threatened to inflict fatal wounds on "an island" with "noe other way to inrich it selfe but by trade."[59] Country and Whig authors concurred that the center of gravity for French ambitions lay rather in Western Europe than in the colonial zones. They argued, however, that this change made the security of European borders now *more* important to the tranquillity of Christendom than any contests fought out in the Atlantic or the East Indies. The ascent of the court of Versailles to political and material splendor, while its colonies remained underdeveloped, offered evidence, for Slingsby Bethel, that monarchs reaped "more benefit by keeping their people at home to Manufactures," than by sending subjects "abroad for Silver and Gold."[60] Accordingly, the Low

Countries had become the battleground that would determine the prospects for French "universal monarchy": compelling proof of the danger and fatuity of continuous Anglo-Dutch antagonism. For Bethel, the "subduing of *Holland* cannot be a benefit but loss to *England,* and may be of great advantage to *France,* and the Church of *Rome,* against which they are impregnable Fortresses."[61]

Viewing the world through this lens, Whig authors resurrected lost strategic orthodoxies, holding up the "balance of Europe" and the preservation of the "outworks" in Holland and Flanders as prerequisites for English security.[62] The colonial policies favored by the court of Charles II could be attacked for pitting the country against the wrong enemies in the wrong parts of the world. By subsuming itself in "fruitless battles at sea," argued the Whig MP Henry Powle in 1678, England had "contributed to the French greatness more than any other nation." He traced the malady back to the court's decision to part with Dunkirk, and to funnel resources instead into Tangier and Jamaica, thus letting "the French into our bowels," and rendering England and its neighbors "prey to a conqueror."[63]

If Country and Whig protests impugned the "reason of state" behind colonialist foreign policy, they struck just as vehemently at its moral foundations. The changes in European politics raised new questions over the validity of the old Protestant colonialist ideology, nourished by the Elizabethan sea raids and the Cromwellian Western Design, which had presented English overseas expansion as an instrument for upholding true religion against popery. By 1672, when the court of Spain appeared to have been becalmed, and when colonial conflicts were more likely to be fought out against fellow-Protestant "Netherlanders," the confessional and strategic logic that had justified English ventures outside Europe was cast into serious doubt. As Sir Hugh Cholmley recalled, critics of the Tangier experiment argued that colonial designs rested on an outdated view of the world, one upended when "Spain was already in a low condition, and under such necessities of a friendship with England, as made farther dependence needless."[64]

Most of the foreign policy manifestos released by Country and, latterly, Whig authors tempered religious interests with pragmatism—preferring strategic identification of the most likely "universal monarch" over indiscriminate hostility toward every individual Catholic prince.[65] Sketching out a future for Carolina free of raids and piracy, Anthony Ashley Cooper avowed himself to be "of all the English nobility the most affectionate to the Spaniards."[66] This stance, however, did not signify an abandonment of the religious rulebook for English foreign policy. "The Protestant Interest abroad must be Heartily Espoused," Richard Temple maintained, "not only in order to the Supporte of the True Religion . . . but in order to the maintenance of the civill state," against the tyranny of popish princes.[67] Rather than jettisoning the "Protestant cause," Whig commentators relocated it, swivelling their attentions away from the colonies—which, they believed, could be stabilized through Anglo-Spanish peace—and focusing instead on the parlous position of Huguenot, Vaudois, and Palatinate Protestants: on the threat of France in Europe, rather than Spain in America.[68]

These arguments reactivated an alternative lineage in godly, Protestant literature, which had long questioned the merit of sinking blood and treasure into "these windblown conquests of ours," as Sir Philip Sidney had put it, in favor of seeking out a "generall league among free princes" for the preservation of liberty and true religion.[69] Into the later seventeenth century, cohorts of Puritans, Dissenters, and even a considerable strand of opinion in the Restoration Church submerged the elect status of the English people within a wider ocean of ideas and allegiances, and judged the godliness of the nation by its capacity to protect spiritual brethren beyond its borders.[70] For the earl of Shaftesbury, it was "the foreign Protestants" who supplied the "walls and defences" of the English kingdom—the scaffold on which the realm could build its "palaces of silver" further afield.[71] On this foundation, Whig critics exhorted the Crown at least to temper its dreams of territorial expansion, and concentrate instead on uniting the godly: at home, through liberty of conscience for Dissenters, and abroad, by the elevation of Charles II as "the Champion, and vindicator of the Protestant Religion throughout Christendom," in the words of Carew Reynell.[72] Even if, as Richard Temple argued, it served material interests to "swallow up the Dutch nation, and to make ourselves Masters of their people & trade," the way to do so was not to wage wars and take territory, but to welcome in Protestant migrants, and establish the kingdom of England as a "sanctuary" for the persecuted "trading and mercantile people" of the reformed religion.[73] By this means, agreed Roger Coke, "we Conquer without a War: we make no man miserable, or impose any unwilling subjection," but "encrease the Treasure and Trade of the Nation."[74] At best, for opposition commentators, the court's obsession with distant colonial outposts appeared to be a fatal distraction from more vital moral obligations. At worst it was a smokescreen put up by "popish" courtiers, acting in the pay of Versailles and fomenting divisions within the Protestant world. The spiritual appeal of expeditions into the New World, Africa, and Asia was being superseded by an alternative mapping of England's confessional bonds and obligations.

Slow-burning discontent against Stuart foreign policy erupted in the pamphlet and parliamentary denunciations of the Tangier colony. "Wee are as jealous of the increaseing Grandure of some European kings, as others of our own European neighbours," professed one critique produced in manuscript, and "consequently are not a little troubled to find the King of England diverted from preventing it," by using the finest vessels in the navy "merely as scarecrows to fight Pyrats" in the Straits.[75] "It is our Fortune to sit here in a critical Time, when not only the Affairs of this Nation, but the Protestant Religion abroad need our Countenance," agreed Sir William Temple, speaking in the Commons. In neglecting "the deplorable state" of Dutch, Huguenot, and Vaudois co-religionists, he warned, "we have not made ourselves fit for what God has appointed us."[76] For the more strident critics, the design of a Mediterranean empire was not merely contaminated by Catholic leadership, but had become popish in its very incarnation, by dragging the attentions of the court away from the imperiled frontlines of Protestant Europe. So perverse was England's concentration on the Straits of Gibraltar while Bourbon armies set the Continent aflame, believed the MP William Love, that "popish and French counsels" alone "could have put the King upon these vast expences . . . as they have done in the war with Algiers, on purpose to impoverish the Nation."[77] The kingdom was faced with an urgent decision over how to act within the world, and Whigs chose the Protestant Reformation and the balance of Europe over the needs of a crumbling garrison in the Mediterranean. If England could recuperate the continental alliances needed "to destroy the power of France," Love concluded, then "we shall have no need of Tangier."[78]

These attacks completed the moral, political, and economic argument against overseas expansion, initiated by Country authors in the early 1670s.

Since the reign of Queen Elizabeth, the case for colonization had rested on twin premises: first, that England had a superfluous population more fruitfully employed in cultivating the wastelands of the New World; and second, that the threat of Spanish power rendered America and other places of colonial competition the essential battlegrounds for arresting the growth of universal monarchy and securing the survival of true religion. Now, both assumptions were in danger of being dismantled. The colonizing visions of the court of Charles II had collided with an alternative call to arms, a different analysis of England's material interests, and a rival strategic and ideological reading of world affairs.

Overseas Expansion and the Tory View of Foreign Policy

The arguments of the opposition did not go unchallenged. While the court briefly reeled in the face of the Whig assault, the emerging Tory supporters of the Crown were beginning to spell out a trenchant defense of Stuart foreign and colonial policy, framed in parliament and in print as a moral and strategic vindication of the court of Charles II. Tory authors were not oblivious to concerns over the fiscal improvidence of ceaseless territorial acquisition.[79] Nonetheless, by 1681, the needs of outlying provinces were being made into a totemic part of the anti-Exclusionist case for rallying around the Crown, with the attainment of empire presented as the vital way to secure the realm against internal and foreign enemies. Many of the essential tenets of the loyalist worldview were formulated in defense of the Tangier settlement. Hailing the city as a "jewel of so many extraordinary virtues," the *Discourse Touching Tangier* (1680) produced by Henry Sheres "was so much banded amongst us," feared one Whig author, that it risked deluding "the Ignorant Gazett reader" into appraising the place "the Elixer Vite of the Nation."[80] Tangier, a *casus belli* to the Exclusionist party, had become a litmus test of fidelity to the court by 1680, when the London Presbyterian Roger Morrice recorded loyal peers clustering around the throne to "offer themselves as voluntiers" for the Mediterranean.[81]

The political defense of Tangier was built on a fuller anatomy of international relations developed within court circles through the 1670s. It contested the strategic and ideological premises behind the Country-Whig

view of foreign affairs, and elevated English colonial and maritime interests as more crucial to the wealth and power of the nation than any benefits
stemming from the vaunted "balance of Europe." Many of these arguments
rested on a continuing identification of the Dutch as the gravest peril to
English interests and security. The court was correct to resist the "popular
vogue" against France, believed the East India Company governor Josiah
Child, for the blocks, barriers, and monopolies imposed by the Dutch on
the Asian trade threatened the essential springs of customs revenue that
provided for the defense of the realm.[82] In the West Indies, too, William
Blathwayt concurred, Dutch hostility undermined stable peace, by making
English power appear dangerously fragile. Emboldened by the privateers of
the United Provinces, the court of Spain had failed to address the "muther-
ing Pyracy" still perpetrated by its own subjects against English vessels, and
repudiated the prospect of "uniting Interests with us . . . by suffering us to
be sharers in Trade."[83] Supporters of the Crown did not deny that an anti-
Dutch strategy made English expansion an altogether less "Protestant" affair. Instead, they confronted their opponents with an alternative, and more
worldly, view of the calculations that drove interstate rivalry. The "old war
with Spain for Religion is forgotten, interest now Governs the world,"
opined the merchant George Carew in 1676, "and since trade is become the
religion of Holland, and money their God, no reason or Conscience can
place against them in civilisations, where their interest is concerned."[84]
Seen in this light, Country authors had made a dangerous error in presum-
ing that Protestant affinities would ever moderate the acquisitive instincts
of the United Provinces, as a state that relied on the capture of commerce
for its own preservation. More broadly, the "Protestant interest" represented an unreliable guide to navigating the diplomatic labyrinth created by
European power politics.

The court was not impervious to the challenge from Versailles. Beyond
the public gaze, a lively debate raged within royal circles over how far colonial policy should adapt to accommodate the changes driven by Louis XIV.
From the New World, a lobby of colonial agents pressed the case for revital-
izing the Spanish peace, not least, as one manuscript treatise put it, when
domestic pressures cast doubt on whether the English could afford to sustain any more dominions than those already possessed. If "it is our interest

to have no more land in America," the author maintained, "so it is our advantage that the Spaniards and none but them should keep ye Colonies they have for they are lazy & disingenious and need our Ships, Trade and Manufactures."[85] William Godolphin proposed a similar reorientation of colonial policy around the protection of Spanish territories, in Europe as well as the Americas. If Madrid could be persuaded to open up Central American markets to English traders, he suggested, Charles II could respond in turn with a supply of "eight thousand foot, & two thousand horse . . . English, Scots, & Irish" to defend the Southern Netherlands against Louis XIV.[86] After 1679, the pressure supplied by the Exclusionist Parliament compelled the Lords of Trade to make a show of tethering colonial strategy more tightly to "the present Interests of Europe."[87] The final dismissal of Henry Morgan from public office in Jamaica was forced by the earl of Conway, as secretary of state for the affairs of northern Europe—a move provoked by the admiral's encouragement of anti-Spanish privateering by Brandenburgan adventurers in the Caribbean. These actions threatened an open breach between the court of Madrid and the Hohenzollern Electorate, Conway warned fellow privy councillors, which risked driving Brandenburg "over to the French interest" in Europe.[88]

Yet if the court made some concessions to parliamentary concerns, it nonetheless encouraged a different approach to the problem of French expansion. For Tories the predatory character of world affairs required primarily a strengthening of royal power, and the fortification of the colonies under capable commanders, Catholic soldiers if necessary, to control Catholic populations and repel Catholic enemies. "The French may seize your money now . . . and your Leeward Islands," Sir John Ernle reproached the Commons in 1679. "Is your house on fire, and will you not quench it?"[89] Above all, Tories rejected the idea that interventions in northwestern Europe provided the most effective way to hold the line against Versailles. The more urgent concern, Secretary Coventry advanced, was to make sure that "whilst you secure Flanders, France fall not upon you" in "your islands, and plantations and Jamaica."[90] The slippery reality of world affairs created grave questions regarding the wisdom of subsuming English interests in a grand European alliance against the court of Versailles. It served the tendentious claims of rival powers, Sir Robert Southwell impressed upon his fellow Irish

Protestant Sir John Perceval, to draw England into a looming continental war, "rather than to suffer us by a quiet neutrality to get the Possession and fraight of Europe, as we did before. But if we be allow'd ye Neutrality we covet, the Navigation of England and Ireland will exceedingly increase."[91] No matter how "Covetous or Ambitious" European states might become, the Tory pamphleteer John Nalson argued, they will "difficultly be persuaded to break with us . . . when they shall see the Crown of *England* in capacity, by strong and powerfull *Fleets,* to give Laws to the *Ocean* . . . though in the remotest corners of the *Earth.*"[92] Tory authors presented the "balance of Europe" as an illusory prize, when international friendships were transient and diplomatic agreements insubstantial. On this reading of the world, believed Sir Joseph Williamson, it was folly to "hazard the plantations" by staking "the success of their great interest on every little interest of Germany."[93]

The tone of the Tory argument incubated in the Exclusion Crisis was therefore commercial, strategic, and self-consciously detached from the notion of the international "Protestant interest," with its long latticework of allegiances and obligations. Yet Tories had not entirely relinquished the claim of a providential legitimation for English endeavors overseas. As the gulf between party worldviews widened, so the crises playing out simultaneously in London and the Mediterranean refigured the approved public image of English Tangier. By 1680, Tory authors had begun to raise the city to the center of a rival religious narrative, devised as a counterblast to the moral claims of Protestant Europe. A stream of poems, treatises, and heroic narratives defended the reputation of the Tangier garrison by capturing its members as Christian knights who had "drawn their Swords . . . and serv'd their King and Country," Henry Sheres believed, against the forces of Islam—"the Enemies of our Religion, and of God himself."[94] These authors mobilized all the devotional fears and energies stirred up by the capture and ransoming of English seafarers by Barbary corsairs. They aimed to fix the gaze of their readers on events farther East, when the advance of Turkish forces through the Holy Roman Empire was beginning to vie with anxiety over Louis XIV as a preoccupation in English print.[95] Loyalists repositioned Tangier as a city on the front line against Ottoman expansion, appropriated images of Jerusalem and Lepanto, and represented every shot fired against the besieging forces as a blow struck against the Islamic world. "May not the sins of Barbary be ripe for punishment," intoned Hugh Cholmley, once the proponent of a peaceful free port, now the advocate for Tangier as "a scourge to curb the faithless heads of the men of Algiers."[96] Producing the epitaph for Sir Palmes Fairborne, the lieutenant governor killed in a cavalry charge in October 1680, John Dryden depicted the ascent toward "martyr's glory" of the officers cornered in the Tangier garrison. Engraved on the general's tombstone in Westminster Abbey, the poem was pitched as a lasting memorial to England's contribution toward the defense of Christendom.[97]

These arguments spoke to older lesions in the English confessional imagination. As Peter Marshall has shown, conservative, Laudian, and High Church tendencies within English Protestantism had long nurtured aspects of the old crusading worldview, saluting victories over the Turks achieved even by Catholic powers in Central Europe. The "hotter sort of Protestant," conversely, was apt to prove "the colder sort of Christian," with Calvinists, Puritans, and, latterly, Whigs more absorbed by the threat of the popish cross in Western Europe than the more distant dangers posed by the Crescent.[98] As Tangier ruptured parliamentary opinion, these old fault lines began to appear in the debate over colonial expansion. Tory writings aimed to deflect Whig attacks upon a "popish" colony by accommodating Catholic and Protestant settlers in Tangier in a shared religious struggle, which they represented as far more elemental than the battle for the Low Countries. From this perspective, it was the Whigs who could be accused of weakening the Christian world: their obsession with Catholic plots, Catholic governors, and the exclusion of the duke of York had diverted minds from the onslaught of an alien, conquering religion in the East. Following the polemic through to its logical conclusion, those MPs prepared to see Tangier go down in flames could be considered as morally and spiritually errant as the men of Barbary themselves. English Whigs had become fanatics "worse by half," one Tory poet concluded, "than all the Moors in Fez."[99]

James II and the Revival of the Royal Empire

The Crown's eventual, emphatic victory over the Whig Party came too late for English Tangier. Tumults, local and international, had worn away at court backing for the Mediterranean adventure, and had so disabled its main cheerleader, the duke of York, that Samuel Pepys doubted whether he "be now strong enough to mend things . . . without exposing himself to more envy and complaint." Robert Southwell calculated that to "make the place tenable" would require Charles II to part with £4 million, and finance a garrison of eight thousand men.[100] By September 1683, the king had demurred from meeting such a cost, and an English fleet sailed out to the Straits to begin a formal evacuation.[101] But if the Tangier design was a casualty of a loss of trust in the Crown, the Whig Party had also been weakened, by appearing to put a fixation with domestic conspiracies before the strength of the realm overseas. The "trimming" marquis of Halifax later claimed that a critical moment for tipping his sympathies away from the Exclusionists came when "they were asked what should be done with *Tangier,* to answer with Popery and a Remonstrance."[102] As the evidence of widespread Catholic conspiracies began to collapse, the emerging view that Whig fanaticism imperiled the realm more than Stuart "popery" began to strike fatal blows at the credibility of the opposition.

The defeat of the Exclusionists, and the subsequent collapse of the Whig power base, injected new life into the Crown's program for reforming other centers of the overseas world. Between 1681 and 1685, the rallying of the colonial customs revenues offered Charles II scope to develop his agenda without the constraint of a sitting parliament. Gross receipts from the tobacco inflows had spiralled up to an annual tally of over £700,000, and on the back of these resources, £400,000 annually was made available for the navy: sufficient, according to the earl of Ailesbury, to "put the ships and docks in the greatest order beyond what can be expressed."[103] It was, perhaps, salient that a painting of the siege of English Tangier entered into the collection of William Blathwayt—now appointed auditor-general of the colonies—at Dyrham Park.[104] The call to revive national power, reverse humiliations overseas, and strengthen the Crown through the wealth of its colonies would become an essential fount of policy under the newly enthroned James II.

As I noted in Chapter 5, the new king's colonial policy focused most conspicuously on the creation of centralized dominions in English America. This strategy, however, was only one part of a broader program that was conceived as much to give the Crown authority over the agencies that shaped colonization from *within* the mother kingdom. For William Blathwayt, domestic as well as colonial tranquillity required the plantations to be "united in a more visible and immediate dependence" on royal authority—such was the significance of overseas wealth to the security of the realm. The task for the Lords of Trade was to exhort and advance the spirit of adventure, but also to harness such control over the flows of travel, trade, and overseas settlement as to lay a "foundation for the lasting power of the crown."[105] This approach entailed not merely the reorganization of New World territories, but also closer regulation of the Atlantic commerce. The goal, set out in Blathwayt's "Essay of the Interest of the Crown," was to secure a reliable stream of revenue for the treasury, while also rolling back the authority of the Westminster parliament over affairs relating to the colonies.

Blathwayt's vision expressed itself most clearly in royal policy toward the West Indies. Staffed and steered by members of the royal household, the Royal African Company had held its ground through the years of domestic crisis, against challenges emanating from "separate traders" on the Guinea Coast and their merchant allies in London.[106] "Let them doe in God's name what they find for ye advantage of ye Company, so farre as their Charter will justify," the duke of York had avowed to the Committee of Foreign Affairs in 1677. "The King will stand by them."[107] For the Crown, the significance of the slave-trading monopoly resided not merely in the control exerted over the Caribbean planters, but also in the ability to seal off a significant proportion of the Atlantic trade from parliamentary interference. Where other fields of American commerce could be debated and regulated by MPs through the Navigation Acts, the rights of the "Africa Company" rested on a grant bestowed by the power of the prerogative, and Whig MPs failed in 1679 to make the legal case for bringing the issue before the Commons.[108] Spokesmen for the "Africa Company" played to the Tory gallery through the Exclusion Crisis, representing their monopoly as a vital part of the dignity of the Crown, and attacking commercial "interloping" in Guinea as a Whiggish subversion of the king's just rights. In their printed polemics, company defenders contributed new motifs to the panoply of loyalist imaginative literature.[109] The author of *Certain Considerations Relating to the Royal African Company* (1680) foreshadowed the central plot device of Aphra Behn's *Oroonoko* with the complaint that "separate traders" had undermined English honor in Africa by breaking the rules of the slave exchange. Interlopers, the author claimed, had earned local notoriety by kidnapping "some considerable natives of Guinea" and tricking them into boarding vessels bound for the plantations.[110]

While the fall of the Massachusetts Bay Colony appeared to indicate a push away from company rule, the management of the slave trade illustrated the continuing utility of overseas corporations to the Crown—where the companies themselves possessed more impeccably loyal credentials. The powers of the Royal African Company provided a clear template in 1688 when the Lords of Trade sketched out the terms for a new South American Company, intended to gain exclusive control over the trade in Caribbean commodities, and to finance the Atlantic convoys out of its own profits. This plan brought together courtiers including William Penn and the Catholic merchant-author Henry Neville Payne with London Tories such as Dalby Thomas, and was described in William Blathwayt's 1685 treatise "The Interest of the Crown," which adapted ideas first outlined by his uncle Thomas Povey.[111] In a revealing indication of court thinking, Blathwayt's proposals cast doubt on the effectiveness of the Navigation Acts, given the need to preserve royal power and maintain stability in the West Indies. The acts may have confined commerce to traders arriving on English vessels, but the regulation of markets had otherwise been too slight, he complained, allowing antagonistic relations to develop between planters and merchants, with no guarantee of a regular supply for the islands. The "protection" of the West Indies had been similarly threatened, Blathwayt argued, by the authority ceded to parliament, where members hostile to the planters had threatened colonial trade by forcing through relentless increases in duties on American commodities.[112] Having initially supported a 1685 levy on sugar, the king by 1688 regretted the legislation, according to the earl of Ailesbury. The South American Company offered an extra-parliamentary route toward its reversal.[113]

The proposed new body, to be established on a joint stock "wide and open enough" to offset "the scandalous name of monopolies," fronted an attempt to strengthen the colonies through commercial profits created and managed by the Crown. The South American Company would establish a common factory to expedite the sale and re-export of Caribbean goods in England, with the rate of customs duties to be fixed on the Committee of Trade. Supplemented by the creation of a bank to "supply the needy Planters with mony at the common interest of the Colonies," company revenues would offer the main supply for the defensive infrastructure of the islands, while funding a permanent naval force for "descent upon any troublesome neighbour."[114] The plan for a Caribbean joint-stock company was one of a stream of blueprints raised and never fulfilled through the three-year reign. Yet it cast light on the political and economic revolution plotted by colonial advisers under James II. To fulfill the promise of the colonies, Blathwayt advanced, it would be necessary to "mix" the concerns of the monarchy with the business of overseas commerce, just as past feudal relations had intertwined royal power with the landed interest. The goal of English governments would be to construct a new relationship with merchants and planters, through the mediating authority of privileged corporations. On this foundation, "the stronger foreign trade grows, the stronger the interest of the crown becomes"—with the ultimate effect being to diminish the court's financial dependence on the unruly Westminster parliament.[115]

The bid for closer control over colonial governance, commerce, and revenue underlined the Crown's intention to bring overseas expansion back to the center of English foreign policy. Interests in further territorial enlargement gained their most vigorous expression not in the New World, however, but in the East. In 1681, the loyalist resurgence in London had been followed by a rout of Whig supporters in elections to the East India Company board of directors.[116] The results had prompted the reinvention of the EIC as one of the most vociferous London champions of the house of Stuart. The company's governor, Sir Josiah Child, owned plantations in Jamaica and stocks in the Royal African Company, and aimed to use the "Guinea" precedent of a Crown-corporate partnership to transform English interests on the subcontinent.[117] The convergence between court and company centered on the renewal of an aggressive anti-Dutch strategy, provoked by the VOC's success in drawing local princes into associations against English merchant interests.[118] One such alliance brought the ejection of the EIC from its stronghold at Banten in 1683, eliciting vehement responses in Tory newsletters and heightening Child's conviction that the "designed sole Empire of ye Dutch in India" threatened a "Nationall Gangreene . . . soe fatall to this Kingdom" that it warranted "speedyer & stronger remedyes than can be applyed by any private Merchants."[119] Hitherto, most EIC barons had been content to bolster their settlements behind the shield of *firman* grants from native rulers. Company literature had accentuated the contrast between the Dutch who would make "war for the enlargement of their own Dominion," as one 1672 pamphlet recalled, and the English who remained "content, without affecting new acquests," prioritizing peace and trade alone.[120] This posture, however, was challenged by a growing identification of Indian princes, including the Mughal Aurangzeb, as supine if not complicit in the undermining of the company, and in the incursions of its European rivals. By 1685, decades of cautious negotiation were being supplanted by a new strategic tone set in London, as relentless injunctions from Child enjoined local agents to "doe as the Dutch do" and take the fight to the United Provinces by imitation of the same martial "wisdom" that "has been the cause of all their Sovereign Dominion in India."[121]

The principles fostered under Child's leadership were illustrated in the legal positioning of company settlements, and in the economic strategies that underpinned them. Since its foundation, the EIC had possessed state-like features: its juridical, confessional, and architectural programs were consistent with the civic responsibilities written into the charters of all corporate bodies, within and outside English borders.[122] But in the wake of the Exclusion Crisis, the directors began to justify their activities more vocally through appeals to royal authority than to their own quasi-autonomous corporate liberties. A stream of military officers, judges, and churchmen hitherto unconnected with the Company—and including many Tangier veterans—were lodged within Bombay and Madras. Having disconcerted the merchants at Fort Saint George with the appointment of an outsider, the New Englander Nathaniel Higginson, as governor in 1687, the directors rejoined that specialist local knowledge—"being bred a boy in India, or staying long there & speaking the Language"—may have been enough to hold high office "when we were in the state of mere trading Merchants, but the case is altered from that since his Majestie has been pleased . . . to forme us into the condition of a sovereign state." Now, expertise in "ancient histories of the Greekes and Lattines" offered qualities more apt to "render a man fit for government."[123] Ransacking precedents from across the English world, the directors hired overseers from Caribbean plantations, cast their eyes over the Madagascan slave markets, and sketched plans to boil sugar, plant tobacco, and raise up silkworks and indigo farms.[124] In previous decades, projectors in the Western Atlantic had considered the crops, seeds, and manufacturing processes of the Indian economy as a template for the American colonies. By 1685, the influence was moving in the other direction. Paring down differences between the Eastern and Western "dominions" would, directors anticipated, make EIC operations more "acceptable to . . . all the great men of this Kingdome," as well as "venerable to the Vulgar": rebuffing the canard that the Asian trade represented simply a channel for exotic consumer fancies.[125]

This shift in ideological temper was confirmed by the way in which Crown and company sought to legitimize the East India monopoly in public, against the legal challenges issued by "interloping" separate traders. Pronouncing in favor of the EIC against the merchant Thomas Sandys in 1683, Lord Justice Jeffreys ruled that the organization of the India trade fell within the royal prerogative, because its focus was not just commerce but also dominion, and corporations represented a central part of the way in which "his Majtie and his predecessors have always disposed of their several Plantations abroad."[126] In the East, as in the New World, added the Company's Tory barristers, the monarch was required to regulate overseas enterprises to prevent moral "infection" in pagan domains, a danger much more likely to arise if English traders were permitted to sprawl without oversight across the Indian subcontinent. The Asian trade could reasonably be caged within structures robust enough "to take care of the Christian Religion," as an obligation that overrode all domestic laws against monopolies.[127] In recourse to these arguments, the Company aimed to change the terms of the debate, and draw its opponents into an ideological discussion—much more dangerous after the Exclusion Crisis—over the rights of Christian monarchs and the duties of Christian subjects. Whiggish barristers decried as "monkish, phantastical and phanatical" the "mixing of trade and religiosity" and the erection of "a partition wall . . . as to property and commerce" between Christians and "infidels."[128] But the company was fortifying itself with royal approval, and moving self-consciously into line with the preoccupations of the Stuart court, as it reanimated old blueprints for eastward colonial expansion. Soon its agents were riveting onto Indian holdings the same language, strategies, and ideas that had informed the transition of Tangier from peaceful emporium to would-be seat of Christian conquests. Bombay "is not able to subsist of it selfe, and without Territories annexed to it," the surgeon and Tangier veteran John St. John wrote to James II, because "this Mogull Orangsha is a capital Enemy to all Christians and others who are not Mahometan Votaries . . . and tis very observable how politiquely he laboureth to extirpate & shoulder them out of all India."[129]

By 1685, the EIC had won its court battles, and convinced significant sections of the Privy Council of its strategic as well as commercial value. The cost, as Child reminded his factors, was to move the case for the company onto very different intellectual terrain. The fulfilment of its mandate now obliged the EIC to release its holdings from the shackles of Mughal *firmans* and Dutch military power, and "make ye English Nation in India look like a political governing state, as it is by his Majesty's institution, and ought to be, & must be" in order to "doe our duties to his Maty & our Country."[130] Soon, the Crown was being drawn deeper into the politics of the region, as Dutch forces began to harry English factories on the Malabar Coast, and Aurangzeb's refusal to lift blocks, duties, and impositions on the trade routes used by English merchants provoked new altercations with the imperial court at Delhi.[131] In 1685, James II licensed the departure of a fleet of twelve men-of-war, conveying six hundred troops to reinforce Company recruits.[132] A year later, an enlarged edition of Nathaniel Crouch's *The English Empire* incorporated "acquisitions" in the East Indies and West Africa into the "dominions" claimed by the house of Stuart.[133] In October 1686, the EIC began to launch a sustained assault on Mughal-ruled centers across Bengal. Child and his fellow directors wedded themselves to the creation of a Dominion of India, conceived to honor and emulate the reforms of the Crown in the New World, and to serve as the final component in the king's design for national revival overseas.[134]

The political ruptures in later Stuart Britain cannot be properly understood without appreciation of the project for territorial expansion developed at the courts of Charles II and James II. The instability that climaxed with the

Exclusion Crisis was fomented by larger conflicts over the application of English power overseas: divisions over whether court policy was laying the foundations for liberty and true religion, or whether it was hastening—by emulation and acquiescence—the growth of popery, tyranny, and French universal monarchy. Domestic polarization was interspersed with urgent questions concerning the most appropriate way to govern England's overseas interests, the implications for politics at home, and the virtue of holding colonies outside Europe at all. In a political landscape reordered by the rise of Louis XIV and by fears over the growth of domestic Catholic power, the ideological engine of anti-popery, which had galvanized colonial ventures in the 1580s and 1650s, now threatened to undermine them. Under these conditions, the old, idealized notion of England creating a more irenic kind of dominion—a sovereignty of the seas, a decentralized empire of liberty—fell away before starker political choices. The terms of domestic debate presented an increasingly sharp dichotomy between the centralizing, militaristic projects for colonization supported by the Stuart court, and the preference voiced by many Whigs for no significant territorial empire at all.

By 1688, the turn in domestic and colonial politics appeared to denote a decisive victory for the court. Yet the rout of opponents in England and America had not diminished the political and financial inhibitions on royal actions. The evacuation of Tangier had exposed the dangers besetting foreign ventures that failed to mobilize consensus and secure reliable streams of revenue from the domestic realm. In Massachusetts, Sir Edmund Andros remained dependent on the ability to establish a modus vivendi with local elites, having been furnished with only sixty soldiers under the pay of the royal exchequer. Across the Atlantic, Crown support for the EIC monopoly had provoked bitter opposition within a section of the City of London, while the strike upon "liberties and properties" in New England "makes a strange noise here, in England, to the disadvantage of his Matie," as one Crown agent warned.[135] The legacy of Tangier still simmered through English politics, embodied in the form of the returning military veterans, who created instability on both sides of the Atlantic. The threatened arrival of the "Tangerines" in America intensified local animus toward a centralizing Crown—Francis Nicholson was appointed lieutenant governor of New York in 1688, while Percy Kirke was mooted, but not eventually appointed, as governor general of the Dominion of New England.[136] Conversely, Tangerine disillusionment with the monarch whose religion—they believed—had cost them their colony meant that swordsmen such as Kirke, Charles Trelawney, and Charles Churchill would exert a decisive influence over the eventual withdrawal of Tory backing for the court.[137]

By the latter half of 1688, the imperial vision of James II was being exposed to spiralling local and international threats. In October, the EIC directors warned their factors to anticipate aggression from the United Provinces, with the Dutch fleet "daily expected to invade" England, under such "plausible and popular pretences" as securing "the Establishment of the Protestant Religion."[138] Voyaging across the Atlantic in December, a party of New England lobbyists picked up rumors of "Wars in England," of "the king's death . . . the Pr. of Aurang [Orange] in Salisbury Plain, expected at London," as news was exchanged between passing vessels.[139] By the time their ship reached Chatham, James II had been cast into exile, and the political experiments constructed on both sides of the Atlantic were on the brink of collapse.

PART FOUR

BRITAIN, EUROPE, AND THE POST-REVOLUTIONARY

EMPIRE, 1689–C. 1700

8

Revolution and the Redefinition of Empire

FOR ALL THE STRIDENT CONFIDENCE OF THE schemes and blueprints devised within the Old World, the events of 1688–1689 showed the colonial authority of James II to be paper thin. It took almost two months for news of the flight and subsequent deposition of the king to filter across the Atlantic. But distorted claims and counterclaims of upheavals within the Old World increased the strains running through English America. Across the principal civil and commercial centers, opposition pamphlets, sermons, and moments of public protest were animated not merely by localized hostility to the royal program, but also by a conception of America's place within a global struggle against the rampaging forces of Catholic universal monarchy. From New England to the Chesapeake, rumors of secret alliances between French and Indian assailants outside English borders, and Catholic subversives within, brought the fraying civil order to the breaking point.[1]

The collapse of the Crown's embryonic dominions began in Boston. On April 18, 1689, over a thousand protestors took up arms outside the city's principal fort and secured the detention of Governor Andros, Edward Randolph, and a handful of acolytes associated with the crumbling power base. Power was transferred to a new "Committee of Safety," comprising a roll-call of the old ruling Congregationalists displaced by the Crown in 1685. Confrontation in Massachusetts was averted largely by the overwhelming local consensus behind the revolt: the new government had failed to build up a caucus of supporters sufficiently invested to take up arms in its defense.[2] But in other parts of English America, the dissolution of royal authority brought violent political and religious divisions into the open. Self-proclaimed "Protestant Associators" stormed the Maryland state house, expelled the governor and his Catholic-dominated council, and routed an army hastily raised in allegiance to Lord Baltimore.[3] In New York, Protestant anxieties combined with the longstanding discontents of the Dutch community to accelerate the revolt under the militia captain Jacob Leisler. Forts and garrisons were seized, "popish" officers were purged, and the lieutenant-governor, Francis Nicholson, was driven from the capital.[4] The Revolution was more vigorously contested in the West Indies, where the strength of the Irish population meant that loyalty to James II took a more durable and militant form. Flags were raised for the house of Stuart on Saint Christopher, Nevis, and Montserrat in June 1689, and for over a year the islands stood in the eye of the international storm, as French squadrons swarmed around the Caribbean, and Irish privateers preyed on English merchant vessels.[5] The resistance in the Leeward Islands outlasted by three months the Jacobite defeat at the battle of the Boyne.

The Revolution of 1688–1689 was an imperial crisis—first because of the waves of instability that swept through the English overseas world; and second, because ideological divisions on both sides of the Atlantic were inflected with questions over how the kingdom should act beyond its borders, and how outposts on distant continents should best be governed. It is now widely accepted that the Revolution amounted to a decisive moment in the political history of English America.[6] The consequences for the way in which colonization was debated in the Old World have been subject to comparably limited scholarly attention. Yet regime change exposed the future of the English overseas empire to serious uncertainty. In England, the overthrow of James II brought the rehabilitation of the Whig Party, ushering into government many leaders of a faction that had dissented openly against territorial expansion since the 1670s. The tone of English foreign policy was now set by the concerns of a Dutch prince—William III—whose public pronouncements showed at best limited engagement with dominions outside Europe. In the following century, the Williamite expansion of the English state, and its accompanying fiscal innovations—the creation of the Bank of England and the institutionalized national debt—would eventually release funds and resources to empower the realm overseas. In the 1690s, however, the purpose behind these reforms was not to underwrite colonial expeditions, but to funnel English manpower onto the continent closer to home. The kingdom of England was recast as a guardian of the "balance of Europe," to be achieved through sustained intervention against the court of Versailles. The affairs of Europe, not empire, supplied the strategic impetus that quickened the growth of the English fiscal-military state—even if that state relied to a considerable extent on the customs garnered through colonial commerce.[7]

The Revolution fomented questions over the English dominions that were closely intertwined with the new uncertainties sweeping through domestic politics. How far would the defense of the overseas territories remain a viable priority for the Crown, when its foreign policy now pointed elsewhere? Would new governments seek to reform, retrench, or retreat entirely from their outposts outside Europe? If colonial possessions were to be secured, did the change in England's ruling order mean an end to the centralizing political and economic orthodoxies that had underpinned overseas expansion since the 1660s? These dilemmas became unavoidable as statesmen contemplated prospects for a new settlement in the colonies that had gone into revolt against James II. As Whig and Tory statesmen responded to the tumults in New York and Boston, they found themselves unable to address the meaning of revolution in America without considering the nature of their own revolution at home.

Debates over the governance, religion, and political economy of the English colonies remained a divisive feature of domestic and parliamentary politics through the following decade, as Whig statesmen tightened their hold on government. Lobbyists from the colonies played to the splits in Whitehall and Westminster, pitching rival manifestos in London, in competing attempts to redefine the civil and military relationship with the Old World. Radical hopes for a new settlement that would enlarge colonial liberties vied against the pressures of international warfare and the call for closer oversight of England's overseas possessions. After 1695, the new supervisory Board of Trade became a particular locale for disputes over the organization of empire and the rationale behind overseas expansion.[8] In this context, circles of Whig thinkers took up the challenge of creating a vision of empire better suited to the post-revolutionary landscape—distinct at once from the anti-colonial politics of the old Country Party, and from the expansionist absolutism of the reign of James II. Statesmen, political economists, and moral philosophers looked for ways to reconstitute civil and religious virtue in settler populations, reduce the burden on the mother kingdom, and address the problems that had undermined the reputation of the colonies in England. By equipping English America to play a fuller part in the struggle against French universal monarchy, they sought to re-establish the case for the colonies on the legitimizing authority of the international Protestant cause.

Empire and the Meaning of Revolution

By 1689, the expansion of the realm as a feature of English foreign policy was a stance indelibly associated with the personal and ideological priorities of James II. Hence a backlash against colonialist excesses soon added to the polemical reaction against Stuart "despotism," as commentators connected the growth of tyranny in England to the imperial models—popish, classical, or Asiatic—seen to have inspired royal policy. "Our constitution is not design'd for conquest . . . by being very fortunate, we should run the Risque of becoming very unhappy, and endanger our Liberties, in extending our Empire," the Whig author John Dennis informed his readers.[9] For many of the new MPs elected into parliament in 1689, the link between colonization and arbitrary government was symbolized by the fate of the "Protestant slaves" who had been transported into Jamaica and Barbados after the Monmouth Rebellion, and denied release by councils reluctant to part with much-needed labor.[10] Oligarchy, as well as tyranny, was seen to have sprung out of the corrupted politics of overseas expansion. For the Whig MP Edward Clarke, the "Rich Men" of the joint-stock companies had threatened a contamination of the constitution akin to the Medici subversion of Florence.[11] Critics of Josiah Child's East India Company melded anti-monopolistic arguments with attacks on the "wicked aspiring to territories and dominion" and on the "injustices & Robberies committed on ye Indians"—all identified as part of the design to "enslave us both at home and abroad to the Absolute will and pleasure of the late King."[12] By the summer of 1689, these complaints had been bolstered by the ignominious end to the war against the Mughal emperor—a run of defeats culminating in the siege and occupation of Bombay, which forced the EIC to sue for peace with Aurangzeb, at the cost of a 500,000-rupee fine.[13]

The critique of recent overseas adventures was strengthened because the Williamite state possessed a rival set of international priorities. As early as January 1689, the king announced his intention to dispatch eight thousand troops onto the Continent, as participants in the Grand Alliance against Louis XIV. For the following eight years, the three kingdoms were cast into the storm of an international war, which obliged the king to spend almost 40 percent of his reign across the Channel. Whig pamphlets, poems, and artistic productions defined the redemption of the liberties of Europe as the providential mandate of the 1688 Revolution.[14] The consequence was to bring England and the United Provinces into a union as close as was politically possible, and—in effect—to terminate the old strategic goal of chasing the "sovereignty of the seas" in regions contested with Dutch traders. "Tis certainly the interest of England to preserve and cherish the States of Holland," believed the Whig merchant-scholar Henry Martin, for all that "it has been the craft of Ministers to cajole the People" with "antient stories" serving "other interests."[15] Jacobites, such as the exiled earl of Ailesbury, professed their amazement at compatriots' amnesia over "the treatment of our poor factors at Amboyna . . . [the Dutch] burning of our ships at Chatham and their kicking us out of the pepper trade in the Indies."[16] But with the Williamite Crown aiming to transform conceptions of the English interest, advocates for the colonies were placed on the defensive.

Yet if its political compass pointed in another direction, the new government was unable to insulate itself entirely from colonial affairs. With naval warfare intensifying in the West Indies in 1689, the implosion of Crown authority in Boston and New York had created a power vacuum, opening up a potential channel for conquests running deep into English America, should Louis XIV choose to mount an assault. While the northern colonies stood, convulsed by fears of French invasions, a bitter battle was breaking out across the Atlantic over what kind of government could best secure the provinces formerly included within the Dominion of New England. At the point of the Revolution, a contingent of Bay Colonists was already present in London, lobbying the court of James II for religious liberty in Massachusetts. The overturnings in English politics, and the robust Whig majority delivered in the new Convention Parliament, emboldened the leaders of this expedition to widen their ambitions, and bid for the complete recovery of the dissolved 1629 Charter.[17] Increase Mather and Samuel Sewall worked with the MP and New England Company patron Henry Ashurst to pitch their case before Whig circles in coffeehouses, Dissenting chapels, and aristocratic households.[18] In all their efforts, they sought to lift the public image and reputation of the Bay Colony, countering the claims of doctrinal error and temporal self-aggrandizement that had threatened to estrange the Congregationalists from their "godly" support base in the Old World. New England campaigners sought to establish a platform for dialogue with "our Honoured and Beloved Brethren the Renowned Church of Scotland," now brought back into Presbyterian hands.[19] They threw themselves into fundraising to support Presbyterian communities under assault from Jacobite armies in Ulster.[20] Overtures were also extended to receptive Anglicans, including the new Whig bishops John Tillotson and Gilbert Burnet.[21] But the aim of these activities was nonetheless to build a coalition of Nonconformist Protestants, and tilt the confessional balance away from the Church of England across the British dominions. For Bay Colony lobbyists, the events of 1688–1689 amounted to a triumph for all the "dissenting" peoples of the British dominions; it could be identified as part of a greater international struggle for true religion, in which Massachusetts was a legitimate, and even vital, participant.

For the first six months of 1689, colonial lobbyists capitalized on the radical impetus within the Convention Parliament, as MPs pushed for the reclamation of domestic liberties perceived to have been stifled since the end of the Exclusion Crisis. The new coronation oath obliged William III and Mary II to "governe the People of this Kingdome of England *and the Dominions thereto belonging*" according to parliamentary statute and constitutional custom.[22] Anticipating a bill for overturning the Corporations Act, Henry Ashurst prepared an amendment "to include New England, and the other Forraigne Plantations" and so restore the Bay Colony charter liquidated under Charles II.[23] But in England and America, the reformist agenda rested on unstable foundations. By October 1689, the displaced Dominion officeholders, Andros, Randolph, and Nicholson, were back in London, avowing their loyalty to William III.[24] In February 1690, the Convention Parliament fell, and the new election brought a counterrevolutionary resurgence. The retention of William Blathwayt on the Committee of Trade, and the rehabilitation of the Tory earls Nottingham and Danby (the latter now marquis of Carmarthen), brought the colonial agents in London face to face with "old courtiers" who had adumbrated the program of imperial centralization under Charles II.[25] Re-established in government, the Tories immediately set about mobilizing a force to reclaim control of New York City. The new Crown governor, Henry Sloughter, arrived in the city in March 1691, dispersed the insurgent faction, and expedited the trial and execution of Jacob Leisler on grounds of treason.[26] With colonial business now wrenched away from parliament, the "great affaire touching New England," as the Presbyterian minister Roger Morrice put it, moved toward final resolution within the Committee of Trade—which was itself split along party lines— in a year-long joust of petitions and complaints, lobbying and counter-campaigning.[27]

The clash on the Committee of Trade began with a failed attempt by New Englanders and their Whig allies to indict Edmund Andros on a charge of misconduct in office. It developed rapidly, however, into a wider contest over the future settlement of Massachusetts and over the correct principles behind English overseas governance. As reports from America ramified through English news networks, assailants and defenders of the Dominion of New England deployed public channels in their bid to construct the approved narrative of the colonial revolts. The Massachusetts agents printed over five hundred copies of Increase Mather's *A Brief Relation of the State of New England* for dissemination in London and Edinburgh, accompanied by a stream of loyal addresses to William III from the provisional councils in Boston and New York. Samuel Sewall took to print in 1691, collaborating with Edward Rawson, the secretary of the ruling committee in Massachusetts, to produce *The Revolution in New England Justified*.[28] Their antagonists responded in kind, with counter-histories assembled by Edward Randolph and the Tory judge John Palmer, in concert with their allies in Whitehall, which included point-by-point anatomies of the "laws of New-England," as passed by Congregationalists in the General Court, "which are either contrary, or not agreeable to the laws of England."[29] These confrontations heightened the ideological stakes of the transatlantic clash over the New England charters. Rival combatants presented politically incompatible understandings of the foundation, development, and correct governance of the English overseas dominions. But their arguments also hurtled into a political and intellectual vacuum in Whitehall and Westminster, when domestic debate had left unsettled the basic grounds of William and Mary's right to wear their crowns, and when the 1688 Revolution was still imagined from different standpoints as a moment of radical popular election, a foreign conquest, or a pragmatic solution to fill a vacant throne.[30] Divided responses to "revolutions" in America became inseparable from rival attempts to shift the political ground in Old England, and to settle the meaning and implications of "revolution" within the three kingdoms.

Advocates for the Dominion of New England delivered robust defenses of the Crown's policies in America since the early 1680s.[31] Tories invoked precedents, ancient and contemporary, to contend that no expanding domain had allowed its colonies to approach constitutional parity with the central law-giving institutions. The Dutch no less than the Romans had constructed "despoticall and absolute" relationships with outlying territories, John Palmer argued. The principle of "first discovery" was invoked to portray New England as "King's Land," occupied by migrant subjects only at the benevolence of the sovereign authority that had licensed the original settlements.[32] Concurrently, opined a 1689 paper "humbly offered to the Parliament," the *quo warranto* issued against Massachusetts by Charles II was "quite different" to any of the alleged breaches of the constitution by James II within England itself. The tethering of the Bay Colony was not "popery and arbitrary government," but a reassertion of the lawful precedence of the mother kingdom over a people violating the "very Laws and Navigation of *England,* and making themselves as it were Independant to this Crown."[33]

Veterans of the dominion proclaimed their loyalty to William III and to the 1689 settlement. But their arguments rested on a highly conservative interpretation of the downfall of James II, framed to accentuate the contrast with risings in Boston and New York, and to delegitimize the interim authorities seated in both cities. For Palmer, the "revolution" in England amounted simply to the replacement of one prince with another, after the voluntary flight of James II. "We do not finde," he averred, "that the people of England took up armes to right themselves," nor that that "the Lords Spirituall & Temporall assumed any Authority, for which they had no colour of Law . . . they never left their Duty and Allegiance to his late Majesty, untill he first left the Kingdome." Instead, people and legislators "became humble suppliants" to William of Orange, who came not to "subvert and destroy the Lawfull Government; but to maintaine & support the same in a peaceable manner."[34] This chain of events created no precedent for popular mobilization, no reduction in royal authority, and, above all, no grounds to impugn the policies of the Crown in America before 1688. The insurrections in the colonies could not credibly be linked to any part of the political upheaval in the Old World, but instead became the localized inflammation of "fanatick" spirits: Congregationalists imposing false claims of "dominion by grace" to sustain their illegitimate grip over government.[35]

Responding to these charges, the advocates for Massachusetts and Leislerian New York accepted that events in America constituted an act of popular resistance.[36] But they argued that this action followed logically from the deposition of James II in England—the "late glorious enterprise against tyranny and slavery" that the colonists had both honored and completed by disposing of the fallen monarch's placemen.[37] Bay Colony pamphleteers alleged that it was their opponents—not the Congregationalist clergy—who had staked an unfounded claim of "dominion by grace" over America. Samuel Sewall accused James II's officers of licensing absolutism with recourse to the "popish principle, disowned by all Protestants," which placed the right to America in the hands of Christian princes who had endorsed the conquest of "heathen" terrain. The "revolution in New England," he argued, had destroyed this false doctrine and transferred colonial property back to the "king's subjects": the people who had first cleared and planted the vacant wasteland. New England lobbyists appraised the Massachusetts Bay charter as not a flimsy document to be enacted or rescinded at the pleasure of the prince, but an "original contract" that installed inviolable structures for self-government—"the hedge to protect us from the wild beasts of the field."[38] The insurgents of 1689, Sewall affirmed, were engaged with their compatriots in Old England in a common struggle to uphold a God-given system of government by consent, against the "doctrine of Obedience and Non-Resistance, which a sort of men did of late . . . cry up as Divine Truth." The defense of Massachusetts and New York therefore hinged on the creation of a radical Whig orthodoxy within the domestic realm. As Sewall concluded, "no man does really approve of the Revolution in England, but must justifie that in New England also; for the latter was effected in compliance with the former."[39] Sewall, Mather, and their fellow authors concurred with Palmer that the legitimacy of actions in New England depended on the existence of a prior revolution in the three kingdoms. Where they differed was in the insistence that such an event had, indeed, happened.

Neither side was able to claim victory in the altercation over Massachusetts. The compromise charter, unveiled by the Committee of Trade in 1691, restored the rights of the Boston General Court as a colonial assembly, with power to nominate the governing council. All land grants issued by the court prior to 1685 were upheld, and the property rights of the occupants reaffirmed. The Committee of Trade recognized the territorial reach of the province by adding Maine, Plymouth, and newly conquered parts of French Acadia to its jurisdiction. But the Crown also arrogated to itself the right to appoint a governor, deputy governor, judges, and sheriffs, and to put these officers in control of military affairs not merely in Massachusetts, but also in Connecticut and Rhode Island. The arrangement finally struck a blow at the old godly commonwealth by mandating toleration for all Protestants in Massachusetts, and transferring the basis of suffrage from church membership to a property qualification.[40] Although the Bay Colony had re-established rights more extensive than those given to New York, New Hampshire, and Maryland—all now subject to a Crown-imposed governor *and* council—royal power had been made a permanent part of the political landscape, and jubilant claims of a return to rule by the Saints looked increasingly hollow.[41]

The Colonial Lobby and the Call for a Reformed Empire

The 1691 settlement forced a long-term alteration in the political strategy of the Bay Colony. Since, as Increase Mather believed, even the partial reinstatement of chartered liberties had owed to the intervention of domestic

Whig supporters, the Boston magistracy were now obliged to tighten the umbilical cord with the mother kingdom, in order to keep those networks of support intact. Voices across New England kept up the pressure on their Whig allies, seeking to nurture within the party a colonial vision that rejected at once the blanket animosities of the old Country commentators and the centralizing predilections of Tory courtiers. Representatives for Massachusetts and Connecticut entered the lobbying spaces in Whitehall and Westminster: active, as Henry Ashurst put it, "before ye Lords of Trade and ye Treasury . . . standing at ye stake, and fencing against friends & Enemies in yr cause."[42] Dispensing gifts, and organizing addresses of thanks to political allies, Ashurst joined a growing throng of lobbyists for the major colonies who were attempting to capitalize on the pressures of war and the lengthier parliamentary sessions in order to renegotiate the fiscal and military relationship with the Crown. A campaign by agents for Jamaica and Barbados overturned the raised duties on sugar and tobacco when the act of 1685 was due for renewal in 1693, convincing the Crown of the need to incentivize production when Atlantic markets were threatened by conflict.[43] As Douglas Bradburn has shown, wartime regulations empowered the Council of Virginia, through its London agents, to regulate the size and timing of the returning tobacco fleet, by limiting the approved quantities of hogsheads in such a way as to benefit large-scale planters, whose prices had collapsed amid the booming market of the 1680s.[44] The pressures and opportunities of a time of international conflict enlarged some areas of the English state, but also revealed its reliance on dispersed networks of agents—the more ingenious of whom found ways to align the public good with the advancement of their own particular interests.

In seeking out a new rubric for William's empire, agents for Massachusetts daringly made a virtue of the most contentious feature of their colony —its capacity to act as supplier and manufacturer of native commodities. This native economic potential, they argued, could be converted to the benefit of the mother kingdom if appropriate freedoms were extended to the merchants of Boston and other local ports. Entering into dialogue with the Committee of Trade in 1692, Henry Ashurst made the case for redirecting the English timber supply chain away from Scandinavia and the Baltic, promoting the firs of New England as a resource fit for the construction of the royal fleet.[45] By demonstrating its capability as a producer of naval stores, Ashurst and Increase Mather hoped ultimately that Massachusetts would gain license to develop its own shipbuilding industry, together with rights of command over maritime defense—making it a place of civil, military, and commercial authority within the frame of a decentered empire.[46] Proponents of the Bay Colony were able to engage in England a circle of Whig thinkers who had begun to question the more rigid features of the Navigation Acts, in recognition of the co-dependency of provinces and mother kingdom in a time of conflict. The political economist Francis Brewster advanced that Massachusetts should be set free to compete with Scandinavian timber merchants, and to export its native supplies directly into Spain and the Levant, where merchants could reel in "considerable returns in Bullion" and so increase the stock of coins circulating through the English territories.[47]

Among some authors, as Steve Pincus has shown, these attitudes denoted an emerging Whig openness toward freer trade in general, and a challenge to the "mercantilist" notion of the world's wealth as fixed and finite. If shipbuilders in Massachusetts or silk-throwers in the East Indies could produce useful material more economically than the English workforce, believed Henry Martin, then they should be encouraged, since imports conserved domestic labor, and allowed able hands in England to be put to more effective use.[48] For most of its newfound champions, however, support for Massachusetts rested less on a shift in economic philosophy than an expanded vision of the colony as now more fully a part of the English realm: worthy, after 1689, of being furnished with equivalent civil and commercial liberties. Overturning a prior animosity toward Massachusetts, Francis Brewster saw the Revolution as marking a moment of convergence between England and its colonies: a shared experience of tyranny vanquished and liberty reclaimed. The loyal participation of the Bostoners meant that the Crown should follow "the wisdom of the Romans," he believed, in "making the Privilege of a Roman Universal, through their whole Conquest."[49] Because the Bay Colony was now demonstrably working toward the same national and Protestant interest, it should be entrusted with greater commercial freedoms, and accepted as a suitable destination for English migrant labor.

Over the following generation, exchanges with supporters in the Old World gradually altered the public self-fashioning of the New England elites. In literature pitched at Old World readers, Bay Colonists strove to strip back old shades of "creolean" otherness, and refigured themselves as Whigs, Englishmen, and Europeans, now anxious to attain "loving converse with our Protestant Brethren, not be strange to them."[50] Dedicating his spiritual biography of his father to the scholars of Glasgow University in 1723, Cotton Mather recast the Boston magistracy as pillars of "polite" learning: admonishing in retrospect the excesses of the Salem witch trials and the "rash things done unto the Quakers" of Massachusetts, and linking the springs of piety in New England to the health of "the European waters that nourish it."[51] Through the 1690s, paeans in Boston print to the revolutionary actions of 1688–1689 were counterpoised by declarations of obedience to William as "emperor of America" that overturned the qualified and conflicted stance taken toward royal authority during previous reigns.[52] New Englanders positioned themselves as co-architects of the cleansed Protestant realm, welcoming its interventions in the New World, and often advocating policies of expansion in Canada or Central America that far exceeded the instincts of domestic Whigs.[53] Military protection from England could be given "encouragement and assistance," Henry Ashurst assured his Boston correspondents, since "wee are now happy in a Prince yt makes the Lawes his rule."[54]

Party Divisions and Colonial Policy, 1689–1695

While the Revolution in England was seen to have benefited Whigs disproportionately, the scope to enact a new vision of empire, one more conducive to the interests of party supporters, was constrained. It took until 1694 for Whig leaders to gain ascendancy in government. Before then, the political landscape on both sides of the Atlantic was conditioned as much by the influence of the "court Tory" persuasion, fronted by Nottingham and Carmarthen, that sought to reconstitute under William III many of the centralizing principles followed by the pre-Revolution Lords of Trade. The goal of tying colonies more closely to the Crown animated a new crop of governors who had been sent into the provinces on a mandate to establish more effective defenses against France, and was reflected in vocal opposition among Tory authors toward any idea of entrusting dominions with rights over defense and manufacturing. In America, as in the Old World, "industry has it first foundation in liberty," Charles Davenant accepted, but licensing naval bases in Boston and other colonial ports tipped the balance too far: raising the danger of disorderly colonies becoming like "offensive arms wrested from a nation, to be turn'd against it, as occasion may serve."[55] Running with this diagnosis, William's Tory ministers presided over the rehabilitation of the men emblematically associated with the Dominion of New England. Edward Andros, appointed governor of Virginia in 1691; Francis Nicholson, who gained supreme command over Maryland in 1693; and Edward Randolph, returning as surveyor general of the mainland colonies in 1691, were all positioned at a tactful distance from their old theaters of operation. But their promotions added to the anxieties raised in New England that an unprotected "Revolution" could slide all too smoothly into a "restoration."[56]

Many of the emerging confrontations took place within the confessional arena: a reflection of the ambiguous dual legacy left by the Revolution for Protestants across the English overseas world. At home, the 1689 Toleration Act had weakened the powers of the bishops, and delivered a precedent to encourage opponents of Anglican supremacy within the New World. In the overseas dominions, however, the specific measures that followed the fall of James II strengthened the Church of England—principally at the expense of Catholics, with the conversion of Maryland into a royal colony, and the purge of the Irish Caribbean interest, but also in directives imposed on New England and the Middle Colonies to grant Anglicans legal parity with other Protestants.[57] Bishop Compton of London, another Tory "survivor" of the Revolution, worked with privy councillors and Anglican merchants to promote a program of church-building and lay education in Maryland and the Middle Colonies.[58] These activities climaxed in 1701 with the creation of the Society for the Propagation of the Gospel (SPG), the missionizing arm of the Anglican episcopate. Its tripartite remit of evangelical activity among Indians, slaves, and settlers would be accompanied by a confrontational approach toward rival Protestants in colonial territories.[59] America, a locale for the threatened "godly" through much of the seventeenth century, figured in the 1690s as an arena for an embattled strain of High Churchmanship—confirmed when a smattering of English Non-jurors and Scottish Episcopalians, purged from the Presbyterian Kirk, crossed the seas to bolster the ranks of the colonial ministry.[60] Pennsylvania and the Jerseys provided especially contested ground, and church patrons campaigned to uproot the officeholding power of the Quakers, capitalizing on the allegations of illegal trade that followed the rise of Philadelphia as a commercial rival to New York.[61] A decade after the Revolution, William Penn complained that the "awful and charming words Church and King" still resounded across English America, creating "a dust wch weak eyes cannot see well through."[62]

By the middle of the 1690s, colonial policy had become a battleground for contending interpretations of political and religious orthodoxy in post-Revolution Britain. Allegations of Jacobitism, flung at Willian Penn as an erstwhile ally of James II, were cordially returned against local Tory leaders by their Quaker and Congregationalist opponents. Whig supporters in America played on reports of Jacobite toasts drunk by Crown officials in taverns and mansions in Virginia, judging Andros, Randolph, and their coevals to be so steeped in the inheritance of the Dominion of New England as to render their allegiance to William III distinctly questionable.[63] As conflicting groups looked for allies in the Old World, clashes in the dominions soon spun back into the parliamentary arena. In 1695, Henry Ashurst steered into the Commons the bill seeking posthumous reversal of the attainder placed on the New York insurgent Jacob Leisler, and framed the exoneration of the rebels as a defense of the principle of popular action against tyranny. While the preservation of a mixed Whig-Tory ministry under William III had blurred some of the party dividing lines, the Leisler debate restored old political alignments in their brightest colors. The veteran Whig Exclusionists William Brockman, John Arnold, and Sir Walter Yonge acted as tellers for the bill, which was pitted against a united cadre of Tory opponents.[64] Though Leisler's attainder was reversed on a slender majority, the New York experiences of revolution and counterrevolution had created domestic splits that crackled with the tensions of recent political history.

While Tory Anglicans regained the political momentum in the New World, Whig statesmen within the Williamite ministry struggled against the charge of indifference to the colonial interest, set against the higher priority they attached to upholding the Grand Alliance in Europe. Alarm over the expense of continental warfare, and the consequent disruption to the Atlantic and Mediterranean trade, had engendered Tory-colonialist disquiet as early as 1689. "Had we attended the sea, the French could have done little in Flanders," lamented the MP Thomas Clarges. "It goes to my heart that the king of England should be at the head of a Confederate Army."[65] These criticisms mounted as commitments in Europe took precedence over the provision of naval convoys and the fortification of colonial defenses, leaving merchant fleets prey to French privateers. "As to Traffick & the Navigation," fulminated a Bristol merchant in 1695, "there needs no information how wretchedly that hath been managed . . . & what an immense Treasure have the French taken in this War by our cursed negligence."[66] Before the cessation of the war in 1697, the size of British armies in Flanders swelled to 56,000. By contrast, a single marine regiment serviced the defense of the Caribbean, failed in an attempt to capture Martinique, and was withdrawn altogether in 1695, forcing colonists to draft servants and slaves into their own hastily raised militias.[67] Concern over England's shrinking "dominion of the seas" hastened the convergence of Tories outside the court and "Old Whig" dissidents into a new Country opposition, broadcasting its grievances in parliament and the pamphlet press.[68] Setting themselves up as defenders of the colonial interest, Country authors and MPs set out to reclaim old, idealized images of an English maritime empire. They presented an Atlanticist war strategy as an alternative to the emerging "Leviathan" state, with its taxes, impressments, and rising public expenditure. "A powerfull fleet at Sea . . . to be compassed by the help of trade," Charles Davenant maintained, was better suited to the English constitutional temperament than "a great standing army" that "will be dangerous to liberty," as well as doubtful in its value to the national interest.[69]

These clashes came to a head in 1695, after the king announced plans for the creation of a new, supervisory Board of Trade, to be allocated greater independence from the Privy Council in devising colonial and commercial policies.[70] While the reform responded to longstanding merchant complaints over the narrowness and inaccessibility of the old Committee of

Trade, the timing of the king's decision—shortly after he removed the remaining Tories from the Crown administration—together with the unsettled powers and uncertain accountability of the board, was a provocation to opponents of government policy. In a blast against "ministerial despotism," the new Country alliance precipitated a near crisis by seeking to impose parliamentary control over the appointment, management, and executive actions of the new body.[71] Their initiative, as a group of Bristol Whigs protested, would have unbalanced authority within the kingdom, putting the entire overseas apparatus out of the hands of the king's ministers, with "Cruizers and Convoys & Seamen" placed at the disposal of "a separate power" in parliament.[72] While the action was defeated, it confirmed the change in how colonial policy would be decided and debated. From the Leisler revolt to the beginnings of the Board of Trade, questions over the organization of the overseas world—which successive Stuart monarchs had determinedly kept out of Westminster—were now subject to the heat of the parliamentary arena. Disputes over the colonies had reopened the old schism between maritime and continental conceptions of England's national interest and national identity. The same debates stirred up animosities among opposition MPs toward a Dutch monarch, and shone a light on the unsettled state of the constitution in post-Revolution England.

The Board of Trade and the Persistence of Imperial Power

Ultimately, the structure of the Board of Trade represented less radical a break with the past than many supporters and critics had imagined. Disappointing widespread expectations of an enlarged unit that would include representatives of major port towns and the different spheres of overseas trade, the king instead plucked eight Lords Commissioners from within the Crown administration and made them accountable to both parliament and the Privy Council. Where the new board differed from the old Committee of Trade was in its clear Whig preponderance. Seven commissioners were publicly aligned with the party, with John Locke, veteran of the Shaftesbury patronage network, soon standing out among the most active appointees. The Tory identity of the eighth member, William Blathwayt—sole survivor of the previous regime—was already starting to weaken.[73] For

Whig leaders, the creation of the board offered a chance to wrest back the initiative in colonial affairs, challenging claims of party indifference toward the dominions, and heading off the grievances of merchants and planters by giving them a channel to the policymaking machinery. The activity of the commissioners intensified after the northern theater of conflict re-opened in 1696, with Anglo-French clashes in Newfoundland, Acadia, the Hudson Bay, and northwestern New York. Behind these actions was the looming reality of a Spanish succession crisis, with Louis XIV lodging claims over the Crown of Madrid, and all of its overseas dominions, on behalf of his grandson, the duke of Anjou. The Americas were becoming more central to the clash of European states. In adjusting to these realities, the board raised the importance of the New World in government deliberations, pushed the king into closer engagement with the overseas territories, and hastened the diminution of the old anti-colonial strain within the Whig Party.

More uncertain was the extent to which commissioners had altered the basic Restoration rulebook for colonial government, as many Whig supporters had counselled in 1689. The complexities of the new approach would be revealed in policies toward the overseas corporations that had been subject to especially lively Whig invectives after the Revolution. Ministers gratified the lobbying coalition of planters and "separate traders" in 1698 by breaking apart the monopoly of the Royal African Company and throwing open the West African markets to competition, subject to a 10 percent tax on goods other than gold and slaves, to support the coastal castles maintained by the old corporation.[74] In the same year, the government raised radical expectations by stripping the directors of the EIC of their corporate privileges. Yet, far from opening up the Asian trade, the Crown opted to create an entirely new East India Company, replete with Whig and Dissenting capital, but furnished with all the familiar monopoly powers.[75] Ministers engaged more readily with other forms of old Whig animosity toward the East India trade. A succession of statutes culminating in the Calico Act of 1700 banned the import of finished or printed Indian cloth, with a view to protecting domestic weavers and silk workers, and dampening demand for invasive luxury fabrics.[76] But while the customs burgeoned through sales in tea, coffee, and a spice trade revived with

Anglo-Dutch peace, the government proved unwilling to end commercial—and, to a more limited extent, territorial—enterprises in India, and remained attached to the principle of a monopoly company as a means to achieve those goals.[77] The effect of the reorganization was, ironically, to draw the Crown deeper into Asian affairs—conferring royal commissions on officials of the new company as "presidents" and "consuls for the English nation," in a bid to dignify their presence on the subcontinent.[78]

As William Pettigrew and George Van Cleve have shown, the terms of the Williamite debate over West Africa and the East Indies centered less on a battle between the virtues of free trade or monopoly power than the question of where corporations stood in relation to the needs of a European state at war. Beyond the preservation of forts and castles, the Royal African Company offered limited strategic and financial assets to the Crown. The East Indian interest, by contrast, was perceived to lend itself more readily toward company oversight, as a trade resting on the managed export of English bullion and requiring intensive regional diplomacy. The new directors supplied rapid confirmation of their value with a loan of £2 million to the exchequer.[79] Across the overseas world, the board's deregulation of the African slave trade proved the exception rather than the rule in Crown commercial policy. Traders and colonists had to fall into line with a legislative agenda focused on the protection of domestic manufacturing, against a background of rising concern over the loss of bullion through illegal coin-clipping, wartime expenditure, and diminished export markets.[80] Heeding the clamor of domestic producers, the Board of Trade maintained fiscal disincentives toward Caribbean sugar refining, blocked shipbuilding in New England, and singled out Massachusetts woollen manufactures as a particular threat to the customs and labor force of the mother kingdom, banning their export from the colony in 1698.[81]

The call for the Crown to strengthen its regulatory arsenal was heightened by the provocation of illegal trading in the Middle Colonies, and by colonial links to the Red Sea and Madagascar pirate networks that had brought Asian silks illicitly into New York and Philadelphia. A new Navigation Act of 1696 sanctioned the creation in America of admiralty courts staffed by Crown-appointed judges, and equipped to make sure, as the board commissioner John Pollexfen put it, that "all back doors could be shut" to unlicensed traffic, "and those Collonies made to have their whole dependance on England."[82] In an apt sign that centralization remained the basic premise of Crown policy, the moving spirit behind the reform was the veteran surveyor-general Edward Randolph: still "huffing & bouncing" his way through Whitehall, to the disgust of the governor of Pennsylvania.[83]

In the policies of the Board of Trade, the colonists encountered less of the expansion of political and economic liberties anticipated in 1689 than another aspect of the Whig worldview—the regulatory commercial model sketched out by Country thinkers like Roger Coke and Richard Temple, who had been deeply suspicious of the trading interests amassed by overseas dominions. The political thinking behind the new economic measures was illustrated when a body of Whig authors close to the board attempted to define the correct relationship between the Crown and the colonies, and aimed retrospectively to write any revolutionary implications for English America out of the events of 1688–1689. When a prince took possession of territory outside Europe, he was under no obligation to transfer all the "Rights and Priviledges" of the domestic realm, insisted William Atwood, a commonwealthman in 1689 whose radicalism did not extend beyond the borders of the English kingdom. Atwood backed the continuation of an EIC monopoly, and rose through the admiralty courts to become chief justice of New York in 1701. Appropriating and subverting radical Whig arguments, he professed that it would even be *improper* to export English common law and its attendant liberties overseas—no less errant than if William I had made England an "accession to Normandy" or for William of Orange to have imposed the writ of the Dutch States-General on the three kingdoms.[84]

These arguments echoed in many Whig circles. With a nod to old anti-colonial sensibilities within the party, the Bristol author and trader John Cary conceded that "all Plantations setled abroad out of our own People must needs be a loss to this Kingdome except they are imployed there to serve its Interest."[85] The only way to make sure that England "may not split upon the same rock" as the depopulated kingdom of Spain was to entrench colonial dependence on "the Head of this Empire, from whence all its Members do derive their Being, and must depend for their Support and Protection."[86] Cary identified the Revolution as a vital *domestic* moment: a restitution of the ancient constitution, and an affirmation that the "supreme imperial authority" resided collectively in "the King, House of Lords, and House of Commons in England." But if the sovereign form of the realm had been set back to rights, its relationship with outlying territories was unaffected. Indeed the establishment of a king-in-parliament monarchy brought the chance to convert colonial entities from disconnected Crown dominions into coordinated parts of an "empire of England," governed legislatively from Westminster. Legal rectitude and "reason of state," Cary concluded, still obliged English governments to follow the practices of "the Romans," from whose "Mighty Empire and Vast Dominions . . . we have principally learn'd the way of Settling and Managing of Colonies."[87] Colonial liberties, however desirable, could only ever remain a gift of the Crown, to give or to take away.

The reality of centralization and standardization gained some acquiescence in America by the later 1690s, as colonial leaders navigated the borderline between the defense of civil privileges and appeals to the Crown to bolster security in expectation of further international conflict. In 1698, William Penn collaborated with the Tory Charles Davenant in a plan for a "national assembly" that would seek out two delegates from every colony, under the oversight of the governor of New York, to "consider of wayes and meanes to support the Union and safety of these Provinces" through common subsidies and military quotas.[88] But where Penn's supporters were adamant that English America could be fortified by "better Correspondence & Commerce" between existing authorities, the Board of Trade was increasingly receptive to the argument, voiced by the New York anti-Leislerians Richard Daniel and John Nelson, that the intrinsic problem lay in the very existence of "so many petty governments," and their "independency" not merely from Whitehall, but from each other. It was this state of fragmentation, Nelson believed, that had made the English vulnerable before French Canada, where governors-general had been able to reap fuller resources from only a fraction of the number of settlers.[89] In this climate, political pressure would be placed on the "immunities and priviledges" claimed by the remaining proprietary colonies—Pennsylvania, Carolina, the Bahamas, and the Jerseys—and even the newly circumscribed chartered authorities of Massachusetts, Connecticut, and Rhode Island, which, the Lords Commissioners concluded by 1700, "have no ways answered the cheif design for which such large Tracts of Land" had been granted.[90] "Unamerican understandings," Penn lamented, had turned "our great men" against the "Constitution of these parts." The implications broke on the colonists in April 1701, when a Reunification Bill, drafted by the board, was put before the House of Lords, proposing to place every single "Independent Colony" under direct and permanent Crown control.[91]

At this point, in a sharp reversal of the colonial politics of twenty years, voices among the Tories now provided the most forceful resistance to the centralizing reforms mapped out by privy councillors. "Use the plantations in America very kindly, because they being so remote will soon be too strong to be forced," urged the jurist Edmund Bohun, appointed chief justice of Carolina in 1698.[92] Out of office and gravitating toward Country politics, a growing contingent of Tories were susceptible to these arguments. With party elders such as the earl of Bath and Lord Berkeley holding rights as proprietors in Carolina and the Jerseys, the privileges of "private governments" could be identified—together with the rights of the old East India and Royal African companies—as part of the panoply of "liberties and properties" threatened by the ever-encroaching, high-taxing Williamite state.[93] Employing the Jacobite polemicist Charlwood Lawton as his agent, William Penn assembled a cohort of Tory and opposition MPs to assist the lobbying initiatives that stalled and eventually strangled the Reunification Bill. Its passage remained unresolved until March 1702, when the death of the king terminated the parliamentary session and put an end to all bills not yet passed.[94]

Political Economy, Colonial Liberty, and the Whig View of Empire

Continuities in colonial policy through the 1690s serve, ostensibly, to back up the traditional view of English imperialism as a development that transcended shifts in regular politics—and support the equally well-worn case that Whigs jettisoned their old ideological allegiances once they gained opportunities to enter government. A closer examination reveals a more complex picture. Ministers certainly sat at odds with the interests of American landowning proprietors, and looked askance at the rights accrued by powerful families such as the Penns and the Calverts. Yet unlike the architects of the Dominion of New England, the Lords Commissioners still envisaged the political liberties of settlers, enshrined by robust and frequent colonial assemblies, as the lynchpin of civil life overseas. Appointed in 1698 as combined governor of New York and Massachusetts, the earl of Bellomont centralized the military affairs of the two provinces, but also cultivated support among old Leislerian magistrates and within the General Court in Boston, where he was identified as the chief protector of the Bay Colony against Tory and High Church attentions.[95] There was no better mechanism than representative assemblies, Bellomont's friend John Locke contended, for enabling the Crown "to know the true State of ye Country, or to try ye fitness of a Governor to manage ye people."[96] These arguments spoke to the practical limitations on the reach of the Board of Trade. While the king's "fiscal-military state" was focused on domestic and European goals, colonial governors remained dependent on established local elites for the creation of a basic defensive and bureaucratic apparatus, including the provision of troops and staffing of the admiralty courts.[97] But the stance of the board also reflected a diagnosis of the ills that had held back colonial development over the previous half century. Locke's analysis of the "Grievances of Virginia," written together with the clergyman James Blair in 1697, advocated an increase in regal power as the "prudent restraint" necessary not to subdue but to *support* settler freedoms, counteracting the influence of despotic governors, absentee elites, and profiteering patronage networks.[98] The extension of English liberties, for Locke, would consist not in grants to powerful landholders, but in legal arrangements that replicated the terms of the king-in-parliament monarchy at home, to the benefit of individual colonists.

In economic affairs, Whig ministers similarly sought to increase opportunities for local self-sufficiency, by encouraging new forms of productive activity within the framework of the Navigation Acts. The board conceded the right of settlers to "employ themselves" in "such things . . . as should be wanting for their own sustenance," and engaged with colonial spokesmen who sought to relieve planters from dependence on staple crops, which were deemed excessively vulnerable to glutted markets and seasonal blight.[99] John Locke's design for Virginia invited authorities to replenish the region with vineyards, silk works, and exports of hemp and flax: these suggestions reclaimed older, discarded visions of colonial development in a bid to temper the power of the tobacco barons, and restore vitality to economic life.[100] Turning their attention to the northern colonies, board commissioners resisted the idea of a licensed shipbuilding industry in Boston. But they pushed nonetheless toward a new economic partnership between Old and New England, centered on the production of "naval stores" (timber, pitch, tar, cordage) that would be ferried out for manufacture in English dockyards. The earl of Bellomont believed that "factories" in southern Connecticut would alter the regional flows of trade and maritime activity, steering the underemployed labor force northward from the Middle Colonies, and breaking the hold of piracy and illegal commerce over coastal communities.[101]

The aim of Whig ministers was to direct the colonial economy, but not to narrow it. Indeed, attempts to wean Middle Colonists away from the Red Sea pirates brought an exemption for the dominions from the 1700 Calico Act, opening up American markets to Asian imports now barred from the domestic realm.[102] Bringing together many of these ideas, it was no coincidence that Locke's notes gestured back to the Whigs' "Country" inheritance, containing as they did extensive transcripts of the works of Carew Reynell and Roger Coke.[103] By accommodating the old complaints, Whig authors aimed to show how colonies could be converted from a drain on the nation's resources into realms of "improvement." Breaking from the anti-colonial critiques of the 1670s, they now maintained that the goal of a state was not so much a large population in itself, as a population productively employed. By working to "excite Industry and Ingenuity," believed the Bristol merchant John Cary, governors of the overseas dominions would offer "a double Imployment to the People of England, first to those who raise them there, next to those who prepare Manufactures here wherewith they are supplied." As places of "earth, sea and labour," colonial economies would be re-founded on the supply of materials useful for domestic manufacturing.[104] Their peoples would be encouraged to prioritize virtuous industry over monolithic production of sugar and tobacco, privilege the practical over the luxuriant in the commodities they developed, and eschew the capture of territory for national self-aggrandizement alone.

These intuitions sat in some tension, nonetheless, with the long-term economic implications of decisions taken by the board in 1696–1698. The breaking of the Royal African Company monopoly was the prerequisite for the expansion of the slave trade, triggering a boom that forced 400,000 Africans into English America through the first quarter of the eighteenth century, to toil for the production of staple crops. Abigail Swingen has pinpointed the 1690s as the decade when the centrality of unfree labor to colonial development became a consensus: the single shared assumption uniting both sides in the vociferous clash over the powers of the Royal African Company. William Pettigrew has seen the proliferation of slave traffic as the logical result of a Revolution settlement centered on the civil and economic liberties of white Europeans, which left Englishmen accordingly "free to enslave."[105] The economic nostrums debated within the Board of Trade suggest, perhaps, a more fitful and contradictory relationship between coerced labor and the colonial ideologies of Williamite Whigs. Recent work by Holly Brewer has pressed the case for seeing the years between the formation of the Board of Trade and the collapse of the Whig Junto in 1702 as a thwarted radical moment, one that would incubate challenges to the sociopolitical primacy of English slaveownership as part of a larger confrontation with the Virginian tobacco lobby. As early as 1696, the board tried to overturn the Virginia law that enshrined hereditary slave status through the maternal bloodline. Under pressure from Whitehall, Virginian authorities overturned the "headright" system that awarded grants of land in return for the import of black Africans—which was blamed by Locke for the profligate parceling out of colonial land without regard to its proper cultivation.[106] Calls for the conversion of Chesapeake "negroes," which honored Locke's friendships with the evangelical lobbyists Morgan Godwyn and Robert Boyle, struck equally at the theological underpinnings of unfree labor.[107]

The ultimate failure of all these plans to arrest the growth of Chesapeake slavery pointed to the limits on the reach of the Lords Commissioners, as well as their own political inhibitions.[108] Any attempts to undermine slavery in Virginia were, in any case, absent from ministerial discussions of the West Indies, where bonded labor had struck deeper economic and cultural roots. The weakness of Locke's proposals was the lack of any answer to the demographic shortfall afflicting great tracts of English America. When the Board of Trade gave no public encouragement to migration out of England, even committed Whig supporters of economic diversification, such as Francis Brewster and John Poyntz, would still envisage a role for labor wrenched out of Africa.[109] Locke and his associates had, however, started a debate over colonial development that stretched beyond the party conflicts and ministerial overhauls of the early 1700s, and was echoed in the strong opposition voiced by Boston magistrates toward any extension of slavery into New England.[110] The debates on the Board of Trade kept alive competing political and moral economies: alternative visions of the way to shift plantations from large-scale, unprofitable estates toward bustling communities of independent smallholders. Into the mid-eighteenth century, Whig authors crossed swords over whether the better route lay in widening the slave markets and lowering prices on trafficked people, or in stimulating alternatives to staple-crop production that would enable planters to be fruitful and multiply, and to sustain larger families through greater economic autonomy.[111]

Politically and economically, Whig thinkers of the 1690s viewed the colonies through the lens of international conflict. For most statesmen and authors aligned with the party, conceptions of the English interest still focused on the continent closer to home—protecting the borders of Protestant states, fortifying Protestant minorities, and preserving pragmatic alliances with the Habsburg Crowns of Austria and Spain against the court of Versailles.[112] John Dennis's 1704 play *Liberty Asserted* took as its subject the territorial struggle for North America, and the plight of the Indian Five Nations menaced by French expansion. But its preface foregrounded "the Liberties of Europe" as the theater of world affairs most endangered by universal monarchy. The Iroquois tribes were made analogous to European polities, and the English acclaimed not as conquerors of the New World, but as liberators of all "free states" falling under the French yoke.[113]

Whig ministers rejected calls for further expansion in America. At the 1697 Peace of Ryswick, colonial territories were returned to pre-1689 boundaries, revoking conquests made by New Englanders in Acadia and—despite opposition from some board commissioners—restoring the French half of Saint Christopher, in return for guarantees from Louis XIV over the security of the Netherlands and the Protestant royal succession.[114] As we will see in Chapter 9, the same strategy produced fatally consequential opposition to the Scottish design for conquests on the Isthmus of Panama in 1698. If the Spanish Empire began to collapse, or even if the disputed succession fell to the Bourbons, William Blathwayt's preference was to transfer Central American dominions to the Habsburg house of Austria, on a pledge of free trade, rather than undergo the risk of bringing them "into our own hands."[115] A Lockean focus on "usefull Improvements" to existing colonies over the seizure of any new territories therefore abided by the needs of international politics.[116] The role of the colonies, reimagined by Whig authors, was to help the kingdom sustain its commitments across the Channel: to restore "the Ballance of Christendom . . . to its Proper Standard," as the merchant James Whiston put it, and equip England once more to "hold the Scales of Europe."[117]

These priorities gained expression in the confessional program devised by Whig ministers for English America. The Lords Commissioners championed the revival of the Protestant mission as a means to secure the Iroquois alliance, reaffirming the centrality of "religion" as "one of the strongest bonds of union" within an expanding domain.[118] But ministers also aimed to internationalize the initiative, integrating the spiritual labor of foreign Protestants as part of a larger project to rebuild links between the Church of England and reformed congregations overseas.[119] Pressured by Whig bishops, the newly formed SPG endeavored to "communicate their good designs to other Protestant Nations," sending fund-raising representatives to the reformed churches of Grisons, Geneva, and Saint Gallen, and mobilizing experienced Dutch and Huguenot missionaries for work with Amerindians in northwestern New York.[120] In line with this ethos, the board threw its weight behind programs—encouraged by Whig Churchmen, Congregationalist preachers, and Quaker leaders—to usher communities of Huguenot, Palatinate, and Vaudois refugees into America's uncultivated colonial spaces. Between 1698 and 1714, Crown policy provided transit into the New World for over ten thousand émigrés from "places where Protestants are grievously oppressed," with the Lords Commissioners appealing to Virginian authorities to support their resettlement through the public purse. Crown governors such as Lord Bellomont encouraged harmonious co-existence between established and newly arriving congregations, and chastised Anglican and Congregationalist authorities alike where they discerned signs of obstruction or recalcitrance.[121]

The presentation of colonial Christianity as a broadly Protestant, rather than specifically Anglican, entity would sit uneasily with the consciences of many SPG-backed ministers. Crown-sponsored pluralism was a scarcely easier prospect for members of the Congregationalist establishment in Boston, who still sought to maintain ascendancy over other Protestants in New England.[122] Yet for the Board of Trade, the assimilation of "foreign Protestants" into the colonial population supplied a vital part of the answer to doubts cast over the moral and economic value of the overseas dominions. Colonial America was in need of "improving" influences, professed William Penn, in rare agreement with Whitehall, for in too many enclaves, "the common people . . . are ill examples to the natives, little comfort to themselves, and not half the benefit they might be, to the Collonys & the Crowne."[123] Refugee Protestants would reinvigorate material and spiritual lives in English America, helping to rebalance colonial economies with their dexterity in silk work, wine production, and shipbuilding. The availability of new populations would allay domestic fears over migration out of the mother kingdom.[124] Above all, the opening of a new international refuge would strengthen the contribution of the colonies to the greater task impinging on the Protestant world. In the shadow of the French bid for the universal monarchy, John Locke believed, the future of the English dominions rested on the will of Protestants to rise above congregational differences, and to prove themselves "vigorous in their joint endeavours for the maintenance of the Reformation" wherever they were situated.[125]

By the later 1690s, the Whig champions of the Revolution found themselves in control of an empire toward which many members of their party were ambivalent. How resolutely ministers wedded themselves to the colonial interest is uncertain. The Board of Trade aimed to limit the quantity of territory taken by English subjects. Rejecting the "blue water" vision of detachment from the Continent, Whigs devised a colonial policy within a European context, with expansion tempered by the obligation to support foreign Protestant minorities and maintain the "balance" in the Old World and the New. But the management of the dominions remained an inescapably high priority, in view of the fiscal significance of American trade, the eruption of warfare across the Atlantic, and the host of interest groups that vied for supremacy in the Stuarts' overseas world. To this end, Whig commentators focused on the renovation rather than acquisition of colonies, and on the foundation of a moral and political economy to sustain the Revolution settlement outside Europe.

Ministers recuperated older ideas—from Protestant missionizing to mixed plantation economies—that had fallen from Crown policy in previous decades. They fixed their primary focus, however, on the virtue of the settlers themselves. Since the later 1660s, colonization had fallen into association with debauchery, disorder, and despotism: it had been indicted by its critics as an act of "carnal" vainglory, and as a venture that put "trade before religion," with ill effects for the mother kingdom as well as for the dominions themselves. Whig statesmen aimed to confute these accusations, with the "instructing and reforming of our own people," and with the revival of civil life through the integration of pious Protestant refugees. The goal of the Board of Trade was to wrench fragile dominions back into the service of liberty and true religion, restore the moral health of their populations, and reinvent English America as the possession of a wider Protestant world.[126]

9

The Colonies and the
Meaning of "Britain"

WHILE COMMENTATORS CONSIDERED THE VALUE AND VIABILITY of the colonies against the background of changing events in Europe, the English Atlantic world was being influenced simultaneously by shifting relations between the three kingdoms of the British Isles. In the early seventeenth century, the expansion of the Stuart realm had been neither conceived nor conducted as an exclusively English affair. Samuel Purchas may have focused on the creation of "Englandes out of England," but he also imagined "Royal Scotland, Ireland and Princely Wales, multiplying new Sceptres to his Majesty and his heirs in a New World."[1] Even after 1660, when the Navigation Acts defined the overseas world as more explicitly "English," scholars including James Howell, Edward Chamberlayne, and James Whiston spoke of the three kingdoms and the colonies collectively as parts of a "British Empire," bound under royal power.[2] Cohorts of Scottish and Irish compatriots were sprinkled through the overseas settlements. They were active in royal vessels and regiments; visible within commercial fleets; and, in many locales, absorbed within a loose colonial or creolean identity, which accommodated the blurred edges of religion and nationality. These inflows reflected the wider cosmopolitan realities of the Atlantic world. Through the course of the century, Dutch, Huguenot, German, and Sephardi Jewish communities had all entered and settled in the English overseas territories. But the ambitions of Scottish and Irish colonists carried especially potent implications because of the unsettled architecture of the polity from which they emerged.

By 1689, the terms of the dynastic union between England, Ireland, and Scotland were still contested, and many of the most delicate constitutional anomalies were being exposed in debate over the management of colonies. Unresolved conundrums persisted over whether colonial spaces were accessible to all subjects of the Crown, or whether a larger set of legal and commercial privileges accrued to the people of England, whose adventurers had pioneered the original settlements. If other kingdoms were *not* granted parity within the English colonies, were they at liberty to seek alternative spheres of interest outside Europe? These questions had brought dissension into Stuart politics through the seventeenth century. The scope for tension, however, rose to a head after the revolutions of 1688–1689, when the closer, wartime regulation of English overseas interests collided with the birth of patriotic, militantly Protestant movements in Scotland and Ireland, giving voice to calls for equal access to the Atlantic commerce, and seeking a release from the imperial stranglehold of the Westminster parliament. The famous product of these developments was the Darien design of 1697–1700, the failed attempt by Scottish adventurers to seize the Isthmus of Panama from Spain, and the trigger for a diplomatic crisis that shone a light on the danger of competing colonial policies emerging from within the British Isles.[3]

The political thought and political economy that informed colonial enterprises devised in Scotland and Ireland has been extensively considered by scholars including Allan MacInnes, Jane Ohlmeyer, David Armitage, and Louis Cullen.[4] Less well studied is the reception of these ventures in England, and their impact on debate over the colonies within the southern kingdom. Colonial schemes formed within Scotland and Ireland were infused with a rhetoric of national self-assertion, and the Darien design has, especially, been totemic to Scotland's older national narrative—traditionally characterized as the last stand of a waning, independent kingdom before its absorption into the Union of 1707.[5] But the politics of "Greater Britain" cannot be understood purely in terms of clashing national interests, or even rigid national identities. Advocates for Scotland and Ireland relied on networks of support within the English dominions, and even in England itself. Scottish and Irish voices inserted their arguments into divisions over colonial strategy, and contributed to the growth of colonial lobbies and colonial debates within the southern kingdom. The Darien design, conceived originally in London, was as much an intervention in English colonial affairs as a patriotic mission; an attempt to revive territorial and economic blueprints marginalized under Williamite governments, and challenge the direction of policy under the Board of Trade.

The colonization of the New World is commonly understood as an experience that entrenched structural inequalities within the Atlantic Archipelago, accelerating the political and economic domination of England over its neighbors.[6] That trajectory, however, appeared far from self-evident during the seventeenth century itself. In later Stuart Britain, political controversy was generated as much by the perceived danger of English colonies falling into dependence upon Scottish and Irish participation, and by the potential vulnerability of English trade in the face of competition from the other two kingdoms. Authors in all three kingdoms were united in the belief that prosperity rested on the ability to harness the markets of the New World, and establish favorable patterns of commerce outside Europe. Conversely, they shared the anxiety that overseas expansion, inadequately regulated, would unbalance the political and constitutional equilibrium within the composite monarchy. These disputes threw open the unexamined frictions of a loose dynastic union, which had failed to bind its component parts together within a common national interest, let alone a single state apparatus.

The Nature and Limits of English Power, 1660–1688

A powerful turn in modern historiography has brought an understanding of English settlement in the New World as resting on foundations of conquest and colonization *within* the Atlantic Archipelago. In particular, the English plantation of Munster and Ulster between 1558 and 1625 has been identified as the crucible for colonizing practices exported across the Atlantic: large-scale settlement, the transference of landholding and juridical structures, and a taxonomy of civility and barbarism that was applied to anatomize indigenous peoples and so justified their subjugation.[7] Connections between colonizing enterprises in Ireland and America still flickered through the later seventeenth century. From the lords Baltimore to William Penn, and the organizers of the New England mission, Robert Boyle and

Daniel Gookin, projectors and promoters quarried fiscal resources, human capital, and ideological stimulus out of previous Irish enterprises to fortify their American designs.[8] But by 1660, contemporaries were just as alive to the differences between the two environments. Lacking the centuries of contact and familiarity that preceded Elizabethan plantations in Ireland, the English in the New World had failed to integrate Amerindians in a manner comparable to the co-option of Gaelic and "Old English" peoples as laborers, tenants, officials, and even, in some cases, political leaders in the Irish administration. Conversely, Ireland drew in no enslaved labor force, and yielded no lucrative staple crop.[9] By the point of the Restoration, moreover, it was increasingly difficult to see the Irish kingdom as offering a settled, prescriptive model for English America. Through the 1640s, the bloodshed of the Civil Wars and the thwarted Catholic resurgence had exposed the insecure foundations of Elizabethan and Jacobean reforms—and, in the eyes of many projectors, returned the country to virgin conditions.[10]

After 1660, Ireland stood more commonly in a competitive than in a complementary relationship with the Western Atlantic colonies, with "improvers" in the two zones often bidding against each other for finite Crown resources. The one ostentatious attempt under Charles II to transfer strategies from east to west—the planned imposition of Poynings' Law on Virginia and Jamaica—was discarded as unsuited to the management of more distant territories, if not inimical to the liberties of English settlers.[11] Instead, as the New World colonies came into greater maturity, political influences were as liable to travel in the opposite direction, with developments in America serving to unsettle the delicate relationship between the English and Irish kingdoms. This trend became especially apparent when cohorts of Ireland's "colonized" peoples began to enter into the imperial venture farther west, identifying the dominions as a place to advance Catholic power and prosperity. As we have seen, the development of the Leeward Islands as an Irish Catholic enclave gave vent to the firestorms erupting in the 1670s over the growth of "popery and arbitrary government." Equally vigorous controversies arose in Westminster over the trading patterns that established America as the marketplace for over half of Ireland's beef exports. The Irish had "interloped" without legal warrant into the commerce of the Caribbean, complained the MP and former Leeward

Islands governor Sir Charles Wheeler in 1672. Their actions, he warned, threatened not merely to raise the wealth and ambition of Irish Catholics, but also to slice the English realm apart from a vital stream of commercial revenue.[12] These attacks exacerbated the tension between English parliamentarians and West Indian planter elites, who largely welcomed the competition provided by Irish imports—a politically safer alternative, Governor Thomas Lynch believed, than dependence on supplies from New England.[13]

In an ideological environment where "every nation is endeavouring to possess the trade of the whole world . . . every city to draw all to itself," as the Scottish scholar Andrew Fletcher put it, the concern that colonial wealth could upend domestic political balances raised controversy *within* as well as between the Stuarts' kingdoms.[14] In 1695, a lobbying force of Bristol merchants took to parliament their anxieties over "the growing greatness of London," as a force that threatened to "swallow up the Trade of England" to the impoverishment of other communities.[15] Disputes between English and Irish interests brought additional peril, however, because they exposed ambiguities within the constitutional framework of the polity. Nominally, Ireland was a sovereign kingdom: the Henrician settlement of 1541–1542 had affirmed its status as a polity governed through autonomous legislative institutions. Yet the commercial freedoms ceded to Irish subjects in America had been offered on an entirely different premise—that Ireland was a conquered and planted province: a country "not onely under one King with us," as the Council of Trade averred, "but [which] belongs to & is an appendix of the Crowne of Engl," so that "Lawes made in Parliament . . . doe bind them."[16] Imagined in these terms, the relationship conferred upon parliament the right to control the trade of Ireland, and to take legislative action if it threatened to drag commerce away from English ports.

MPs flexed their muscles with amendments to the Navigation Acts in 1671–1672, banning the direct import of valuable American commodities into Irish markets, on grounds, recorded by Edward Dering, that "we have the same power to charge Ireland that we have of other plantations," and, "since we maintain it, it is but reason we should govern it."[17] Such measures were not, however, enough to allay English merchant anxieties; Irish *exports* to America remained lawful, and many Catholic traders simply acquired London leasehold properties in order to continue their involvement with the Atlantic import markets.[18] By 1695, the Irish still "supply all ye West Indies wth provisions, & have beat us out of that Trade by the Exchange," declared a petition presented to the Bristol MP Sir Thomas Day. If these activities continued unabated, the effect would be to "make England depend on Ireland when our Trade is removed thither, wch will also draw over our People."[19] The Irish penetration of markets and plantations was exposing the contradictions within a colonial experiment that relied on the resources of a composite monarchy, and all of its subject populations, but demanded the subordination of one component by another.

Scotland presented a contrasting picture. While the northern kingdom was recognized as a sovereign polity, "wholly independant of it selfe and not subject to ye Crowne of England," in the words of the Restoration Council of Trade, the consequence of separate status was legal exclusion from the colonial domain.[20] After the Navigation Acts were passed, individual Scots could still enter into the colonies, on English-owned vessels with a three-quarters English crew. Some were able to hold public offices, following the precedent of Calvin's case (1608), which had extended rights of common nationality to English and Scottish subjects within each other's territories. But, like members of all other foreign nations, Scots were denied the right to export manufactured materials on their own ships, or to ferry back American goods without prior passage through an English port. These terms reflected, in part, demographic realities. As late as 1700, only about ten thousand Scots resided in the Stuarts' colonies. But Scottish interests in America had widened through the century: merchant settlers had entered Barbados in the 1640s, while the earls of Stirling and the ducal house of Hamilton had staked claims over contested land in Long Island and southern Connecticut.[21] A slow but distinct rise in Atlantic activity stirred the belief that Scotland possessed rights to the emergent colonial territories equal to those held by the other Stuart kingdoms. In 1670, the Edinburgh Parliament acted on the idea, endorsing the transportation of felons and "delinquents" to "His Majesties Plantations," in imitation of English use of the overseas territories.[22]

In this context, the Navigation Acts would be portrayed in Scottish commentaries as a declaration of economic warfare, condemning the northern kingdom to decline by stifling "Foreign Trade, which gives Life to all Manufactures, and increases the value of Land, by giving Encouragement to Improve it," in the words of one parliamentarian.[23] As Allan MacInnes and Esther Mijers have shown, the actual impact on the Scottish economy is questionable.[24] Old merchant links with the United Provinces remained buoyant through the seventeenth century, while Scots developed acumen in the Baltic carrying trade, and stretched commercial fingertips into Sweden, Poland, and Westphalia—the principal magnets for a "forgotten diaspora," which eventually included around forty thousand people.[25] Neither were the bars imposed by English parliaments sufficient to prevent Scottish involvement in the Atlantic world. Associations with several colonies were kept alive by a bustling community of Scottish merchants resident in London.[26] Just as Spanish affiliations had provided avenues for Irish Catholics into the Caribbean, so the Dutch free ports at Curacao and Tobago created openings for Scots to break into the trade of English America.[27] A sizeable quantity of plantations in Scottish hands on Nevis and Antigua had reached prosperity by the later 1670s, and through the connections forged with Glasgow merchant houses and sugar refineries, traces of West Indian wealth wound back into the kingdom.[28] "Famous are the Scots," mused John Houghton, "who tho they have no Plantation, yet run about, and disperse themselves, to take possession of every corner of the known World."[29]

Yet if the economic consequences of the Navigation Acts could be contested, a public *perception* had arisen, nonetheless, that Scotland's material weaknesses flowed from a failure to create regulated colonies on the English model. "What matters," believed the Chesapeake merchant John Stewart, was whether a Scotsman enriched himself only from labor in the English dominions, in which case he worked mainly to enlarge the traffic of the southern kingdom—or, more beneficially, "if he gains riches from goods Imported to Scotland from a Scots Colony," or, at least from "an English Colony belonging to a Scotsman living in Scotland." Following this logic, it was only when Scotland possessed sovereign powers over colonial settlements, and economic liberties to develop them as its interests demanded, that individual trading exploits would nourish the greater body politic.[30] For Stewart and sundry other commentators, the problems seeping into later seventeenth-century Scotland—perceived overpopulation, underemployment, and civil and religious broils—replicated the maladies afflicting England at the beginnings of the Elizabethan colonial venture. Accordingly, they required the same remedy: a centrally planned undertaking to recover the balance of trade through managed migration, the export of native manufactures into overseas plantations, and then the import and re-export of colonial produce.[31] On this reasoning, the Edinburgh parliament slashed duties on imported tobacco in 1673.[32] In 1681, a committee of trade was convened on the order of the Council of Scotland, with an appeal to projectors to put forward designs for national enrichment overseas.[33] Under ideological pressure, if not economic necessity, a consensus had been created, believed the East Jersey promoter George Scot, "that it is a Nationall Interest to advance in generall the design of a Plantation, hence to America."[34]

Provocative as this rhetoric was, the two Scottish designs that came to fruition in the 1680s—the settlement of former Covenanters in southern Carolina, and the Quaker-led migration into East Jersey—were constructed, more cautiously, under the umbrella of English imperial authority.[35] Crucially, both endeavors capitalized on currents of pro-Scottish sympathy within the overseas dominions, among governors and assemblymen anxious about shortages of white labor and ill-disposed toward the regulatory restrictions that had allowed London and Bristol merchants to narrow markets and dictate prices. With hundreds of potential soldiers and servants left to "wander in Poland & Germany to serve other Princes," Governor Lynch complained, the Navigation Acts had cut off "the Nerves & Sinews" of Jamaica, to the benefit of regional adversaries.[36] For other voices, Scots became vital to the moral armoring of the English dominions. The clergyman John Beale envisaged the "plaine and hardy breeding" of Scottish frontiersmen as a restorative influence over colonies struggling to sustain their Protestant virtue, and a counterpoise to the luxuriant influences borne in from London and Dublin.[37] In 1689, the planter Edward Lyttleton would propose, only semi-satirically, that Barbados be handed over to Scottish governance: the northern kingdom, he believed, having demonstrated a more generous appetite in "working merrily for the Plantations," free of the anti-colonial prejudices vented in the Westminster parliament.[38] For some critics, the defense of Scottish and Irish participation excited challenges to the entire philosophy of statutory constraints on colonial commerce. The Tory jurist Edmund Bohun lacerated the Navigation Acts as inimical to "the great Designe . . . to spread Commerce, Arts, Manufactures, and by them Christianity from Pole to Pole." If the Crown returned to the proper Roman model of extending empire through acquiring land rather than forging commercial monopolies, Bohun maintained, further New World conquests would create "trade enough for England, Scotland and Ireland," so that all three kingdoms "may drive all they can wthout envying each being three sisters under one common father."[39]

More consequentially, many Scottish and Irish enterprises came with a level of backing from within the Stuart court. James, duke of York handed out licenses to Scottish merchants active in his New York proprietary, and promoted Scottish settlers onto the provincial council.[40] The second earl of Clarendon, appointed to the Irish lord lieutenancy in 1685, imagined the scent of spices in the air at the port of Kinsale, and hoped that "I shall not be thought less an Englishman for proposing what is for the benefit of Ireland . . . since it is his Majesty's."[41] For twenty years, the Crown pushed sporadically to widen the imperial infrastructure. The governance of Tangier— outside the Navigation Acts—provided a microcosm of an alternative, "British" pathway for the overseas dominions, with lawyers, surgeons, soldiers, and traders drawn out of Scotland and Ireland into the governing infrastructure.[42] For some circles at court, these developments forced a contemplation of deeper changes to the structure of the monarchy. Between 1661 and 1670, the abortive push for first a commercial, and then a full parliamentary, union between England and Scotland was shot through with colonialist political and economic ideology—perceptions of the advantage to be gained from "an encrease of traders," as one treatise argued, when "the English Plantations want people, and yet England [is] too much dispeopled by them" to surrender more of its own subjects.[43] Some Tory scholars called for the integration of Irish representatives into Westminster, as the best way to control the kingdom. Full union provided the route through which "a conquered nation" could be "restored to all Civill and Military Powers," as William Petty proposed; "twisted in a Cord with England and Scotland," in the words of John Houghton, the combined polity would become "too strong for all Forreign Powers either to break or weaken."[44] For these authors, the logic of decentering colonial trade pointed toward political *centralization* and the creation of a constitutional framework that could tie separate places of commerce into a shared national endeavor.

By 1689, the Stuarts' overseas world had been exposed to two, colliding constitutional visions. Westminster parliamentarians imagined the infant empire as an arena forged from the sacrifices of the southern kingdom, and the Navigation Acts as a blessing "wch the English are bound to cherish as a Childe of their owne," in the words of the Council of Trade, to prevent "the fruits of the English Labour" being whisked out of the realm.[45] By contrast, the advocates of a pluralized British vision captured the colonies as *monarchical* rather than English: as places properly open to all subjects, at the dispensation of Stuart princes. The "manadgment of forraign trade," believed the duke of Lauderdale, as secretary of state for Scotland, was a privilege that belonged "to the king as his prerogative."[46] The Crown, on this analysis, would be diminishing its imperial authority at home, as well as its manpower abroad, if it allowed any single parliament to sequester authority over the territories established outside Europe.

The Three Kingdoms, the Atlantic World, and the Revolution Settlement

The revolutionary experiences of 1688–1689 opened the sluice gates for all the suppressed national tensions festering within the English Atlantic world. In Irish Jacobite circles, the military resistance by planters in the Leeward Islands gave stimulus to calls for fuller separation from the English realm, and a comprehensive rearrangement of the imperial framework, in the event of a second Restoration. The Catholic scholar Nicholas Plunkett believed that the buoyancy of Irish commerce, and the "parcel of privateers" at its disposal, gave his country the means to "overtop" English competitors, and to flourish in imitation of "those master traders, the Hollanders" as an "independent nation" within the "British Empire."[47] Though Jacobitism was defeated in Scotland and Ireland by 1692, the Crown enjoyed scarcely more comfortable relations with the militantly Protestant parties now brought to ascendancy, in the name of the Revolution, in both kingdoms. Through the 1690s, the radicalism unleashed within the Edinburgh Parliament caused particular disquiet among Williamite loyalists, who were confronted with the resurrection of the Presbyterian Church, and an invocation of the language of godly, elective monarchy, to justify the deposition of James VII. "Adieu any temper of moderation, adieu unione," lamented the earl of Tweeddale, "as the men are mor violent then those who went befor soe will ther government."[48] Many of the tensions between competing post-revolutionary regimes spilled out into the Atlantic setting, as authors in all three kingdoms sought to reconceptualize their interests in the commerce and politics of the overseas dominions.

While Irish Catholic planters were purged from public office in the Caribbean, the more pragmatic post-Revolution governors proved successful at reintegrating the community into the lawful life of the islands. Spared the expected wave of confiscations and expropriations, Catholic settlers retained a stake in the tranquillity of the domain. Planting families and their relatives were well represented among the signatories to the Articles of Limerick, who in 1691 struck terms for peace and submission to the Crown.[49] A smattering of Irishmen served loyally in the Caribbean militias through the reign of Queen Anne, when war returned to the West Indies, and governors in the Leeward Islands were compelled to mobilize against French invasions in 1710, 1711, and 1712.[50]

Opportunities for individuals did not, however, translate into any greater leverage for the Irish kingdom itself. The legislative restrictions on the Irish economy were enlarged under the Board of Trade, with the 1696 Navigation Act barring the import into the kingdom of *any* American goods that had not first made landfall in England.[51] During the decade of wartime disruption, MPs from both parties began to graft onto Ireland the same economic anxieties—over shortages of English bullion and declines in exports—that had previously hardened attitudes against the American colonies. Ireland was bracketed together with Massachusetts as two territories with wayward political tendencies, merchant fleets, and broad-based manufacturing economies that, if unchecked by political intervention, could take the traffic of the Atlantic world out of English hands.[52] These sentiments took legislative form in 1698–1699 with the passing of the Woollen Acts— blocks on the export of wool out of Ireland and the American colonies, with encouragement for landowners to turn instead toward linen production, which was considered less threatening to English producers.[53] The political provocation of the law lay in its challenge to an industry in which Irish Protestants had a visible stake. The constitutional implications of English MPs legislating for Irish affairs were even more inflammatory, in a decade when Protestants had gained ascendancy over the Dublin parliament and were becoming increasingly protective of that body as a means of safeguarding their own privileges.[54]

The reaction to the Woollen Acts, voiced in polemical campaigns in Dublin and London, forced into the open half-buried questions over the legal consequences for Ireland arising from the Elizabethan plantations, and over the relationship between that kingdom and the colonies developing in America. The Protestant scholar William Molyneux, author of the most famous intervention in the debate, denounced the woollen restraints as the culminating point of a chain of "innovations" from Westminster, beginning with the Navigation Acts, which had cut a swathe through the sovereign liberties guarded for over four centuries. Molyneux enunciated a vision of Ireland as an autonomous trading kingdom within the Stuart empire, with "New English" planters bolstered by the constitutional freedoms won originally by Gaelic princelings and Norman barons. By acting without regard to these ancient privileges, he argued, English ministers had stripped the kingdom illegally down to the status of the American provinces: violating just as brazenly the "gothick" principle of government by consent, and the more recent inheritance of the 1688 Revolution.[55] While these civic republican strains did not command consensus among all Irish Protestant commentators, the crux of opposition to the Woollen Acts was nonetheless a reassertion of fundamental distinctions between Ireland and the American plantations. The Dublin jurist Richard Cox conceded the "provincial" and dependent status of his kingdom, but distinguished between "colonies for trade" and "colonies for empire," putting Ireland into the latter of the two categories. American dominions, as "colonies for trade," could legitimately have their commerce tethered because their rationale was to advance the economic interests of the mother kingdom. Conversely, the function of a "colony for empire" was to "keep great countries in subjection" and prevent "the charge and hazard of constant standing Armies" falling to the Crown.

The only way to fulfill this goal in Ireland, Cox believed, was to empower the colonists (the Protestants) and enable them, through commerce and manufacturing, to provide for their own defense.[56]

These arguments met with a condemnatory resolution in Westminster and a stream of confrontational ripostes from defenders of English merchant interests—including many of the same authors who had taken to print to support restraints on the trade of the American colonies.[57] Since the reign of Elizabeth, Ireland, no less than English America, had been a place of conquest and plantation, maintained the Bristol merchant John Cary— and it was on this foundation alone, more than any set of mythologized medieval liberties, that Protestant magnates could legitimize their landed possessions. Colonies across the world, he advanced, were designated in different ways—some, like Ireland, had been dignified as "kingdoms," while others had been denoted as provinces, dependencies, and viceroyalties "according to the Humour or Fancy of Princes." But whatever the appellation, every dominion created by conquest and settlement was subject to the same "higher kind of law" inherent in the "Imperial Constitution," which demanded submission to a "supream legislature." Law-making institutions in Ireland, as in America, existed to *shadow* the constitution of the mother kingdom. But these arrangements did *not* allow the "criolians" to operate independently of the power that had put them in their place. Otherwise, by the same logic, there could be no reason to deny the same enlargement of liberties to "those who settled in our Plantations in America . . . and what a Jumble of Laws should we have then?"[58]

Responses by Cary and other proponents of the new laws echoed controversies emerging in America: in particular, the conflicts over illegal trade and insubordination by proprietary governments that had sparked the 1696 Navigation Act, and would prepare the ground for the Reunification Bill of 1701. The passing of the Woollen Acts was driven by English fears over loss of authority in the Atlantic world, in the face of competing institutions and alternative centers of commerce, from Boston and Philadelphia to Dublin. "Since I see they are so apt to be forgetful of their Duty," suggested the political economist Simon Clement, the Crown should place an inscription on the wall of every parliament or assembly in Ireland and America, to affirm:

that this Island (or Province) is a Colony; that England is our Mother Countrey; that we are ever to expect Protection from her in the Possession of our
Lands; which we are to cultivate and improve for our own Subsistence and
Advantage, but not to Trade to or with any other Nation without her Permission; and that 'tis our incumbent Duty to pay Obedience to all such Laws as
she shall Enact concerning Us.[59]

At the close of the seventeenth century, the politics of English plantation in
Ireland and America remained—as in the reign of Queen Elizabeth—
closely intertwined. But if Ireland had once been the laboratory for imperial designs and colonial ideologies, the relationship was being inverted. As
the management of the Atlantic economy became more critical to Crown
finances, so the pressures and precedents of English America were refram-
ing government policy within Britain itself, and altering the language and
practice of debate over the future of the composite monarchy.

The Darien Design and the Appeal to English Opinion

In sketching out the idea of Ireland as a distinct kingdom, immune from
interference by Westminster, William Molyneux reached instinctively for
the example of Scotland.[60] Through the later seventeenth century, however,
the practical meaning of Scottish sovereignty was falling into doubt, amid
anxiety over the disproportion in riches between the northern and southern
kingdoms, and the impact of English colonial wealth on the balance of the
dynastic union. These strains heightened through the Williamite-Jacobite
War of 1689–1692, which came close to bankrupting the administration in
Edinburgh, and when successive harvest failures created a devastating fam-
ine that over a decade would decrease the Scottish population by more than
10 percent. Out of these pressures emerged the Darien design; the plan
concocted by the newly formed Company of Scotland to plant a colony on
the Isthmus of Panama (Darien) and establish an independent settlement
in America, as a means to reclaim providential favor and material prosperity for the nation.[61] In appealing to the sensibilities of Edinburgh parliamentarians, the scheme was introduced as a patriotic call to arms. But
Darien was also the brainchild of many of the same networks of aristocratic
patrons, merchants, and political speculators who had versed themselves in

the commerce of the Stuarts' overseas world through the previous generation, and had formed affinities with English governors in the West Indies,
East and West Jersey, and Carolina.[62] The Company of Scotland relied on
political connections south of the border, channeled the vocabulary of English debates over empire, and developed its design in expectation of eventual English support.

With English, Dutch, and Sephardi Jewish merchants accounting for ten
of its nineteen-strong board of directors, the origins of the company were
not exclusively or identifiably Scottish at all.[63] Its original focus was the
capture of colonies in southwest India, with agents seizing on the disarray
of the Asian trade as the EIC monopoly came under political pressure, and
raising £600,000 from appeals concentrated among "separate traders" in
England.[64] When its activities were exposed, and summarily denounced in
the Westminster parliament, several critics cast doubt on the integrity of
the company's name, claiming to detect an English interloping unit that
advanced itself behind the *shield* of Scottish sovereign rights.[65]

The shift toward the Americas corresponded with the reinvention of the
company as a vehicle for the national interest, after the directors reopened
their subscription books in Edinburgh in February 1696, to much public
fanfare.[66] These actions were in part a response to provocation from the
Westminster parliament. The 1696 Navigation Act moved to bar Scots
from entering into public positions in America, in a decree overturned
three years later on the advice of the attorney general.[67] But under the guid-
ance of William Paterson, the London-based banker and former agent
for the Massachusetts Bay Colony, the altered design still drew heavily on
English influences.[68] Since the 1650s, English authors had cast eyes over
Panama as an apparently weak link in the chain of the Spanish Empire,
as a place of restive Indians and unsettled colonial authority, and—most
importantly—as the "doorway" for a possible Pacific route through to the
trading stations of India, China, and Japan. Many of these possibilities had
been introduced to domestic opinion by the buccaneers' raid under Henry
Morgan in 1671: in the wake of the attack, Governor Lynch had worked
strenuously to suppress reports of the riches and vulnerability of the isthmus.[69] By the 1690s, English interest had been revived amid doubt over
the future of the Habsburg colonial territories, against the background of

the disputed Spanish succession. The literature produced by Morgan's associates—Lionel Wafer, William Dampier, Basil Ringrose—circulated on the Board of Trade in London, as it had within the Company of Scotland. Its reception gave rise to the near-identical conclusion: that "it would be no very difficult matter for any European Prince or State to make some secure settlement . . . and by a faire correspondence with the natives to ingage them in Treaties of Friendship and defence against all manner of Enemies."[70]

Pushing their plans into the public domain, projectors for the Company of Scotland appropriated these older readings of power and geography in the Americas. In sketching out ideas for their new settlement, they aimed simultaneously to recuperate certain blueprints for empire that had been sidelined under the Board of Trade, appealing to constituencies of English traders and planters whose profits had been attenuated by warfare. In homage to his original Eastern strategy, Paterson turned to the model of the free port—which had been marginalized after the passing of the Navigation Acts, and discredited by failure at Tangier, but kept alive within the EIC— as the commercial model for Bombay and Madras.[71] Paterson identified Darien as the potential "Emporium and Staple for the Trade of both Indies," an entrepôt coaxing in merchants of all religions and nationalities, on the anti-mercantilist premise that "trade is capable of increasing trade, and money of begetting money to the end of the world." Reclaiming the cosmopolitan language of the "empire of the seas," he pictured an open Panamanian market as the "magnet" to "bring Empire home to its proprietors Doors," reeling in the treasures of disparate continents without incurring for its possessors "the fatigues, the expences . . . the Guilt and the blood" of territorial conquest.[72]

Yet, as it cast around for support, the company also reopened other, much more militant colonial designs persistent among the pirates, treasure-seekers, and Campeche-log-cutters in the English Caribbean. For these audiences, Darien could be vaunted in a very different light, as a vantage point over the passage of the Spanish treasure fleet; even as a springboard for conquests deep into mine-rich South America.[73] In successive treatises, and addresses to the Church of Scotland, the blueprint for an irenic emporium gave way to a fiery, martial Protestantism, transmitting visions of Spanish America as "the Antichrist's pouch by which he main-taines his War against the Church," and calls to liberate and convert the Indians, laced with rebukes of English colonists for their neglect of missionary duties.[74] On these foundations, the company invited English projectors to participate in an enterprise that would overcome all the frustrations of a century of New World colonization.[75] The seizure of Panama by combined Anglo-Scottish arms became a means to "increase the strength and riches of the Isle of Brittain," the directors insisted to the Privy Council in 1698, in a memorial subsequently put into the public domain. The benefits would be felt equally on both sides of the border, they maintained, as befitting a realm "under the Government of one Monarch, of one Religion and interest and [which] can have no different friends or enemies without endangering the whole."[76]

Beneath the patina of Presbyterian patriotism, the Darien design represented not simply a project for Scotland's particular regeneration, but one of an array of competing attempts to remoralize and revitalize the colonial enterprise after the 1688 Revolution. The Presbyterian radical Robert Ferguson, a former subscriber to the New England Company, imagined the propagation of the Gospel among the Panama Indians as a Protestant ecumenical moment, an essential part of the common struggle against popery and universal monarchy that transcended the splits between reformed congregations. Anglicans, he professed, should "be thankful to God, that the *Reformed Religion* is like to obtain some footing where it never had any," even if it was to flower on the isthmus under "a Form of Ecclesiastical Government and Discipline ... different from those of the *Church* of *England*."[77] In view of Paterson's New England associations, it was unsurprising that these arguments gained an especially fervent reception in Massachusetts, where they capitalized on the post-revolutionary moment of reengagement between the Bay Colony and the greater Protestant world. Prayers pronounced in Boston chapels in 1698 showed an enthusiasm for Darien that dwarfed the ambivalent reaction, forty years earlier, to Cromwell's Western Design.[78] Scouring the Bible for portents, Cotton Mather began the composition of "a Compleat System of the Christian Religion ... back'd with irresistible Sentences of Scripture," and "turn'd into the Spanish Tongue." Anticipating triumph in Panama, he readied himself to "cast this Treatise, into the midst of the Spanish Indies . . . not knowing how great a matter a little Fire may kindle."[79] Paterson and Mather envisaged at once the expansion and decentering of the empire, as ways to bring about its purification by Protestant virtue. Involvement in new conquests would raise up Boston and Edinburgh as places of authority equal to London, with a proportionate right to influence the direction of the Stuart realm.

Darien and the Crisis of Dynastic Union

Freighted with these hopes, the company had mobilized overwhelming consensus and harvested almost a quarter of the money in Scotland by July 1698, when 1,200 settlers sailed out from the port of Leith.[80] While "I believe . . . that it will not succeed so well as expected," confessed the secretary of state, Viscount Seafield, "no man [that] desires to be well esteemed of in his own country will be persuaded to oppose what is for the interest of the company."[81] The political provocation proved, however, to be too great a gamble. As late as August 1697, the Board of Trade debated the possibility of lending support to the scheme.[82] But by the end of the year, commissioners had swung toward opposition, faced with a project that not merely challenged English commercial interests, but also assailed the basic tenets of Williamite foreign policy and the approved prescriptions for colonial development. Court hostility was driven by fears of English Caribbean settlers being coaxed away from plantation farming, and back into Central American piracy, with Scottish activities rekindling old, self-destructive cravings for "mines and treasure."[83] For the Board of Trade, the destabilizing nature of the enterprise was embodied by the plan to set up Darien as a free port— since such spaces were ever distinguished, one critic opined, as no more than "sanctuaries for buccaneers, pyrates and such Vermin" that sought to escape the bonds of civil society.[84] Above all, the venture came into collision with the European priorities that now shaped and tempered English overseas expansion, and the exigency in particular of preserving the Spanish Empire as a dependent ally under a Habsburg succession, rather than risking its disintegration or diplomatic drift toward France.[85]

The combined Anglo-Spanish opposition may not have directly caused the catastrophe that unfolded on the isthmus. But it certainly compounded the toll levied by disease, climatic challenge, and failed supply lines. The eventual loss of two thousand subjects made Darien by far the costliest of all the failed colonial schemes devised in seventeenth-century Britain.[86] In Scotland, appeals for days of prayer and penitence swiftly gave way to a mood of vehement recrimination, vented out through the realm of urban popular politics with tirades against English MPs and a monarch who had chosen to endorse territorial claims springing from the Bulls of Donation over the aspirations of his northern, Protestant subjects.[87] A wounded national feeling had been set ablaze, fueled by appeals to the spirits of Wallace and Bruce, though the situation was rather more redolent, for many observers, of more recent Covenanting mobilization. "God help us, we are ripening for destruction," warned one officer of the beleaguered Edinburgh garrison in August 1701, after a night of rioting in the city. "It looks very like [sixteen] Forty-one."[88]

The Darien venture may not have been born of separatist politics, but its outcome inflamed the sentiment. The loyalist earl of Melville feared that events in America had made the prospect of closer union ever more remote, stirring across the country a perception that "the crowns of England and Scotland are incompatible."[89] By 1701, when company supporters began to sound the clarion call for a new colonial venture, they identified the prerequisite as a radical redistribution of power within the British Isles. Scottish colonial enterprises, for the duke of Hamilton, were now unthinkable without "the makeing of such Lawes to clear & Extricat uss from this too visible misfortune," and to prevent any monarch from privileging one kingdom so crudely over another.[90] Scots could "not think our selvs secure," agreed Lord Belhaven, simply because we "burne a pamphlet and say wee are independent" while doing "noe more to show that yt is soe."[91]

Paradoxically, the Darien venture had exactly the opposite effect on a section of opinion at the court of Whitehall. The failed strike on the Spanish Empire began to stimulate a more explicit *English* interest in the possibility of closer union, seen now in some quarters of the political nation as a strategic necessity to preserve peace within the British Isles and safeguard European alliances. This argument was prompted in part by fears over the royal succession, with the exiled Jacobite court now pivoting toward the grievances of the northern kingdom, and playing on the "betrayal" on the isthmus in pamphlets scattered through Lowland towns and cities.[92] But Darien also forced English statesmen to address the danger of their northern fellow subjects forging an independent colonial policy, and to recognize the potential vulnerability of their own kingdom to shifting patterns of power and wealth within the Atlantic world. Should Scottish adventurers succeed in taking American territory, John Cary had warned in 1695, it was all the more imperative for the English government "to take care of *Ireland,* and by reducing it to the terms of a Colony" prevent Scots "selling the Product there," for that "I am apt to think is the main thing they aim at."[93] As early as January 1701, the future of the British monarchy was being considered on the Privy Council in London. "Every body was for ye union," reported Lord Basil Hamilton, and the marquis of Halifax signaled his frustration that "this came in being neither from the Throne, nor ye Scottish Nation."[94] The sentiment echoed among colonial notables like William Penn, who regretted to the duke of Hamilton that Englishmen had not "found it to have been our Interest, as Brittans and Protestants, to have endured your endeavours better in this part of the world." The blocks placed on Scottish enterprise weakened the empire as a whole, Penn believed, in view of the debt owed to the kingdom's Atlantic traders as "the most considerable merchants," and those who brought "the greatest returns . . . for England" from the Middle Colonies.[95]

These conversations registered inside Scotland, and set the stage for a major political confrontation through the forthcoming decade. There was no teleological link between the Darien project and the eventual parliamentary union with England, and certainly no unanimity in the political direction taken by patrons of the Company of Scotland. Radicalized by the collapse of the colony and his own family's financial losses, the duke of Hamilton was adamant that any form of union sketched out in London was a trap that would tend only to "make us greater slaves than the Irish."[96] Conversely, many of the long-term, ideologically committed Scottish unionists based their position less on imperial dreams than on older *European* preoccupations—the necessity of Protestant states bonding closer together against the "designs & power of the Romish party" on the Continent, as the earl of Melville put it. From Melville's perspective, colonial opportunities jeopardized rather than advanced the cause of union, offering at best "palliative remedies" to the economic ills of the northern kingdom, while sowing "jealousies" between England and Scotland that blinded subjects to the commonalities between "Nations who dwell in the same Island . . . who are of the same language, of the same profession of Religion."[97] Yet, by 1702 and the succession of Queen Anne, the prospect of a new settlement was "on the table," as Hamilton conceded, and English overtures would meet with a small but receptive audience of merchants and projectors inside Scotland.[98] The unionist party was now enlarged by colonial investors such as Secretary of State Tarbat, who believed that the commercial and demographic frailties of the English plantations gave the Scots their strongest negotiating hand, and the best chance of extracting a favorable settlement from Whitehall.[99] The most conspicuous convert to this line of argument was William Paterson—now recasting and republishing his manifesto for the conquest of Panama as a design best pursued under *British* direction: a potential prize for a newly formed nation, and a way to fashion its fraternal bonds.[100]

On the back of this analysis, Scottish commissioners took their case to London in 1702, and foregrounded the call for free trade in English America over any constitutional conditions on an act of union.[101] Against this agenda, the opposition to union resounded among Scottish commentators who doubted the wisdom of seeking overseas colonies, who saw closer ties with the Dutch as a superior foundation for overseas ventures, or who believed that the politics of the English Atlantic world offered scant reassurance, should Scotland find herself incorporated. The "temper, conduct, and inclinations of your people," the patriot author Andrew Fletcher addressed one English interlocutor, militated against any hope of union for Scotland on equal footing, for "how your colonies in America are treated is well known to all men."[102] The result of the Darien venture may not have determined the outcome of the new Anglo-Scottish negotiations, let alone the form of union eventually settled in 1707. But the overseas dominions would now become pivotal to the terms of the debate, in a crisis of nationhood, empire, and Protestant succession that would rage far beyond the first decade of the eighteenth century.

The English overseas world was born out of a polity unsettled in its governing apparatus, and still wrestling with constitutional uncertainties flowing from the plantation of Ireland and the union of the English and Scottish Crowns. Through the seventeenth century, these uneasy dynamics were quickened as subjects in each of the Stuart realms developed competing colonial interests and grasped the significance of overseas commerce for the balance of power within the three kingdoms. If imperial ideologies in Stuart England had emerged partly as the product of conquests and unions within Britain and Ireland, the relationship was now reversed, with the demands of overseas empire placing pressure on state structures *inside* the Atlantic Archipelago. For some commentators, the colonial wealth amassed by the English realm threatened to eclipse all the legal niceties and customary observances that upheld the rights of Scotland and Ireland as sovereign kingdoms. For their English counterparts, acts of self-assertion in Dublin and Edinburgh risked setting dangerous precedents for American colonial assemblies and drowning out the voice of the Westminster parliament in a monarchy that was expanding outside its constitutional, as well as territorial, boundaries.

By 1700, a growing number of commentators believed that the challenges of overseas expansion would force changes in the structure of the Stuart monarchy. The need to manage the unwieldy riches of the Atlantic world had exposed the limits of a narrowly dynastic union, in a climate marked by warfare, commercial protectionism, and territorial competition. The pressure was heightened by voices from America, where a Britannic future was posited as the long-term solution to the gaping shortfalls created when England's geographic outreach had exceeded the demographic resources—and the level of domestic consensus—at its disposal. English ministers were confident enough in the robustness of the status quo to reject union with Ireland, when the notion was put into print by circles of Protestant scholars and Dublin parliamentarians in 1702–1703.[103] But Scotland presented a more dangerous proposition—a kingdom that could not so easily be "reduced to a colony," and a potential competitor nourished by commerce in Europe and the Western Atlantic. The Darien design, treated in retrospect as a clumsily quixotic affair, caused convulsions in its own time because of the perception that it could, quite viably, have succeeded.

Conclusion

BY 1702, THE FINAL YEAR OF THE reign of William III, serious cracks had emerged in the authority of England's ruling Whig Junto. New ructions over domestic and foreign policy, exacerbated by allegations of misconduct in public office, had unleashed a parliamentary war of attrition, giving rise to a series of impeachments that would conclude after the accession of Queen Anne with the ejection of all leading Whig ministers from government. A striking feature of these controversies was the visibility of colonial and Atlantic affairs. The Junto lords were accused of selling off English vessels and cargo for personal enrichment and of receiving bribes from the king of Spain to turn a blind eye toward Spanish attacks on merchant shipping. The government was excoriated for its sponsorship of William Kidd—the privateer who had abused a commission to tackle the New York pirate networks and emerged subsequently as one of the most notorious Atlantic freebooters. The Partition Treaty of 1700, which set out a planned division of the Spanish Empire, rankled primarily for its secrecy, but also clashed with a growing clamor for England to renew its own territorial ambitions in Central America.[1] Behind much of this agitation, the Whig MP Henry Ashurst warned his American correspondents, lay transatlantic networks connecting Tory opponents in Westminster to the New York anti-Leislerians—the "same party that have allwayes been Enemies to New England"—who saw an opportunity, in the upheavals of the mother kingdom, to regain control of colonial government.[2] The collapse of the Junto showed how a more interconnected Atlantic world did not tend necessarily toward greater stability. The danger of growing parliamentary engagement was to turn the dominions into combustible material for party conflict, and to sharpen local tensions by connecting colonial appointments to the ebb and flow of the contest at Westminster.

Behind the sound and fury of these contests, there were, still, many grounds for seeing the empire of Queen Anne as a more secure entity than the overseas world bequeathed to Charles II in 1660. With England's eastern interests fading into the political background, its colonial strategy became more clearly and unanimously focused on the Americas. While New York developed, under royal governance, as the political "Centre of her Majesty's Plantations on the Continent," the staple-crop-producing colonies of the Chesapeake and the West Indies had become the economic hothouses of the Atlantic world, powered by the human carnage of the African slave trade.[3] With merchants becoming confident enough to sink credit and capital into American ventures, the New England colonies were also being woven into the web of Crown-supported overseas commerce. Overcoming the challenges posed by international conflict, naval convoys, backed up by greater coordination between ministers and colonial governing regimes, kept the supply lines intact so that flows of American trade continually and reliably swelled the royal coffers. In 1708, the Whig scholar John Oldmixon could introduce his history of the American colonies with the insistence that there were "no Hands . . . more usefully employ'd for the Profit and Glory of the Common-Wealth" than those active within the dominions of the New World.[4]

Yet for all these advances, commentators familiar with the older strains and fractures in colonial development could discern some unsettling continuities. In much of the New World, English imperial power was more apparent than real: falsified more than it was illuminated by the maps, memoranda, and scholarly histories dispatched into the Plantation Office. Queen Anne's mainland dominions stretched nominally for over a thousand miles, but most settler communities clung close to the Atlantic shoreline. Farther west, territorial control fell away into a "back country" controlled by unconquered Indian princes, who were still seen by many governors as the decisive actors in conflicts between Europe's colonizing powers.[5] Though English *naval* power had intensified in the Atlantic, the average number of redcoats serving in America rarely exceeded three hundred under Queen Anne and her successor George I, whereas more than ten thousand troops were posted regularly in Ireland.[6] Strategically and administratively, William Blathwayt complained in 1702, "we proceed so awkwardly in these matters as if ye New World were to be discovered again."[7]

Set against these chinks in the armor of the state, private interest groups —merchants, mercenaries, missionaries, and adventurers—remained vital components in the expansion and consolidation of English authority, even while the power of corporate and proprietary governments contracted. Detached from episcopal oversight, the religion of English America was similarly conditioned by voluntarist initiatives, regional partnerships of clergy and laity, and evangelical programs fostered by competing congregations, who drew upon the resources of empire but maintained often tense relations with the authority that was underwriting the colonial enterprise.[8] The unresolved fragilities of English power in the New World meant that alternative pathways to global dominion persisted in the imaginations of statesmen and projectors. The "blue water" strategy, embedded by Tory ministers into the Peace of Utrecht in 1713, was directed as much toward the Mediterranean as the Atlantic, with the acquisition of Gibraltar and Minorca gesturing back to the old strategic visions that had inspired the taking of Tangier.[9] The limits of state power in America explained, too, the mockery dispensed in many eighteenth-century commentaries toward "that modern assum'd stile," as Daniel Defoe put it, "by which some Authors think they do us an Honour when they call the extended scattered Colonies and Dominions . . . the *English Empire.*"[10]

But if English imperialism was a flimsy and contested phenomenon in many places outside Europe, the effects of overseas expansion were exerting more decisive changes over the colonizing kingdom itself. By the reign of Queen Anne, wider swathes of English life were being defined by their involvement in a global arena of political and economic activity, shaped by international rivalries and complex movements of people, commodities, and cultural practices. The impact of the overseas world was clearest in practices of commerce and consumption, but its importance was rising, too, in the cut and thrust of parliamentary business. Between 1689 and

1784, as Steve Pincus, Tiraana Bains, and Alec Zuercher Reichardt have calculated, over 70 percent of the days of debate at Westminster were dominated by colonial and maritime affairs.[11] At the same time, the possibility of empire was bursting ever more conspicuously into the realms of imaginative literature, popular tastes, and aesthetic sensibilities.[12] "Traces of the colonized," as Philip Morgan has put it, reached into the language and landscape of domestic life, even if England's encounters with non-European peoples were defined as much by what was kept silent, or forgotten, as by the connections made visible.[13] Colonial exposures were most vividly apparent in the capital, and across the string of Atlantic port towns and cities. But colonial influences extended further into the English shires and provinces, as regional and kinship networks mobilized for commercial enterprises, church patrons collected for the SPG, and scholarly anatomies of the overseas dominions circulated through the studies of country gentlemen.[14]

This deepening familiarity extended to the colonists themselves, who were working ever more vigorously to assert their credentials as participants in domestic politics.[15] While "creole" cultures were demonstrating greater political maturity and self-confidence by the end of the seventeenth century, conceptions of civility and authority in English America still rested on the links binding settlers to their mother kingdom. By 1690, the Virginia Tory William Fitzhugh could acquire a Huguenot tutor for his son, as a substitute for schooling in the Old World. But the regimen was guided by grammars, prayerbooks, and works of natural philosophy imported from suppliers and correspondents across the Atlantic.[16] Farther north, growing fears of materialism, luxury, and spiritual "declension," voiced among the clergy of Massachusetts, provided ironic testament to the narrowing of the cultural gulf between Old and New England.[17] Expressing an English Whig perspective, John Oldmixon confessed to distaste over the Puritan excesses of the northern colonies, but applauded the stand taken in Boston against "the criminals" imposed on America by James II. In his view, the loyalty of Massachusetts to "the Crown of England," through privation and provocation, proved that there could be no viable "notion of any more Difference between Old-England and New, than between Lincolnshire and Somersetshire."[18] For all their periodic frustrations with royal policy, most colonial leaders agreed that the surest route toward preserving laws and liberties lay in closer involvement with the mother kingdom, and opportunities to influence its internal direction.[19] Cotton Mather imagined "the vine which God has here planted" in Massachusetts sending "its boughs into the Atlantic Sea eastward," to replenish the realm of England, just as its branches burgeoned west "unto the Connecticut River."[20] Paid agencies, patrons, and returning migrants labored toward the creation of a more mutually responsive political environment, which offset the spatial distance between England and its dominions. At the very least, by 1700, political divisions that straddled the entire Stuart world mattered more than the question of which side of the Atlantic an individual happened to live on.

By the beginning of the new century, there were some glimmerings of English domestic consensus over the management of the colonial interest. The most important of these concerned the essential validity of maintaining dominions overseas. Since the 1670s, projectors had been forced to reformulate the case for the colonies, after the discrediting of the two paramount assumptions—permanent Anglo-Spanish enmity and domestic overpopulation—that had justified Elizabethan and Jacobean enterprises. Anti-colonial sentiment had broken into domestic politics during the reigns of Charles II and James II, animated by controversies over the moral, financial, and demographic costs of empire, and by rumored practices of "popery and arbitrary government" overseas. But despite the expectations of some radicals in 1689, these arguments did not dictate the course of post-Revolution policy. By 1700, moreover, statesmen of both parties were accepting that England's empire would take a conventional territorial form, after the disasters at Darien and Tangier had quietly put paid to any hope that English monarchs might construct a radically alternative "empire of the seas." Now most Whig authors could support at least the nurturing and protection of the existing territorial possessions as potential—if often unfulfilled—ways to advance the national interest. John Oldmixon agreed with Tory commentators that the decline of imperial Spain had stemmed rather from religious persecution, despotism, and economic mismanagement, than the inevitable effect of accumulating overseas colonies.[21]

Conversely, authors across the political spectrum endorsed the Lockean diagnosis that it was not simply acquisition of land in itself, but "what is put upon its surface, as usefull Buildings, Trees, Quarries," as the Tory merchant Dalby Thomas surmised, that would make overseas experiments successful.[22] "Industry and skill," advised the Tory Charles Davenant, would render a people richer than "mines of gold and silver," and—in mainland North America at least—it was imperative for statesmen to avoid "aiming at more Provinces, and a greater Tract of Land, than we can either cultivate or defend."[23] Defined by these maxims, England's empire would be a polity of laboring bodies designed to complement the Old World through its self-sealed commercial arrangements, and through offering cheaper and more effective management of the English population, but not to overwhelm it with territorial burdens.[24]

Under the cover of these broad, unifying maxims, however, many of the old divisions remained alive and intact. The shift toward an empire of manufacturing labor left open the question of what forms of productive activity could safely be encouraged within the overseas territories, and with what kind of labor force.[25] Unresolved strategic questions were reopened in 1702, when the resumption of international warfare brought disputes over the future of Spanish America back into English politics. The shadow of Walter Raleigh, the Western Design, and the Jamaican buccaneers lingered long over English debate, and many Tories shared William Paterson's judgment that, without preemptive conquest, the mountainous storehouses of gold and silver would remain a "razor att the throat" of Protestant Europe, awaiting only "the rising of some great prince" to bring the nightmare of universal monarchy into being.[26] Yet the greater part of the War of the Spanish Succession was fought on the other side of the English Channel. Between 1702 and 1713, the campaigns in the Low Countries and the Iberian Peninsula sealed within parts of the Whig Party a political perspective that made overseas expansion subordinate to the greater national interest of protecting "foreign Protestants" and preserving the "balance of Europe." The domestic furor that followed the Peace of Utrecht, and the Tory withdrawal from conflict in return for colonial gains, dramatized deep-seated divisions in English thought over whether the triumph of liberty would take place at sea or on the Continent.[27] Behind the heat of party conflict lurked an older inheritance of confessional and ideological controversies over the destiny and identity of the English realm.

If the anti-colonial arguments of the 1670s had been winnowed down in English politics, they nonetheless left a trail of moral, economic, and cultural anxieties that haunted debate over the enlargement of the realm. In 1708, John Oldmixon still felt obliged to defend colonial endeavors against "the arguments brought from antiquity" and the aspersion "that by draining England of her People, they weaken us at Home."[28] Colonial promoters continually sought ways to roll back the unappetizing associations of empire, and to prove the compatibility of territorial expansion with English customs, laws, and liberties.[29] If the political reality of English colonization was subject to fewer challenges, its legal and intellectual architecture remained unsettled. "The terms British Empire are not the language of common law, but the language of newspapers and political pamphlets," as John Adams later asserted—given that successive ministers had failed to settle on a form or even theory of government that could comprehend all of England's scattered possessions.[30] The result was that every major new acquisition created grounds for constitutional uncertainty, as well as potential for public commotion. The traumas of earlier decades were memorialized in the City of London, where an especially dismal wing of Newgate Prison bore the sobriquet "Tangier."[31] Above all, commentators still grappled with the disturbing possibility that the challenge of occupying distant continents lay beyond the power of the kingdom altogether. "Hath not England's Plantations dispeopled England too much? And yet do not their Plantations rather deserve the Name of Solitudes, than Colonies?" jibed the Scottish secretary of state Viscount Tarbat in 1700.[32] The ceaseless call to populate and fortify new settlements drove the push toward union with Scotland, and the conversion of English dominions into a British Empire. Through the following decades, demographic pressures would also quicken the trade in slave labor and render the growth of the colonies as much an expansion of Africa as of Europe.

Later Stuart England was a nation shaped by overseas expansion before it had acquired a settled territorial empire, and certainly before the birth of the imperial state that would evolve under later monarchs and governments. The idea of empire outstripped the reality—a case of clarity of mind being thwarted by an absence of means—and the crystalline visions of colonial projectors and promotors ran all too frequently into experiences of defeat and frustration, and accusations of overreach. But while statesmen clashed over the wisdom and virtue of territorial outgrowth, the colonial adventure was beginning to cast a different complexion on the realm of England itself. Cultural, religious, and political debates stirred on the colonial frontier crept back into a kingdom that was still wrestling with its own inner divisions, even as it extended itself across the seas. Between 1660 and 1700, domestic controversies over the affairs of church and constitution, consumer taste and moral reform, became weighted with the pressures and possibilities created by overseas expansion. The implications would still be unfurling nearly a century later.

Unless otherwise stated, all pre-1750 works were printed in London.

Abbreviations

BL	British Library
BL Add MSS	British Library Additional Manuscripts
BL, IOR	British Library, India Office Records
Bodl.	Bodleian Library, Oxford
CO	Colonial Office Papers, National Archives, Kew, London
CSPC	*Calendar of State Papers Colonial*
CSPD	*Calendar of State Papers Domestic*
CRO	County Record Office
HMC	Historical Manuscripts Commissions
IOR	India Office Records, British Library
NLS	National Library of Scotland, Edinburgh
NRS	National Records of Scotland, Edinburgh
USPG	Papers of the United Society for the Propagation of the Gospel, Rhodes House Library, Oxford
W&MQ	*William and Mary Quarterly*

Introduction

1. "An Essay of the Interest of the Crown in American Plantations & Trade," 1685, BL Add MSS, 47, 131, 60–72. For the attribution to Blathwayt, see Malcolm Gaskill, *Between Two Worlds: How the English Became Americans* (Oxford: Oxford University Press, 2014), 338.

2. Julian Baggini, "One and a Half Cheers for the Statue Topplers," *Prospect*, 9 June 2020; Jeremy Black, "The Facts and the Fury," *The Critic*, 10 June 2020.

3. Tony Claydon, *Europe and the Making of England, 1660–1760* (Cambridge: Cambridge University Press, 2007); Steven Pincus, *Protestantism and Patriotism: Ideologies and the Making of English Foreign Policy, 1650–1668* (Cambridge: Cambridge University Press, 1996); Patrick Collinson, "England and International Calvinism, 1558–1640," in Menna Prestwich, ed., *International Calvinism, 1541–1715* (Oxford: Clarendon Press, 1985).

4. See especially David Armitage, *The Ideological Origins of the British Empire* (Cambridge: Cambridge University Press, 2000); Anthony Pagden, *Lords of All the World: Ideologies of Empire in Spain, Britain, and France, c. 1500–c. 1800* (New Haven: Yale University Press, 1995); J. H. Elliott, *Empires of the Atlantic World: Britain and Spain in America, 1492–1830* (New Haven: Yale University Press, 2006).

5. David Armitage and Michael Braddick, eds., *The British Atlantic World* (Basingstoke: Palgrave Macmillan, 2002); Elizabeth Mancke and Carole Shammas, eds., *The Creation of the British Atlantic World* (Baltimore: Johns Hopkins University Press, 2005).

6. For comments on this trend, see David Armitage, "Greater Britain: A Useful Category of Analysis?" *American Historical Review* 104, no. 2 (April 1999): 427–445; Nicholas Canny, "Writing Atlantic History; or, Reconfiguring the History of Colonial British America," *Journal of American History* 86, no. 3 (December 1999): 1093–1114.

7. Brendan Simms, *Three Victories and a Defeat: The Rise and Fall of the First British Empire* (London: Penguin, 2007); Claydon, *Europe and the Making of England*.

8. See, for instance, J. H. Elliott, "Party Politics and Empire in the Early Eighteenth Century," in Jason Peacey, ed., *Making the British Empire, 1660–1800* (Manchester: Manchester University Press, 2020), 45.

9. George Louis Beer, *The Old Colonial System, 1660–1754*, part 1: *The Establishment of the System, 1660–1688* (New York: Macmillan, 1912); Charles McLean Andrews, *The Colonial Period of American History*, 4 vols. (New Haven: Yale University Press, 1934–1937).

10. John Robertson, "Empire and Union: Two Concepts of the Early Modern European Political Order," in Robertson, ed., *A Union for Empire: Political Thought and the British Union of 1707* (Cambridge: Cambridge University Press, 1996), 5–8; Pagden, *Lords of All the World*, 12–14.

11. John Palmer, *The Present State of New-England* (1689), 7, 9; Maura Jane Farrelly, *Papist Patriots: The Making of an American Catholic Identity* (Oxford: Oxford University Press, 2012), 38–39.

12. This figure was calculated from the English Short Title Catalogue, available at https://estc.ucr.edu.

13. James Muldoon, *Empire and Order: The Concept of Empire, 800–c. 1800* (Basingstoke: Macmillan, 1999), 139; Michael W. Doyle, *Empires* (Ithaca: Cornell University Press, 1986), 19.

14. Pagden, *Lords of All the World*, 17; Armitage, *Ideological Origins*, 29–36.

15. Samuel von Pufendorf, *Of the Law of Nature and Nations* (1703), book 7, 141.

16. Nicholas Barbon, *A Discourse of Trade* (1690), 57.

17. Charles Davenant, *An Essay upon the Probable Methods of Making a People Gainers in the Ballance of Trade* (1699), 100–101, 119–120.

18. Mary Maples Dunn and Richard S. Dunn, eds., *The Papers of William Penn*, 5 vols. (Philadelphia: University of Pennsylvania Press, 1981–1986), vol. 3, 605–606.

19. Richard Koebner, *Empire* (Cambridge: Cambridge University Press, 1961), 59–60.

20. Jack P. Greene, *Peripheries and Center: Constitutional Development in the Extended Polities of the British Empire and the United States, 1607–1788* (Athens: University of Georgia Press, 1987); Bernard Bailyn, *The New England Merchants in the Seventeenth Century* (Cambridge: Harvard University Press, 1979).

21. Carla Gardina Pestana, *The English Atlantic in an Age of Revolution, 1640–1661* (Cambridge: Harvard University Press, 2004); Owen Stanwood, *The Empire Reformed: English America in the Age of the Glorious Revolution* (Philadelphia: University of Pennsylvania Press, 2011); Evan Haefeli, "Toleration and Empire," in Stephen Foster, ed., *British North America in the Seventeenth and Eighteenth Centuries* (Oxford: Oxford University Press, 2013), 128–130; David. S. Lovejoy, *The Glorious Revolution in America* (New York: Harper & Row, 1972).

22. Karin Wulf, "Vast Early America: Three Simple Words for a Complex Reality," *Humanities* 40, no. 1 (Winter 2019).

23. Steve Pincus, "Rethinking Mercantilism: Political Economy, the British Empire, and the Atlantic World in the Seventeenth and Eighteenth Centuries," *W&MQ* 69, no. 1 (January 2012): 3–34.

24. Abigail L. Swingen, *Competing Visions of Empire: Labor, Slavery, and the Origins of the British Atlantic Empire* (New Haven: Yale University Press, 2015); William A. Pettigrew, *Freedom's Debt: The Royal African Company and the Politics of the Atlantic Slave Trade, 1672–1752* (Chapel Hill: University of North Carolina Press, 2013); Susan Dwyer Amussen, *Caribbean Exchanges: Slavery and the Transformation of English Society, 1640–1700* (Chapel Hill: University of North Carolina Press, 2007); Holly Brewer, "Slavery, Sovereignty, and 'Inheritable Blood': Reconsidering John Locke and the Origins of American Slavery," *American Historical Review* 122, no. 4 (October 2017), 1038–1107.

25. Amussen, *Caribbean Exchanges*, 179–225.

26. Stanwood, *Empire Reformed*, 27.

27. Alison Games, *The Web of Empire: English Cosmopolitans in an Age of Expansion, 1560–1660* (Oxford: Oxford University Press, 2008), 289–299; Stephen Saunders Webb, *1676: The End of American Independence* (New York: Knopf, 1984).

28. Ken MacMillan, " 'Bound by Our Regal Office': Empire, Sovereignty, and the American Colonies in the Seventeenth Century," in Foster, *British North America*, 67–102.

29. L. H. Roper, *Advancing Empire: English Interests and Overseas Expansion, 1613–1688* (Cambridge: Cambridge University Press, 2017).

30. J. M. Sosin, *English America and the Restoration Monarchy of Charles II: Transatlantic Politics, Commerce, and Kinship* (Lincoln: University of Nebraska Press, 1980);

Michael J. Braddick, *State Formation in Early Modern England, c. 1550–1700* (Cambridge: Cambridge University Press, 2000), 398; Michael J. Braddick, "The English Government, War, Trade and Settlement, 1625–1688," in Nicholas Canny, ed., *The Oxford History of the British Empire*, vol. 1: *The Origins of Empire* (Oxford: Oxford University Press, 1998), 286–308.

31. George Smith to George Oxenden, 8 March 1665/6, BL Add MSS, 40712, fol. 40; Donald Akenson, *If the Irish Ran the World: Montserrat, 1630–1730* (Montreal: McGill-Queen's University Press, 1997), 31.

32. Philip Stern, "British Asia and the British Atlantic: Comparisons and Connections," *W&MQ*, 3rd ser., vol. 63, no. 4 (October 2006): 693–712; Jonathan Eacott, *Selling Empire: India in the Making of Britain and America, 1600–1830* (Chapel Hill: University of North Carolina Press, 2016).

33. Om Prakash, *European Commercial Enterprise in Pre-Colonial India* (Cambridge: Cambridge University Press, 1998), 144–151. For recent literature on the East India Company, see Philip Stern, *The Company-State: Corporate Sovereignty and the Early Modern Foundations of the British Empire in India* (Oxford: Oxford University Press, 2011); and Emily Erikson, *Between Monopoly and Free Trade: The English East India Company, 1600–1757* (Princeton: Princeton University Press, 2014).

34. Mark G. Hanna, *Pirates' Nests and the Rise of the British Empire* (Chapel Hill: University of North Carolina Press, 2015), 183–221; Alison Games, "Beyond the Atlantic: English Globetrotters and Transoceanic Connections," *W&MQ*, 3rd ser., vol. 63, no. 4 (October 2006), 675–692.

35. John Seeley, *The Expansion of England* (London, 1883), 12.

36. Trevor Burnard, *Planters, Merchants, and Slaves: Plantation Societies in British America, 1650–1820* (Chicago: Chicago University Press, 2015), 98.

37. Bridget Orr, *Empire on the English Stage, 1660–1714* (Cambridge: Cambridge University Press, 2001); Karen O'Brien, "Poetry Against Empire: Milton to Shelley," *Proceedings of the British Academy* 117 (London: British Academy, 2002), 269–296.

38. Nuala Zahedieh, *The Capital and the Colonies: London and the Atlantic Economy, 1660–1700* (Cambridge: Cambridge University Press, 2010); Ralph Davis, *English Overseas Trade, 1500–1700* (London: Macmillan, 1973); David Harris Sacks, *The Widening Gate: Bristol and the Atlantic Economy, 1450–1700* (Berkeley: University of California Press, 1991).

39. Claydon, *Europe and the Making of England*; Steve Pincus and Alan Houston, eds., *A Nation Transformed: England after the Restoration* (Cambridge: Cambridge University Press, 2001); Steven Pincus, "The English Debate over Universal Monarchy," in Robertson, *Union for Empire*, 37–62; Braddick, *State Formation*, 278.

40. Carl Bridenbaugh, ed., *The Pynchon Papers: Letters of John Pynchon, 1654–1700*, 2 vols. (Boston: Colonial Society of Massachusetts, 1982), vol. 1, 78–79; John J. McCusker, "The Demise of Distance: The Business Press and the Origins of the Information Revolution in the Early Modern Atlantic World," *American Historical Review* 110, no. 2 (April 2005): 295–321.

41. Marion Tinling, ed., *The Correspondence of the Three William Byrds of Westover, Virginia, 1684–1776*, 2 vols. (Charlottesville: Virginia Historical Society, 1977), vol. 1, 136–137.

42. Mark Knights, *Representation and Misrepresentation in Later Stuart Britain: Partisanship and Political Culture* (Oxford: Oxford University Press, 2005).

43. Linda Colley, *Britons: Forging the Nation, 1707–1837* (New Haven: Yale University Press, 1992); Kathleen Wilson, *The Sense of the People: Politics, Culture, and Imperialism in England, 1715–1775* (Cambridge: Cambridge University Press, 1995).

44. Charles Davenant, *Essays upon I. The Balance of Power. II. The Right of Making War, Peace and Alliances. III. Universal Monarchy* (1701), 285.

Chapter 1. The Restoration and the Geography of English Overseas Expansion

1. Thomas Povey to Daniel Searle, 20 October 1659, BL Add MSS 11,411, fol. 90.

2. Thomas Povey to Richard Povey, 29 October 1659, BL Add MSS 11,411, fol. 25.

3. Carla Gardina Pestana, *The English Conquest of Jamaica* (Cambridge: Harvard University Press, 2017); Abigail L. Swingen, *Competing Visions of Empire: Labor, Slavery, and the Origins of the British Atlantic Empire* (New Haven: Yale University Press, 2015), 18–53; Robert Brenner, *Merchants and Revolution: Commercial Change, Political Conflict, and London's Overseas Traders, 1550–1653* (Princeton: Princeton University Press, 1993), 115–166, 170–185.

4. William Morice, Instructions for Thomas, Lord Windsor, 21 March 1661/2, Bodl., Rawlinson MSS, A347, fols. 7–11.

5. David Armitage, "The Cromwellian Protectorate and the Languages of Empire," *Historical Journal* 35, no. 3 (September 1992): 542; Blair Worden, "Oliver Cromwell and the Sin of Achan," in Derek Beales and Geoffrey Best, eds., *History, Society, and the Churches: Essays in Honour of Owen Chadwick* (Cambridge: Cambridge University Press, 1985), 125–146.

6. Thomas Povey to Edward D'Oyley, n.d. 1659, BL Add MSS, 11411, fol. 87.

7. John Scott, "Account of the English colonies," 1661, BL Sloane MSS, 3662, fol. 10.

8. Thomas Povey to Edward D'Oyley, n.d., BL Add MSS, 11411, fol. 87.

9. Thomas Povey to Richard Povey, 14 July 1661, BL Add MSS, 11411, fol. 33.

10. John Ogilby, *The relation of his Majesties Entertainment Passing through the City of London, To His Coronation* (1661); Blair Hoxby, "The Government of Trade: Commerce, Politics and the Courtly Art of Restoration," *ELH* 66, no. 3 (Fall 1999): 591–627.

11. William de Britaine, *The interest of England in the present war with Holland* (1672), 20–21.

12. Thomas Sprat, *The History of the Royal Society* (1667), 19–21, 87–88.

13. James Howell, *Proedria Vasilike: A discourse concerning the precedency of kings* (1664), 3–15; Winifred Joy Mulligan, "The British Constantine: An English Historical Myth," *Journal of Medieval and Renaissance Studies* 8 (1978): 257–279.

14. John Evelyn, *Navigation and Commerce. Their original and progress* (1674), 67; Ken MacMillan, " 'Bound by Our Regal Office': Empire, Sovereignty, and the American Colonies in the Seventeenth Century," in Stephen Foster, ed., *British North America in the Seventeenth and Eighteenth Centuries* (Oxford: Oxford University Press, 2013), 72–73.

15. Richard Hakluyt, *A Discourse concerning Western Planting. Written in the year 1584*, 2 vols. (Cambridge, 1877), vol. 1, 118–119.

16. See, for instance, Roger Boyle, first earl of Orrery, *Henry the Fifth* (1664), 39–43; Paper on rights to the New World, 1663, *CSPC, 1661–1668*, 622.

17. Evelyn, *Navigation and Commerce*, 1, 5.

18. Richard Braybrooke, ed., *Memoirs of Samuel Pepys*, 5 vols. (London, 1828), vol. 5, 133; Linda Colley, *Captives: Britain, Empire, and the World* (London: Jonathan Cape, 2002), 38.

19. William Paterson, "A brief view of the weight and consequence of the general trade, and of some considerable places in the Indies," n.d., Rawlinson MSS, C840, fols. 39–40.

20. Alison Games, *The Web of Empire: English Cosmopolitans in an Age of Expansion, 1560–1660* (Oxford: Oxford University Press, 2008), 47–115.

21. Nabil Matar, *Turks, Moors, and Englishmen in the Age of Discovery* (New York: Columbia University Press, 1999), 86–87; Elizabeth Mancke, "Empire and State," in David Armitage and Michael Braddick, eds., *The British Atlantic World* (Basingstoke, UK: Palgrave Macmillan, 2002), 175–195.

22. Benjamin Worsley to Anthony Ashley Cooper, 14 August 1668, National Archives, PRO 30/24/49, fols. 225–226.

23. Mary B. Campbell, *The Witness and the Other World: Exotic European Travel Writing, 400–1600* (Ithaca: Cornell University Press, 1991), ch. 6; Anna Suranyi, *The Genius of the English Nation: Travel Writing and National Identity in Early Modern England* (Newark: University of Delaware Press, 2008), 17–18, 38–39.

24. L. B. Cormack, *Charting an Empire: Geography at the English Universities, 1580–1620* (Chicago: University of Chicago Press, 1991), 84; David Harris Sacks, "Richard Hakluyt's Navigations in Time: History, Epic, and Empire," *Modern Language Quarterly* 67, no. 1 (March 2006): 31–62.

25. Lords of Trade, Accounts, BL Add MSS, 9767, fols. 14–15; "A List of all Books in the Plantation Office treating of New England," n.d. [c. 1677], BL Egerton MSS, 2395, fol. 573; John Cholmley to Sir William Langhorne, 20 December 1671, Northallerton, North Yorkshire, CRO, ZCG/V/3; HMC, *The Manuscripts of S. H. Le Fleming* (London, 1890), 106, 112.

26. Henry Gale to anonymous correspondent, 5 August 1703, BL Stowe MSS 748, fol. 12.

27. *London Gazette*, no. 2343 (April 1688); William Bray, ed., *The Diary of John Evelyn*, 2 vols. (London, 1901), vol. 2, 199; *Musaeum Tradescantianum: or, A Collection of Rarities. Preserved . . . by John Tradescant* (1656), 1, 6; Andrew Hadfield, *Literature, Travel and Colonial Writing in the English Renaissance, 1545–1625* (Oxford: Oxford University Press, 1998), ch. 1.

28. Samuel Purchas, *Purchas His Pilgrimes. In Five Bookes* (1625), 1.
29. George Alsop, *A Character of the Province of Maryland* (1666), 61; Robert Beverley, *The History and Present State of Virginia* (1705), preface.
30. John Ogilby, *An Embassy from the East India Company of the Netherlands* (1669), 3.
31. *The Golden Coast; or, A Description of Guinney* (1665), 1–2.
32. Thomas Fuller, *The History of the Worthies of England* (1662), 40.
33. Richard Dunn, *Sugar and Slaves: The Rise of the Planter Class in the English West Indies, 1624–1713* (Chapel Hill: University of North Carolina Press, 1972), 11–123; Kenneth R. Andrews, *Elizabethan Privateering* (Cambridge: Cambridge University Press, 1964), 159–199.
34. Thomas Povey, "Overtures touching a Councell to bee erected for forreigne plantations," n.d. [1659], BL Egerton MSS 2395, n.d., fols. 270–271, reissued 1660, fols. 272–273.
35. Howell, *Proedria Vasilike*, 160.
36. William Godolphin to Leoline Jenkins, 15/25 March 1675/6, National Archives, SP, 94/63, fol. 243. The principal medicinal commodities acquired from the Americas were sassafras and sarsaparilla.
37. Barbara H. Stein and Stanley J. Stein, *Silver, Trade, and War: Spain and America in the Making of Early Modern Europe* (Baltimore: Johns Hopkins University Press, 2000).
38. Henry Goodricke to Henry Coventry, 21 September 1679, Longleat, Coventry MSS, 80/283.
39. Andrew Fitzmaurice, "The Commercial Ideology of Colonization in Jacobean England: Robert Johnson, Giovanni Botero, and the Pursuit of Greatness," *W&MQ*, 3rd ser., vol. 64, no. 4 (October 2007): 791–820; Steven Pincus, "The English Debate over Universal Monarchy," in John Robertson, ed., *A Union for Empire: Political Thought and the British Union of 1707* (Cambridge: Cambridge University Press, 1996), 37–62.
40. "An Essay of the Interest of the Crown in American Plantations & Trade," 1685, BL Add MSS, 47131, 60.
41. Peter Heylin, *Cosmographie* (1652), 290.
42. Karen Ordahl Kupperman, "Errand to the Indies: Puritan Colonization from Providence Island Through to the Western Design," *W&MQ* 45, no. 1 (1988): 70–99; Bruce Lenman, *England's Colonial Wars, 1550–1688: Conflicts, Empire and National Identity* (London: Longman, 2001), 147–148, 174–175.
43. Anthony Pagden, *Lords of All the World: Ideologies of Empire in Spain, Britain, and France, c. 1500–c. 1800* (New Haven: Yale University Press, 1995), 63–65.
44. Carla Gardina Pestana, *The English Atlantic in an Age of Revolution, 1640–1661* (Cambridge: Harvard University Press, 2004), 225; Hilary McD. Beckles, "The 'Hub of Empire': The Caribbean and Britain in the Seventeenth Century," in Nicholas Canny, ed., *The Oxford History of the British Empire*, vol. 1: *The Origins of Empire* (Oxford: Oxford University Press, 1998), 218–240; Alison Games, "Migration," in Armitage and Braddick, *British Atlantic World*, 32–33.

45. Sir William Berkeley, "A Discourse and View of Virginia," 1662, BL Egerton MSS, 2395, fols. 357–358.

46. Thomas Povey, "Proposition for a Council for the Plantations to be selected from the Privy Council, with a permanent secretary," 1660, BL Egerton MSS, 2395, fol. 276.

47. J. H. Elliott, *Empires of the Atlantic World: Britain and Spain in America, 1492–1830* (New Haven: Yale University Press, 2006), 235–238; Michael Zuckerman, "Identity in British America: Unease in Eden," in Nicholas Canny and Anthony Pagden, eds., *Colonial Identity in the Atlantic World, 1500–1800* (Princeton: Princeton University Press, 1987), 120–121.

48. Susan Hardman Moore, *Pilgrims: New World Settlers and the Call of Home* (New Haven: Yale University Press, 2010), 9–13; Matar, *Turks, Moors,* 89–90.

49. John Hammond, *Leah and Rachel; or, the Two Fruitfull Sisters Virginia and Maryland* (1655), epistle dedicatory.

50. Berkeley, "Discourse and View," fol. 257.

51. Minutes of Council of Foreign Plantations, 10 January 1660/1, BL Egerton MSS, 2395, fols. 289–290; Swingen, *Competing Visions,* 32–33.

52. R. Latham and W. Matthews, eds., *The Diary of Samuel Pepys,* 11 vols. (London: HarperCollins, 1970–1983), vol. 3, 115; Thomas Povey to Edward D'Oyley, n.d. 1659, BL Add MSS, 11411, fol. 87; Slingsby Bethel, *The World's Mistake in Oliver Cromwell* (1668), 9–10; Stephen Saunders-Webb, *The Governors-General: The English Army and the Definition of the Empire, 1569–1681* (Chapel Hill: Published for the Institute of Early American History and Culture, Williamsburg, VA, by the University of North Carolina Press, 1987), 153–155.

53. C. H. Firth, ed., *The Memoirs of Edmund Ludlow,* 2 vols. (Oxford, 1894), vol. 2, 3; Latham and Matthews, *Diary of Samuel Pepys,* vol. 3, 15.

54. "A Proposition for the better securing of his Maty's interest in Dunkirk," Bodl., Clarendon MSS, 75, fol. 456.

55. George Downing to Earl of Clarendon, 20 February 1661, Clarendon MSS, 106, fols. 111–114.

56. Earl of Lauderdale to earl of Cassilis, 14 January 1660/1, Edinburgh, NRS, Ailsa MSS, GD 25/9, box 30/2.

57. Privy Council Register, National Archives, PC/2/55, 10, 14, 39.

58. Latham and Matthews, *Diary of Samuel Pepys,* vol. 5, 264; Thomas Povey to Timothy Temple, 3 April 1660, BL Add MSS 11,411, fol. 27.

59. J. E. Farnell, "The Navigation Act of 1651, the First Dutch War and the London Merchant Community," *Economic History Review* n.s. 16, no. 3 (1964): 439–454; Brenner, *Merchants and Revolution,* 115–166.

60. Francis, Lord Willoughby to Roger Osborne, 19 February 1660, BL Add MSS, 11411, fol. 31; Barbara Murison, "Thomas Povey," *Oxford Dictionary of National Biography,* https://www.oxforddnb.com.

61. Richard Fanshaw to Earl of Clarendon, 30 July 1662, Clarendon MSS, 77, fols. 100–101.

62. "The State of Affaires of the English in Jamaica," 27 March 1660/1, BL Egerton MSS, 2395, fol. 241; Thomas Povey to Edward D'Oyley, n.d., BL, Add MSS, 11411, fols. 87–88.

63. Patent for a Committee of Trade, 1 November 1660, CO, 389/1, 2; Privy Council Register, 10 September 1662, PC/2/55, 62; Paul Slack, *The Invention of Improvement: Information and Material Progress in Seventeenth-Century England* (Oxford: Oxford University Press, 2014), 94–99; Thomas Leng, *Benjamin Worsley (1618–1677): Trade, Interest, and the Spirit in Revolutionary England* (Woodbridge, UK: Boydell and Brewer, 2008), 35–36, 41–52, 75–77.

64. Povey, "Overtures touching a Councell," fol. 272.

65. "Instructions for the Councill of Trade," 1660, BL Egerton MSS, 2395, fols. 268–269; ibid.; John Bland, *Trade Revived* (1659), 45; Perry Gauci, *The Politics of Trade: The Overseas Merchant in State and Society, 1660–1720* (Oxford: Oxford University Press, 2001), 181–182.

66. Edward Hyde, Paper on negotiations with Portugal, February 1661, Clarendon MSS, 75, fols. 204–205; Proposals from the crown of Portugal to Charles II, n.d. [February 1660/1], Clarendon MSS, fols. 217–218; *The Life of Edward, earl of Clarendon*, 3 vols. (Oxford, 1827), vol. 1, 491; Latham and Matthews, *Diary of Samuel Pepys*, vol. 3, 91.

67. Conde de Ponte to Charles II, 4 February 1660/1, Clarendon MSS, 74, fols. 111–112; Francis Parry to James Ball, 20 September 1668, BL Add MSS, 35100, fol. 7; Lorraine Madway, "Rites of Deliverance and Disenchantment: The Marriage Celebrations for Charles II and Catherine of Braganza, 1661–62," *The Seventeenth Century* 27, no. 1 (March 2012): 82–84.

68. Alexander Mackenzie to Lord Rutherford, 18 June 1662, *CSPD, 1661–1662*, 56/74; Crown of Spain to Charles II, March 1660/1, Clarendon MSS, 74, fols. 280–283; William Cobbett, ed., *The Parliamentary History of England*, 36 vols. (1806–1820), vol. 4, 190–191.

69. Richard Russell, "Motives for Peace and Commerce with Portugal," n.d., Durham, UK, Ushaw College, Russell papers, A25/54.

70. E. S. De Beer, ed., *The Diary of John Evelyn*, 6 vols. (Oxford: Oxford University Press, 1955), vol. 3, 324.

71. HMC, *The Manuscripts of J.M. Heathcote* (London, 1899), 23–24.

72. Edward Hyde, Draft reply from Charles II to crown of Portugal, February 1661, Clarendon MSS, 75, fols. 204–205; East India Company, Report to the Council of Trade, n.d., Coventry MSS, 101, fols. 81–82; "On what terms of advantage to ye King & his Subjects it may be fitt for ye King to undertake ye protection of ye Portugall in East India," n.d., Coventry MSS, 101, fols. 81–82.

73. Cobbett, *Parliamentary History*, vol. 4, 190.

74. Edward Hyde, Draft reply to crown of Portugal, February 1661, Clarendon MSS, 75, fols. 204–205.

75. Glenn Ames, "The Role of Religion in the Transfer and Rise of Bombay, c. 1661–87," *Historical Journal* 46, no. 2 (June 2003): 317–340.

76. Gerald Aungier to Oxenden, n.d. 1662, BL Add MSS, 40708, 1.

77. Robert Markley, *The Far East and the English Imagination, 1600–1730* (Cambridge: Cambridge University Press, 2006), 30–64; Robert Batchelor, *London: The Selden Map and the Making of a Global City, 1549–1689* (Chicago: Chicago University Press, 2014), 1–14, 48–57.

78. David A. Boruchoff, "Piety, Patriotism, and Empire: Lessons for England, Spain, and the New World in the Works of Richard Hakluyt," *Renaissance Quarterly* 62, no. 3 (Fall 2009): 809–858, at 824.

79. Philip Stern, "British Asia and the British Atlantic: Comparisons and Connections," *W&MQ*, 3rd ser., vol. 63, no. 4 (October 2006): 704; Sir David Kirke, Report on Newfoundland, n.d., BL Egerton MSS, 2395, fols. 259–260.

80. Carew Reynell, *The true English interest* (1674), 13.

81. Purchas, *Pilgrimes*, 21.

82. Games, *Web of Empire*, 4, 6, 117–120.

83. Philip Lawson, *The East India Company: A History* (London: Longman, 1993), 18–41.

84. Robert Ferguson, *The East India Trade the most profitable Trade to the Kingdom* (1677), 7; John Fryer, *A New Account of India and Persia* (1682), 86; K. N. Chaudhuri, *The Trading World of Asia and the English East India Company, 1660–1760* (Cambridge: Cambridge University Press, 1978), 1–10, 41–56.

85. Philip Stern, *The Company-State: Corporate Sovereignty and the Early Modern Foundations of the British Empire in India* (Oxford: Oxford University Press, 2011), 3–25.

86. Michael J. Braddick, *State Formation in Early Modern England, c. 1550–1700* (Cambridge: Cambridge University Press, 2000), 398–399.

87. Richard Hakluyt, *Principal Navigations* (1589), 243–244, 267–272.

88. Purchas, *Pilgrimes*, 590–591.

89. Lenman, *England's Colonial Wars*, 193–199.

90. "The East India Companies Charter," 13 April 1661, Rawlinson MSS, A303; Hoxby, "Government of Trade," 601–610; Stern, *Company-State*, 21–25, 155.

91. Ferguson, *East India Trade*, 17–19.

92. Jonathan I. Israel, *Dutch Primacy in World Trade, 1585–1740* (Oxford: Oxford University Press, 1990), 175–185, 244–250.

93. William Temple, *Observations upon the United Provinces of the Netherlands* (1673), 204; Charles Molloy, *Holland's Ingratitude* (1666), 11; Anthony Milton, "Marketing a Massacre: The East India Company, the Amboyna Incident, and the Public Sphere in Early Stuart England," in Peter Lake and Steven Pincus, eds., *The Politics of the Public Sphere in Early Modern England* (Manchester: Manchester University Press, 2012), 168–190.

94. Samuel Maverick, "The Government of the New Netherlands," 1664, Clarendon MSS, 74, fols. 235–236.

95. Scott, "Account of the English colonies," fol. 60; Robert M. Bliss, *Revolution and Empire: English Politics and the American Colonies in the Seventeenth Century* (Manchester: Manchester University Press, 1990), 73–74.

96. Thomas Mun, *England's treasure by forraign trade* (1664), 196.

97. J. N. Hillgarth, *The Mirror of Spain, 1500–1799: The Formation of a Myth* (Ann Arbor: University of Michigan Press, 2003).

98. Molloy, *Holland's Ingratitude*, 1–2.

99. Steven Pincus, *Protestantism and Patriotism: Ideologies and the Making of English Foreign Policy, 1650–68* (Cambridge: Cambridge University Press, 1996), 222–236.

100. Henry Stubbe, *A justification of the present war against the United Netherlands* (1672), 1–2.

101. Arnold Browne to Oxenden, 14 January 1662/3, BL Add MSS 40,708, 27–28; Earl of Southampton and Lord Ashley to Oxenden, 27 March 1663, BL Add MSS 40,711, 62–63.

102. George Downing to Clarendon, 30 December 1661, Clarendon MSS, 106, fols. 6–16; Clarendon to Downing, 20 January 1662, Clarendon MSS, 106, fols. 50–51.

103. East India Company, report to the Council of Trade, n.d., Coventry MSS, 101, fols. 81–82; Council of Trade to the King, 13 January 1660/1, Coventry MSS, 103, fol. 20; Edward Hyde, Draft reply to crown of Portugal, February 1661, Clarendon MSS, 75, fols. 204–205.

104. William Ryder to Oxenden, 26 March 1663, BL Add MSS, 40711, 51–52.

105. Colley, *Captives*, 41–50; Tristan Stein, "Tangier in the Restoration Empire," *Historical Journal* 54, no. 4 (December 2011): 985–1011.

106. Gilbert Burnet, *History of his own time*, 2 vols. (1724–1734), vol. 1, 173.

107. Hakluyt, *Discourse*, vol. 1, 14–15.

108. David Hancock, ed., *The Letters of William Freeman, London Merchant, 1678–1685* (London: London Record Society, 2002), vii, xxi, 2, 15, 78–79.

109. William Godolphin to earl of Arlington, 28 August 1671, SP 94/58, fol. 190.

110. Nathaniel Bradley to Samuel Pepys, 5 December 1676, Rawlinson MSS, A185, fol. 175; James Houblon, "A Discourse touching the Grounds of ye Decay of ye English Navigation," n.d., Rawlinson MSS, A171, fol. 285; Richard Grassby, *The English Gentleman in Trade: The Life and Works of Sir Dudley North, 1641–1691* (Oxford: Oxford University Press, 1994), 23–24.

111. Howell, *Proedria Vasilike*, 140.

112. Sandwich to Hyde, May 1661, Clarendon MSS, 75, fols. 464–465; *A Description of Tangier, the country and people adjoyning* (1664), 6.

113. [Bland], *The Present Interest of Tangiers* (1679), 2.

114. Earl of Sandwich to duke of York, 1662, BL Sloane MSS 3509, fols. 26–27; Hyde, Memorandum on Braganza match, 1661, Clarendon MSS, 78, fol. 158.

115. M.S. Anderson, "Britain and the Barbary States in the Eighteenth-Century," *Bulletin of the Institute of Historical Research* 29, no. 79 (May 1956): 87–107; Colley, *Captives*, 49–50.

116. G. A. Starr, "Escape from Barbary: A Seventeenth-Century Genre," *Huntington Library Quarterly* 29, no. 1 (November 1965); Nabil I. Matar, *Britain and Barbary, 1589–1689* (Gainesville: University of Florida Press, 2005); Tony Claydon, *Europe and the Making of England, 1660–1760* (Cambridge: Cambridge University Press, 2007), 132–150.

117. Hugh Cholmley, "Severall Discourses Concerning the Interest of Tangr," n.d, Rawlinson MSS, A341, fol. 45.

118. Sandwich to York, 1662, BL Sloane MSS 3509, fols. 26–27.

119. David Armitage, *The Ideological Origins of the British Empire* (Cambridge: Cambridge University Press, 2000), 100–124.

120. *A Discourse Written by Sir George Downing* (1672), 44–45; E. S. Reinert, "Emulating Success: Contemporary Views of the Dutch Economy before 1800," in Oscar Gelderbloom, ed., *The Political Economy of the Dutch Republic* (Aldershot: Ashgate, 2009), 19–40.

121. Temple, *Observations*, 228.

122. Samuel Lambe, *Seasonable Observations humbly offered to His Highness the Lord Protector* (1657), 11.

123. Mun, *England's treasure*, 190.

124. Thomas P. Slaughter, ed., *Ideology and Politics on the Eve of the Restoration: Newcastle's Advice to Charles II* (Philadelphia: American Philosophical Society, 1984), 36.

125. Scott, "Account of the English colonies," fol. 10. See also Captain John Smith, *The trade & fishing of Great-Britain* (1661).

126. David J. B. Trim, "Seeking a Protestant Alliance and Liberty of Conscience on the Continent," in Susan Doran and Glenn Richardson, eds., *Tudor England and Its Neighbours* (Basingstoke: Macmillan, 2005), 139–176; Brendan Simms, *Three Victories and a Defeat* (London: Penguin, 2007), 11–17.

127. Mun, *England's treasure*, 198–199, 204–205.

128. Sir Richard Fanshaw, "A Narrative concerning the Margaretta Prize," 1 August 1665, Clarendon MSS, 83, fols. 186–187; George Downing, "Paper on the king's revenue," 16/26 August 1661, Clarendon MSS, 104, fols. 252–253; Lauren Benton, *A Search for Sovereignty: Law and Geography in European Empires, 1400–1900* (Cambridge: Cambridge University Press, 2010), 104–160.

129. Armitage, *Ideological Origins*, 108.

130. *CSPC, East Indies,* January 1601, ii, 118–121; John Dryden, *Annus Mirabilis. The Year of Wonders* (1667); William Davenant, *Poem to the King's Most Sacred Majesty* (1663); C. G. Roelofsen, "Grotius and the International Politics of the Seventeenth Century," in Hedley Bull, Benedict Kingsbury, and Adam Roberts, eds., *Hugo Grotius and International Relations* (Oxford: Oxford University Press, 1990), 104–112.

131. George Downing to Clarendon, 20 November 1663, Clarendon MSS, 107, fols. 121–122.

132. Downing, *Discourse*, 108–113.

133. See especially John Selden, *Of the dominion, or ownership of the sea . . . translated into English by Marchamont Nedham* (1652); John Selden, *Mare Clausum. The right and dominion of the sea in two books . . . perfected and restored by J.H.* (1663).

134. Howell, *Proedria Vasilike*, 15, 35; Downing, *Discourse*, 108–113.

135. See especially James Howell, "Touching the late Rendition of Dunkirk," Clarendon MSS, 78, fols. 121–134.

136. Mun, *England's treasure*, 189.

137. News from Lisbon, 7 September 1661, Clarendon MSS, 75, fols. 183–185.

138. Cholmley, "Severall Discourses," Rawlinson MSS, A341, fol. 47.

139. Howell, *Proedria Vasilike*, 85–89.

140. John Ogilby, *The Entertainment of His Most Excellent Majestie Charles II* (1661), 10–12; Batchelor, *London*, 152–161.

141. *Aqua triumphalis, being a true relation of the honourable the city of Londons entertaining Their Sacred Majesties upon the river of Thames* (1662), 2–6.

142. Cobbett, *Parliamentary History*, vol. 4, 266.

143. "Estimate," 19 August 1661, Clarendon MSS, 75, fols. 97–98; Edwin Chappell, ed., *The Tangiers Papers of Samuel Pepys* (London, 1935), 76–77.

144. Latham and Matthews, *Diary of Samuel Pepys*, vol. 3, 319; "The Generall Survey of his Majesties Royall Citty of Tang," 31 December 1676, Rawlinson MSS A185, 37; E. M. G. Routh, *Tangier: England's Lost Atlantic Outpost, 1661–1684* (London, 1912), 194.

145. "Accompt of the Limits & Trade for ye African Company," 1672, CO 268/1, fols. 5–6; K. G. Davies, *The Royal African Company* (London: Longmans Green, 1957), 40–45, 63–64; Bliss, *Revolution and Empire*, 127.

146. Paper on negotiations with Portugal, February 1661, Clarendon MSS, 75, fols. 204–205; Downing to Clarendon, 30 September 1664, Clarendon MSS, 108, fols. 111–116; "Articles of Agreement between the Royal Company and the East India Company," October 1662, BL, IOR, E/3/86 fols. 171–172.

147. Davies, *Royal African Company*, 256; Latham and Matthews, *Diary of Samuel Pepys*, vol. 4, 152; vol. 5, 48, 52.

148. Sir Abraham Shipman to Oxenden, 21 September 1663, BL Add MSS 40709, 4–5; Pepys, Notes on Tangier, Rawlinson MSS, D916, fols. 84–85.

149. Sir Hugh Cholmley to Sir Richard Fanshaw, 19 July 1665, North Yorkshire CRO, ZCG, V, 1/1/1, fol. 175; Cholmley, "Some discourses further stating the several interests of Tangier," in *Memoirs of Sir Hugh Cholmley* (1870), 83–84.

150. *Life of Edward, Earl of Clarendon*, 2 vols. (Dublin, 1759 ed.), vol. 1, 96.

151. *Calendar of Treasury Books*, vol. 1: *1660–1667*, ed. William A. Shaw (London, 1904), 458–459, 493, 518.

152. M. de Bastide to Clarendon, 2 April 1661, Clarendon MSS 75, fols. 99–102; Pepys, notes on Tangier, Rawlinson MSS, D916, fols. 84–85; Howell, "Touching the late Rendition," fols. 132–133.

153. Clarendon to Sir Richard Fanshaw, March 1664/5, Clarendon MSS, 78, fol. 170.

154. Russell, "Motives for Peace and Commerce," A25/54.

155. William Ryder to George Oxenden, 26 March 1663, BL Add MSS 40,711, 52.

156. *Life of Edward, Earl of Clarendon*, vol. 1, 107–108; Downing to Clarendon, 22 July/ 1 August 1664, Clarendon MSS, 108, fols. 39–41.

157. Petition of Royal Adventurers to Charles II, 15 June 1664, *CSPD, 1664–1665*, 99/83; Register of the Privy Council, 19 March 1661, PC/2/55, 294; 31 October 1662, PC/2/56, 96; 11 November 1662, PC/2/56, 105.

158. "Animadversion of Tangier," 17 June 1664, Clarendon MSS, 81, fols. 284–285.

159. Sir William Coventry, Paper on the Dutch War, 1667, Coventry MSS, 102, fols. 4–7; Latham and Matthews, *Diary of Samuel Pepys,* vol. 5, 160.

160. Latham and Matthews, *Diary of Samuel Pepys,* vol. 5, 108, 159–160; Pincus, *Protestantism and Patriotism,* 277–317.

161. Earl of Peterborough to Williamson, 15 April 1665, *CSPD, 1664–1665,* 118/37; Privy Council Register, 25 October 1663, PC/2/56, 297; Paulina Kewes, "Dryden's Theatre and the Passions of Politics," in Stephen N. Zwicker, ed., *Cambridge Companion to John Dryden* (Cambridge: Cambridge University Press, 2006), 140–141.

162. *Life of Edward, Earl of Clarendon,* vol. 1, 195.

163. Sir Richard Ford, Paper on grounds for war, Clarendon MSS, 83, fols. 373–374.

164. "A Brief Narrative of the Late Passages between his Majesty and the Dutch, and his Majesty's preparations thereunto," 1664, Clarendon MSS, 83, fols. 375–381.

165. *Life of Edward, Earl of Clarendon,* vol. 1, 94–95; Downing to Clarendon, 25 March 1663/4, Clarendon MSS, 107, fol. 143.

166. Dryden, *Annus Mirabilis,* 44, 73.

167. Ames, "Role of Religion," 330–340.

168. Bliss, *Revolution and Empire,* 194–198.

169. "Copie of a Privy Seal for £1,000 p. annee for New York," 10 August 1670, BL Egerton MSS, fol. 108–109; Richard Nicolls to Clarendon, February 1665/6, Clarendon MSS, 84, fols. 118–122.

170. Hugh Cholmley to Henry Cholmley, 7 May 1666, Cholmley MSS, ZGC V/1/1/319.

171. Cobbett, *Parliamentary History,* vol. 4, 228–229.

Chapter 2. The Moral Image of Empire in Restoration England

1. Margaret Cavendish, *The Description of a New World, Called The Blazing-World* (1666), 121–122; Jason Scott-Warren, *Early Modern English Literature* (Cambridge: Cambridge University Press, 2005), 138–146.

2. Cavendish, *Blazing World,* 11, 144.

3. David Armitage, "Literature and Empire," in Nicholas Canny, ed., *The Oxford History of the British Empire,* vol. 1: *The Origins of Empire* (Oxford: Oxford University Press, 1998), 99–108; Frank E. Manuel and Fritzie P. Manuel, *Utopian Thought in the Western World* (Cambridge: Harvard University Press, 1979), 181–203, 243–288; Lauren Benton, *A Search for Sovereignty: Law and Geography in European Empires, 1400–1900* (Cambridge: Cambridge University Press, 2010), 162–163.

4. Cavendish, *Blazing World,* 97–98.

5. Thomas Sprat, *Observations on Monsieur de Sorbier's Voyage into England* (1665), 89, 91.

6. Thomas Povey to Edward Digges, 2 March 1660/1, BL Add MSS, 11411, fol. 24.

7. *Memoirs of Sir Hugh Cholmley* (1870), 95.

8. Arthur H. Williamson, "An Empire to End Empire: The Dynamic of Early Modern British Expansion," *Huntingdon Library Quarterly* 68, nos. 1–2 (March 2005): 227–256; Karen O'Brien, "Poetry Against Empire: Milton to Shelley," *Proceedings of the British Academy* 117 (London: British Academy, 2002), 269–296.

9. William Loddington, *Plantation-Work: The Work of this Generation* (1682), 3.

10. David Armitage, *The Ideological Origins of the British Empire* (Cambridge: Cambridge University Press, 2000), 61–98; Steven Pincus, "From Holy Cause to Economic Interest: The Study of Population and the Invention of the State," in Pincus and Alan Houston, eds., *A Nation Transformed: England after the Restoration* (Cambridge: Cambridge University Press, 2001), 272–298.

11. Edmund Bohun to John Cary, 15 February 1696, BL Add MSS, 5540, fols. 60–61.

12. George Scot, *Model of the Government of the Province of East New Jersey* (1682), 25–26.

13. John Hammond, *Leah and Rachel; or, the Two Fruitfull Sisters Virginia and Maryland* (1655), 1.

14. William Davenant, *Gondibert, an heroick poem* (1651), 35.

15. James Howell, *Proedria Vasilike: A discourse concerning the precedency of kings* (1664), 159.

16. Roger Whitley, Commonplace book, Bodl., MS Eng. Hist. e. 303, 2; Andrew Fitzmaurice, *Humanism and America: An Intellectual History of English Colonisation* (Cambridge: Cambridge University Press, 2003), 20–56.

17. Sprat, *Observations*, 17, 59–63.

18. George Lane to Sir John Percival, 6 June 1682, BL Add MSS, 47022, fol. 82.

19. John Evelyn, *Navigation and Commerce. Their original and progress* (1674), 18; *CSPC, 1661–1668,* 739.

20. Davenant, *Gondibert,* 35.

21. David A. Boruchoff, "Piety, Patriotism, and Empire: Lessons for England, Spain, and the New World in the Works of Richard Hakluyt," *Renaissance Quarterly* 62, no. 3 (Fall 2009): 809–811; Peter Burke, "America and the Rewriting of World History," in Karen Ordahl Kupperman, ed., *America in European Consciousness, 1493–1750* (Williamsburg: Omohundro Institute of Early American History and Culture, University of North Carolina Press, 1995), 40–41.

22. Anthony Pagden, *Lords of All the World: Ideologies of Empire in Spain, Britain, and France, c. 1500–c. 1800* (New Haven: Yale University Press, 1995), 32, 46–47, 51; J. H. Elliott, *Empires of the Atlantic World: Britain and Spain in America, 1492–1830* (New Haven: Yale University Press, 2006), 184–206.

23. Howell, *Proedria Vasilike,* 161.

24. John Dryden, *The Indian Emperor; or, The Conquest of Mexico by the Spaniards* (1667), preface, 5–6; Bridget Orr, *Empire on the English Stage, 1660–1714* (Cambridge: Cambridge University Press, 2001), 143.

25. John Robertson, "Empire and Union: Two Concepts of the Early Modern European Political Order," in Robertson, ed., *A Union for Empire: Political Thought and the British Union of 1707* (Cambridge: Cambridge University Press, 1996), 17;

Sofia Guthrie, "Antoine Garissoles' *Adolphid* (1649), a Huguenot Latin Epic," MA diss., University of Warwick, 2014.

26. *An epitome of Mr. John Speed's theatre of the empire of Great Britain and of his prospect of the most famous parts of the world* (1676), 189–196.

27. Charles Molloy, *De Jure Maritimo et Navali: or, A Treatise of Affaires Maritime, and of Commerce* (1676), A3.

28. Cavendish, *Blazing World*, 60.

29. David Armitage, "Milton: Poet against Empire," in David Armitage, Armand Himy, and Quentin Skinner, eds., *Milton and Republicanism* (Cambridge: Cambridge University Press, 2005), 206–225; Williamson, "Empire to End Empire," 233–234.

30. O'Brien, "Poetry against Empire," 269–279; J. Martin Evans, *Milton's Imperial Epic:* Paradise Lost *and the Discourse of Colonialism* (Ithaca: Cornell University Press, 1996).

31. Paul Rycaut, *The present state of the Ottoman Empire* (1667), 5, 7–8.

32. Henry Martin, *Considerations upon the East-India Trade* (1701), 86.

33. Linda T. Darling, "Ottoman Politics through British Eyes: Paul Rycaut's *The Present State of the Ottoman Empire*," *Journal of World History* 5, no. 1 (Spring 1994): 71–97; Robert Markley, *The Far East and the English Imagination, 1600–1730* (Cambridge: Cambridge University Press, 2006), 30–69.

34. John Dryden, *Aureng-Zebe* (1675), 31.

35. Rycaut, *Present state*, 2, 78–79, 81.

36. For the fullest account, see Orr, *Empire on the English Stage*, 49–75.

37. Dryden, *Aureng-Zebe*, 2, 44; Dryden, *Indian Emperor*, 1.

38. John Milton, *Areopagitica* (1644), 6–7.

39. *The tears of the Indians being an historical and true account of the cruel massacres and slaughters of above twenty millions of innocent people* (1656); William S. Maltby, *The Black Legend in England* (Durham, NC: Duke University Press, 1971), 18–21; Boruchoff, "Piety, Patriotism," 813–816.

40. John Clerk to James Clerk, 1679, NRS, GD 28/5177/36, fol. 3.

41. Heylin, *Cosmographie*, 1082–1083.

42. John Davies and César Rochefort, *The history of the Caribby-islands* (1666), preface, 256; Dryden, *Indian Emperor*, 57–59.

43. Fabian Philipps, *The antiquity, legality, reason, duty and necessity of prae-emption and purveyance* (1663), 454.

44. Dryden, *Indian Emperor*, 61.

45. William Godolphin to earl of Arlington, 28 June/5 July 1670, SP 94/56, fol. 217.

46. William Paterson to the directors of the Company of Scotland, 15 January 1700, Edinburgh, National Library of Scotland, Adv. MSS 83.7.5, 56.

47. Heylin, *Cosmographie*, preface; Pagden, *Lords of All the World*, 63–71; Armitage, "Literature and Empire," 109–110.

48. Rycaut, *Present state*, 7, 8, 78–79.

49. *Europae modernae speculum; or, A view of the empires, kingdoms, principalities, seigneuries, and common-wealths of Europe* (1666), 258.

50. J. G. A. Pocock, *The Ancient Constitution and the Feudal Law* (Cambridge: Cambridge University Press, 1957); Richard Helgerson, *Forms of Nationhood: The Elizabethan Writing of England* (Chicago: Chicago University Press, 1994), 36–39.

51. James Howell, "Touching the late Rendition of Dunkirk," Bodl., Clarendon MSS, 78, fol. 133.

52. Sprat, *Observations*, 82.

53. Thomas Jordan, *London Triumphant* (1672), 7.

54. "Reasons to justifie the first Designe into the West Indies," BL Harley MSS, 3361, fols. 46–47.

55. "A breife survey of Jamaica," BL Egerton MSS, 2395, fol. 614.

56. Armitage, *Ideological Origins*, 68–71.

57. See, for instance, Richard Eburne, *A Plaine Pathway to Plantations* (1624), preface, 4–5; *A Declaration of his Highness* (1655); Cotton Mather, *Magnalia Christi Americana*, 2 vols. (1702), vol. 1, 41–42; Douglas Bradburn, "The Eschatological Origins of the English Empire," in Douglas Bradburn and John C. Coombs, eds., *Early Modern Virginia: Reconsidering the Old Dominion* (Charlottesville: University of Virginia Press, 2011), 15–56.

58. *An Abstract or abbreviation of some few of the many (later and former) testimonys from the inhabitants of New-Jersey* (1681).

59. Heylin, *Cosmographie*, 1000.

60. Pagden, *Lords of All the World*, 46–51; Andrew Fitzmaurice, *Sovereignty, Property and Empire 1500–2000* (Cambridge: Cambridge University Press, 2014), 45–50.

61. Francis Parry to earl of Arlington, 16/26 November 1672, BL Add MSS, 35100, fol. 240.

62. Hakluyt, *Discourse*, vol. 1, 11; vol. 2, 8–9.

63. Richard S. Dunn and Mary Maples Dunn, eds., *The Papers of William Penn*, 5 vols. (Philadelphia: University of Pennsylvania Press, 1981–1986), vol. 2, 473; Papers concerning the English right to Nova Scotia, BL Egerton MSS, 2395, fols. 20–21; Anthony Pagden, "The Struggle for Legitimacy and the Image of Empire in the Atlantic to c. 1700," in Canny, *Oxford History of the British Empire*, vol. 1, 34–54.

64. E. E. Rich, ed., *Minutes of the Hudson's Bay Company, 1671–1674* (London: Champlain Society, 1942), 132.

65. Earl of Arlington to Richard Fanshaw, 6 October 1664, in Thomas Bebington, ed., *The Right Honourable the Earl of Arlington's Letters*, 2 vols. (1701), vol. 2, 49.

66. Dunn and Dunn, *Papers of William Penn*, vol. 2, 473, emphasis mine. Penn would later backtrack on that claim in the same exchange with the Committee of Trade.

67. Howell, *Proedria Vasilike*, 160–161; Scott, *Model of the Government*, 32–33.

68. Richard Eburne, *A Plaine Pathway to Plantations* (1624), preface, 4–5; Heylin, *Cosmographie*, 99–100.

69. See especially John Beale to John Evelyn, 12 June 1669, BL Add MSS 15948, fol. 137; Michael Hunter, Antonio Clericuzio, and Lawrence M. Principe, eds., *The Correspondence of Robert Boyle, 1636–1691*, 6 vols. (London, 2004), v, 243 [henceforth *Boyle Correspondence*]; Draught of a scheme . . . drawn up for Dr Daniel Cox," n.d., Rawlinson MSS, A305, fols. 2–5.

70. Samuel Maverick to earl of Clarendon, 1665, Clarendon MSS, 74, fol. 249.

71. Joseph Hall, *Resolutions and Decisions of Divers Practical Cases of Conscience* (1659 ed.), 234–235, 247–248.

72. Fitzmaurice, *Sovereignty*, 59–83; Pagden, *Lords of All the World*, 47–51.

73. Hall, *Resolutions*, 247.

74. James Axtell, *The Invasion Within: The Contest of Cultures in Colonial North America* (Oxford: Oxford University Press, 1985); Elliott, *Empires*, 80–81.

75. R. W. Cogley, *John Eliot's Mission to the Indians before King Philip's War* (Cambridge: Harvard University Press, 1999); William Kellaway, *The New England Company, 1649–1776* (London: Longmans, Green, 1961), 5–8; David S. Lovejoy, "Satanizing the American Indian," *New England Quarterly* 67, no. 4 (December 1994): 603–621.

76. *The soveraignty & goodness of God . . . being a narrative of the captivity and restauration of Mrs. Mary Rowlandson* (1682), 64.

77. Francis J. Bremer, *John Winthrop: America's Forgotten Founding Father* (Oxford: Oxford University Press, 2003), 178.

78. Daniel Denton, *A Brief Description of New York* (1670), 6–7.

79. John Cotton, *God's Promise to his Plantation* (1630); John Winthrop, "General Considerations for Planting New England," in Alexander Young, ed., *Chronicles of the First Planters of the Colony of Massachusetts Bay, 1623–1636* (Boston, 1846), 272; Samuel Sewall and Edward Rawson, *The Revolution in New England Justified* (1691), 13.

80. Hammond, *Leah and Rachel;* Ellen Chirelstein, "Lady Elizabeth Pope: The Heraldic Body," in Lucy Gent and Nigel Llewellyn, eds., *Renaissance Bodies* (Chicago: Chicago University Press, 1990), 36–59; James Tully, "Rediscovering America: The Two Treatises and Aboriginal Rights," in G. A. J. Rogers, ed., *An Approach to Political Philosophy: Locke in Contexts* (Cambridge: Cambridge University Press, 1993), 137–176.

81. Dunn and Dunn, *Papers of William Penn*, vol. 2, 498–499; vol. 3, 61; *CSPC, 1685–1688*, 456.

82. Molloy, *De Jure*, 421–422.

83. Carla Gardina Pestana, *Protestant Empire: Religion and the Making of the British Atlantic World* (Philadelphia: University of Pennsylvania Press, 2009), 69–71.

84. Carl Bridenbaugh, ed., *The Pynchon Papers. Letters of John Pynchon, 1654–1700*, 2 vols. (Boston: Colonial Society of Massachusetts, 1982), vol. 1, 23, 61, 105–106; Jenny Hale Pulsipher, *Subjects unto the Same King* (Philadelphia: University of Pennsylvania Press, 2005), 62–65, 70–72, 79–81.

85. David Pulsifer, ed., *Acts of the Commissioners of the United Colonies* (Boston, 1859), vol. 2, 255–259; Harold W. Van Lonkhuyzen, "A Reappraisal of the Praying Indians: Acculturation, Conversion, and Identity at Natick, Massachusetts, 1646–1730," *New England Quarterly*, 63, no. 3 (September 1990): 396–428.

86. Increase Mather, *A brief history of the war with the Indians in New-England* (1676), 1–3; Helen Smith, "'Wilt Thou Not Read Me, Atheist?' The Bible and Conversion," in Kevin Killeen, Helen Smith, and Rachel Willie, eds., *The Oxford Handbook of*

the Bible in Early Modern England, c. 1530–1700 (Oxford: Oxford University Press, 2015), 350–365; Mark Häberlein, "Protestantism Outside Europe," in Ulinka Rublack, ed., *The Oxford Handbook of the Protestant Reformations* (Oxford: Oxford University Press, 2016), 353–356.

87. Philipps, *Antiquity, legality*, 42; George Alsop, *A Character of the Province of Maryland* (1666), 59–61; Karen Ordahl Kupperman, "Presentment of Civility: English Reading of American Self-Presentation in the Early Years of Colonization," *W&MQ* 54, no. 1 (January 1997): 193–228.

88. Colin Kidd, *The Forging of Races* (Cambridge: Cambridge University Press, 2006), 65–68.

89. John Oldmixon, *The British Empire in America*, 2 vols. (1708), vol. 1, 161; John Ogilby, *America* (1670), 17–18; Heylin, *Cosmographie*, 1004; Richard Cogley, " 'Some other kinde of being and condition': The Controversy in Mid-Seventeenth-Century England over the Peopling of Ancient America," *Journal of the History of Ideas* 68, no. 1 (January 2007): 35–56; Richard W. Cogley, "John Eliot and the Origins of the American Indians," *Early American Literature* 21, no. 3 (Winter 1986/1987): 210–225.

90. Alsop, *Character of the Province of Maryland*, 59, 71; Kidd, *Forging of Races*, 39, 67.

91. Heylin, *Cosmographie*, 1004; "Col Scott's Preface to an Intended History of America," Rawlinson MSS, A175, fol. 382; Roger Greene, *Virginia's Cure; or, An advisive narrative concerning Virginia* (1661), 5–8.

92. Anthony Pagden, *European Encounters with the New World* (New Haven: Yale University Press, 1993), 185–187; Alden T. Vaughan and Virginia Mason Vaughan, "England's 'Others' in the Old and New Worlds," in Francis J. Bremer and Lynne A. Botelho, eds., *The World of John Winthrop: Essays on England and New England, 1588–1649* (Boston: Massachusetts Historical Society, 2005), 22–74.

93. Roger Williams, *The hirelings minister none of Christs* (1652), 2–4; *A Petition of WC Exhibited to the High Court of Parliament* (1641).

94. Patrick S. McGhee, " 'Heathenism' in the Protestant Atlantic World, c. 1558–1700," PhD diss., University of Cambridge, 2019.

95. Thomas Thorowgood, *Iewes in America* (1650); Andrew Crome, "The Jewish Indian Theory and Protestant Use of Catholic Thought in the Early Modern Atlantic," in Crawford Gribben and Scott Spurlock, eds., *Puritans and Catholics in the Trans-Atlantic World, 1600–1800* (Basingstoke: Palgrave Macmillan, 2015), 112–130.

96. John Oxenbridge, *A seasonable proposition of propagating the gospel by Christian colonies in the continent of Guaiana* (1670), 5–6.

97. Sir Henry Bennett to the Governor of Massachusetts, 1661, Clarendon MSS, 103, fols. 1–2.

98. Jeremy Gregory, "The Later Stuart Church and America," in Grant Tapsell, ed., *The Later Stuart Church, 1660–1714* (Manchester: Manchester University Press, 2012), 152; Mattie E. E. Parker, ed., *North Carolina Charters and Constitutions* (Raleigh, NC: Carolina Charter Tercentenary Commission, 1963), 76; Charter of Rhode Island and Providence Plantations, 8 July 1663, *CSPC, 1661–1668*, 512.

99. Matthew Sylvester, ed., *Reliquiae Baxteriana* (1696), bk. 1, pt. 2, 290; *Boyle Correspondence*, ii, 44–45; Kellaway, *New England Company*, 41–50; Linda Gregerson, "The Commonwealth of the Word: New England, Old England, and the Praying Indians," in Linda Gregerson and Susan Juster, eds., *Empires of God: Religious Encounters in the Early Modern Atlantic* (Philadelphia: University of Pennsylvania Press, 2010), 70–83.

100. Robert Gray, *A good speed to Virginia* (1604), 3–4.

101. Loddington, *Plantation-Work*, 3. See also Oxenbridge, *Seasonable proposition*, 5; William Crashaw, *A sermon preached in London* (1609).

102. "Col. Scott's Preface to an Intended History of America," Rawlinson MSS, A175, fol. 383; Davies and Rochefort, *History of the Caribby-Islands*, preface, 256; Morgan Godwyn, *A Supplement to the Negro's & Indian's Advocate* (1681), 32–35.

103. F. J. Powicke, *Some Unpublished Correspondence of the Reverend Richard Baxter and the Reverend John Eliot* (Manchester: Manchester University Press, 1931), 55.

104. "Col. Scott's Preface," fols. 382–383; "Writers of Carolina," PRO 30/24/48, fols. 277–278; Green, *Virginia's Cure*, 12–13; Jorge Cañizares-Esguerra, "The 'Iberian' Justifications of Territorial Possession by Pilgrims and Puritans in the Colonization of America," in Cañizares-Esguerra, ed., *Entangled Histories: The Anglo-Iberian Atlantic, 1500–1830* (Philadelphia: University of Pennsylvania Press, 2018), 161–177.

105. Patent of Incorporation, 7 February 1661/2, *CSPC, 1661–1668*, 223.

106. Roger Whitley, "Plantation," Bodl., MS Eng. Hist. e. 309, c. 712, fol. 608.

107. *Boyle Correspondence*, iv, 427; Report of the committee of the East India Company, 1672, Bodl., Tanner MSS 36, fol. 67.

108. Thomas Leng, "'A Potent Plantation well armed and Policeed'": Huguenots, the Hartlib Circle, and British Colonization in the 1640s," *W&MQ* 66, no. 1 (January 2009): 173–194; Sarah Irving, *Natural Science and the Origins of the British Empire* (London: Pickering & Chatto, 2008), 47–68.

109. Thomas Sprat, *The History of the Royal Society* (1667), 86, 382.

110. A. Rupert Hall and Marie Boas Hall, eds., *The Correspondence of Henry Oldenburg*, 10 vols. (London: Mansell, 1966), vol. 3, 525–526.

111. John Evelyn to Henry Oldenburg, 18 July 1676, BL Evelyn MS, 39a, fol. 382; Michael Hunter, *Science and Society in Restoration England* (Cambridge: Cambridge University Press, 1981).

112. Answers to Henry Oldenburg, July 1664, Royal Society Archives, CLP 19, 9; Oldenburg, "A Memoriall for Sir Robert Southwell in Portugall," 20 September 1665, RSA, CLP 19, 15.

113. Thomas Birch, *The History of the Royal Society of London* (London, 1756–1757), 397; C. R. Weld, *A History of the Royal Society* (London, 1848), vol. 1, 349–350; Sprat, *History*, 215.

114. Lorenzo Magalotti, *Travels of Cosmo the Third, Grand Duke of Tuscany, through England* (London, 1821), 176–177.

115. Marquis of Lansdowne, ed., *The Petty–Southwell Correspondence, 1676–1687* (London, 1928), 144–145, 161, 233.

116. Thomas Povey to Edward Digges, 2 March 1660/1, BL Add MSS, 11411, fol. 24.

117. Mary Astell, *An essay in defence of the female sex* (1696), 96–97, 102–103.

118. Hall and Hall, *Oldenburg Correspondence*, vol. 3, 276–277.

119. Thomas Lynch to Sir Robert Moray, 2 March 1671/2, BL Add MSS, 11410, fols. 239–242.

120. Thomas Lynch to Sir Robert Moray, 25 December 1672, BL Add MSS 11,410, fol. 297; BL Egerton MSS, 2395, fol. 648.

121. Hall and Hall, *Oldenburg Correspondence*, vol. 4, 144–145.

122. Ashley Cooper to Thomas Lynch, 29 October 1672, PRO 30/24/48 fol. 194.

123. *Boyle Correspondence*, vol. 2, 172.

124. Cavendish, *Blazing World*, 48, 156.

125. Sprat, *Observations*, 49–50.

126. Thomas Hariot, *Briefe and True Report of the New Found Land of Virginia* (1588), 27.

127. Toby Barnard, "The Hartlib Circle and the Cult and Culture of Improvement in Ireland," in Mark Greengrass, Michael Leslie, and Timothy Raylor, eds., *Samuel Hartlib and Universal Reformation* (Cambridge: Cambridge University Press, 1995), 283–286; Toby Barnard, *Improving Ireland? Projectors, Prophets, and Profiteers, 1641–1786* (Dublin: Four Courts Press, 2008).

128. Joseph M. Levine, *The Battle of the Books: History and Literature in the Augustan Age* (Ithaca, NY: Cornell University Press, 1994), 13–46.

129. Sprat, *History*, 16–17. See also John Ogilby, *An Embassy from the East India Company of the Netherlands* (1669), 3.

130. *Life of Edward, Earl of Clarendon*, vol. 1, 153.

131. Cavendish, *Blazing World*, 139–145.

132. Thomas Leng, *Benjamin Worsley (1618–1677): Trade, Interest, and the Spirit in Revolutionary England* (Woodbridge, UK: Boydell and Brewer, 2008), 187–191; Paul Slack, *The Invention of Improvement: Information and Material Progress in Seventeenth-Century England* (Oxford: Oxford University Press, 2014), 100–101.

133. John Flavel, *Navigation Spiritualiz'd; or, A New Compass for Seamen* (1664), preface.

134. Marquis of Lansdowne, *Petty–Southwell Correspondence*, 154–155.

135. Ibid., 46; Ted McCormick, *William Petty and the Ambitions of Political Arithmetic* (Oxford: Oxford University Press, 2009), 42–43, 288–289.

136. *Boyle Correspondence*, vol. 2, 167–168, vol. 5, 241; Michael Hunter, *Robert Boyle: Between God and Science* (New Haven: Yale University Press, 2009), 5, 65, 129–131, 170–171.

137. Henry Sheres, "A Discourse touching the Current in the Streight of Gibraltar," 1676, Rawlinson MSS, A341, fols. 178–193.

138. Langdon Cheves, ed., *The Shaftesbury Papers* (Charleston, SC: Tempus Publishing, 2000), 82.

139. Oldenburg, "Queries for his Excellency ye Lord Henry Howard of Norfolk, Embassador for his Majty to Morocco," 1669, RSA, CLP 19, 33.

140. Molloy, *De Jure*, preface.

141. Flavel, *Navigation Spiritualiz'd*, 37–39.

142. James Whiston, "To the King's most Excellent Maty," 1686, BL Sloane MSS, 3984, fol. 198.

143. Edmund Waller, *A Panegyrick to my Lord Protector* (1655), 5.

144. Williamson, "Empire to End Empire," 241.

145. Rycaut, *Present state*, 213.

146. William Davenant, *Poem to the King's Most Sacred Majesty* (1663), 20.

147. Earl of Peterborough to the subjects of Tangier, 22 February 1661/2, Rawlinson MSS, D941, fol. 3; *Memoirs of Sir Hugh Cholmley*, 10, 98.

148. William J. Bulman, *Anglican Enlightenment: Orientalism, Religion and Politics in England and Its Empire, 1648–1715* (Cambridge: Cambridge University Press, 2015), 43–70.

149. Hugh Cholmley to Richard Fanshaw, 19 July 1665, Northallerton, North Yorkshire CRO, Cholmley MSS, ZCG, V/1/1/I, 175.

Chapter 3. Conflict, Commerce, and Political Economies of Empire

1. Samuel Lambe, *Seasonable Observations humbly offered to His Highness the Lord Protector* (1657), 5.

2. Thomas Sprat, *History of the Royal Society* (1667), 407; see also Thomas Mun, *England's treasure by forraign trade* (1664), 2–9.

3. *The Character and Qualifications of an Honest Loyal Merchant* (1686), preface.

4. Nuala Zahedieh, *The Capital and the Colonies: London and the Atlantic Economy, 1660–1700* (Cambridge: Cambridge University Press, 2010), 35–53, 57–64; Alison Gilbert Olson, *Making the Empire Work: London and American Interest Groups, 1690–1790* (Cambridge: Harvard University Press, 1992), 52; Ian K. Steele, *The English Atlantic, 1675–1740* (Oxford: Oxford University Press, 1986), 88–95.

5. Perry Gauci, *The Politics of Trade: The Overseas Merchant in State and Society, 1660–1720* (Oxford: Oxford University Press, 2001), 76–86, 166–175; Richard Grassby, *The Business Community of Seventeenth-Century England* (Cambridge: Cambridge University Press, 1995).

6. Abigail L. Swingen, *Competing Visions of Empire: Labor, Slavery, and the Origins of the British Atlantic Empire* (New Haven: Yale University Press, 2015), 11–31, 82–107; Steven Pincus, " 'From Holy Cause to Economic Interest': The Study of Population and the Invention of the State," in Pincus and Alan Houston, eds., *A Nation Transformed: England after the Restoration* (Cambridge: Cambridge University Press, 2001), 272–298; Leslie Theibert, "Reconciling Empire: English Political Economy and the Spanish Imperial Model, 1660–90," in Jason Peacey, ed., *Making the British Empire, 1660–1800* (Manchester: Manchester University Press, 2020), 100–120.

7. Emily Erikson and Mark Hamilton, "Companies and the Rise of Economic Thought: The Institutional Foundations of Early Economics in England, 1550–1720," *American Journal of Sociology* 124, no. 1 (2018): 142.

8. John Evelyn, *Navigation and Commerce. Their original and progress* (1674), 10–11.

9. Ernest Barker, ed., *The Politics of Aristotle* (Oxford: Clarendon Press, 1946), 301.

10. James Harrington, *The Commonwealth of Oceana*, ed. J. G. A. Pocock (Cambridge: Cambridge University Press, 1992), 5, 21; J. G. A. Pocock, *Virtue, Commerce and History* (Cambridge: Cambridge University Press, 1985), 68.

11. Andrew Fitzmaurice, *Humanism and America: An Intellectual History of English Colonisation* (Cambridge: Cambridge University Press, 2003), 39–86.

12. Craig Muldrew, *The Economy of Obligation: The Culture of Credit and Social Relations in Early Modern England* (London: Palgrave Macmillan, 1998); Natasha Glaisyer, *The Culture of Commerce in England, 1660–1720* (Woodbridge, UK: Boydell & Brewer, 2006), 100–142.

13. Henry Sheres, *A discourse touching Tanger in a letter to a person of quality* (1680), 10–11.

14. Christine R. Johnson, "Commerce and Consumption," in Ulinka Rublack, ed., *The Oxford Handbook of the Protestant Reformations* (Oxford: Oxford University Press, 2016), 708–722; Haig Smith, "Religious Governance in England's Overseas Companies c. 1601–1698," PhD diss., University of Kent, 2017, 4–6.

15. John Donne, *Foure sermons upon speciall occasions* (1625), 28.

16. Benjamin Worsley to Anthony Ashley Cooper, "Some Considerations about the Commission for Trade," [1668], PRO 30/24/49, fols. 90–92; Thomas Leng, *Benjamin Worsley (1618–1677): Trade, Interest, and the Spirit in Revolutionary England* (Woodbridge, UK: Boydell and Brewer, 2008), 141–143.

17. Proposal concerning admiralty courts, 1665, BL Add MSS 28,079, fols. 26–7; Joyce Appleby, *Economic Thought and Ideology in Seventeenth-Century England* (Princeton: Princeton University Press, 1987).

18. Letter from Hamburg, 2 August 1680, Bodl., Carte MSS, 69, fol. 387.

19. Johann von Friesendorff, "Proposals," 20 August 1661, Clarendon MSS, fols. 75, 108–113; C.K., *Some seasonable and modest thoughts* (1696), 5; Roger Coke, *A Discourse of Trade* (1670), preface; Andrew Fletcher, *An Account of a Conversation, concerning a Right Regulation of Governments, for the Common Good of Mankind* (1703), 40.

20. Istvan Hont, *Jealousy of Trade: International Competition and the Nation-State in Historical Perspective* (Cambridge: Harvard University Press, 2005), 185–190.

21. Worsley to Ashley Cooper, "Some considerations," fol. 92.

22. R. Latham and W. Matthews, eds., *The Diary of Samuel Pepys*, 11 vols. (London: HarperCollins, 1970–1983), vol. 5, 95. Basil Henning, in *The History of Parliament: The House of Commons, 1660–1690*, 2 vols. (London: Secker and Warburg, 1983), vol. 1, 10, puts the figure at 7 percent for the Cavalier Parliament, rising to 11 percent by the 1680s.

23. James Whiston, "To the King's most Excellent Maty," 1686, BL Sloane MSS, 3984, fol. 198.

24. Celia Fiennes, *Through England on a Side Saddle* (London, 1888), 233; P. K. O'Brien and P. A. Hunt, "The Rise of a Fiscal State in England, 1485–1815," *Historical Research* 66, no. 160 (June 1993): 129–176.

25. Kenneth Morgan, "Mercantilism and the British Empire, 1688–1815," in Donald Winch and Patrick O'Brien, eds., *The Political Economy of British Historical Experience* (Oxford: Oxford University Press, 2002), 165–191; David Ormrod, *The Rise of Commercial Empires: England and the Netherlands in the Age of Mercantilism* (Cambridge: Cambridge University Press, 2003), 17–18.

26. Philip J. Stern and Carl Wennerlind, "Introduction," in Stern and Wennerlind, eds., *Mercantilism Reimagined: Political Economy in Early Modern Britain and Its Empire* (Oxford: Oxford University Press, 2013), 3–22.

27. Steve Pincus, "Rethinking Mercantilism: Political Economy, the British Empire, and the Atlantic World in the Seventeenth and Eighteenth Centuries," *W&MQ* 69, no. 1 (January 2012): 15–17.

28. Richard Hakluyt, *A Discourse concerning Western Planting. Written in the year 1584*, 2 vols. (Cambridge, 1877), vol. 1, 13–14, 160–161; G. D. Ramsay, "Clothworkers, Merchant Adventurers and Richard Hakluyt," *EHR*, 92, no. 364 (July 1977): 504–521; Nuala Zahedieh, "Economy," in David Armitage and Michael Braddick, eds., *The British Atlantic World* (Basingstoke: Palgrave Macmillan, 2002), 53–57.

29. William Smith, *To the King's Most Excellent Majesty . . . an essay for recovery of trade* (1661), 39–42.

30. Hakluyt, *Discourse*, vol. 1, 14–15.

31. Benjamin Worsley to Anthony Ashley Cooper, 14 August 1668, PRO 30/24/49, fol. 225.

32. John Scott, "Account of the English colonies," 1661, BL Sloane MSS, 3662, fol. 4; Evelyn, *Navigation and Commerce*, 16, 18, 26–30; John Fryer, *A New Account of India and Persia* (1682), preface.

33. Worsley to Ashley Cooper, 14 August 1668, fol. 227; "Certaine Propositions for the better accomodating the forreigne plantations with servants," 1661, BL Egerton MSS, 2395, fol. 277; Journal of Lords of Trade, CO 391/1, 32.

34. Richard Blome, *A description of the island Jamaica* (1672), 58–59; Roger Whitley, "Plantation," Bodl., MS Eng. Hist. c. 712, 608; John Bland, *Trade Revived* (1659), 12.

35. Langdon Cheves, ed., *The Shaftesbury Papers* (Charleston, SC: Tempus Publications, 2000), 14–15.

36. Thomas Lynch, "The true state of the manufacture of sugar within our plantations," n.d., BL Egerton MSS, 2395, fol. 639; Rawlinson MSS, A478, fol. 68.

37. Fabian Philipps, *The antiquity, legality, reason, duty and necessity of prae-emption and purveyance* (1663), 311.

38. Worsley to Ashley Cooper, 14 August 1668, PRO 30/24/49, fol. 224.

39. Ibid., fol. 225.

40. "Instructions for the Councill of Trade," 1660, BL Egerton MSS, 2395, fol. 268; Anthony Ashley Cooper, "The Generall Account of the trade of the Kingdom," n.d., PRO 30/24/49, fol. 118; Paul Slack, *The Invention of Improvement: Information and Material Progress in Seventeenth-Century England* (Oxford: Oxford University Press, 2014), 84–86; Appleby, *Economic Thought*, 47–51.

41. Scott, "Account of the English colonies," fol. 4; Andrea Finkelstein, *Harmony and the Balance: An Intellectual History of Seventeenth-Century English Economic Thought* (Ann Arbor: University of Michigan Press, 2000), 84–89.

42. *The Character and Qualifications of an Honest, Loyal Merchant* (1686), 4.

43. Pincus, "Rethinking Mercantilism," 15–16.

44. Charles II, "Instructions" for the Council of Trade, c. 1670, PRO 30/24/49, fol. 120; E. E. Rich, ed., *Minutes of the Hudson's Bay Company, 1671–1674* (London: Champlain Society, 1942), 139.

45. Humphrey Giffard to George Oxenden, London, 25 March 1662/3, BL Add MSS, 40711, 47; Earl of Cassilis to earl of Lauderdale, 20 December 1660, NRS, Ailsa MSS, GD 25/9, box 30/2; K. G. Davies, *The Royal African Company* (London: Longmans, Green, 1957), 44–47.

46. Warrant to Sir Ralph Freeman and Henry Slingsby, 24 December 1663, *CSPC, 1661–1668*, 615; H G. Stride, "The Gold Coinage of Charles II," *British Numismatic Journal* 28 (1955): 386–393.

47. Sir Walter Raleigh, *The Discovery of the Large, Rich, and beautiful Empire of Guiana* (London, 1848), 82–83, 96–97.

48. Roger Whitley, "Plantation," Bodl., MS Eng. Hist. e. 309, fol. 608.

49. Sir William Berkeley, "A Discourse and View of Virginia," 1662, BL Egerton MSS, 2395, fol. 259; Berkeley to anon. correspondent, 30 March 1663, BL Egerton MSS, 2395, fol. 362.

50. Nuala Zahedieh, "Trade, Plunder and Economic Development in Early Jamaica, 1655–1689," *Economic History Review* 39, no. 2 (May 1986): 205–222; Saunders Webb, *Governors-General*, 233.

51. "The relation of Collonell Doyley upon his returne from Jamaica directed to the Lord Chancellor," 1662, BL Add MSS, 11411, fol. 10.

52. Edmund Hickeringill, *Jamaica viewed, with all their ports, harbours, and their several surroundings* (1661), 34.

53. "A Proposition for the Improving the interest of this Common Wealth in America," n.d., BL Egerton MSS, 2395, fols. 91–92; "Certeine queries concerning his Highnesse Interest in the West Indies," 1658, BL Egerton MSS, 2395, fol. 88.

54. Hickeringill, *Jamaica Viewed*, 53.

55. Mark G. Hanna, *Pirates' Nests and the Rise of the British Empire* (Chapel Hill: University of North Carolina Press, 2015), 102–143; Nuala Zahedieh, " 'A Frugal, Prudential and Hopeful Trade': Privateering in Jamaica, 1655–1689," *Journal of Imperial and Commonwealth History* 18, no. 2 (1990), 145–168.

56. R. Latham and W. Matthews, eds., *The Diary of Samuel Pepys*, 11 vols. (London: HarperCollins, 1970–1983), vol. 4, 41.

57. Swingen, *Competing Visions*, 74–78; Saunders Webb, *Governors-General*, 214–233.

58. Samuel von Pufendorf, *An Introduction to the History of the Principal Kingdoms and States of Europe* (1695), 73–75.

59. William Godolphin to Leoline Jenkins, 8 April 1676, SP 94/63, fol. 266.

60. Godolphin to Jenkins, 2/12 February 1675/6, SP 94/63, fol. 238.

61. Heylin, *Cosmographie*, 1053.

62. James Houblon, "A Discourse touching the Grounds of ye Decay of ye English Navigation," Rawlinson MSS A171, fol. 285.

63. Smith, *To the King's Most Excellent Majesty*, 45.

64. Pincus, "Rethinking Mercantilism," 16.

65. Register of the Privy Council, 11 March 1662, PC 2/56, 172–173.

66. Hickeringill, *Jamaica Viewed*, 18.

67. "On France and Spayne," 1661, Clarendon MSS, 73, fols. 71–72; "A breif survey of Jamaica," n.d., BL Harley MSS 3361, fols. 41–45; "Considerations about the peopling and settlement of the island of Jamaica," n.d., BL Egerton MSS, 2395, fols. 283–286.

68. "Whither the English now upon Jamaica may yet properly be understood to be a Collonie," 1660, BL Egerton MSS, 2395, fols. 289–290.

69. "Mr Worsley's Discourse of the Privateers of Jamaica," n.d., BL Add MSS, 11410, fols. 303–313.

70. Thomas Lynch, "Accompt of the English Sugar Plantations," PRO 30/24/49, fol. 20.

71. "Instructions . . . for the disposeing of the Regiment of Foot," 14 March 1670/1, CO 153/1, fols. 27–28; Sarah Barber, "Power in the English Caribbean: The Proprietorship of Lord Willoughby of Parham," in L. H. Roper and B. van Ruymbeke, eds., *Constructing Early Modern Empires: Proprietary Ventures in the Atlantic World, 1500–1750* (Leiden: Brill, 2007), 197.

72. Samuel Fortrey, *England's Interest and Improvement* (1673), 39.

73. Journal of the Lords of Trade, 18 October 1677, CO 391/2, fols. 64–65.

74. Anthony Langston, Account of Virginia, 1663, BL Egerton MSS, 2395, fol. 366.

75. William Berkeley to anonymous correspondent, 28 March 1663, BL Egerton MSS, 2395, fol. 360; Elizabeth Mancke, "Chartered Enterprises and the Evolution of the British Atlantic World," in Elizabeth Mancke and Carole Shammas, eds., *The Creation of the British Atlantic World* (Baltimore: Johns Hopkins University Press, 2005), 243–244.

76. Richard Beale Davis, ed., *William Fitzhugh and His Chesapeake World, 1676–1701* (Chapel Hill: University of North Carolina Press, 1963), 39–43.

77. James Tully, "Rediscovering America: The *Two Treatises* and Aboriginal Rights," in Tully, *An Approach to Political Philosophy: Locke in Contexts* (Cambridge: Cambridge University Press, 1993), 137–176; Barbara Arneil, *John Locke and America: The Defence of English Colonialism* (Oxford: Oxford University Press, 1996).

78. Journal of the Lords of Trade, 18 October 1677, CO 391/2, fols. 64–65.

79. Langston, Account of Virginia, 1663, BL Egerton MSS, 2395, fol. 366.

80. "A Shorte Memoriall to the Right Honourable Henry Coventry," 1675, Coventry MSS, 77, fol. 29; Francis Moryson and Thomas Ludwell to Coventry, 21 June 1676, 77 fol. 140; Journal of the Lords of Trade, CO, 391/2, fols. 64–65.

81. Mark Goldie, "Locke and America," in Matthew Stuart, ed., *A Companion to Locke* (Oxford: Oxford University Press, 2016), 561–562; Stephen Buckle, "Tully, Locke, and America," *British Journal for the History of Philosophy* 9, no. 2 (2001): 245–281.

82. Fortrey, *England's Interest*, 39; Bland, *Trade Revived*, 48; Journal of the Lords of Trade, CO, 391/1, fol. 102; Lynch, "Accompt of the English Sugar Plantations," PRO 30/24/49, fols. 230–236.

83. James Horn, *Adapting to a New World: English Society in the Seventeenth-Century Chesapeake* (Chapel Hill: University of North Carolina Press, 1994), 6; Zahedieh, *Capital and the Colonies*, 208–209; Carole Shammas, *The Pre-Industrial Consumer in England and America* (Oxford: Oxford University Press, 1990), 75–80.

84. Journal of Sir Edward Dering, BL Add MSS, 22467, fol. 92; Anchitel Grey, *Debates of the House of Commons, from the year 1667 to the year 1694*, 10 vols. (London, 1763), vol. 1, 286; Berkeley, "Discourse and View," fol. 257; Alvin Rabushka, *Taxation in Colonial America* (Princeton: Princeton University Press, 2008), 237–238.

85. Lynch, "An Accompt of the English Sugar Plantations"; Richard Ligon, *A true & exact history of the island of Barbados* (1657), 108.

86. *CSPC, 1669–1674*, 520.

87. Zahedieh, "Economy," 59; C. D. Chandaman, *English Public Revenue, 1660–1688* (Oxford: Clarendon, 1975), 9–36; Ralph Davis, "English Foreign Trade, 1660–1700," *Economic History Review*, n.s. 7, no. 2 (1954): 152–153.

88. "The relation of Collonell Doyley," 1662, BL Add MSS, 11410, fols. 11–12; Sir Richard Ford to earl of Clarendon, 1664, Clarendon MSS, 83, fols. 373–374; Davies, *Royal African Company*, 44–60.

89. David Eltis, "The Volume and Structure of the Transatlantic Slave Trade: A Reassessment," *W&MQ*, 3rd ser. 58, no. 1 (January 2001): 17–46; www.slavevoyages. org/assessment/estimates (accessed 17 July 2020).

90. *CSPC, 1700*, 565; Richard Dunn, *Sugar and Slaves: The Rise of the Planter Class in the English West Indies, 1624–1713* (Chapel Hill: University of North Carolina Press, 1972), 155, 312.

91. Dunn, *Sugar and Slaves*, 112; Richard Dunn, "The Barbados Census of 1680," *W&MQ* 26, no. 1 (January 1969), 3–30; Swingen, *Competing Visions*, 67, 162.

92. Anthony S. Parent, *Foul Means: The Formation of a Slave Society in Virginia, 1660–1740* (Chapel Hill: University of North Carolina Press, 2003), 74; Horn, *Adapting to a New World*, 148–149.

93. Lynch to Arlington, 27 June 1671, BL Add MSS, 11410, fol. 183; Trevor Burnard, *Planters, Merchants, and Slaves: Plantation Societies in British America, 1650–1820* (Chicago: University of Chicago Press, 2015), 24, 50, 70–71; Michael Craton, "Property and Propriety: Land Tenure and Slave Property in the Creation of a British West Indian Plantocracy, 1612–1740," in John Brewer and Susan Staves, eds., *Early Modern Conceptions of Property* (London: Routledge, 1996), 503–508.

94. Zahedieh, *Capital and the Colonies*, 208–209; Rabushka, *Taxation*, 237–238.

95. William Cobbett, ed., *The Parliamentary History of England*, 36 vols. (1806–1820), vol. 4, 167–168; L. F. Stock, ed., *Proceedings and Debates of the British Parliaments Respecting North America*, 5 vols. (Washington, DC, 1924), vol. 1, 283, 373–374; *Lords Journal*, vol. 11, 233; William Molyneux, *The case of Ireland's being bound by acts of Parliament in England* (1698), 103.

96. Davies, *Royal African Company*, 59–64, 103; William A. Pettigrew, *Freedom's Debt: The Royal African Company and the Politics of the Atlantic Slave Trade, 1672–1752* (Chapel Hill: University of North Carolina Press, 2013), 11–43.

97. "Worsley's Discourse of the Privateers," 317–318.

98. Benjamin Worsley to Ashley Cooper, 14 August 1668, PRO 30/24/49, fol. 227.

99. Thomas Povey to Edward Digges, 2 March 1660/1, BL Add MSS, 11411, fol. 24; Berkeley, "Discourse and View," fols. 354–357.

100. Samuel Clarke, *A true and faithful account of the four chiefest plantations of the English in America* (1670), 15–16; John Oldmixon, *The British Empire in America*, 2 vols. (1708), vol. 1, 248.

101. Slack, *Invention of Improvement*, 109; Simon Schaffer, "The Earth's Fertility as a Social Fact in Early Modern Britain," in Mikulas Teich, ed., *Nature and Society in Historical Context* (Cambridge: Cambridge University Press, 1997), 124–147.

102. John Poyntz, *The present prospect of the famous and fertile island of Tobago* (1683), 37–38.

103. Register of the Privy Council, 26 May 1662, PC 2/55, fol. 326; Register of the Privy Council, 10 June 1662, PC 2/56, fol. 10.

104. Benjamin Worsley to Ashley Cooper, 14 August 1668, fol. 227; Berkeley, "Discourse and View," fol. 357.

105. J. W. M. Lee, ed., *The Calvert Papers*, 3 vols. (Baltimore, 1889), vol. 1, 208–211.

106. Charles II, "Instructions" for the Council of Trade, 1670, PRO 30/24/49, fol. 120; William Bray, ed., *The Diary of John Evelyn*, 2 vols. (London, 1901), vol. 2, 75; Sir Richard Ford, "A Proposall for removing spices and other plants from the East to the West Indies," 1661, BL Egerton 2395, fols. 337–338; Hall and Hall, *Oldenburg Correspondence*, vol. 2, 151–159.

107. "New Plantation at Cape Florida," 1666, PRO 30/24/48, fols. 278–279; Cheves, *Shaftesbury Papers*, 440–441; Thomas Leng, "Shaftesbury's Aristocratic Empire," in John Spurr, ed., *Anthony Ashley Cooper, First Earl of Shaftesbury* (Farnham: Ashgate, 2011), 105–117.

108. Cheves, *Shaftesbury Papers*, 440–441.

109. Ibid., 13, 125, 188–189.

110. Ibid., 315–316.

111. "Worsley's Discourse of the Privateers," 320–321.

112. Cheves, *Shaftesbury Papers*, 81–82.

113. George Milner, "Proposals in order to the improvement of the county of Albemarle," 1664, BL Egerton 2395, fols. 661, 664.

114. Berkeley, "Discourse and View," fols. 356–357.

115. *London Gazette*, 13 December 1666.

116. *CSPC, 1661–1668*, 739.

117. B.W., *Free Ports. The Nature and Necessitie of them stated* (1652); Benjamin Worsley, "Breife Heads of some of the most Considerable Advantages that will be promoted by ffree Ports," 1661, Clarendon MSS, 92, fol. 248; Leng, *Worsley*, 73–75.

118. B.W., *Free Ports*, 7.

119. Lynch, "An accompt of the English Sugar Plantations," fol. 20.

120. Worsley, "Breife Heads," fol. 248.

121. John Shattock, Description of Madeira, n.d., BL Egerton MSS, 2395, fol. 649; *Memoirs of Sir Hugh Cholmley*, 96; Hugh Cholmley, "Discourse of Tangier," 1672, BL Lansdowne MSS, fol. 95.

122. Cholmley, "Severall Discourses Concerning the Interest of Tangr," n.d., Rawlinson MSS, A341, fol. 45; John Luke to the earl of Middleton, 16 June 1671, BL Sloane MSS, 3511, fols. 13–15.

123. Lord Belassis to Sir Henry Bennett, 13 April 1665, CO 279/4, 71; Samuel Pepys, Papers on Tangier, n.d., Rawlinson MSS, D916, fol. 84; *Memoirs of Sir Hugh Cholmley* (1870), 10, 98.

124. Cholmley, "Discourse of Tangier," fol. 95.

125. *To the Kings most Excellent Majesty, The humble Remonstrance of John Blande of London* (1661), 3.

126. Richard Nicolls to Clarendon, February 1666, Clarendon MSS, 84, fols. 118–122; Council of Barbados, "The heads of Addresses," 22 December 1669, BL Egerton MSS, 2395, fol. 465.

127. Earl of Sandwich to the Duke of York, 1662, BL Sloane MSS 3509, fols. 26–27; Earl of Sandwich, paper on Tangier, May 1661, Clarendon MSS, 75, fols. 464–465; Resolutions of the royal commissioners for Tangier, 14 January 1668/9, Clarendon MSS, 87, fols. 22–23; Christian J. Koot, " 'A Dangerous Principle': Free Trade Discourses in Barbados and the English Leeward Islands, 1650–1689," *Early American Studies* 5, no. 1 (Spring 2007): 132–163.

128. Worsley, "Breife Heads," fol. 248.

129. Henry Coventry, "About E. Ind Company," August 1681, Coventry MSS, 101, fol. 83.

130. John Pollexfen, *Discourse of trade, coyn and paper credit* (1697), 56–57.

131. Lambe, *Seasonable Observations*, 3–4; Gauci, *Politics of Trade*, 115–116.

132. Farnell, "Navigation Act," 439–441; Charles Wilson, *England's Apprenticeship* (London: Longmans, Green, 1965), 64; Bliss, *Revolution and Empire*, 58–60.

133. Tristan Stein, "Tangier in the Restoration Empire," *Historical Journal* 54, no. 4 (December 2011): 1000–1002.

134. Meeting of English commissioners, 16 February 1667, Oxford, All Souls College MSS, 229, fol. 81.

135. Answers to ye Demands of ye Commissioners of Trade for Scotland, 1667, BL Egerton MSS, 3340, fols. 4–5.

136. Smith, *To the King's Most Excellent Majesty*, 26.

137. Sir Francis Brewster, *Essays on trade and navigation in five parts* (1695), 92, 100.

138. Committee for Foreign Affairs, 18 December 1670, SP 104/176, 267.

139. Register of the Privy Council, 13 February 1660/1, PC 2/55, fol. 68.

140. Worsley, "Some Considerations about the Commission for Trade," 1668, PRO 30/24/49, fol. 86.

141. "Worsley's Discourse of the Privateers," 328.

142. "Reasons for the permitting the productions of the English plantations in America to bee brought directly to Tanger," 1668, BL Egerton 2395, fol. 656.

143. Cholmley, "Discourse of Tangier," 97; Henry Norwood to Clarendon, 29 May 1667, Clarendon MSS, 85, fols. 391–393.

144. Latham and Matthews, *Diary of Samuel Pepys*, vol. 5, 352–353.

145. Thomas Blackerby to George Oxenden, 11 March 1666/7, BL Add MSS 40,713, 8–9.

146. Carl Bridenbaugh, ed., *The Pynchon Papers. Letters of John Pynchon, 1654–1700*, 2 vols. (Boston: Colonial Society of Massachusetts, 1982), vol. 1, 73–74.

147. Willoughby to Sir William Coventry, 15 July 1666, Clarendon MSS, 84, fols. 215–216.

148. Downing to Clarendon, 15/25 January 1663/4, Clarendon MSS, 107, fols. 65–66.

149. Bridenbaugh, *Pynchon Papers*, vol. 1, 71–72.

150. *Europae modernae speculum; or, A view of the empires, kingdoms, principalities, seignieuries, and common-wealths of Europe* (1666), 91–92.

151. Lynch, "Accompt of the English sugar plantations," fol. 638.

152. *CSPC, 1669–1674*, 975.

153. Godolphin to Arlington, 1/11 July 1669, SP 94/54, fol. 194; Godolphin to Henry Coventry, 14/24 August 1678, Coventry MSS, 60, fol. 235.

154. Godolphin to Arlington, 11/21 September 1667, SP 94/53, fol. 49; Sir John Werden to Arlington, 1 May 1669, SP 94/54, fol. 155; Thomas Bebington, ed., *The Right Honourable the Earl of Arlington's Letters*, 2 vols. (1701), vol. 1, 371.

155. Godolphin to Arlington, 13/23 July 1670, SP 94/57, fol. 17; Godolphin to Arlington, 19/29 October 1670, SP 94/ 57, fol. 117; Godolphin to Francis Parry, 25 September 1670, MS Eng. Lett. C. 328, fols. 52–53; Barbara H. Stein and Stanley J. Stein, *Silver, Trade, and War: Spain and America in the Making of Early Modern Europe* (Baltimore: Johns Hopkins University Press, 2000), 63–64, 122.

156. Arlington to Godolphin, 12 August 1670, BL Add MSS, 35100, fol. 96.

157. *CSPC, 1669–1674*, 138; Bliss, *Revolution and Empire*, 161–163.

158. "Worsley's Discourse of the Privateers," fol. 310.

159. Godolphin to Arlington, 11/21 September 1667, SP 94/53, fol. 49; Godolphin to Charles II, 19/29 July 1670, SP 94/57, fol. 35.

160. Swingen, *Competing Visions*, 63; Lynch, "Considerations about the Spaniards buying Negros of the English at Jamaica," 2 February 1674, BL Egerton MSS, 2395, fol. 501.

161. Cheves, *Shaftesbury Papers*, 327.

162. "Worsley's Discourse of the Privateers," fol. 313.

163. Lynch to Henry Slingsby, 29 November 1671, BL Add MSS 11,410, fols. 200–201.

164. Lynch, "Considerations about the Spaniards," fol. 501.

165. Godolphin to Arlington, 13/23 July 1670, SP 57/94, fol. 20.

166. Lynch to the Council of Trade and Plantations, 20 August 1671, BL Add MSS, 11410, fols. 187–189.

167. Belassis to Clarendon, 5/15 September 1665, Clarendon MSS, 83, fols. 196–197; Cholmley to Henry Norwood, 24 December 1666, Cholmley MSS, ZCG, V,

1/1/2, fol. 5; Cholmley to Clifford, 28 April 1670, Cholmley MSS, ZCG, V, 1/1/2, fol. 31.

168. Martin Westcombe to John Fitzgerald, 27 October 1663, CO 279, 2/130; Bebington, *Arlington Letters*, vol. 2, 39, 42.

169. Middleton to the Lords Commissioners, 9 October 1672, BL Sloane MSS, 3511, fols. 160–161; Thomas Maynard to Edward Nicholas, 8/18 December 1661, National Archives, SP 89/5, fol. 73.

170. E. M. G. Routh, *Tangier: England's Lost Atlantic Outpost, 1661–1684* (London, 1912), 23–24, 49, 69; Linda Colley, *Captives: Britain, Empire, and the World* (London: Jonathan Cape, 2002), 52.

171. Cholmley, "Discourse of Tangier," fol. 94.

172. James Wilson, "His account of Tangier and Barbary," 1661, BL Sloane MSS 3509, fols. 11–14; Earl of Sandwich to the duke of York, 1662, BL Sloane MSS 3509, fols. 26–27.

173. Sandwich to Clarendon, May 1661, Clarendon MSS, 76, fols. 464–465.

174. Cholmley to Henry Norwood, 1 November 1667, Cholmley MSS, V/1/1/2, 108; Cholmley to Christopher Wren, 28 April 1670, Cholmley MSS, V/1/1/3, 38. See also Henry Norwood to Clarendon, 29 May 1667, Clarendon MSS, 85, fol. 291.

175. Anna Suranyi, *The Genius of the English Nation: Travel Writing and National Identity in Early Modern England* (Newark: University of New Hampshire Press, 2008), 75–76, 78; Nabil Matar, *Turks, Moors, and Englishmen in the Age of Discovery* (New York: Columbia University Press, 1999), 134–135.

176. Charles Molloy, *De Jure Maritimo et Navali: or, A Treatise of Affaires Maritime, and of Commerce* (1676), 422.

177. Daniel Defoe, *A Plan of the English Commerce* (1727), 1.

Chapter 4.　"People of Another World"

1. "Overtures touching a Councell to bee erected for forreigne plantations," 1660, BL Egerton MSS, 2395, fol. 272; "Proposition for a Council for the Plantations," 1660, BL Egerton MSS, 2395, fol. 276.

2. Mary Maples Dunn and Richard S. Dunn, eds., *The Papers of William Penn*, 5 vols. (Philadelphia: University of Pennsylvania Press, 1981–1986), vol. 2, 64; Clarence S. Brigham, ed., *British Royal Proclamations Relating to America, 1603–1763* (Worcester, MA, 1911), 52–55.

3. "Overtures touching a Councell," fol. 272.

4. Anthony Pagden, *Lords of All the World: Ideologies of Empire in Spain, Britain, and France, c. 1500–c. 1800* (New Haven: Yale University Press, 1995), 15–17.

5. See especially Daniel Defoe, *A Plan of the English Commerce* (1727), 71.

6. William Cobbett, ed., *The Parliamentary History of England*, 36 vols. (1806–1820), vol. 4, 128–129.

7. Peter Moogk, "Reluctant Exiles: Emigrants from France in Canada before 1760," *W&MQ* 46, no. 3 (July 1989): 465–466.

8. John Josselyn, *An account of two voyages to New-England* (1673), 152.

9. Richard Koebner, *Empire* (Cambridge: Cambridge University Press, 1961), 50–60.

10. Jack P. Greene, "Negotiated Authorities: The Problem of Governance in the Extended Polities of the Early Modern Atlantic World," in Greene, *Negotiated Authorities: Essays in Colonial, Political and Constitutional History* (Charlottesville: University of Virginia Press, 1994), 1–23.

11. L. H. Roper, *Advancing Empire: English Interests and Overseas Expansion, 1613–1688* (Cambridge: Cambridge University Press, 2017), 161–190. See also Elizabeth Mancke, "Negotiating an Empire: Britain and Its Overseas Peripheries, c. 1550–1780," in Christine Daniels and Michael V. Kennedy, eds., *Negotiated Empires: Centers and Peripheries in the Americas, 1500–1820* (London: Routledge, 2002), 244–246.

12. Carla Gardina Pestana, *The English Atlantic in an Age of Revolution, 1640–1661* (Cambridge: Harvard University Press, 2004), 225; Alison Games, "Migration," in David Armitage and Michael Braddick, eds., *The British Atlantic World* (Basingstoke: Palgrave Macmillan, 2002), 32–33.

13. Randall H. Balmer, *A Perfect Babel of Confusion: Dutch Religion and English Culture in the Middle Colonies* (Oxford: Oxford University Press, 1989); Robert Home, *Of Planting and Planning: The Making of British Colonial Cities* (London: Routledge, 2013), 68.

14. Kristen Block and Jenny Shaw, "Subjects Without an Empire: The Irish in the Early Modern Caribbean," *Past and Present* 210, no. 1 (February 2011): 33–60; Louis Cullen, "The Irish Diaspora of the Seventeenth and Eighteenth Centuries," in Nicholas Canny, ed., *Europeans on the Move: Studies in European Migration, 1500–1800* (Oxford: Clarendon Press, 1994), 113–152.

15. Bridget Orr, *Empire on the English Stage, 1660–1714* (Cambridge: Cambridge University Press, 2001), 224–230.

16. J. M. Sosin, *English America and the Restoration Monarchy of Charles II: Transatlantic Politics, Commerce, and Kinship* (Lincoln: University of Nebraska Press, 1980), 41–43; Michael J. Braddick, "Government, War, Trade, and Settlement," in Nicholas Canny, ed., *The Oxford History of the British Empire*, vol. 1: *The Origins of Empire* (Oxford: Oxford University Press, 1998), 286–308.

17. *Life of Edward, Earl of Clarendon*, vol. 1, 197.

18. Privy Council Register, 26 February 1661, 55/2, fol. 284; Robert M. Bliss, *Revolution and Empire: English Politics and the American Colonies in the Seventeenth Century* (Manchester: Manchester University Press, 1990), 145.

19. Worsley to Ashley Cooper, 14 August 1668, PRO 20/34/49, fol. 228.

20. R. P. Bieber, "The British Plantation Councils of 1670–4," *English Historical Review* 40, no. 157 (January 1925): 93–106; Charles M. Andrews, "Committees, Commissions, and Councils of Trade and Plantations, 1622–1675," *Johns Hopkins University Studies in Historical and Political Science*, ser. 26, nos. 1–3 (1908): 15–19.

21. E. S. De Beer, ed., *The Diary of John Evelyn*, 6 vols. (Oxford: Oxford University Press, 1955), vol. 3, 578.

22. Worsley to Ashley Cooper, 14 August 1668, fol. 228.

23. William Penn, *A Brief Account of the Province of Pennsylvania* (1681), 1.

24. John Palmer, *The Present State of New-England* (1689), 7, 9; Maura Jane Farrelly, *Papist Patriots: The Making of an American Catholic Identity* (Oxford: Oxford University Press, 2012), 9–10.

25. Jack P. Greene, *Peripheries and Center: Constitutional Development in the Extended Polities of the British Empire and the United States, 1607–1788* (Athens: University of Georgia Press, 1986), 23–24.

26. Dunn and Dunn, *Papers of William Penn*, vol. 2, 472–474.

27. Josselyn, *An account of two voyages,* 45–46; "The Royal Charter Incorporating the Hudson's Bay Company," in E. E. Rich, ed., *Minutes of the Hudson's Bay Company,* 139; Company of Adventurers to the Bahamas, "Articles of Agreement," 4 September 1672, BL Add MSS, 15640, fols. 1, 9, 11.

28. Privy Council Register, 20 March 1661, PC 2/55, fol. 97; Tristan Stein, "Tangier in the Restoration Empire," *Historical Journal* 54, no. 4 (December 2011): 1006.

29. Samuel Maverick to Clarendon, n.d., Clarendon MSS, 74, fol. 253.

30. Palmer, *Present State of New-England,* 7, 9.

31. Sir John Werden to James Dyer, 30 November 1676, CO 5/1112, fol. 19.

32. Notes explanatory of some of the heads annexed to the petition of the Virginia Agents, 1675, Coventry MSS, 77, fol. 44.

33. Richard Beale Davis, ed., *William Fitzhugh and His Chesapeake World, 1676–1701* (Chapel Hill: University of North Carolina Press, 1963), 156–158.

34. Jack P. Greene, " 'The Same Liberties and Privileges as Englishmen in England': Law, Liberty and Identity in the Construction of Colonial English and Revolutionary America," in Rebecca Starr, ed., *Articulating America: Fashioning a National Political Culture in Early America* (Lanham: Rowman & Littlefield, 2000), 45–90.

35. Charles II, "A grant of Bombay with all its rights forever to our East India Company," 1668, Rawlinson MSS, B516, fol. 32.

36. Earl of Peterborough, "To all his Majesty's subjects in the aforesaid Dominions," 5 February 1661/2, Rawlinson MSS, D491, fol. 2; Hugh Cholmley, "Discourse of Tangier," 1672, BL Lansdowne, 192, fol. 95; John Luke to the Archbishop of Canterbury, n.d., BL Sloane MSS, 3509, fol. 64.

37. Ken MacMillan, " 'Bound by Our Regal Office': Empire, Sovereignty, and the American Colonies in the Seventeenth Century," in Stephen Foster, ed., *British North America in the Seventeenth and Eighteenth Centuries* (Oxford: Oxford University Press, 2013), 76–77.

38. Directors to Deputy-Governor and Council at Bombay, BL, IOR, 28 July 1686, E/3/91, fol. 83.

39. *The laws of Virginia, now in force* (1662); "Sir Thomas Muddiford's Commission as Governor of Jamaica," 1664, Rawlinson MSS, A347, fol. 84; Dunn and Dunn, *Papers of William Penn*, vol. 2, 66.

40. Ashley Cooper to Major Tolhurst, 17 July 1671, PRO 30/24/48, fol. 181; Ken MacMillan, *Sovereignty and Possession in the English New World: The Legal Foundations of Empire, 1576–1640* (Cambridge: Cambridge University Press, 2006), 14; MacMillan, "Bound by Our Regal Office," 89–90.

41. Roper and Van Ruymbeke, *Constructing Early Modern Empires,* 20–13; William Pettigrew, "Corporate Constitutionalism and the Dialogue Between the Global and Local in Seventeenth-Century English History," *Itinerario* 39, no. 3 (January 2016): 487–501.

42. Farrelly, *Papist Patriots,* 64.

43. Phil Withington, "Public Discourse, Corporate Citizenship and State-Formation in Early Modern England," *American Historical Review* 112, no. 4 (October 2007): 1016–1038; Michael J. Braddick, *State Formation in Early Modern England, c. 1550–1700* (Cambridge: Cambridge University Press, 2000), 11–46.

44. Langdon Cheves, ed., *The Shaftesbury Papers* (Charleston, SC: Tempus Publications, 2000), 382.

45. Paul D. Halliday, *Dismembering the Body Politic: Partisan Politics in England's Towns, 1650–1730* (Cambridge: Cambridge University Press, 1998), 276–303.

46. Thomas P. Slaughter, ed., *Ideology and Politics on the Eve of the Restoration: Newcastle's Advice to Charles II* (Philadelphia: American Philosophical Society, 1984), 41; Thomas Hobbes, *Leviathan; or, The Matter, Forme and Power of a Common-Wealth Ecclesiasticall and Civill,* ed. C.B. MacPherson (London: Penguin, 1968), 375.

47. Bliss, *Revolution and Empire,* 45–64; Pestana, *English Atlantic,* 157–167.

48. "Overtures touching a Councell," fol. 272.

49. "An Essaie or overture for regulating the Affaires of his Highness in the West Indies," n.d., BL Add MSS, 11411, fols. 11–12.

50. Earl of Cassilis to earl of Lauderdale, 28 December 1660, NRS, Ailsa MSS, GD 25/9, box 30/2; "Proposals for the advancement of the plantation of Jamaica," PRO 30/24/49, fols. 31–3; *CSPC, 1661–1668,* 56.

51. Register of the Privy Council, 20 February 1660/1, PC 2/55, fol. 74.

52. *Life of Edward, Earl of Clarendon,* vol. 1, 236.

53. Rich, ed., *Minutes of the Hudson's Bay Company,* 139; Perry Gauci, *The Politics of Trade: The Overseas Merchant in State and Society, 1660–1720* (Oxford: Oxford University Press, 2001), 116.

54. Company of Adventurers to the Bahamas, "Articles of Agreement," fol. 1; W. H. Miller, "The Colonization of the Bahamas, 1647–1670, *W&MQ,* 3rd ser. 2, no. 1 (1945): 33–46.

55. Rich, *Minutes of the Hudson's Bay Company,* 182–183, 217, 222; P. E. H. Hair and Robin Law, "The English in West Africa to 1700," in Canny, *Oxford History of the British Empire,* vol. 1, 255; K. G. Davies, *The Royal African Company* (London: Longmans, Green, 1957), 63–65, 101–104; Roper, *Conceiving Carolina,* 72–73.

56. Elizabeth Mancke, "Negotiating an Empire," in Christine Daniels and Michael V. Kennedy, eds., *Negotiated Empires: Centers and Peripheries in the Americas, 1500–1820* (London: Routledge, 2002), 235–265; Jack P. Greene, "Transatlantic Colonization and the Redefinition of Empire in the Early Modern Era," in Daniels and Kennedy, *Negotiated Empires,* 267–282.

57. Thomas Woodward to Anthony Ashley Cooper, 2 June 1665, PRO 30/24/48, fol. 7; Earl of Sandwich to Edward Hyde, May 1661, Clarendon MSS, 75,

fols. 464–465; Patricia Seed, *Ceremonies of Possession in Europe's Conquest of the New World, 1492–1640* (Cambridge: Cambridge University Press, 1995); Jane Ohlmeyer, "Eastward Enterprises: Colonial Ireland, Colonial India," *Past & Present* 240, no. 1 (August 2018): 98.

58. Cotton Mather, *The wonders of the invisible world* (1693), preface.

59. T. H. Breen, "Persistent Localism: English Social Change and the Shaping of New England Institutions," *W&MQ*, 3rd ser. 32 (January 1975): 3–28; T. H. Breen, "Creative Adaptations: Peoples and Cultures," in J. P. Greene and J. R. Pole, eds., *Colonial British America: Essays in the New History of the Early Modern Era* (Baltimore: Johns Hopkins University Press, 1984), 195–232.

60. Bliss, *Revolution and Empire*, 210–211; Thomas Leng, "Shaftesbury's Aristocratic Empire," in John Spurr, ed., *Anthony Ashley Cooper, First Earl of Shaftesbury* (Farnham: Ashgate, 2011), 106–107.

61. George Scot, *Model of the Government of the Province of East New Jersey* (1682), 211, 214–217.

62. Dunn and Dunn, *Papers of William Penn*, vol. 1, 390–395, vol. 2, 149–151, 224; William Penn, *A further account of the province of Pennsylvania and its improvements* (1685), 17.

63. Scot, *Model of the Government*, 27.

64. Sir William Berkeley, "A Discourse and View of Virginia," 1662, BL Egerton MSS, 2395, fol. 354.

65. Dunn and Dunn, *Papers of William Penn*, vol. 3, 456–457, 565–568; Roper, *Conceiving Carolina*, 47–48, 61–62; Sosin, *English America*, 136–138, 213–216.

66. Dunn and Dunn, *Papers of William Penn*, vol. 3, 633.

67. Michael Craton, "Reluctant Creoles: The Planters' World in the British West Indies," in Bernard Bailyn and Philip Morgan, eds., *Strangers Within the Realm: Cultural Margins of the First British Empire* (Williamsburg: Omohundro Institute of Early American History and Culture, University of North Carolina Press, 1991), 314–362.

68. *CSPC, 1661–1668*, 764.

69. Register of the Privy Council, 26 May 1662, PC 2/55, fol. 326; Register of the Privy Council, 12 June 1668, PC 2/56, fol. 10; Alison Gilbert Olson, *Making the Empire Work: London and American Interest Groups, 1690–1790* (Cambridge: Harvard University Press, 1992), 29–30.

70. Marion Tinling, ed., *The Correspondence of the Three William Byrds of Westover, Virginia, 1684–1776*, 2 vols. (Charlottesville: Virginia Historical Society, 1977), vol. 1, 32–34; Romney R. Sedgwick, "John Bromley," in Romney Sedgwick, ed., *The History of Parliament: The House of Commons, 1715–1754* (Oxford: Oxford University Press, 1970).

71. Carl Bridenbaugh, ed., *The Pynchon Papers: Letters of John Pynchon, 1654–1700*, 2 vols. (Boston: Colonial Society of Massachusetts, 1982), vol. 1, 108–110.

72. William Smith, *To the King's Most Excellent Majesty . . . an essay for recovery of trade* (1661), 45. See also John Houghton, *Collection of Letters for the improvement of husbandry and trade*, 2 vols. (1681–1683), vol. 2, 28.

73. Report of the grand committee, March 1670, BL Add MSS 22,467, fols. 91–92; L. F. Stock, ed., *Proceedings and Debates of the British Parliaments Respecting North America*, 5 vols. (Washington, DC, 1924), vol. 1, 369, 373–374; Cobbett, *Parliamentary History*, vol. 4, 368–369.

74. *The Interest of the Nation, the Sugar Plantations, and the Refiners of Sugars, stated* (1691), 6.

75. "Reasons against the management of the East India trade as now driven under the present Joint Stock," All Souls MS 238, fol. 162; *The allegations of the Turky Company and others against the East-India-Company* (1681), 4.

76. For these ideas, see Henry Oldenburg, "Inquiries Recommended to Colonel Linch going to Jamaica," 16 December 1670, BL Sloane MSS 3984, fol. 194.

77. *Lords Journal*, vol. 12: *1666–75*, 486–487, 494–495, 502–503; Stock, *Proceedings and Debates*, vol. 1, 368–371, 382–383, 386; Anchitel Grey, *Debates of the House of Commons, from the year 1667 to the year 1694*, 10 vols. (London, 1763), vol. 1, 312–313, 435–437.

78. Edward Lyttleton, *The Groans of the Plantations* (1689), 2; *To the Kings most Excellent Majesty, The humble Remonstrance of John Blande of London* (1661).

79. John Scott, "Account of the English colonies," 1661, BL Sloane MSS, 3662, fol. 10.

80. *The Case of His Majesties Sugar Plantations* (1670), 3.

81. Cobbett, *Parliamentary History*, vol. 4, 382–383.

82. *Lords Journal*, vol. 12, 502–503.

83. Cobbett, *Parliamentary History*, vol. 4, 368–369; Sugar bakers of Bristol to Thomas Day and John Yate, 15 January 1695/6, BL Add MSS, 5540, fol. 95; *The Interest of the Nation*, 9.

84. Sugar bakers of Bristol to Day and Yate, fol. 92.

85. Cobbett, *Parliamentary History*, vol. 4, 386–387.

86. For petitions, see Mark Knights, "Petitioning and the Political Theorists: John Locke, Algernon Sidney and London's 'Monster' Petition of 1680," *Past and Present* 38, no. 1 (1993): 94–111.

87. Journal of Sir Edward Dering, March 1670, BL Add MSS, 22467, fol. 91.

88. Cobbett, *Parliamentary History*, vol. 4, 371.

89. Lee, ed., *Calvert Papers*, vol. 1, 290; David Galenson, "The Seventeenth-Century Chesapeake," in Barbara Solow, ed., *Slavery and the Rise of the Atlantic System* (Cambridge: Cambridge University Press, 1991), vol. 1, 287; Dunn, *Sugar and Slaves*, 111–114.

90. *Life of Edward, Earl of Clarendon*, vol. 1, 236.

91. "Wm Byam's Journall of Guiana from 1665 to 1667," BL Sloane MSS, 3662, fols. 27, 37.

92. James Drake, *King Philip's War: Civil War in New England 1675–6* (Amherst: University of Massachusetts Press, 1999), 169–195.

93. James Horn, *Adapting to a New World: English Society in the Seventeenth-Century Chesapeake* (Chapel Hill: University of North Carolina Press, 1994), 158–159, 373–377.

94. See, for example, *London Gazette* 1058, January 1675/6; *A Continuation of the state of New-England being a farther account of the Indian war* (1676); William Hubbard, *The present state of New-England* (1677); *Strange News from Virginia* (1677); HMC *Le Fleming*, 129.

95. Grey, *Debates*, vol. 4, 225, 237.

96. Henry Morgan to Henry Coventry, 30 January 1675/6, Coventry MSS, 74, fol. 167; Abigail L. Swingen, *Competing Visions of Empire: Labor, Slavery, and the Origins of the British Atlantic Empire* (New Haven: Yale University Press, 2015), 90; Stephen Saunders Webb, *1676: The End of American Independence* (New York: Knopf, 1984), 198–207.

97. Joseph Hall, *Quo Vadis? A just censure of travell as it is commonly undertaken by the gentlemen of our nation* (London, 1617); Andrew Hadfield, *Literature, travel*, 4–6; Orr, *Empire on the English Stage*, 225–230.

98. Worsley to Ashley Cooper, 14 August 1668, fol. 225.

99. John Stewart to the duke of Hamilton, 1 February 1701/2, NRS, GD 406/1/11870, fol. 11; William Lithgow, *The totall discourse, of the rare adventures, and painefull peregrinations of long nineteene yeares travailes from Scotland* (1632), 151; Edmund Spenser, "A View of the Present State of Ireland," 1596, in *The Works of Edmund Spenser*, vol. 4 (London, 1750), 120; Nabil Matar, *Islam in Britain, 1558–1685* (Cambridge: Cambridge University Press, 1998), 63–64; Linda Colley, *Captives: Britain, Empire, and the World* (London: Jonathan Cape, 2002), 52–61.

100. Worsley to Ashley Cooper, 14 August 1668, fol. 225.

101. Michael Zuckerman, "Unease in Eden," in Nicholas Canny and Anthony Pagden, eds., *Colonial Identity in the Atlantic World, 1500–1800* (Princeton: Princeton University Press, 1987), 120–121; Karen Ordahl Kupperman, "Introduction," in Kupperman, ed., *America in European Consciousness, 1493–1750* (Williamsburg: Omohundro Institute of Early American History and Culture, University of North Carolina Press, 1995), 22.

102. Povey to D'Oyley, 1659, BL Add MSS, 11411, fol. 87; Robert Sanford, *Surinam Justice* (1662), epistle dedicatory.

103. Lynch to Lord Cornbury, 29 March 1671/2, BL Add MSS, 11410, fol. 257.

104. Dunn, *Sugar and Slaves*, 101–160.

105. Lynch to Arlington, June 1671, BL Add MSS, 11410, fols. 183–184.

106. George Milner, "Proposals in order to the improvement of the county of Albemarle," n.d., BL Egerton MSS, 2395, fols. 661.

107. Ibid., 663–664; J. H. Elliott, *Empires of the Atlantic World: Britain and Spain in America, 1492–1830* (New Haven: Yale University Press, 2006), 180.

108. Francis Borland, *Memoirs of Darien* (1715), 50–51; Hammond, *Leah and Rachel*, 3–4.

109. Aphra Behn, *The Widdow Ranter; or, The history of Bacon in Virginia a tragicomedy* (1690), 3–4.

110. Ibid., 10, 43; Derek Hughes and Janet Todd, "Tragedy and Tragicomedy," in Hughes and Todd, eds., *Cambridge Companion to Aphra Behn* (Cambridge: Cambridge University Press, 2004), 83–98.

111. Scot, *Model of the Government*, 8, 12.

112. Henry Neville, *The Isle of Pines; or, A late Discovery of a fourth island near Terra Australis, Incognita* (1668), 26, 31; John Scheckter, *The Isle of Pines: Henry Neville's Uncertain Utopia* (Farnham: Ashgate, 2016).

113. Edward Randolph to the Lords of Trade, 1676, Coventry MSS, 77, fols. 247–248; Louise A. Breen, "Praying with the Enemy: Daniel Gookin, King Philip's War and the Dangers of Intercultural Mediatorship," in Martin Daunton and Rick Halpern, eds., *Empire and Others: British Encounters with Indigenous Peoples, 1600–1850* (Philadelphia: Pennsylvania University Press, 1999), 101–122.

114. Increase Mather, *A Discourse concerning the danger of apostacy* (1685), 102–105.

115. John Davies and César Rochefort, *The history of the Caribby-islands* (1666), 270; "Virginia's Deplorable Condition; or, An impartiall Narrative of the murthers committed by the Indians there," 1676, Coventry MSS, fol. 173.

116. Morgan Godwyn, *Trade preferr'd before religion and Christ* (1685), 21–25.

117. Farrelly, *Papist Patriots*, 289.

118. Earl of Sandwich's journal, x, p. 404, Mapperton House Archives, Beaminster, UK. I am very grateful to Dr. Tom Leng for this reference.

119. Nathaniel Johnson to the Lords of Trade, 1686, CO 152/37, fol. 17.

120. Alden T. Vaughan, "From White Man to Redskin: Changing Anglo-American Perceptions of the American Indian," *American Historical Review* 87, no. 4 (October 1982): 917–953; David S. Lovejoy, "Satanizing the American Indian," *New England Quarterly* 67, no. 4 (December 1994): 603–621.

121. Neville, *Isle of Pines*, 17–18; *CSPC, 1661–1668*, 1785; Donald Akenson, *If the Irish Ran the World: Montserrat, 1630–1730* (Montreal: McGill-Queen's University Press, 1997), 87.

122. Dunn, *Sugar and Slaves*, 239–253.

123. Imtiaz Habib, *Black Lives in the English Archives, 1500–1677* (Farnham: Ashgate, 2017), 185–187; V. C. D. Mtubani, "African Slaves and English Law," *Pula: Botswana Journal of African Studies* 3, no. 2 (November 1983): 71–72; David Brion Davis, *The Problem of Slavery in Western Culture* (Oxford: Oxford University Press, 1988), 208–209. The three contrary cases were *Chamberlain v. Harvey* (1697), *Smith v. Brown and Cooper* (1701) and *Smith v. Gould* (1706).

124. C. B. Macpherson, *The Political Theory of Possessive Individualism* (Oxford: Clarendon Press, 1962); Lewis E. Hill, "On Laissez-Faire Capitalism and Liberalism," *American Journal of Economics and Sociology* 23, no. 4 (October 1964): 393–396; John Quiggin, "Leave John Locke in the Dustbin of History," *Jacobin Magazine* (June 2019).

125. Holly Brewer, "Slavery, Sovereignty, and 'Inheritable Blood': Reconsidering John Locke and the Origins of American Slavery," *American Historical Review* 122, no. 4 (October 2017): 1038–1078.

126. Dunn and Dunn, *Papers of William Penn*, vol. 3, 65–66.

127. *Satyr against coffee* (1662), 1.

128. George Wither, *A Sigh for the Pitchers* (1666), 29.

129. Michael Guasco, *Slaves and Englishmen. Human Bondage in the Early Modern Atlantic World* (Philadelphia: University of Pennsylvania Press, 2014), 2.

130. Ruth Paley, Cristina Malcolmson, and Michael Hunter, "Parliament and Slavery, 1660–c. 1710," *Slavery and Abolition* 31, no. 2 (March 2010): 257–281.

131. Richard Baxter, *Chapters from a Christian Directory*, ed. Jeanette Tawney (London, 1925), 28–35; De Beer, *Diary of John Evelyn*, vol. 4, 471; Journal of the Lords of Trade, 17 August 1680, CO 391/3, fol. 97; Katharine Gerbner, "The Ultimate Sin: Christianising Slaves in Barbados in the Seventeenth Century," *Slavery & Abolition* 31, no. 1 (2010), 57–73.

132. *CSPC, 1661–1668*, 1212, 1488, 1692.

133. Thomas Tryon, *The planter's speech to his neighbours & country-men* (1684), 33–34; Thomas Tryon, *The merchant, citizen and country-man's instructor* (1701), 183–185; Philippe Rosenberg, "Thomas Tryon and the Seventeenth-Century Dimensions of Antislavery," *W&MQ*, 3rd ser. 61, no. 4 (October 2004): 609–642.

134. Edmund White to Joseph Morton, London, 27 February 1687, NLS, Dunlop papers, MSS 9250, fol. 40.

135. Guasco, *Slaves and Englishmen*, 41–69.

136. Aphra Behn, *Oroonoko. The History of the Royal Slave* (1688), 93, 109, 140.

137. Godwyn, *A Supplement to the Negro's & Indian's Advocate* (1681), 6–7; James Farr, "Locke, Natural Law, and New World Slavery," *Political Theory* 36, no. 4 (May 2008): 495–522; Owen Stanwood, "Captives and Slaves: Indian Labor, Cultural Conversion, and the Plantation Revolution in Virginia," *Virginia Magazine of History and Biography* 114, no. 4 (2006): 434–463.

138. Rowan Strong, "A Vision of an Anglican Imperialism: The Annual Sermons of the Society for the Propagation of the Gospel in Foreign Parts, 1701–1714," *Journal of Religious History* 30, no. 2 (May 2006): 189–196; Katharine Gerbner, *Christian Slavery: Conversion and Race in the British Atlantic World* (Philadelphia: Pennsylvania University Press, 2018), 92–111.

139. Lyttleton, *Groans of the Plantations*, 17–23; William A. Pettigrew, "Free to Enslave: Politics and the Escalation of Britain's Transatlantic Slave Trade, 1688–1714," *W&MQ*, 3rd ser. 64, no. 1 (2007): 3–38; Robin Blackburn, *The Making of New World Slavery: From the Baroque to the Modern, 1492–1800* (London: Verso, 1997), 9–10, 63–64; Winthrop D. Jordan, *White over Black: American Attitudes toward the Negro, 1550–1812* (Chapel Hill: University of North Carolina Press, 1968).

140. Kathleen Brown, "Native Americans and Early Modern Concepts of Race," in Daunton and Halpern, *Empire and Others*, 79–100; Guasco, *Slaves and Englishmen*, 184–194, 225–227, 295.

141. Godwyn, *Supplement to the Negro's and Indians Advocate*, 3. See, for evidence of this attitude, Journal of the Lords of Trade, 8 October 1680, CO 391/3, fol. 3

142. Behn, *Oroonoko*, 20–22.

143. Samuel Sewall, *The Selling of Joseph. A Memorial* (1700), 1–2; *Diary of Samuel Sewall*, 3 vols., Collections of the Massachusetts Historical Society, 5th ser. (1898), vol. 2, 16; Brion Davis, *Problem of Slavery*, 345.

144. Sewall, *Selling of Joseph*, 2.

145. Hammond, *Leah and Rachel*, 1–2, 19.

146. Journal of the Lords of Trade, 1675/6, CO 391/1, fol. 33; Swingen, *Competing Visions*, 25–26.

147. Shaftesbury to Governor and Council at Charles Town, 10 June 1675, PRO 30/24/48, fol. 212.

148. Cheves, *Shaftesbury Papers*, 365.

149. Charles II, "Instructions" for the Council of Trade, c. 1670, PRO 30/24/49, fol. 120.

150. Thomas Povey to William, Lord Willoughby, 15 March 1672, BL Egerton MSS, 2395, fol. 487.

Chapter 5. Protestantism, Pluralism, and the Politics of Allegiance in the Restoration Empire

1. James Fawcett to Archbishop Sancroft, 21 January 1686/7, Bodl., Tanner MSS, 29, fol. 126.

2. Tim Harris, *Rebellion: Britain's First Stuart Kings, 1567–1642* (Oxford: Oxford University Press, 2014), 36.

3. Francis, Lord Willoughby to Clarendon, 18 February 1663/4, Clarendon MSS, 81, fols. 110–111.

4. "Instructions to our trusty and welbeloved Sir William Berkeley," 1662, Coventry MSS, 76, fol. 63.

5. Roger Greene, *Virginia's Cure; or, An advisive narrative concerning Virginia* (1661), 16–17.

6. James Houblon to Samuel Pepys, n.d., Rawlinson MSS, A185, fol. 107.

7. Greene, *Virginia's Cure*, preface.

8. Morgan Godwyn, *A supplement to the Negro's [and] Indian's advocate* (1681), 8.

9. Brent S. Sirota, *The Christian Monitors: The Church of England and the Age of Benevolence, 1680–1730* (New Haven: Yale University Press, 2014), 223–247; David Manning, "Anglican Religious Societies, Organizations, and Missions," in Jeremy Gregory, ed., *The Oxford History of Anglicanism*, vol. 2: *Establishment and Empire, 1662–1829* (Oxford: Oxford University Press, 2017), 429–451.

10. Journal of the Lords of Trade, 13 January 1675/6, CO 391/1, fol. 32.

11. Thomas Lynch to Archbishop Sheldon, 29 November 1671, BL Add MSS, 11410, fol. 199.

12. Richard Eburne, *A Plaine Pathway to Plantations* (1624), preface, 4–5; James B. Bell, *The Imperial Origins of the King's Church in Early America, 1607–1783* (Basingstoke: Palgrave Macmillan, 2004), 3–9.

13. Jeremy Gregory, " 'Establishment' and 'Dissent' in British North America: Organizing Religion in the New World," in Stephen Foster, ed., *British North America in the Seventeenth and Eighteenth Centuries* (Oxford: Oxford University Press, 2013), 136–169.

14. Greene, *Virginia's Cure*, 14; Jon Butler, *Awash in a Sea of Faith: Christianizing the American People* (Cambridge: Harvard University Press, 1990), 37–66.

15. Philip S. Haffenden, "The Anglican Church in Restoration Policy," in J. M. Smith, ed., *Seventeenth-Century America: Essays in Colonial History* (Chapel Hill: University of North Carolina Press, 1959), 179–181.

16. John Hammond, *Leah and Rachel; or, the Two Fruitfull Sisters Virginia and Maryland* (1655), 5.

17. Carla Gardina Pestana, *The English Atlantic in an Age of Revolution, 1640–1661* (Cambridge: Harvard University Press, 2004), 185–193, 210–217; Patricia Bonomi, *Under the Cope of Heaven: Religion, Society and Politics in Colonial America* (Oxford: Oxford University Press, 2003), 13–38, 105–118.

18. Butler, *Awash in a Sea of Faith*, 56–59; Mark Peterson, *The Price of Redemption: The Spiritual Economy of Puritan New England* (Stanford: Stanford University Press, 1997).

19. *Boyle Correspondence*, vol. 4, 349–350; Samuel Sewall and Edward Rawson, *The Revolution in New England Justified* (1691), preface; Stephen Foster, *The Long Argument: English Puritanism and the Shaping of New England Culture, 1570–1700* (Chapel Hill: University of North Carolina Press, 1991), 138–174.

20. George Cartwright to Sir Henry Bennett, 1665, BL Egerton MSS, 2395, fol. 433.

21. Langdon Cheves, ed., *The Shaftesbury Papers* (Charleston, SC: Tempus Publications, 2000), 31, 344; George Milner, "Proposals in order to the improvement of the county of Albemarle," n.d., BL Egerton MSS, 2395, fols. 661–663; Mark Peterson, *The City-State of Boston: The Rise and Fall of an Atlantic Power, 1630–1865* (Princeton: Princeton University Press, 2019), 27–36.

22. Richard Nicolls to William Morice, 24 October 1668, Rawlinson MSS, A175, fol. 75; Robert Mason to Danby, 5 March 1675/6, BL Egerton, 3340, fol. 155; John Josselyn, *An account of two voyages to New-England* (1673), 182, 198, 272.

23. Richard Ligon, *A true & exact history of the island of Barbados* (1657), 113; Memorial on New England, n.d., BL Add MSS 63,773, fol. 190; Vaughan to Danby, 20 September 1675, BL Egerton, 2240, fol. 141; Bernard Bailyn, *The New England Merchants in the Seventeenth-Century* (Cambridge: Harvard University Press, 1955), 84–90.

24. "A Representation of the state of affaires in New England," February 1662, Clarendon MSS, 79, fols. 77–78; Samuel Maverick, "The Government of the New Netherlands," n.d., Clarendon MSS, 74, fols. 230–236.

25. "Notes explanatory of some of the heads annexed to the petition of the Virginia Agents," 1675, Coventry MSS, 77, fol. 44; Journal of the Lords of Trade, 4 April 1677, CO 391/2, fol. 9.

26. Earl of Sandwich, "Upon New England," in F. R. Harris, *The Life of Edward Montague, K.G., First Earl of Sandwich, 1625–1672*, 2 vols. (London, 1912), vol. 2, appendix K.

27. *A short account of the present state of New-England* (London, 1690), 9; Josselyn, *Account of two voyages*, 182, 198, 272.

28. Jenny Hale Pulsipher, *Subjects unto the Same King* (Philadelphia: University of Pennsylvania Press, 2005), 196–198; Robert M. Bliss, *Revolution and Empire: English Politics and the American Colonies in the Seventeenth Century* (Manchester: Manchester University Press, 1990), 82–83, 147.

29. Alison Games, *Migration and the Origins of the English Atlantic World* (Cambridge: Harvard University Press, 1999), 158–161; April Lee Hatfield, *Atlantic Virginia: Intercolonial Relations in the Seventeenth Century* (Philadelphia: University of Pennsylvania Press, 2004), 54–57, 60, 117; Carla Gardina Pestana, *Protestant Empire: Religion and the Making of the British Atlantic World* (Philadelphia: University of Pennsylvania Press, 2009), 88.

30. Henry Gardener, *New-England's Vindication* (1660), 1–2, 5.

31. Worsley to Ashley Cooper, 14 August 1668, PRO 20/34/49, fol. 227.

32. HMC, *The Manuscripts of His Grace the Duke of Portland*, 10 vols. (London, 1891–1931), iii, 279; Robert Sanford, *Surinam Justice* (1662), 9, 44; Sarah Barber, *A Revolutionary Rogue: Henry Marten and the English Republic* (Stroud: Sutton, 2000), 134–135.

33. Cheves, *Shaftesbury Papers*, 50; John Cotton, "Note" on New England, n.d., Clarendon MSS, 75, fol. 451; John Oxenbridge, *A seasonable proposition of propagating the gospel by Christian colonies in the continent of Guaiana* (1670), 11.

34. George Cartwright, Memorial on Massachusetts, 1665, Clarendon MSS, 83, fols. 335–336; Pestana, *English Atlantic*, 86–87; Michael Winship, *Hot Protestants: The History of Puritanism in England and America* (New Haven: Yale University Press, 2019), 104–109, 191.

35. Susan Hardman Moore, *Pilgrims: New World Settlers and the Call of Home* (New Haven: Yale University Press, 2010), 78, 144.

36. Cartwright to Bennett, fol. 433; Samuel Maverick to Clarendon, 1661, Clarendon MSS, 74, fol. 239; Bliss, *Revolution and Empire*, 147.

37. Fabian Philipps, *The ancient, legal, fundamental, and necessary rights of courts of justice* (1676), 312.

38. Paul D. Halliday, *Dismembering the Body Politic: Partisan Politics in England's Towns, 1650–1730* (Cambridge: Cambridge University Press, 1998), 17–18, 109, 117; *Boyle Correspondence*, vol. 2, 355–356.

39. E. S. De Beer, ed., *The Diary of John Evelyn*, 6 vols. (Oxford: Oxford University Press, 1955), vol. 3, 582.

40. Earl of Cassilis to earl of Lauderdale, 28 December 1660, NRS, Ailsa MSS, GD 25/9, box 30/2.

41. Cheves, *Shaftesbury Papers*, 304.

42. Vincent Gookin, *The Great case of Transplantation in Ireland discussed* (1659), 3.

43. *CSPC, 1661–1668*, 512. See also Adrian Chastain Weimer, "The 'Contynuance of our Civell and religious Liberties': Plymouth Colonists' 1665 'Humble Addresse' to the King," *Early American Literature* 56, no. 1 (2021): 219–232; Adrian Chastain Weimer, "The Resistance Petitions of 1664–1665: Confronting the Restoration in Massachusetts Bay," *New England Quarterly* 92, no. 2 (2019): 221–262.

44. "Declaration to encourage settlement in Carolina," 25 August 1663, in William L. Saunders, ed., *Colonial and State Records of North Carolina,* 10 vols. (Raleigh, 1886–1890), vol. 1, 43–46.

45. *The Fundamental Constitutions of Carolina* (London, 1669), 21–22.

46. N.H. Keeble and Geoffrey F. Nuttall, eds., *Calendar of the Correspondence of Richard Baxter,* 2 vols. (Oxford: Oxford University Press, 1991), vol. 2, 65; Matthew Sylvester, ed., *Reliquiae Baxteriana* (1696), bk. 1, pt. 2, 290; William Kellaway, *The New England Company, 1649–1776* (London: Longmans, Green, 1961), 36–41.

47. *Boyle Correspondence,* vol. 2, 268; vol. 4, 458; Gabriel Glickman, "Protestantism, Colonization and the New England Company in Restoration Politics," *Historical Journal* 59, no. 2 (June 2016): 365–391.

48. John Spurr, *The Restoration Church of England* (New Haven: Yale University Press, 1991), 31–42; Paul Seaward, *The Cavalier Parliament and the Reconstruction of the Old Regime, 1661–1667* (Cambridge: Cambridge University Press, 1988), 30–42.

49. Sylvester, *Reliquiae,* bk. 1, pt. 2, 207.

50. Thomas Thorowgood, *Jews in America* (1661); " 'God preserve . . . New England': Richard Baxter and His American Friends," *Journal: United Reformed Church History Society* 5 (1993): 146–153.

51. Peterson, *Price of Redemption,* 12–14, 20, 47–48.

52. Anthony Milton, "The Unchanged Peacemaker? John Dury and the Politics of Irenicism in England, 1628–1643," in Mark Greengrass, Michael Leslie, and Timothy Raylor, eds., *Samuel Hartlib and Universal Reformation* (Cambridge: Cambridge University Press, 1995), 95–117.

53. Report of the committee of the East India Company, Bodl., Tanner MSS 36, fol. 67; "To the Right Honourable the Lords of His Maties most Honoble Privy Council," 1663, Royal Society Archives, RB1/4/18l; Payment for Samuel Chylinsky, 3 March 1664/5, National Archives, Privy Council Register, 2/58, fol. 34; Nicholas Tyacke, "From Laudians to Latitudinarians: A Shifting Balance of Theological Forces," in Grant Tapsell, ed., *The Later Stuart Church, 1660–1714* (Manchester: Manchester University Press, 2012), 51–52; Fiona A. MacDonald, *Missions to the Gaels: Reformation and Counter-Reformation in Ulster and the Highlands and Islands of Scotland, 1560–1760* (Edinburgh: John Donald, 2006), 209–210.

54. Sylvester, *Reliquiae,* bk. 1, pt. 2, 295–297.

55. Morgan Godwyn, *A supplement to the Negro's [and] Indian's advocate* (1681), 4.

56. Lynch to Sheldon, 29 November 1671, BL Add MSS, 11410, fol. 199; *CSPC, 1681–1685,* 188.

57. Jacqueline Rose, "By Law Established: The Church of England and the Royal Supremacy," in Tapsell, *Later Stuart Church,* 25–28.

58. Mark Goldie, *Roger Morrice and the Puritan Whigs: The Entring Book, 1677–1691* (Rochester: Boydell Press, 2016), 12; David J. Appleby, *Black Bartholomew's Day: Preaching, Polemic and Restoration Nonconformity* (Manchester: Manchester University Press, 2009).

59. Sylvester, *Reliquiae*, bk. 1, pt. 2, 298; Cotton Mather, *A letter of advice to the churches of the non-conformists* (1700), 3–4, 28.

60. Baxter to Eliot, 30 November 1663, in Keeble and Nuttall, *Calendar*, vol. 2, 40–41; Morgan Godwyn, *Trade preferr'd before religion and Christ* (1685), 24–25.

61. Thomas Shephard to anonymous correspondent, 9 July 1673, NLS, Wodrow Quarto CV, fol. 114; John Scott, "Account of the English colonies," 1661, BL Sloane MSS, 3662, fol. 23.

62. Cartwright to Bennett, 1665, BL Egerton MSS, 2395, fols. 433–435.

63. *Boyle Correspondence,* appendix 6, 446; Godwyn, *A Supplement,* 4; Katharine Gerbner, "The Ultimate Sin: Christianising Slaves in Barbados in the Seventeenth Century," *Slavery & Abolition* 31, no. 1 (2010): 57–73.

64. Baxter to Eliot, 30 November 1663, in Keeble and Nuttall, *Calendar,* vol. 2, 40–41.

65. Cotton Mather, *India Christiana* (1721), 37–40; David Silverman, *Faith and Boundaries* (Cambridge: Cambridge University Press, 2005), 174–181; Peterson, *Price of Redemption,* 185–188.

66. *Boyle Correspondence,* vol. 2, 470–471; *CSPC, 1661–1668,* 283; Francis J. Bremer, *The Puritan Experiment: New England Society from Bradford to Edwards* (Lebanon, NH: University Press of New England, 1995), 150–151.

67. Henry Oxenden to George Oxenden, 1 April 1666, BL Add MSS, 40712, fol. 9.

68. George Southcombe, "Dissent and the Reformation Church," in Tapsell, *Later Stuart Church,* 209–210.

69. Ann Hughes, *Gangraena and the Struggle for the English Revolution* (Oxford: Oxford University Press, 2004), 250, 402; Pestana, *English Atlantic,* 67–68, 71.

70. Alison Gilbert Olson, *Making the Empire Work: London and American Interest Groups, 1690–1790* (Cambridge: Harvard University Press, 1992), 83.

71. *Boyle Correspondence,* v, 225; Pulsipher, *Subjects,* 180.

72. "Sketch of a plan to establish an English bishopric," 1670, All Souls MS 238, fol. 152; William J. Bulman, *Anglican Enlightenment: Orientalism, Religion and Politics in England and Its Empire, 1648–1715* (Cambridge: Cambridge University Press, 2015), 220–221.

73. William Gibson, "A Bishop for Virginia in 1672: A Fragment from Bishop Ward's Papers," *Archives* 34, no. 10 (2009): 36–41; Bell, *Imperial Origins,* 12–15.

74. Haffenden, "Anglican Church," 177, 182.

75. "A Journal kept by Col William Beeston," BL Add MSS 12,430, fol. 22; Instructions to Sir Charles Wheeler, 31 January 1670/1, CO 153/1/11; *CSPC, 1677–1680,* 1058.

76. Gregory, " 'Establishment' and 'Dissent,' " 138–168.

77. Spurr, *Restoration Church,* 56–58.

78. *CSPC, 1661–1668,* 739; *CSPC, 1669–1674,* 270; Kenneth Lane Carroll, *John Perrot: Early Quaker Schismatic* (London: Friends' Historical Society, 1971).

79. Sir Abraham Shipman to George Oxenden, 21 September 1663, BL Add MSS, 40709, fol. 4.

80. *CSPC, 1669–1674,* 1425.

81. *CSPC, 1661–1668,* 512–513; James, duke of York, "Instructions for Edm. Andros," 1678, CO 5/1112, fol. 5; Evan Haefeli, *New Netherland and the Dutch Origins of American Religious Liberty* (Philadelphia: University of Pennsylvania Press, 2012), 263.

82. Gregory, "Later Stuart Church and North America," 236–237; Nathaniel B. Shurtleff, ed., *Records of the Governor & Company of the Massachusetts Bay in New England,* 5 vols., (Boston: William White, 1853–1854), vol. 4, pt. 2, 74–80, 164–165.

83. "Preuilleges graunted to the People of the Hebrew Nation that are to goe to the Wilde Cust," n.d, BL Egerton MS 2385, fol. 46; Lynch to Henry Slingsby, 29 November 1671, BL Add MSS, 11410, fols. 200–201; Cranfield to Coventry, 4 August 1675, Coventry MSS, 76, fol. 378; Samuel Oppenheim, "An Early Jewish Colony in Western Guiana, 1658–1666, and Its Relation to the Jews in Surinam, Cayenne and Tobago," *Publications of the American Jewish Historical Society* 16 (1907), 95–186.

84. Charles II, Sir Henry Bennett, "Instructions for the Earle of Teviot," 1663, Rawlinson MSS, C423, fols. 71–72.

85. Philip Calvert to Richard Nicolls, 22 March 1667/8, Huntington Library, BL59. I am indebted to Dr. Mark Williams for this reference.

86. Memorial by Portuguese ambassador, May 1661, Clarendon MSS, 75, fols. 460–461; Bequest of Bombay to East India Company, 1668, Rawlinson B5156, fol. 17.

87. Karin Schuller, "Irish-Iberian Trade from the Mid-Sixteenth to the Mid-Seventeenth Centuries," in David Dickson, Jan Parmentier, and Jane Ohlmeyer, eds., *Irish and Scottish Mercantile Networks in Europe and Overseas in the Seventeenth and Eighteenth Centuries* (Ghent: Academia Press, 2006), 175–196.

88. William Godolphin to Coventry, 7/17 November 1678, Coventry MSS, 60, fol. 257.

89. *CSPC, 1677–1680,* 574, 741; Donald Akenson, *If the Irish Ran the World: Montserrat, 1630–1730* (Montreal: McGill-Queen's University Press, 1997), 111.

90. Ibid., 47–53; Natalie Zacek, *Settler Society in the English Leeward Islands, 1670–1776* (Cambridge: Cambridge University Press, 2010), 45–48; Ryan Dominic Crewe, "Brave New Spain: An Irishman's Independence Plot in Seventeenth-Century Mexico," *Past and Present* 207 (May 2010): 53–87.

91. William, Lord Willoughby to anon correspondent, 18 September 1667, BL Stowe MSS 755, fol. 19.

92. Lynch to Arlington, 27 December 1672, BL Add MSS 11,410, fol. 301; Henry Goodricke to Coventry, 24 October 1679, Coventry MSS, 60, fol. 295; William Stapleton to Committee of Trade, 14 April 1676, CO 153/2/129; Nuala Zahedieh, "The Merchants of Port Royal, Jamaica, and the Spanish Contraband Trade, 1655–1692," *W&MQ* 43, no. 4 (October 1986): 570–593.

93. Kevin Whelan, "An Underground Gentry? Catholic Middlemen in Eighteenth-Century Ireland," *Eighteenth-Century Ireland* 10 (1995): 7–68; Louis M. Cullen, "Galway Merchants in the Outside World, 1650–1800," in Louis M. Cullen, *Economy, Trade and Irish Merchants at Home and Abroad, 1600–1988* (Dublin: Four Courts Press, 2012), 169–181.

94. Hugh Cholmley to Thomas Maynard, 15 March 1664/5, Cholmley MSS, V/1/1/1, fol. 50; Cholmley to Lord Henry Howard, 14 August 1670, Cholmley MSS, V, 1/1/3, fol. 115.

95. Henry Norwood to Clarendon, 1666, Clarendon MSS, 84, fols. 406–410; Gabriel Glickman, "Empire, 'Popery,' and the Fall of English Tangier, 1662–1684," *Journal of Modern History* 87, no. 2 (June 2015): 258–259, 264–265.

96. "Public accounts of the island of Montserrat," March 1673, Manchester, John Rylands Library, Stapleton MSS, 2/3.

97. Kristen Block and Jenny Shaw, "Subjects Without an Empire: The Irish in the Early Modern Caribbean," *Past and Present* 210, no. 1 (February 2011): 33–60.

98. Richard Langhorne to Christopher, Lord Hatton, 12 June 1673, BL Add MSS, 29,554, fol. 170.

99. William Stapleton, "Answers to the Council for Plantations," March 1672, Stapleton MSS, 2/2; Minutes of the Council of Antigua, 27 April 1681, Stapleton MSS (uncatalogued); Akenson, *If the Irish Ran the World*, 127–130; Gabriel Glickman, "Catholic Interests and the Politics of English Overseas Expansion, 1660–1689," *Journal of British Studies* 55, no. 4 (October 2016): 693–694.

100. Alexandra Walsham, *Charitable Hatred: Tolerance and Intolerance in England, 1500–1700* (Manchester: Manchester University Press, 2006), 48–50; Mark Knights, " '*Meer Religion*' and the 'Church-State' of Restoration England: The Impact and Ideology of James II's Declarations of Indulgence," in Steven Pincus and Alan Houston, eds., *A Nation Transformed: England after the Restoration* (Cambridge: Cambridge University Press, 2001), 41–70.

101. *CSPC, 1677–1680*, 121; Sandwich, "Upon New England," in Harris, *Edward Montague*, vol. 2, appendix K.

102. Farrelly, *Papist Patriots*, 98–100.

103. Akenson, *If the Irish Ran the World*, 93–95.

104. Cholmley to Lord Henry Howard, 14 August 1670, Cholmley MSS, V, 1/1/3, fol. 115.

105. Lynch to Slingsby, 29 November 1671, BL Add MSS, 11410, fols. 200–201.

106. Charles Molloy, *De Jure Maritimo et Navali* (1676), A3.

107. De Beer, *Diary of John Evelyn*, vol. 3, 579–580.

108. For the fullest accounts of the actions of the committee, see Philip S. Haffenden, "The Crown and the Colonial Charters, 1675–1688," parts 1 and 2, *W&MQ* 15, no. 3 (July 1958): 298–311, and 15, no. 4 (October 1958): 452–486; J. M. Sosin, *English America and the Restoration Monarchy of Charles II: Transatlantic Politics, Commerce, and Kinship* (Lincoln: University of Nebraska Press, 1980); Stephen Saunders Webb, *1676: The End of American Independence* (New York: Knopf, 1984), 199–244; Bliss, *Revolution and Empire*, 179–189.

109. "Overture for the better regulation of the forreigne plantations," fol. 149; Journal of the Lords of Trade, 24 September 1675, CO 391/1, fol. 21; Journal of the Lords of Trade, 23 December 1675, CO 391/1, fols. 30–31; Sir William Stapleton to Committee of Trade, 20 December 1675, CO 153/2, fols. 78–79.

110. K. H. D. Haley, *The First Earl of Shaftesbury* (Oxford: Clarendon Press, 1968), 345–365.

111. Journal of the Lords of Trade, 1 June 1676, CO 391/1, fol. 65.

112. Sir John Werden to Edmund Andros, 30 November 1676, CO 5/1112, fols. 18–19.

113. Edward Randolph to the Lords of Trade, 13 April 1681, BL Add MSS 63,773, fols. 145–146; Henry Coventry to earl of Essex, 2 October 1676, Coventry MSS, 84, fol. 47.

114. Journal of the Lords of Trade, 18 April 1678, CO 391/2, fol. 122.

115. Journal of the Lords of Trade, 11 September 1677, CO 391/2, fols. 54–55; John C. Rainbolt, "A New Look at Stuart 'Tyranny': The Crown's Attack on the Virginia Assembly, 1676–1689," *Virginia Magazine of History and Biography* 75, no. 4 (October 1967): 387–406.

116. "The Report of the Right Honourable the Lords of the Committee for Trade and Plantations to the King," 28 May 1679, BL Add MSS, 12429, fols. 87–88; Richard S. Dunn, "Imperial Pressures on Massachusetts and Jamaica, 1675–1700," in A. G. Olson and R. M. Brown, eds., *Anglo-American Political Relations, 1660–1775* (New Brunswick, NJ: Rutgers University Press, 1970), 52–75.

117. Journal of the Lords of Trade, 12 June 1677, CO 391/2, fols. 29–30; "An overture for the better regulation of the forreigne Plantations," 1675, BL Egerton MSS, 3340, fols. 148–149.

118. Journal of the Lords of Trade, 16 May 1678, CO 391/2, fols. 125–126.

119. Barbara C. Murison, "The Talented Mr Blathwayt: His Empire Revisited," in Nancy L. Rhoden, ed., *English Atlantics Revisited: Essays Honouring Professor Ian K. Steele* (Montreal: McGill-Queen's University Press, 2014), 42–43; Journal of the Lords of Trade, 22 November 1680, CO 391/3, fol. 155; Earl of Clarendon to earl of Carlisle, 27 August 1681, BL Add MSS, 2724, fol. 106; Richard R. Johnson, "The Imperial Webb: The Thesis of Garrison Government in Early America Considered," *W&MQ*, 3rd ser. 43, no. 3 (July 1986): 408–430.

120. Journal of the Lords of Trade, 20 May 1679, CO 391/3, fols. 4–9; Journal of the Lords of Trade, 16 September 1680, CO 391/3, fol. 99; Journal of the Lords of Trade, 14 October 1680, CO 391/3, fols. 108–109; "The Earl of Carlisle's answer," 1680, BL Add MSS, 12429, fol. 105.

121. *CSPC, 1681–1685*, 663, 696; "A Paper given to my Ld Chamberlaine by Mr Shepheard from ye Earle of Shaftesbury," 28 September 1681, Clarendon MSS, 88, fol. 5.

122. Peterson, *City-State of Boston*, ch. 3; Richard Johnson, *Adjustment to Empire: The New England Colonies, 1675–1715* (New Brunswick, NJ: Rutgers University Press, 1981), 71–134.

123. Richard S. Dunn, "The Glorious Revolution and America," in Nicholas Canny, ed., *The Oxford History of the British Empire*, vol. 1: *The Origins of Empire* (Oxford: Oxford University Press, 1998), 452.

124. Lords of Trade to Nathaniel Johnson, 28 May 1687, CO 153/3, fol. 262; "The Humble Petition and address of your Majesty's most Loyall and obedient subjects of Barbados," 1685, BL Sloane MSS, 3984, fol. 221; John Cary, *An Answer to Mr Molyneux* (1698), 143.

125. "Col Dongan's answer to Heads of Inquiry," 1687, CO 5/1113, fols. 12, 17; Dongan to earl of Sunderland, 8 September 1687, CO 5/1113, fol. 76; Daniel K. Richter, *The Ordeal of the Long-House: The Peoples of the Iroquois League in the Era of European Colonization* (Chapel Hill: University of North Carolina Press, 1992), 149–159.

126. "Mr Worsley's Discourse of the Privateers of Jamaica," n.d., BL Add MSS, 11410, fols. 312.

127. Owen Stanwood, *The Empire Reformed: English America in the Age of the Glorious Revolution* (Philadelphia: University of Pennsylvania Press, 2011), 54–55.

128. See especially ibid., 53–102; Johnson, *Adjustment to Empire*; David. S. Lovejoy, *The Glorious Revolution in America* (New York: Harper & Rowe, 1972).

129. Mark Goldie, "Danby, the Bishops and the Whigs," in Tim Harris, Paul Seaward, and Mark Goldie, eds., *The Politics of Religion in Restoration England* (Oxford: Basil Blackwell, 1990), 75–105.

130. Tim Harris, *Politics under the Later Stuarts: Party Conflict in a Divided Society, 1660–1715* (Harlow, UK: Longman, 1993), 93–108.

131. Edward Randolph to Henry Coventry, 17 June 1676, *CSPC, 1675–1676*, 953; R. N. Toppan and A. T. S. Goodrick, eds., *Edward Randolph: Including his Letters and Official Papers*, 7 vols. (Boston, 1898–1909), vol. 4, 272.

132. Journal of the Lords of Trade, 21 January 1675/6, CO 391/1, fol. 34; Haffenden, "Anglican Church," 166–191; Bell, *Imperial Origins*, 13–27.

133. *CSPC, 1681–1685*, 1129; Toppan and Goodrick, eds., *Randolph*, vol. 3, 288; Jeremy Gregory, "The Later Stuart Church and America," in Tapsell, ed., *Later Stuart Church*, 251.

134. *CSPC, 1681–1685*, 414.

135. Ned C. Landsman, "The Middle Colonies: New Opportunities for Settlement, 1660–1700," in Canny, *Oxford History of the British Empire*, vol. 1, 355–363; Pestana, *Protestant Empire*, 111–112.

136. Dunn and Dunn, *Papers of William Penn*, vol. 1, 386, 396, 418, 542, vol. 2, 23; *CSPC, 1681–1685*, 1479; Ned C. Landsman, *Scotland and Its First American Colony, 1683–1765* (Princeton: Princeton University Press, 1985), 99–129; G. P. Insh, *Scottish Colonial Schemes, 1620–1686* (Glasgow, 1922), 148–169, 182–183.

137. John J. McCusker, "Colonial Statistics," in Susan B. Carter et al., eds., *Historical Statistics of the United States*, vol. 5: *Governance and International Relations* (Cambridge: Cambridge University Press, 2006), 561–562.

138. Mary K. Geiter, "The Restoration Crisis and the Launching of Pennsylvania, 1679–81," *English Historical Review* 112, no. 446 (April 1997): 300–318.

139. George Scot, *Model of the Government of the Province of East New Jersey* (1682), epistle dedicatory, 47–48; George Scot of Pitlochie and James, earl of Perth, *A brief advertisement concerning East-New-Jersey, in America* (1685), 1.

140. Journal of the Lords of Trade, 22 January 1680/1, CO 391/3, fols. 126–127; Journal of the Lords of Trade, 24 February 1680/1, CO 391/3, fol. 128; Dunn and Dunn, *Papers of William Penn*, vol. 2, 73.

141. Richard Wharton to Edward Randolph, 2 February 1684/5, Bodl., Tanner MSS, 31, fol. 6.

142. Michael Garibaldi Hall, *Edward Randolph and the American Colonies, 1676–1703* (Chapel Hill: University of North Carolina Press, 1960), 21–58; Bell, *Imperial Origins*, 30–33.

143. Toppan and Goodrick, eds., *Randolph*, vol. 3, 165, 317; "An humble memorial of the present Condition of the Dissenters of New England," July 1688, BL Egerton MSS, 3340, fol. 179; Cotton Mather, *Parentator. Memoirs of remarkables in the life and the death of the ever-memorable Dr. Increase Mather* (1724), 109, 113–115.

144. Edward Randolph to Bishop Lloyd, 28 March 1685/6, Tanner MSS, 31, fol. 7; Butler, *Awash in a Sea of Faith*, 61–62.

145. Thomas Dongan to committee touching New York, 1684, CO 5/113, fols. 12–13; Dongan to Sunderland, 8 September 1687, CO 5/113, fol. 77; Peter R. Christoph, ed., *The Dongan Papers* (New York, 1993), 82, 90.

146. *CSPC, 1685–88*, 1027, 1429, 1430; Robert Ritchie, *The Duke's Province* (Chapel Hill: University of North Carolina Press, 1977), 173; Carl Bridenbaugh, ed., *The Pynchon Papers. Letters of John Pynchon, 1654–1700*, 2 vols. (Boston: Colonial Society of Massachusetts, 1982), vol. 1, 89, 176–177.

147. Marion Tinling, ed., *The Correspondence of the Three William Byrds of Westover, Virginia, 1684–1776*, 2 vols. (Charlottesville: Virginia Historical Society, 1977), vol. 1, 55–56.

148. M. G. Hall, ed., "The Autobiography of Increase Mather," *Proceedings of the American Antiquarian Society* (New York, 1961), 325; Mather, *Parentator*, 114–115.

149. Mark Goldie, "Sir Peter Pett, Sceptical Toryism and the Science of Toleration in the 1680s," in W. J. Sheils, ed., *Persecution and Toleration: Studies in Church History*, vol. 21 (Oxford: Blackwell, 1984), 247–273.

150. Henry Neville Payne, *The persecutor expos'd* (1685), 37, 39; Paul Hopkins, "Payne, Henry," *Oxford Dictionary of National Biography*.

151. Marquis of Lansdowne, ed., *The Petty Papers*, 2 vols. (London: Reprints of Economic Classics, 1997), vol. 1, 59–63, 256–257; Marquis of Lansdowne, ed., *The Petty-Southwell Correspondence, 1676–1687* (London: Reprints of Economic Classics, 1997), 187; Ted McCormick, *William Petty and the Ambitions of Political Arithmetic* (Oxford: Oxford University Press, 2009), 275–280.

152. [William Petyt,] *Britannia Languens; or, A Discourse of Trade* (1680), 245–246.

153. Richard Tuck, *Thomas Hobbes. Philosophy and Government, 1572–1651* (Cambridge: Cambridge University Press, 1993), 341; Jon Parkin, "Hobbism in the Later 1660s: Daniel Scargill and Samuel Parker," *Historical Journal* 42, no. 1 (March 1999): 93; McCormick, *William Petty*, 37–38.

154. Caroline Robbins, ed., *The Diary of John Milward* (Cambridge: Cambridge University Press, 1938), 216.

155. Steve Pincus, *1688: The First Modern Revolution* (New Haven: Yale University Press, 2009), 320, 378; Scott Sowerby, *Making Toleration: The Repealers and the Glorious Revolution* (Cambridge: Harvard University Press, 2013), ch. 2.

156. Leoline Jenkins, paper on trade, 1685, All Souls, MS 264, fol. 224. See also James Whiston, "To the King's most Excellent Maty," 1686, BL Sloane MSS, 3984, fol. 198.

157. *Declaration of Indulgence, 1687*, in Andrew Browning, ed., *English Historical Documents*, vol. 6: *1660–1714* (London: Routledge, 1996), doc. 149.

158. Peter Pett, *The Happy Future State of England* (1688), 184, 200; Chappell, ed., *Tangiers Papers*, 317. See also Thomas Sheridan, *A discourse . . . of the interest of England* (1678), 139, 162.

159. William Penn to James II, 24 May 1687, BL Add MSS 5540, fol. 43.

160. Patrick Gordon, *Geography Anatomiz'd* (1699), 401–402.

161. Edward Stillingfleet, *A sermon preached on the fast-day, November 13, 1678* (1678), 46–47.

Chapter 6. Warfare, Luxury, and the Domestic Critique of English Overseas Expansion

1. John Dryden, *The prologue and epilogue to the History of Bacon in Virginia* (1689), 1; Bridget Orr, *Empire on the English Stage, 1660–1714* (Cambridge: Cambridge University Press, 2001), 55.

2. R. Latham and W. Matthews, eds., *The Diary of Samuel Pepys*, 11 vols. (London: HarperCollins, 1970–1983), vol. 3, 95–96; Imtiaz Habib, *Black Lives in the English Archives, 1500–1677* (Farnham: Ashgate, 2017), ch. 3; Susan Dwyer Amussen, *Caribbean Exchanges: Slavery and the Transformation of English Society, 1640–1700* (Chapel Hill: University of North Carolina Press, 2007), 179, 215–225.

3. James Walvin, *Fruits of Empire: Exotic Produce and British Taste, 1660–1800* (Basingstoke: Macmillan, 1997), 14–37, 120–127.

4. Gary S. De Krey, *Restoration and Revolution in Britain: Political Culture in the Era of the Glorious Revolution* (Basingstoke: Macmillan, 2007), 99–116.

5. Paul Slack, "The Politics of Consumption and England's Happiness in the Later Seventeenth Century," *English Historical Review* 112, no. 497 (June 2007): 609–631; Christopher Berry, *The Idea of Luxury: A Conceptual and Historical Investigation* (Cambridge: Cambridge University Press, 1994).

6. James Houblon, "A Discourse touching the Grounds of ye Decay of ye English Navigation," n.d., Rawlinson MSS, A171, fol. 280.

7. "Att two conferences with Sir Charles Wheeler," 7 and 10 December 1672, CO 153/1, fol. 53; "Sir Robert Southwell's report concerning planters," CO 153/2, 23 June 1675, fols. 12–15.

8. E. E. Rich, ed., *Minutes of the Hudson's Bay Company, 1671–1674* (London: Champlain Society, 1942), 131; "Newfoundland business," PRO 30/24/49, fol. 209.

9. Earl of Arlington to the court of Spain, 1670, SP 94/54, fol. 79.

10. John Werden to Arlington, 23 September/3 October 1668, SP 94/53, fol. 321; Godolphin to Arlington, 4/14 May 1670, SP 94/56, fols. 124–125.

11. Lynch to Arlington, 9 March 1671/2, BL Add MSS 11,410, fol. 250.

12. *CSPC, 1661–1668,* 739, 744; Richard Dunn, *Sugar and Slaves: The Rise of the Planter Class in the English West Indies, 1624–1713* (Chapel Hill: University of North Carolina Press, 1972), 154–156.

13. "A narrative humbly presented to His Majesty by Sir Thomas Modyford," 1671, BL Egerton MSS 3340, fol. 114.

14. Petition to Arlington, September 1671, SP 94/58, fols. 201–202; Godolphin to Arlington, 4/14 May 1670, SP 94/56, fols. 124–125.

15. "The Relation of Admirall Henry Morgan touching the service done his Matie in ye late expedition against ye Spaniards," 29 June 1671, Clarendon MSS, 87, fols. 90–93; Peter Earle, *The Sack of Panama: Captain Morgan and the Battle for the Caribbean* (New York: St. Martin's, 1981).

16. Godolphin to Arlington, 14/24 June 1671, SP 94/58, fol. 104.

17. Godolphin to Arlington, 2/12 October 1672, SP 94/60, fol. 132.

18. Lynch to Sir Robert Moray, 2 March 1671/2, BL Add MSS, 11410, fol. 237; Lynch to Sir Charles Lyttelton, 5 March 1671/2, BL Add MSS, 11410, fols. 243–245.

19. Langdon Cheves, ed., *The Shaftesbury Papers* (Charleston, SC: Tempus Publications, 2000), 182–183.

20. Ibid., 197–201.

21. *Journal of Committee of Foreign Affairs,* 10 October 1669, SP 104/176, fol. 205.

22. *Journal of Committee of Foreign Affairs,* 8 August 1669, SP 104/176, fol. 188.

23. "The propositions of the East India Company," 1672, Rawlinson MSS, A 302, fols. 8–11; "Concerning the Trade of Pepper," March 1672/3, BL Add MSS, 28079, fol. 2.

24. Clarendon to the earl of St. Albans, 25 March 1667, Clarendon MSS, 85, fols. 167–168; Bebington, ed., *Arlington Papers,* vol. 1, 371.

25. *Journal of Committee of Foreign Affairs,* 22 January 1671/2, SP 104/176, fol. 268.

26. William A. Pettigrew, *Freedom's Debt: The Royal African Company and the Politics of the Atlantic Slave Trade, 1672–1752* (Chapel Hill: University of North Carolina Press, 2013), 11–43; *Certain Considerations relating to the Royal African Company* (1680), 4.

27. E. S. De Beer, ed., *The Diary of John Evelyn,* 6 vols. (Oxford: Oxford University Press, 1955), vol. 3, 585.

28. Lynch to Sir Charles Lyttelton, 5 March 1671/2, BL Add MSS, 11410, fol. 245.

29. Lynch to Sir Joseph Williamson, 7 March 1671/2, BL Add MSS, 11410, fol. 248.

30. Charles II to Louis XIV, 1669, BL Add MSS, 65138, fols. 30–32; "A project of a secret treaty between the King of Great Brittain and the most Christian King," 1669, BL Add MSS, 65138, fols. 77–80; Ronald Hutton, "The Making of the Secret Treaty of Dover," *Historical Journal* 29, no. 2 (June 1986): 297–318.

31. Committee for Foreign Affairs, 18 November 1671, SP 104/176, fol. 320; "Proposalls concerning the West Indies, by the Lord Willoughbie," November 1671, BL Egerton MSS, 2395, fol. 477.

32. Michael J. Braddick, *State Formation in Early Modern England, c. 1550–1700* (Cambridge: Cambridge University Press, 2000), 417.

33. Clarendon, Memorial, 1663, Clarendon MSS, 79, fol. 35; Tim Harris, *Restoration: Charles II and His Kingdoms, 1660–1685* (London: Allen Lane, 2005), 59–60.

34. Richard Nicolls to Clarendon, February 1666, Clarendon MSS, 84, fols. 118–119; Cholmley to Henry Norwood, 24 December 1666, Cholmley MSS, ZCG, V, 1/1/2, 5; Lynch to the Council of Trade, 20 August 1671, BL Add MSS, 11410, fol. 185.

35. *CSPC, 1669–1674,* 1066; "A narrative humbly presented to His Majesty by Sir Thomas Modyford," BL Egerton MSS, 3340, fol. 114.

36. George Downing, "Paper concerning the King's revenue," 16/26 August 1661, Clarendon MSS, 104, fols. 252–258; *Life of Edward, Earl of Clarendon,* vol. 1, 151.

37. *Life of Edward, Earl of Clarendon,* vol. 1, 152–153.

38. Cholmley to Christopher Wren, 28 April 1670, Cholmley MSS, ZCG, V/1/1/3, 38.

39. Godolphin to Arlington, 8 November 1673, SP 94/62, fol. 208.

40. Nicolls to Clarendon, February 1666/7, Clarendon MSS, 84, fols. 119–120.

41. Cholmley to Norwood, 2 September 1667, Cholmley MSS, ZCG V 1/1/2, 71.

42. Gilbert Burnet, *History of his own time,* 2 vols. (1724–1734), vol. 1, 171; De Krey, *Restoration and Revolution,* 97, 101.

43. Godolphin to Arlington, 13/23 November 1672, SP 94/60, fol. 179.

44. Thomas Blackerby to Oxenden, 11 March 1666/7, BL Add MSS, 40713, 8–9.

45. Latham and Matthews, *Diary of Samuel Pepys,* vol. 8, 268–269.

46. Robbins, ed., *Milward Diary,* 123; *Life of Edward, Earl of Clarendon,* vol. 1, 236; William Cobbett, ed., *The Parliamentary History of England,* 36 vols. (1806–1820), vol. 4, 377–378, 383.

47. George Wither, *A Sigh for the Pitchers* (1666), 13, 29, 32; Stephen Bardle, *The Literary Underground in the 1660s* (Oxford: Oxford University Press, 2012), 83–87.

48. Godolphin to Arlington, 13/23 November 1672, SP 94/60, fol. 179.

49. Tim Harris, *Politics under the Later Stuarts: Party Conflict in a Divided Society, 1660–1715* (Harlow: Longman, 1993), 52–64; Steven Pincus, "From Butterboxes to Wooden Shoes: The Shift in English Popular Sentiment from Anti-Dutch to Anti-French in the 1670s," *Historical Journal* 38, no. 2 (June 1995): 333–361.

50. Slingsby Bethel, *The World's Mistake in Oliver Cromwell* (1668), 7–8; *A Discourse of Trade* (1675), 10; *The Interest of Princes and States* (1680), 68–69.

51. Sir Richard Temple, "An Essay upon Government," 1669, Bodl., Eng. Hist. c. 201, fols. 10–11.

52. Roger Coke, *England's Improvements in two parts* (1675), 5–6.

53. Charles II, "Instructions" for the Council of Trade, 1668, PRO 30/24/49, fol. 120.

54. William Penn, *A Brief Account of the Province of Pennsylvania* (1681), 7.

55. Worsley to Charles II, 1668, PRO 30/24/49, fol. 88, E. A. Wrigley and R. S. Schofield, *The Population History of England, 1541–1871* (Cambridge: Cambridge University Press, 1981), 228.

56. Abigail L. Swingen, *Competing Visions of Empire: Labor, Slavery, and the Origins of the British Atlantic Empire* (New Haven: Yale University Press, 2015), 104–107; Mark Goldie, "Locke and America," in Matthew Stuart, ed., *A Companion to Locke* (Oxford: Oxford University Press, 2016), 71.

57. Sir William Coventry, "An Essay concerning the decay of Rents and their Remedies," 1670, BL Sloane MSS, 3828, fol. 205.

58. Roger Coke, *A Discourse of Trade* (1670), preface, 7, 9–10.

59. Carew Reynell, *The True English Interest* (1674), preface, 5, 7.

60. Bethel, *Interest of Princes and States*, 62–63.

61. Ibid., 34; Temple, "Essay upon Government," fol. 12.

62. Reynell, *True English Interest*, 5–6.

63. Ibid., 32–34; Temple, "Essay upon Government," fols. 12–13.

64. Reynell, *True English Interest*, 90–91.

65. [William Petyt,] *Britannia Languens; or, A Discourse of Trade* (1680), 176.

66. Coke, *England's Improvements*, 92.

67. Reynell, *True English Interest*, 34; Anchitel Grey, *Debates of the House of Commons, from the year 1667 to the year 1694*, 10 vols. (London, 1763), vol. 1, 116–117.

68. Reynell, *True English Interest*, 8, 34, 44; Coventry, "Essay concerning the decay of Rents," fols. 205–206.

69. Reynell, *True English Interest*, 8, 34, 44; Paul Slack, *Poverty and Policy in Tudor and Stuart England* (London: Longman, 1988), 55; Swingen, *Competing Visions*, 27–31; Ted McCormick, "Population: Modes of Seventeenth-Century Demographic Thought," in Philip J. Stern and Carl Wennerlind, eds., *Mercantilism Reimagined: Political Economy in Early Modern Britain and Its Empire* (Oxford: Oxford University Press, 2013), 25–45.

70. Grey, *Debates*, vol. 2, 133.

71. Petyt, *Britannia Languens*, 153–155, 246.

72. Ibid., 176; Coke, *Discourse of Trade*, 75.

73. Bethel, *World's Mistake*, 7–8.

74. Slingsby Bethel, *A Discourse of Trade* (1675), 10.

75. Petyt, *Britannia Languens*, 172–173.

76. Carl Bridenbaugh, ed., *The Pynchon Papers: Letters of John Pynchon, 1654–1700*, 2 vols. (Boston: Colonial Society of Massachusetts, 1982), vol. 1, 125.

77. Thomas Hutchinson, *The History of the Colony of Massachusetts Bay*, 3 vols. (Boston, 1767), vol. 1, 262.

78. Dunn and Dunn, *Papers of William Penn*, vol. 3, 228–230.

79. Steven Pincus, *Protestantism and Patriotism: Ideologies and the Making of English Foreign Policy, 1650–1668* (Cambridge: Cambridge University Press, 1996), 78–84, 258–272.

80. Temple, "Essay upon Government," fol. 89; Petyt, *Britannia Languens*, 175–176; Bethel, *Interest of Princes and States*, 78.

81. Bethel, *Interest of Princes and States*, 77–78; Cotton Mather, *A letter of advice to the churches of the non-conformists in the English nation* (1700), preface; Temple, "Essay upon Government," fol. 11.

82. Cobbett, *Parliamentary History*, vol. 4, 504, 514–515, 586; "Concerning the Trade of Pepper," fol. 2.

83. Grey, *Debates*, vol. 2, 199–200; De Beer, *Diary of John Evelyn*, vol. 3, 605–606.

84. Godolphin to Arlington, 27 December and 3 January 1673/4, SP 94/62, fol. 339.

85. De Beer, *Diary of John Evelyn*, vol. 3, 607.

86. Henry Coventry to Princess Elizabeth of the Palatinate, 30 January 1673/4, Coventry MSS, 82, fol. 33.

87. Journal of the Lords of Trade, CO 391/3, 8; George Alsop, *A Character of the Province of Maryland* (1666), 34–35.

88. *CSPC, 1661–1668,* 331, 772, 798; *Journal of the House of Commons,* vol. 8 (London, 1802), 302; Carla Gardina Pestana, *The English Atlantic in an Age of Revolution, 1640–1661* (Cambridge: Harvard University Press, 2004), 185, 209.

89. Sir Charles Sedley, *Bellamira; or, The Mistress. A Comedy* (1687); Leoline Jenkins to James II, 1685, All Souls MS 264, 208; Abbott Emerson Smith, *Colonists in Bondage: White Servitude and Convict Labor in America, 1607–1776* (Williamsburg: Omohundro Institute of Early American History and Culture, University of North Carolina Press, 2012), 67–69.

90. Davenant, *Two Discourses on the Public Revenues and Trade of England* (1698), 203.

91. Thomas Lynch, "Accompt of the English Sugar Plantations," PRO 30/24/49, fol. 20; David Eltis, "Atlantic History in Global Perspective," *Itinerario* 23, no. 2 (July 1999): 141–161; Swingen, *Competing Visions,* 23–27.

92. HMC, *Manuscripts of the Duke of Buccleuch and Queensberry,* 3 vols. (London, 1903), vol. 2, pt. 2, 735.

93. Michael Hunter, "The Cabinet Institutionalized: The Royal Society's 'Repository' and Its Background," in Oliver Impey and Arthur MacGregor, eds., *The Origins of Museums: The Cabinet of Curiosities in Sixteenth- and Seventeenth-Century Europe* (Oxford: Clarendon Press, 1985); Karen Ordahl Kupperman, "Introduction," in Kupperman, ed., *America in European Consciousness, 1493–1750* (Williamsburg: Omohundro Institute of Early American History and Culture, University of North Carolina Press, 1995), 12, 22.

94. William Berkeley to anon. correspondent, 10 April 1663, BL Egerton MSS, 2,395, fol. 365.

95. Marion Tinling, ed., *The Correspondence of the Three William Byrds of Westover, Virginia, 1684–1776,* 2 vols. (Charlottesville: Virginia Historical Society, 1977), vol. 1, 61–62; Ilana Krausman Ben-Amos, *The Culture of Giving: Informal Support and Gift-Exchange in Early Modern England* (Cambridge: Cambridge University Press, 2008).

96. William Blathwayt, Account book, Gloucestershire CRO, Blathwayt MSS, D1799/A320; Inventory, E3254; "A schedule of my estate," 20 June 1717, D1799; J. A. Kenworthy-Browne, *Dyrham Park, Gloucestershire* (London: National Trust, 1980).

97. Carole Shammas, *The Pre-Industrial Consumer in England and America* (Oxford: Oxford University Press, 1990), chaps. 1, 4; Maxine Berg, *Luxury and Pleasure in Eighteenth-Century Britain* (Oxford: Oxford University Press, 2005), 21–84.

98. *A True and perfect description of the strange and wonderful elephant sent from the East-Indies* (1675), 3; Ned Ward, *London Spy,* no. 173 (1678); *The Elephant's Speech to the Citizens and Countrymen of England* (1675), 6; Brian Cowan, *The Social Life of Coffee: The Emergence of the British Coffeehouse* (New Haven: Yale University Press, 2005), 68, 115–120.

99. Lorna Weatherill, *Consumer Behaviour and Material Culture in Britain, 1660–1760* (London: Routledge, 1996), 25, 32–37, 41.

100. Antonio Barrera Ossorio, "Empiricism in the Spanish Atlantic World," in James Delbourgo and Nicholas Dew, *Science and Empire in the Atlantic World* (New York: Routledge, 2008), 184; L. F. Stock, ed., *Proceedings and Debates of the British Parliaments Respecting North America*, 5 vols. (Washington, DC, 1924), vol. 2, 52–53, 55; Nuala Zahedieh, *The Capital and the Colonies: London and the Atlantic Economy, 1660–1700* (Cambridge: Cambridge University Press, 2010), 193–194.

101. *Commons Journal*, vol. 10, 459; vol. 11, 287.

102. EIC directors to Fort St George, 6 June 1687, BL, IOR, E/3/91, fols. 152–153.

103. *Commons Journal*, vol. 11, 44, 504; K. N. Chaudhuri, *The Trading World of Asia and the English East India Company, 1660–1760* (Cambridge: Cambridge University Press, 1978), 280–283; Natasha Glaisyer, *The Culture of Commerce in England, 1660–1720* (Woodbridge, UK: Boydell & Brewer, 2006), 27–68; Giorgio Riello and Beverley Lemire, "East and West: Textiles and Fashion in Eurasia in the Early Modern Period," *Journal of Social History* 41, no. 4 (July 2008): 887–916.

104. Directors to Bombay, 6 June 1686, BL, IOR, E/3/91, fol. 151.

105. John Pollexfen, *Discourse of trade, coyn, and paper credit* (1697), 99.

106. *London Gazette*, no. 2072, 24–28 September 1682; *Coffee-Houses Vindicated* (1673), 2–3; P.J. Marshall, "Taming the Exotic: The British and India in the C17th and 18th," in G. S. Rousseau and Roy Porter, eds., *Exoticism in the Enlightenment* (Manchester: Manchester University Press, 1990), 46–65.

107. John Dryden, *An evening's love; or, The mock-astrologer acted at the Theatre-Royal* (1671), 2.

108. Edward Chamberlayne, *The Fourth Part of the Present State of England* (1683), preface.

109. Henry Martin, *Considerations upon the East-India Trade* (1701), 85–86.

110. *Boyle Correspondence*, vol. 2, 212.

111. Ibid., vol. 5, 309.

112. Berry, *Idea of Luxury*, 43–45, 87–98.

113. Sir George Mackenzie, *The moral history of frugality* (1691), 65.

114. Slingsby Bethel, *The Present Interest of England Stated by a Lover of his King and Country* (1671), 12–13; Bethel, *Interest of Princes and States*, 11–12, 31–32; Reynell, *True English Interest*, 13.

115. Temple, "Essay upon Government," fol. 90.

116. Coventry, "Essay concerning the decay of Rents," fol. 207.

117. Thomas Mun, *England's treasure by forraign trade* (1664), 17, 28, 31.

118. *The Grand concern of England explained in several proposals offered to the consideration of the Parliament* (1673), 9; Samuel Fortrey, *England's Interest and Improvement* (1673), 12–17; Chamberlayne, *Fourth Part of the Present State of England*, Preface.

119. *Commons Journal*, vol. 9, 375, 376.

120. See especially Philip Stubbes, *The Anatomie of Abuses* (1583).

121. "Reasons against the management of the East India trade as now driven under the present Joint Stock," All Souls MS 238, fol. 162; *The allegations of the Turky Company and others against the East-India-Company* (1681), 4.

122. Petyt, *Britannia Languens*, 331–350.

123. Brodie Waddell, *God, Duty and Community in English Economic Life, 1660–1720* (Woodbridge, UK: Boydell & Brewer, 2012), 168–172; Gerald M. MacLean and Nabil Matar, *Britain and the Islamic World, 1558–1713* (Oxford: Oxford University Press, 2011), 211–212.

124. Reynell, *True English Interest*, 10, 12–13.

125. Temple, "Essay upon Government," fol. 90.

126. Pollexfen, *Discourse*, 137.

127. Ibid., 97; *The Allegations of the Turkey Company* (1681), 6–7.

128. John Fryer, *A New Account of East-India and Persia* (1682), 43. See also Peter Heylin, *Cosmographie* (1652), 193–219.

129. Henry Stubbe, *The Indian Nectar; or, A discourse concerning chocolata* (1662), 129–141, 171.

130. Marcy Norton, *Sacred Gifts, Profane Pleasures: A History of Tobacco and Chocolate in the Atlantic World* (Ithaca: Cornell University Press, 2008); Cowan, *Social Life of Coffee*, 18.

131. *An epitome of Mr. John Speed's theatre of the empire of Great Britain and of his prospect of the most famous parts of the world* (1676), 14.

132. Paul Rycaut, *The present state of the Ottoman Empire* (1667), 82.

133. Cowan, *Social Life of Coffee*, 113–145.

134. M.P., *A Character of Coffee and Coffeehouses* (1661), 1.

135. Peter Borsay, *The English Urban Renaissance: Culture and Society in the Provincial Town, 1660–1770* (Oxford: Clarendon Press, 1989); Nuala Zahedieh, "London and the Colonial Consumer in the Late Seventeenth Century," *Economic History Review* 47, no. 2 (May 1994): 239–261.

136. Roger North, *The Lives of the Norths*, 3 vols. (London: Thomas Nelson and Sons, 1972), vol. 1, 250.

137. Marquis of Lansdowne, ed., *The Petty-Southwell Correspondence, 1676–1687* (London: Reprints of Economic Classics, 1997), 235.

138. "Col Scott's Preface to an Intended History of America," Rawlinson MSS, A175, fol. 380.

139. James Houblon, "A Discourse touching the Grounds of ye Decay of ye English Navigation," 1685, Rawlinson MSS, A171, fol. 280; Walvin, *Fruits of Empire*, 69; Ralph Davis, "English Foreign Trade, 1660–1700," *Economic History Review*, n.s. 7, no. 2 (1954): 151–152.

140. Thomas Lynch to Robert Moray, 2 March 1671/2, BL Add MSS, 11410, fol. 239.

141. Thomas Bruce, earl of Ailesbury, *Memoirs . . . written by himself*, ed. W. J. Buckley, 2 vols. (Roxburghe Club, 1890), vol. 2, 105; *Commons Journal*, vol. 9, 742–743; Perry Gauci, *The Politics of Trade: The Overseas Merchant in State and Society, 1660–1720* (Oxford: Oxford University Press, 2001), 199.

142. "Memorial on the East India Company," fol. 89; Council of Trade to Charles II, 11 December 1660, CO 389/1, 16. Davis, "English Foreign Trade," 152, has estimated that two-thirds of the incoming calico supplies gained re-export.

143. Lords Journal, vol. 12, 502–503.

144. Godolphin to Arlington, 28 December/7 January 1670/1, SP 94/57, fol. 202; Godolphin to Arlington, 8 November 1673, SP 94/62, fol. 208.

145. North, *Lives of the Norths,* vol. 1, 353.

146. "Memorial on the East India Company," 1674, Coventry MSS, 73, fol. 89. See also Council of Trade to the King, 11 December 1660, CO 389/1, 17.

147. John Houghton, *England's Great Happiness* (1677), 2–4; Josiah Child, *A New Discourse of Trade* (1693), 136–137, 144, 193; Memorial on the East India Company, fol. 89.

148. "Worsley's Discourse of the Privateers," BL Add MSS 11,410, fol. 322.

149. Slack, "Politics of Consumption," 613–614; Joan Thirsk, *Economic Policy and Projects: The Development of a Consumer Society in Early Modern England* (Oxford: Clarendon Press, 1978).

150. Sprat, *History,* 84; Linda Levy Peck, *Consuming Splendour: Society and Culture in Seventeenth-Century England* (Cambridge: Cambridge University Press, 2005), 314–323.

151. John Houghton, *Collection of Letters for the improvement of husbandry and trade,* 2 vols. (1681–1683), vol. 1, 35–36, 49, 55, vol. 2, 138; Houghton, *England's Great Happiness,* 3; Glaisyer, *Culture of Commerce,* 145–155.

152. Davenant, *Discourses,* 78.

153. Houghton, *Collection of Letters for the improvement of husbandry and trade,* vol. 1, 35–36.

154. Journal of the Lords of Trade, 23 December 1675, CO 391/1, fols. 30–31.

155. Journal of the Lords of Trade, 25 February 1674/5, CO 391/1, fols. 4–5.

156. *The English empire in America; or, A prospect of His Majesties dominions in the West-Indies . . . Printed for Nathaniel Crouch* (1685), preface; Robert Mayer, "Nathaniel Crouch, Bookseller and Historian: Popular Historiography and Cultural Power in Late Seventeenth-Century England," *Eighteenth-Century Studies* 27, no. 3 (Spring 1994): 391–419.

157. Anonymous correspondent to earl of Ormond, Carte MSS, 69, fol. 386.

158. Reynell, *True English Interest,* 34.

159. Houghton, *Collection of letters,* vol. 1, 56–57.

160. Reynell, *True English Interest,* 10.

161. Sir William Temple, *Essay upon Ancient and Modern Learning* (1690), 27–40.

Chapter 7. "Popery," Europe, and the Crisis of English Overseas Expansion

1. Owen Stanwood, *The Empire Reformed: English America in the Age of the Glorious Revolution* (Philadelphia: University of Pennsylvania Press, 2011), 14–27; Trevor Burnard, "Making a Whig Empire Work: Transatlantic Politics and the Imperial Economy in Britain and British America," *W&MQ* 69, no. 1 (January 2012): 51–56.

2. Tony Claydon, *Europe and the Making of England, 1660–1760* (Cambridge: Cambridge University Press, 2007), 173–175; Pincus, *1688,* 309–311, 353.

3. John Houghton, *Collection of Letters for the improvement of husbandry and trade,* 2 vols. (1681–1683), vol. 2, 113.

4. Committee of Foreign Affairs, 9 September 1677, SP 104/179, fol. 152; Robert M. Bliss, *Revolution and Empire: English Politics and the American Colonies in the Seventeenth Century* (Manchester: Manchester University Press, 1990), 176–189; Stephen Saunders Webb, *1676: The End of American Independence* (New York: Knopf, 1984), 188–199.

5. Tim Harris, *Politics under the Later Stuarts: Party Conflict in a Divided Society, 1660–1715* (Harlow: Longman, 1993), 70–72; Saunders Webb, *1676*, 185–188.

6. George Carew, *Severall considerations offered to the Parliament concerning the improvement of trade, navigation and commerce* (1675), 7–8; L. F. Stock, ed., *Proceedings and Debates of the British Parliaments Respecting North America,* 5 vols. (Washington, DC, 1924), vol. 1, 350.

7. Lynch to Sir Robert Moray, 2 March 1672/3, BL Add MSS, 11410, fol. 239.

8. *CSPC, 1681–1685,* 91; Henry Morgan to Henry Coventry, 30 January 1675/6, Coventry MSS, 74, fol. 167; George Carew, *Severall considerations offered to the Parliament* (1675), 6–9.

9. Randolph to the Lords of Trade, 30 April 1681, BL Add MSS 63,773, fol. 145.

10. *The Entring Book of Roger Morrice,* 6 vols. (Woodbridge, UK: Boydell and Brewer, 2007), vol. 2, ed. John Spurr, 216, 236; List of subscribers, 2 May 1683, Tanner MSS 36, fol. 69; Gary S. De Krey, *London and the Restoration, 1659–1683* (Cambridge: Cambridge University Press, 2005), 129; Margaret Priestly, "London Merchants and Opposition Politics in Charles II's Reign," *Bulletin of the Institute of Historical Research* 29 (November 1956): 205–219.

11. *Diary of Samuel Sewall,* 3 vols., Collections of the Massachusetts Historical Society, 5th ser. (1898), vol. 1, 225; Hugh Amory, "British Books Abroad: The American Colonies," in John Barnard, Maureen Bell, and D. F. Mackenzie, eds., *Cambridge History of the Book,* vol. 4 (Cambridge: Cambridge University Press, 2002), 746–747, 750; Alison Gilbert Olson, *Making the Empire Work: London and American Interest Groups, 1690–1790* (Cambridge: Harvard University Press, 1992), 105–107.

12. Roger Coke, *England's Improvements in two parts* (1675), 92–95.

13. *England's slavery, or Barbados merchandize* (1659); Michael Guasco, *Slaves and Englishmen: Human Bondage in the Early Modern Atlantic World* (Philadelphia: University of Pennsylvania Press, 2014), 2.

14. Povey, "Overtures touching the West Indies," 1660, BL Egerton MSS, 2395, fol. 104.

15. William Cobbett, ed., *The Parliamentary History of England,* 36 vols. (1806–1820), vol. 5, 795; Slingsby Bethel, *The World's Mistake in Oliver Cromwell* (1668), 9–11.

16. Anchitel Grey, *Debates of the House of Commons, from the year 1667 to the year 1694,* 10 vols. (London, 1763), vol. 1, 237.

17. Ibid., vol. 2, 365; Chappell, ed., *Tangiers papers,* 98.

18. L. H. Roper, *Conceiving Carolina: Proprietors, Planters and Plots 1662–1729,* (Basingstoke: Palgrave Macmillan, 2004), 72; David Armitage, "John Locke, Carolina,

and the *Two Treatises of Government*," *Political Theory* 32, no. 5 (October 2004): 602–627.

19. Journal of the Lords of Trade, 2 November 1676, CO 391/1, fol. 122; J. E. Buchanan, "The Colleton Family and the Early History of South Carolina and Barbados," PhD diss., University of Edinburgh, 1989, 3–4, 9–11, 161–162, 336.

20. North, *Lives of the Norths*, vol. 2, 121–123.

21. *CSPC, 1677–1680,* 1560; William A. Pettigrew, *Freedom's Debt: The Royal African Company and the Politics of the Atlantic Slave Trade, 1672–1752* (Chapel Hill: University of North Carolina Press, 2013), 49–52; Abigail L. Swingen, *Competing Visions of Empire: Labor, Slavery, and the Origins of the British Atlantic Empire* (New Haven: Yale University Press, 2015), 114–119.

22. William Beeston, "An Account of some affairs in Jamaica during the Government of his Excellency the Earl of Carlisle," n.d., BL Add MSS 12,429, fol. 122; Thomas Newcombe, ed., *The Autobiography of Henry Newcome, M.A.* (Manchester: Chetham Society, 1852), 184; Journal of the Lords of Trade, 14 October 1680, CO 391/3, fols. 108–109.

23. William Penn, *The Case of New Jersey Stated* (n.d.), 1.

24. John Houghton, *Collection of Letters for the improvement of husbandry and trade,* 2 vols. (1681–1683), vol. 2, 113. See also Grey, *Debates*, v, 102.

25. Cholmley to the duchess of Lauderdale, December 1675, Cholmley MSS, V/1/1/III, fol. 298.

26. Edward Pike, ed., *Selections from the Correspondence of Arthur, Earl of Essex, 1675–1677*, Camden Society, 3rd ser., 24 (London, 1913), 87; Stock, *Proceedings and Debates*, vol. 1, 412; Grey, *Debates*, vol. 4, 225, 237.

27. Letter from Hamburg, 2 August 1680, Bodl., Carte MSS 69, fol. 387.

28. Palmes Fairborne to earl of Anglesey, 6 June 1677, BL Add MSS 17,021, fol. 32; Sheres to Pepys, 10 October 1677, Rawlinson MSS A342, 223–224; Nabil I. Matar, *Britain and Barbary, 1589–1689* (Gainesville: University of Florida Press, 2005), 151–169.

29. Samuel Martin to Pepys, August 1676, Rawlinson MSS A173, fols. 135–136; Linda Colley, *Captives: Britain, Empire, and the World* (London: Jonathan Cape, 2002), 52.

30. *His Majesties message to the Commons in Parliament, relating to Tangier* (1680); Grey, *Debates*, vol. 7, 97, 99; vol. 8, 15; Palmes Fairborne to Sheres, 14 April 1679, BL Add MSS 19,872, fols. 45–46.

31. George Wither, *Vox & lacrimae anglorum* (1668), 14.

32. Sir Joseph Trelawney to Joseph Williamson, 6 August 1667, *CSPD, 1667,* 212/88.

33. *An Exact journal of the siege of Tangier* (1680), 13; "Informations against the Earle of Insiquin," n.d., Rawlinson MSS A341, fols. 201–202; *A Full and true account of the barbarous rebellion and rising of the Lord Dunbarton's regiment* (1689).

34. "A catalogue of Books sent to Aleppo," 1678, Bodl., MS Don c. 169, fol. 196; North, *Lives of the Norths*, vol. 1, 349.

35. Earl of Inchiquin to earl of Danby, 13 September 1675, BL Egerton MSS, 2240, fol. 139; "A copy of Mr Giles Bland's letter to Mr Povey, received 28 August 1676,"

BL Egerton 2395, fol. 555; "T.M.," *The Beginning, Progress, and Conclusion of Bacon's Rebellion in Virginia, In the Years 1675 and 1676* (Richmond, 1804), 25.

36. John Bland to earl of Shaftesbury, 1679, BL Sloane MSS, 3512, fol. 283.

37. [Bland], *The Present interest of Tangiers* (1679), 2–4; Gabriel Glickman, "Empire, 'Popery,' and the Fall of English Tangier, 1662–1684," *Journal of Modern History* 87, no. 2 (June 2015): 267–268, 271.

38. *The Observator*, no. 120, 23 August 1684.

39. Grey, *Debates*, vol. 8, 5, 13; Cobbett, *Parliamentary History*, vol. 4, 1258.

40. Grey, *Debates*, vol. 8, 18–19.

41. Godolphin to Coventry, 11/21 December 1678, Coventry MSS 60, fols. 261–262; HMC, *The Manuscripts of the Marquis of Ormonde*, 8 vols. (London, 1895–1899), vol. 4, 477.

42. David Hancock, ed., *The Letters of William Freeman, London Merchant, 1678–1685* (London: London Record Society, 2002), 48–49, 136.

43. Bland to Shaftesbury, 1679, BL Sloane MSS, 3512, fol. 283.

44. Ibid., fol. 283; [Bland], *Present Interest of Tangiers*, preface, 1–2, 4.

45. David Armitage, "John Locke, Carolina and the *Two Treatises of Government*," *Political Theory* 32, no. 5 (October 2004): 608–615.

46. Shaftesbury to Andrew Percival, 9 June 1675, PRO 30/24/48, fol. 228; Lords Proprietors, payments to Samuel Wilson, 10 May 1683, PRO 30/24/48, fol. 333.

47. "Description du Pays nomme Carolina," 1678, PRO 30/24/48, fol. 292.

48. Journal of the Lords of Trade, 29 April 1679, CO 391/3, fol. 3; Accounts of the Lords of Trade, 22 April 1679, BL Add MSS 9767, fol. 61.

49. Thomas Leng, "Shaftesbury's Aristocratic Empire," in John Spurr, ed., *Anthony Ashley Cooper, First Earl of Shaftesbury* (Farnham: Ashgate 2011), 126; "The Report of the Right Honourable the Lords of the Committee for Trade and Plantations to the King," 28 May 1679, BL Add MSS, 12429, fols. 88–92.

50. Duke of York to Anthony Brockholes, 28 March 1681/2, CO 5/1112, fols. 33–34.

51. Letter from Hamburg, 2 August 1680, Bodl., Carte MSS 69, fols. 386–387, 392.

52. Grey, *Debates*, vol. 8, 7.

53. William Loddington, *Plantation-Work: The Work of this Generation* (1682), preface; Mary Maples Dunn and Richard S. Dunn, eds., *The Papers of William Penn*, 5 vols. (Philadelphia: University of Pennsylvania Press, 1981–1986), vol. 1, 515.

54. Grey, *Debates*, vol. 8, 5.

55. Roger Whitley, Commonplace book, Bodl., MS Eng. Hist. e. 310, 36, 51–52; Thomas Sprat, *Observations on Monsieur de Sorbier's Voyage into England* (1665), 9–10, 114; Andrew Hopper, *Black Tom: Sir Thomas Fairfax and the English Revolution* (Manchester: Manchester University Press, 2007), 13–14.

56. Steven Pincus, *Protestantism and Patriotism: Ideologies and the Making of English Foreign Policy, 1650–1668* (Cambridge: Cambridge University Press, 1996), 356, 365, 404–405.

57. Harris, *Politics under the Later Stuarts*, 56–57.

58. Samuel von Pufendorf, *An Introduction to the History of the Principal Kingdoms and States of Europe* (1695), 249.

59. Parry to Arlington, 28 February 1671/2, BL Add MSS, 35100, fol. 184.

60. Slingsby Bethel, *The World's Mistake in Oliver Cromwell* (1668), 7.

61. Slingsby Bethel, *The Interest of Princes and States* (1680), 68–69.

62. Bethel, *World's Mistake*, 10; Edmund Everard, *Discourse on the Present State of the Protestant Princes of Europe* (1677), 13–14; Mark Goldie and Charles-Edouard Levillain, "François-Paul de Lisola and English opposition to Louis XIV," *Historical Journal* 63, no. 3 (June 2020): 559–580.

63. Grey, *Debates*, vol. 4, 312.

64. *Memoirs of Sir Hugh Cholmley* (1870), 11.

65. Grey, *Debates*, vol. 2, 203; Steven Pincus, "From Butterboxes to Wooden Shoes: The Shift in English Popular Sentiment from Anti-Dutch to Anti-French in the 1670s," *Historical Journal* 38, no. 2 (June 1995): 340, 342; Claydon, *Europe*, 154–158.

66. Langdon Cheves, ed., *The Shaftesbury Papers* (Charleston, SC: Tempus Publications, 2000), 376–377.

67. Temple, "Essay upon Government," 13.

68. Bethel, *World's Mistake*, 3–4; Bethel, *Present Interest of England*, 30.

69. Arthur H. Williamson, "An Empire to End Empire: The Dynamic of Early Modern British Expansion," *Huntingdon Library Quarterly* 68, nos. 1–2 (March 2005): 240–241.

70. Tony Claydon and Ian McBride, *Protestantism and National Identity: Britain and Ireland, c. 1650–1850* (Cambridge: Cambridge University Press, 1998), "Introduction," 1–29; Thomas Leng, *Benjamin Worsley (1618–1677): Trade, Interest, and the Spirit in Revolutionary England* (Woodbridge: Boydell and Brewer, 2008), 36–37.

71. Cobbett, *Parliamentary History*, vol. 4, 1116–1117.

72. Reynell, *True English Interest*, 70–71.

73. Temple, "Essay upon Government," fol. 12.

74. Coke, *England's Improvements*, 6.

75. Letter from Hamburg, 2 August 1680, Bodl., Carte MSS 69, fols. 384, 387, 389.

76. Grey, *Debates*, vol. 8, 19.

77. Ibid., vol. 8, 14, 16.

78. Ibid., vol. 8, 15.

79. Edward Chamberlayne, *A Discourse of Trade* (1683), 81–82; *CSPC, 1669–1674*, 1244.

80. Letter from Hamburg, fols. 384, 388; Henry Sheres, *A discourse touching Tanger in a letter to a person of quality* (1680).

81. Morrice, *Entring book*, vol. 2, 229.

82. Directors to "our Generall & Councill of India," 3 August 1687, BL, IOR, E/3/91, fols. 159–160.

83. "An Essay of the Interest of the Crown in American Plantations & Trade," 1685, BL Add MSS, 47131, 62–63.

84. George Carew, *Fraud and oppression detected and arraigned* (1676), 1–2; Duke of Buckingham, *A Letter to Sir Thomas Osborn* (1672), 10–11.

85. "Considerations about the present affaires of the West Indyes," 7 April 1678, BL Egerton MSS, 2395, fols. 574–575. See also "The Present State of Jamaica, in a letter from Mr Nevil to the Earl of Carlisle," 1677, BL Add MSS, 12429, fols. 75–77.

86. Godolphin to Coventry, 5/15 May 1678, Coventry MSS, 60, fols. 187–199.

87. Journal of the Lords of Trade, 9 October 1679, CO 391/3, fol. 38.

88. Earl of Conway to Edmund Poley, 12 April 1681, Yale University, Beinecke Library, OSB MSS 1, box 1/8; Conway to Poley, 22 November 1681, Yale University, Beinecke Library, OSB MSS 1, box 1/15.

89. Cobbett, *Parliamentary History*, vol. 4, 924.

90. Grey, *Debates*, vol. 5, 107.

91. Sir Robert Southwell to Sir John Perceval, 17 March 1683, BL Add MSS, 47022, fol. 108.

92. John Nalson, *The Present Interest of England* (1683), 31.

93. Grey, *Debates*, vol. 4, 314.

94. Sheres, *Discourse*, 29, 33; Samuel Pepys, papers on Tangier, Rawlinson MSS, D916, fols. 89, 109–112; John Ross, *Tangers rescue* (1681).

95. Claydon, *Europe*, 173–180, 223–239.

96. Cholmley, "Severall Discourses," Rawlinson MSS, A341, 45; *Memoirs of Sir Hugh Cholmley* (1870), 21, 39, 43.

97. John Dryden, *An Epitaph to the Memory . . . of Sir Palmes Fairbourn* (1680).

98. Peter Marshall, " 'Rather with Papists than with Turks': The Battle of Lepanto and the Contours of Elizabethan Christendom," *Reformation* 17 (2012): 135–159.

99. *A New song, being the Tories imploration for protection against the Whiggs* (1682).

100. Chappell, ed., *Tangiers Papers*, 244; Southwell to Perceval, 13 November 1683, BL Add MSS, 47022, fol. 132.

101. M. Poseley, *A letter from Tangier to a friend in London* (1683).

102. Marquis of Halifax, *Observations upon a late libel* (1681), 3–4.

103. Thomas Bruce, earl of Ailesbury, *Memoirs . . . written by himself*, ed. W. J. Buckley, 2 vols. (Roxburghe Club, 1890), vol. 1, 107–108; George Louis Beer, *The Origins of the British Colonial System, 1578–1660* (New York: Macmillan, 1908), 171; C. D. Chandaman, *English Public Revenue, 1660–1688* (Oxford: Clarendon, 1975), 8–10, 33–36; L. H. Roper, *Advancing Empire: English Interests and Overseas Expansion, 1613–1688* (Cambridge: Cambridge University Press, 2017), 220–230.

104. Unknown artist, "The Siege of Tangier, 1683," Dyrham Park, Gloucestershire, UK.

105. "Essay of the Interest of the Crown," 64, 66, 68–69.

106. Swingen, *Competing Visions*, 124–125; Pettigrew, *Freedom's Debt*, 23–31.

107. Committee of Foreign Affairs, 9 September 1677, 104/179, fol. 151.

108. Davies, *Royal African Company*, 106–109.

109. James II, *A proclamation to prohibit His Majesties subjects to trade within the limits assigned to the Royal African Company of England, except those of the company* (1685).

110. *Certain Considerations relating to the Royal African Company of England* (1680), 8–11; *Smith's Protestant Intelligence Domestick and Foreign* (7 March 1681).

111. "Proposalls for a South American Company," 28 March 1688, BL Sloane MSS, 3984, 210–211; "Certeine queries concerning His Highnesse Interest in the West Indies," 1657, BL Egerton MSS, 2395, fol. 87; Dalby Thomas, *Historical Account of the rise and growth of the West-India collonies* (1690), 48–53.

112. "Essay of the Interest of the Crown," 64–65.

113. Earl of Ailesbury, *Memoirs*, vol. 1, 112; Samuel Weller Singer, ed., *Correspondence of Henry Hyde, earl of Clarendon and of his brother, Laurence Hyde, earl of Rochester*, 2 vols. (London, 1828), vol. 2, 131–132.

114. "Essay of the Interest of the Crown," 68–72.

115. Ibid., 67.

116. Pincus, *1688*, 387–393.

117. Josiah Child to Earl of Middleton, 1 September 1683, BL Add MSS, 41822, fols. 25–26; William Letwin, *Sir Josiah Child: Merchant Economist* (Cambridge: Harvard University Press, 1959).

118. Bruce Lenman, *England's Colonial Wars, 1550–1688: Conflicts, Empire and National Identity* (London: Longman, 2001), 205–210.

119. John Mountsteven to Edmund Poley, 4 May 1683, Beinecke, Poley papers, OSB MSS 1/30; John Litcott to Sir Robert Throckmorton, 19 March 1682/3, Warwickshire CRO, Throckmorton MSS, LCB/17; Child to Middleton, 1683, 6 September 1683, BL Add MSS, 41822, fols. 28–29.

120. William Beaumont, *The Emblem of Ingratitude* (1672), preface.

121. Directors to Captain Jonathan Unkettell, January 1685/6, BL, IOR, E/3/91, fols. 15–17; Directors to Fort St George, 14 January 1685/6, BL, IOR, E/3/91, fols. 30–33; Directors to Bombay, 3 February 1686/7, BL, IOR, E/3/91, fol. 131.

122. Stern, *Company-State*, 3–25.

123. Directors to Fort St George, 28 September 1687, BL, IOR, E/3/91, fols. 208–209; John Higginson to Josiah Child, 18 July 1692, *Collections of the Massachusetts Historical Society*, vol. 7 (Boston, 1838), 197.

124. Directors to Bengkulu, 31 August 1687, BL, IOR, E/3/91, fols. 191–192; Instructions to our Agent and Councill of Bengall, 14 January 1685/6, BL, IOR, E/3/91, fol. 38; Directors to Pariaman, 21 October 1685, BL, IOR, E/3/91, fols. 1–3; Directors to St Helena, 26 November 1684, BL, IOR, E/3/90, fol. 251; Directors to St Helena, 5 April 1684, BL, IOR, E/3/90, fol. 176.

125. Directors to Surat, 28 October 1685, BL, IOR, E/3/91, fols. 5–6; Directors to Bombay, 3 September 1686, BL, IOR, E/3/91, fols. 85–86.

126. George Jeffreys, Baron Jeffreys, *The Argument of the Lord Chief Justice of the Court of King's Bench concerning the great case of monopolies* (1683), 7.

127. T. B. Howell, ed., *A Complete Collection of State Trials and Proceedings for High Treason and Other Crimes and Misdemeanours*, 21 vols. (London, 1816), vol. 10, 375–376, 380; "East India Company versus Thomas Sandys," Rawlinson MSS, C130, fols. 36, 232.

128. Howell, *Complete Collection of State Trials*, vol. 10, 392, 442–445.

129. John St. John to James II, 18 July 1688, Rawlinson MSS, A171, fols. 52–53.

130. Directors to Bombay, 14 July 1686, BL, IOR, E/3/91, fols. 69–71; Josiah Child, *A treatise wherein it is demonstrated . . . that the East India Trade is the most national of all foreign trades* (1681), 34–35.

131. Report of Fort St George, 30 September 1688, BL Egerton MSS, 3340, fol. 181; *By the King, a Proclamation, For the Recalling all His Majesties Subjects from the Service of Foreign Princes in East India* (1686); Lenman, *England's Colonial Wars*, 209–211; Stern, *Company-State*, 122–124.

132. Directors to Fort St George, 14 January 1685/6, BL, IOR, E/3/91, fols. 30–34; Directors to Admiral John Nicholson, 26 January 1685/6, BL, IOR, E/3/91, fol. 26.

133. *A view of the English acquisitions in Guinea & the East-Indies with an account of this region . . . printed for Nathaniel Crouch* (1686).

134. Directors to Fort St George, 12 December 1687, BL, IOR, E/3/91, fol. 232; Directors to Bombay, 27 August 1688, BL, IOR, E/3/91, fol. 273; Bruce Lenman, "The East India Company and the Emperor Aurangzeb," *History Today* 37, no. 2 (February 1987): 27–29.

135. J. Leslie to Lord Preston, 4 December 1688, BL Add MSS 63, 773, fol. 197; Pincus, *1688,* 381.

136. Toppan and Goodrick, eds., *Randolph*, vol. 2, 248–249, 260–261, vol. 3, 284; *Diary of Cotton Mather*, 2 vols. (New York: F. Ungar, 1957), vol. 1, 113.

137. John Childs, *General Percy Kirke and the Later Stuart Army* (London: Bloomsbury, 2014), 113–132; Stephen Saunders Webb, *Lord Churchill's Coup: The Anglo-American Empire and the Glorious Revolution* (Syracuse: Alfred A. Knopf, 1995), 72, 77–79, 146–156.

138. Directors to Bombay, 8 October 1688, BL, IOR, E/3/91, fol. 295.

139. *Diary of Samuel Sewall*, vol. 1, 242.

Chapter 8. Revolution and the Redefinition of Empire

1. The fullest modern accounts of these events include Owen Stanwood, *The Empire Reformed: English America in the Age of the Glorious Revolution* (Philadelphia: University of Pennsylvania Press, 2011); Richard S. Dunn, "The Glorious Revolution and America," in Nicholas Canny, ed., *The Oxford History of the British Empire*, vol. 1: *The Origins of Empire* (Oxford: Oxford University Press, 1998), 445–466; David. S. Lovejoy, *The Glorious Revolution in America* (New York: Harper & Rowe, 1972); and Jack M. Sosin, *English America and the Revolution of 1688: Royal Administration and the Structure of Provincial Government* (Lincoln: University of Nebraska Press, 1982).

2. Minutes of the Council of Safety at Boston, 20 April 1689, *CSPC, 1689–1692,* 286; Mark Peterson, *The City-State of Boston: The Rise and Fall of an Atlantic Power, 1630–1865* (Princeton: Princeton University Press, 2019), 166–182.

3. Maura Jane Farrelly, *Papist Patriots: The Making of an American Catholic Identity* (Oxford: Oxford University Press, 2012), 129–131.

4. "A Memoriall of what has occurred in their Maties Province of New York," CO 5/1113, fols. 134–137.

5. Petition from the Governor and Council of St Christopher's, 15 July 1689, CO 153/3, fol. 426; "A short remonstrance or account of ye sufferings of the poor inhabitants of St Christopher," CO 153/3, fols. 438–439; Roger Hoare to Edward Clarke, 30 May 1694, Somerset CRO, Clarke of Chipley MSS, DD/SF/7/1/14; James II to John Aylward, Warrant, 6 February 1691, Arundel Castle, Howard of Norfolk MSS, Howard Letters and Papers, vol. 1.

6. Burnard, "Making a Whig Empire Work," 51–56.

7. Pincus, *1688*, 305–364; John Brewer, *The Sinews of Power: War, Money and the English State, 1688–1783* (Cambridge: Harvard University Press, 1990).

8. Peter Laslett, "John Locke, The Great Recoinage, and the Origins of the Board of Trade, 1695–8," *WMQ* 14, no. 3 (July 1957): 370–402; Perry Gauci, *The Politics of Trade: The Overseas Merchant in State and Society, 1660–1720* (Oxford: Oxford University Press, 2001), 185–188.

9. John Dennis, *The Usefulness of the Stage* (1698), 349. See also George Savile, Marquis of Halifax, *A rough draught of a new model at sea* (1694), 13–14.

10. *To the King's most excellent Majestie, The Humble Petition of Sir Walter Yonge, Sir John Guise, Michael Harvey, John Speke, Edward Clarke and diverse other Gentlemen of ye Western Countyes of England* (1689); Edward Clarke, papers concerning Barbados prisoners, 1689–90, Clarke of Chipley MSS, DD/SF/7/1/22.

11. Edward Clarke, "Notes concerning the East India Company," Clarke of Chipley MSS, DD/SF/13/2/32, fol. 40.

12. Ibid., fol. 40; G. White, *A letter to Mr Nathaniel Tenche* (1690), 8; A Discourse Concerning the East India Trade (1693), 4.

13. Bruce Lenman, "The East India Company and the Emperor Aurangzeb," *History Today* 37, no. 2 (February 1987): 27–29; Shafaat Ahmad Khan, *The East India Trade in the XVIIth Century in Its Political and Economic Aspects* (Oxford: Oxford University Press, 1923), 220–233.

14. Tony Claydon, *William III and the Godly Revolution* (Cambridge: Cambridge University Press, 1996).

15. Henry Martin, *Considerations upon the East-India Trade* (1701), 108–109.

16. Thomas Bruce, earl of Ailesbury, *Memoirs . . . written by himself,* ed. W. J. Buckley, 2 vols. (Roxburghe Club, 1890), vol. 2, 640.

17. Gary S. De Krey, "Political Radicalism in London after the Glorious Revolution," *Journal of Modern History* 55, no. 4 (December 1983): 585–617; Mark Goldie, "The Roots of True Whiggism, 1689–1694," *History of Political Thought* 1, no. 2 (Summer 1980): 195–236.

18. Henry Ashurst to William Stoughton, 9 March 1688/9, Ashurst Letterbook, Bodl., MS Don C. 169, fol. 71; *Diary of Samuel Sewall,* 3 vols., Collections of the Massachusetts Historical Society, 5th ser. (1898), vol. 1, 258–269; M. G. Hall, ed., "The Autobiography of Increase Mather," *Proceedings of the American Antiquarian Society* (1961): 326–346; Richard Johnson, *Adjustment to Empire: The New England Colonies, 1675–1715* (New Brunswick, NJ: Rutgers University Press, 1981), 152–156.

19. Mather, *Parentator,* 204.

20. *Diary of Samuel Sewall,* vol. 1, 258.

21. Mather, *Parentator,* 126–127.

22. John Raithby, ed., *Statutes of the Realm,* 9 vols. (London, 1810–1825), vol. 6, 56–57, British History Online, https://www.british-history.ac.uk/statutes-realm/vol6, emphasis mine.

23. L. F. Stock, ed., *Proceedings and Debates of the British Parliaments Respecting North America,* 5 vols. (Washington, DC, 1924), vol. 1, 1; Hall, "Autobiography of Increase Mather," 327.

24. Letter from the Council of New York to the earl of Shrewsbury, 10 June 1689, CO5/1113, fol. 102; Toppan and Goodrick, eds., *Randolph,* vol. 4, 264–265, 281, 290, 298, vol. 5, 7–16.

25. *CSPC, 1689–1692,* 773, 830, 846; Ashurst to unknown correspondent, 18 December 1689, Bodl., MS Don c. 169, fol. 76; Hall, "Autobiography of Increase Mather," 343; Mather, *Parentator,* 166–169; Henry Horwitz, *Parliament, Policy and Politics in the Reign of William III* (Manchester: Manchester University Press, 1977), 50–53.

26. Robert Ritchie, *The Duke's Province* (Chapel Hill: University of North Carolina Press, 1977), 229–231.

27. Morrice, *Entring Book,* v, 18; Narcissus Luttrell, *Brief Historical Relation of State Affairs,* 6 vols. (Oxford, 1857), vol. 2, 32.

28. Increase Mather, *A brief relation of the state of New England* (1689); *Diary of Samuel Sewall,* vol. 1, 269. See also *The Miseries of New England* (1689); *An Account of the Late Revolutions in New England* (1689); *The Declaration of the Gentlemen, Merchants, and Inhabitants of Boston, and the Countrey adjacent, 18 April 1689* (1689); "A Memoriall of what has occurred in their Maties Province of New York," CO 5/1113, fol. 134.

29. John Palmer, *The present state of New-England* (1689); Palmer, *An impartial account of the state of New England* (1690); *An abstract of some of the printed laws of New-England Which are either contrary, or not agreeable to the laws of England* (1689); *A short account of the present state of New-England* (London, 1690).

30. Mark Goldie, "The Revolution of 1689 and the Structure of Political Argument," *Bulletin of Research in the Humanities* 83 (1980): 473–564; John Kenyon, *Revolution Principles: The Politics of Party, 1689–1720* (Cambridge: Cambridge University Press, 1977).

31. M. G. Hall, L. H. Leder, and M. G. Kammen, eds., *The Glorious Revolution in America: Documents on the Colonial Crisis of 1689* (Williamsburg: Omohundro Institute of Early American History and Culture, University of North Carolina Press, 1964), 69–75.

32. Palmer, *Present state,* 8–10.

33. Toppan and Goodrick, eds., *Randolph,* vol. 5, 10–16.

34. Palmer, *Present State,* 21–22, 27.

35. Toppan and Goodrick, eds., *Randolph,* vol. 2, 111, vol. 5, 7–8; *A short account,* 9; Henry Sloughter to the earl of Nottingham, 27 March 1691, CO 5/1113, fol. 148.

36. Samuel Sewall and Edward Rawson, *The Revolution in New England Justified* (1691), 46; *Account of the Late Revolutions,* 1–6.

37. *CSPC, 1689–1692,* 138.

38. Sewall and Rawson, *Revolution in New England Justified,* 14, 42, 45–46; *The Declaration of the Gentlemen, Merchants, and Inhabitants of Boston* (1689).

39. Sewall and Rawson, *Revolution in New England Justified,* 1–2. See also "A Memoriall of what has occurred in their Maties Province of New York," CO 5/1113, fols. 134, 137.

40. Luttrell, *Brief Historical Relation*, vol. 2, 301; Peterson, *City-State of Boston*, 172–173.

41. Johnson, *Adjustment*, 293.

42. Ashurst to William Stoughton, 1 November 1693, Bodl., MS Don c. 169, fols. 90–91; Ashurst to the Council of Massachusetts, 1701, Bodl., MS Don c. 169, fol. 192.

43. "Instructions to Mr Heathcote &c. from the Council & Assembly of Jamaica," 1693, BL Add MSS 12,429, fols. 179–181.

44. Douglas Bradburn, "The Visible Fist: The Chesapeake Tobacco Trade in War and the Purpose of Empire, 1690–1715," *W&MQ* 68, no. 3 (July 2011): 361–386; Trevor Burnard, "Making a Whig Empire Work," 51–56.

45. Luttrell, *Brief Historical Relation*, vol. 2, 152; Nuala Zahedieh, *The Capital and the Colonies: London and the Atlantic Economy, 1660–1700* (Cambridge: Cambridge University Press, 2010), 194–195; Ashurst to the Council for Massachusetts, 7 April 1694, Bodl., MS Don c. 169, fol. 96.

46. Ashurst to William Browne, 12 August 1697, Bodl., MS Don c. 169, fol. 142; Mather, *Brief relation*, 8.

47. Francis Brewster, *Essays on Trade and Navigation* (1697), 87–92.

48. Henry Martin, *Considerations*, 48–51, 56, 115; Steve Pincus, "Addison's Empire: Whig Conceptions of Empire in the Early 18th Century," *Parliamentary History* 31, no. 1 (February 2012): 101, 106–107.

49. Francis Brewster, *A Letter to a member of the House of Commons on a proposal for regulating and advancing the woollen manufactory* (1698), 7; Brewster, *Essays*, 8.

50. Cotton Mather, *Eleutheria; or, An idea of the Reformation in England* (1696), 134.

51. Mather, *Parentator*, 57–59, 86, 165–169.

52. Ibid., 119–122; Hall, "Autobiography of Increase Mather," 333; Cotton Mather, *The wonders of the invisible world* (1693), 45.

53. *Diary of Samuel Sewall*, vol. 1, 437, 484–490; *Diary of Cotton Mather*, 2 vols. (New York: F. Ungar, 1957), vol. 1, 284, 296; Carl Bridenbaugh, ed., *The Pynchon Papers: Letters of John Pynchon, 1654–1700*, 2 vols. (Boston: Colonial Society of Massachusetts, 1982), vol. 1, 205, 211.

54. Ashurst to the Council of Massachusetts, 14 August 1697, Bodl., MS Don c. 169, fol. 145.

55. Charles Davenant, "On the Plantation Trade," in *Discourses on the publick revenues, and on the trade of England* (1698), 206–208, 239–252.

56. Toppan and Goodrick, eds., *Randolph*, vol. 5, 36–38, 41–50; Mary Lou Lustig, *The Imperial Executive in America: Sir Edmund Andros, 1637–1714* (Newark: University of New Hampshire Press, 2002), 227–240; Michael Kammen, *Colonial New York: A History* (New York: Scribner, 1975), 139–141; Stanwood, *Empire Reformed*, 207–210.

57. Evan Haefeli, "Toleration and Empire," in Stephen Foster, ed., *British North America in the Seventeenth and Eighteenth Centuries* (Oxford: Oxford University Press, 2013), 128–130; Council of Maryland to Tenison, 18 October 1694, Lambeth Palace Library, MS 953, 24.

58. "List of Benefactions by Francis Nicholson to 1702," Lambeth Palace Library, SPG Papers, vol. 10, fol. 30; Nicholson to Tenison, 18 March 1696, Lambeth Palace Library, Fulham Papers, vol. 2, fols. 51–52.

59. SPG committee minutes, 19 March 1702/3, 17 March 1703/4, Rhodes House, Oxford, USPG Journal; *Account of the Society for Propagating the Gospel in Foreign Parts* (1706), 20, 38, 66–72; Strong, "Vision of an Anglican Imperialism," 175–198.

60. Lewis Morris to John Chamberlayne, June 1704, Lambeth Palace Library, Fulham Papers, vol. 6, fol. 132; John Blair, Memorial, 1698, Lambeth Palace Library, Fulham Papers, vol. 11, fols. 39–40; Stanwood, *Empire Reformed*, 190–192; David Parrish, *Jacobitism and Anti-Jacobitism in the British Atlantic* (Woodbridge: Boydell Press, 2017), ch. 3.

61. Mary Maples Dunn and Richard S. Dunn, eds., *The Papers of William Penn*, 5 vols. (Philadelphia: University of Pennsylvania Press, 1981–1986), vol. 3, 485–486, 497, 620–621; Andrew R. Murphy, *William Penn: A Life* (Oxford: Oxford University Press, 2018), 216–217.

62. Dunn and Dunn, *Papers of William Penn*, vol. 3, 620–621.

63. Ibid., vol. 3, 473, 526; Toppan and Goodrick, eds., *Randolph*, vol. 2, 140–141; Earl of Bellomont to the Lords of the Treasury, 8 September 1699, Rawlinson MSS, A272, fols. 62–63; Richard Beale Davis, ed., *William Fitzhugh and His Chesapeake World, 1676–1701* (Chapel Hill: University of North Carolina Press, 1963), 287.

64. *Commons Journal*, xi, 328–329; Ashurst to Benjamin Jackson, 6 May 1695, Bodl., MS Don c. 169, fol. 109; Ashurst to Increase Mather, 6 July 1696, Bodl., MS Don c. 169, fol. 121.

65. William Cobbett, ed., *The Parliamentary History of England*, 36 vols. (1806–1820), vol. 5, 788–789.

66. "G.B." to John Cary, 14 February 1695/6, BL Add MSS, 5540, fol. 77.

67. Brewer, *Sinews of Power*, ch. 2; Stephen Saunders Webb, "William Blathwayt, Imperial Fixer: Muddling Through to Empire, 1689–1717," *W&MQ* 26, no. 3 (July 1969): 388–394; "A Narrative of Sir William Beeston, 23 June 1694," BL Add MSS, 12430, fols. 4–12.

68. Julian Hoppitt, *A Land of Liberty? England, 1689–1727* (Oxford: Oxford University Press, 2000), 157–159.

69. Charles Davenant to Sir William Trumbull, 7 February 1695/6, BL Add MSS, 72614, fols. 3–4.

70. Simon Clement, "A Letter to a Member of Parliamt concerning a Committee of Trade," 1696, BL Add MSS, 5540, fols. 105–106; HMC, *Buccleuch*, 738. Ian K. Steele, *Politics of Colonial Policy: The Board of Trade in Colonial Administration, 1696–1720* (Oxford: Clarendon Press, 1968) remains the most comprehensive account.

71. Clement, "Letter to a Member of Parliament," fol. 106; Aldermen of Bristol to Yate and Day, 21 December 1695, BL Add MSS, 5540, fol. 87; Charles Davenant, Paper on a Council of Trade, 1695, BL Harleian MSS, 1223, fol. 186.

72. Thomas Day and John Yate to Aldermen of Bristol, 31 December 1695, BL Add MSS, 5540, fol. 92; Gilbert Burnet, *History of his own time*, 2 vols. (1724–1734), vol. 2, 225.

73. Paula Watson, "William Blathwayt," in Basil Henning, *The History of Parliament: The House of Commons, 1660–1690*, 2 vols. (London: Secker and Warburg, 1983); Ian K. Steele, "The Board of Trade, the Quakers, and Resumption of Colonial Charters, 1699–1702," *W&MQ* 23, no. 4 (October 1966): 16–21; Gauci, *Politics of Trade*, 187–191. The original Whig commissioners were Locke, Charles Montagu, Sir Philip Meadows, John Pollexfen, Abraham Hill, and the earls of Tankerville and Bridgewater.

74. William A. Pettigrew, "Free to Enslave: Politics and the Escalation of Britain's Transatlantic Slave Trade, 1688–1714," *W&MQ*, 3rd ser. 64, no. 1 (2007): 3–38.

75. Notes concerning the East India Company, 1693, Clarke of Chipley MSS, DD/SF/13/2/32, fol. 40; Minutes of examinations before Committee of Lords and Commons, 1693, Clarke of Chipley MSS, DD/SF/13/2/32, fol. 45; Henry Horwitz, "The East India Trade, the Politicians, and the Constitution: 1689–1702," *Journal of British Studies* 17, no. 2 (Spring 1978): 1–18.

76. John Cary, "Queries offered to the House of Commons agst the East India Company," 1697, BL Add MSS, 5540, fol. 115; Representation of the Board of Trade to William III, 23 December 1697, BL Add MSS, 46542, fol. 24; Gerald M. MacLean and Nabil Matar, *Britain and the Islamic World, 1558–1713* (Oxford: Oxford University Press, 2011), 24, 29, 55.

77. Philip Lawson, "Tea, Vice and the English State, 1660–1784," in Lawson, *A Taste for Empire and Glory* (Aldershot, UK: Ashgate, 1997), 1–19; K. N. Chaudhuri, *The Trading World of Asia and the English East India Company, 1660–1760* (Cambridge: Cambridge University Press, 1978), 518–523.

78. Sidney Godolphin to Blathwayt, 25 September 1695, Beinecke, OSB MSS 2, box 4, fol. 74; "An Account of the Memoriall delivered to the Lords Commissioners of the Admiralty by the East India Company," 1697, BL Add MSS, 72572, fol. 65.

79. William A. Pettigrew and George W. Van Cleve, "Parting Companies: The Glorious Revolution, Company Power, and Imperial Mercantilism," *Historical Journal* 57, no. 3 (September 2014): 617–638; William Pettigrew, "Constitutional Change in England and the Diffusion of Regulatory Initiative, 1660–1714," *History* 99, no. 338 (December 2014): 853–855.

80. Joyce Appleby, *Economic Thought and Ideology in Seventeenth-Century England* (Princeton: Princeton University Press, 1987), 219–230; William Farrell, "The Silk Interest and the Fiscal-Military State," in Aaron Graham and Patrick Walsh, eds., *The British Fiscal Military States, 1660–1783* (London: Routledge, 2016), 113–120; April Lee Hatfield, "Slavery, Trade, War, and the Purpose of Empire," *W&MQ* 68, no. 3 (July 2011): 405–408.

81. Sugar bakers of Bristol to Day and Yate, 15 January 1695/6, BL Add MSS, 5540, fol. 95; Vote of the House of Commons, 26 February 1698, Clarke of Chipley MSS, DD/SF/13/2/29; *The Irregular and Disorderly State of the Plantation-TRADE*

Discuss'd, and Humbly Offered to the Consideration of the Right Honourable the LORDS and COMMONS in Parliament Assembled (1695).

82. Representation of the Board of Trade, 23 December 1697, BL Add MSS, 46542, fol. 24; John Pollexfen, *Discourse of Trade* (1697), 87; At the council chamber in Whitehall, 10 September 1696, CO 5/1, fol. 70.

83. Dunn and Dunn, *Papers of William Penn*, vol. 3, 512–513; Michael G. Hall, "The House of Lords, Edward Randolph, and the Navigation Act of 1696," *W&MQ* 14, no. 4 (October 1957): 494–515.

84. William Atwood to John Champante, 1698, Rawlinson MSS, A272, fol. 167; William Atwood, *An apology for the East-India Company with an account of some large prerogatives of the crown of England* (1690), 1–2, 34, 37; *CSPC, 1701*, 1122; *Diary of Samuel Sewall*, vol. 2, 45–46.

85. John Cary to Edmund Bohun, 31 January 1695/6, BL Add MSS, 5540, fol. 59; David Harris Sacks, *The Widening Gate: Bristol and the Atlantic Economy, 1450–1700* (Berkeley: University of California Press, 1991), 339–343.

86. John Cary, *The Irregular and Disorderly State of the Plantation-Trade Discuss'd* (1695), 1.

87. John Cary, *An answer to Mr. Molyneux* (1698), 74–75, 149–150.

88. Dunn and Dunn, *Papers of William Penn*, vol. 3, 418, 479–481, 494; Davenant, "On the Plantation Trade," 259–261. For the parallel ideas that emerged on the Council of Virginia, see "An American," *Essay upon the government of the English Plantations* (1701), 55–56, 68–70.

89. "Mr Nelson's letter to the Duke of Shrewsbury about the North part of America," 1695, BL Add MSS, 47131, fols. 17–21; HMC, *Buccleuch*, 724–727.

90. William Popple to Blathwayt, 11 August 1699, BL Add MSS, 9747, fol. 19; "Answer of the Commissioners of Trade to an order of the Honourable House of Commons," 12 March 1700, BL Add MSS, 46542, fols. 37, 42.

91. Dunn and Dunn, *Papers of William Penn*, vol. 3, 605–606.

92. Edmund Bohun to John Cary, 15 February 1696, BL Add MSS, 5540, fols. 60, 65.

93. "To the King in Council, Petition of the Proprietors and Agents of the Provinces of Carolina, the Bahama Islands, Pennsilvania, East and West Jersey & Conecticott," 5 November 1696, CO 5/1, fol. 73; Hall, "House of Lords," 502–507.

94. Dunn and Dunn, *Papers of William Penn*, vol. 3, 473, 632, 634; Steele, "Board of Trade," 596–619; Alison Gilbert Olson, *Making the Empire Work: London and American Interest Groups, 1690–1790* (Cambridge: Harvard University Press, 1992), 56. For Lawton, see Mark Goldie and Clare Jackson, "Williamite Tyranny and the Whig Jacobites," in Esther Mijers and David Onnekink, eds., *Redefining William III: The impact of the King-Stadtholder in International Context* (Aldershot, UK: Ashgate, 2007), 181–191.

95. Stock, *Proceedings and Debates*, vol. 2, 355–357; Bellomont to the Lords of the Treasury, 8 September 1699, Rawlinson MSS, A272, fols. 62–63; *Diary of Samuel Sewall*, vol. 2, 33; Stanwood, *Empire Reformed*, 187–194.

96. "Some of the Cheif Grievances of the present constitution of Virginia, with an Essay towards the Remedies thereof," Bodl., MS Locke, e.9, fols. 22, 25.

97. Daniel Coxe to William III, 21 January 1696/7, CO 5/1, fol. 93; Dunn and Dunn, *Papers of William Penn*, vol. 3, 469–470.

98. "Cheif Grievances," Bodl., MS Locke, e.9, fol. 25. For recent thought on the authorship of the text, see Jack Turner, "John Locke, Christian Mission, and Colonial America," *Modern Intellectual History* 8, no. 2 (August 2011): 267–297.

99. Stock, *Proceedings and Debates*, vol. 2, 265–266; John Poyntz, *The Present Prospect of the Famous and Fertile Island of Tobago* (1695); Dunn and Dunn, *Papers of William Penn*, vol. 3, 492.

100. "Cheif Grievances," fols. 12–14, 19.

101. "Answers of the Commissioners of Trade and Plantations . . . to the Commons," 1699, Bodl., MS Locke, c. 30, fols. 122–123; Oliver Finnegan, "Piracy in the Age of Projects, 1688–1707," PhD diss., University of Cambridge, 2019, 147–154.

102. "An American," *Essay upon the government*, 23–24; Jonathan Eacott, "Making an Imperial Compromise: The Calico Acts, the Atlantic Colonies, and the Structure of the British Empire," *W&MQ* 69, no. 4 (2012): 731–762.

103. "On Trade," Bodl., MS Locke, c. 30, fols. 18–19.

104. John Cary, *Essay on the State of England in relation to its Trade* (1695), 59–61, 66–68.

105. Swingen, *Competing Visions*, 140–171; Pettigrew, "Free to Enslave"; Pettigrew, *Freedom's Debt*, 31–45.

106. Holly Brewer, "Slavery, Sovereignty, and 'Inheritable Blood': Reconsidering John Locke and the Origins of American Slavery," *American Historical Review* 122, no. 4 (October 2017): 1070–1076; Marion Tinling, ed., *The Correspondence of the Three William Byrds of Westover, Virginia, 1684–1776*, 2 vols. (Charlottesville: Virginia Historical Society, 1977), vol. 1, 188.

107. "Cheif Grievances," fol. 32; Turner, "John Locke," 267–274.

108. Bradburn, "Visible Fist," 361–370.

109. Brewster, *Essays*, 91; Poyntz; *Present Prospect*, 42.

110. *Diary of Samuel Sewall*, vol. 2, 16.

111. Steve Pincus, Tiraana Bains, and A. Zuercher Reichardt, "Thinking the Empire Whole," *History Australia* 16, no. 4 (December 2019): 610–637.

112. Brendan Simms, *Three Victories and a Defeat* (London: Penguin, 2007), ch. 3; Tony Claydon, *Europe and the Making of England, 1660–1760* (Cambridge: Cambridge University Press, 2007), 192–219.

113. John Dennis, *Liberty Asserted: A Tragedy* (1703), epistle dedicatory, 54–55.

114. Lords of Trade to William III, 24 December 1697, CO 5/1, fol. 109.

115. William Blathwayt to George Stepney, 8/18 August 1701, Beinecke, OSB MSS 2, box 2, fol. 33; Blathwayt to Stepney, 9 September 1701, Beinecke, OSB MSS 2, box 2, fol. 33; Pincus, "Addison's Empire," 104–115.

116. "Some of the Cheif Grievances of the present constitution of Virginia, with an Essay towards the Remedies thereof," Bodl., MS Locke, e.9, fol. 1.

117. James Whiston, *A Discourse of the Decay of Trade* (1693), 11.

118. Board of Trade to Archbishop of Canterbury, 25 October 1700, Lambeth Palace Library, Fulham Papers, vol. 8, fols. 3–4; *CSPC, 1696–1697,* 286; E. S. De Beer, ed., *Correspondence of John Locke,* 8 vols. (Oxford: Oxford University Press, 1976), vol. 7, 63–64.

119. Craig Rose, "Providence, Protestant Union and Godly Reformation in the 1690s," *Transactions of the Royal Historical Society* 3 (1993): 151–169.

120. *Account of the Society for Propagating the Gospel in Foreign Parts* (1706), 69, 72; Church of St. Gall to SPG, 11 May 1702, USPG MSS, A1, fol. 13; Synod of the Grisons to SPG, 6 June 1702, USPG MSS, A1, fol. 41; Evan Haefeli and Owen Stanwood, "Jesuits, Huguenots, and the Apocalypse: The Origins of America's First French Book," *Proceedings of the American Antiquarian Society* 116, no. 1 (2006): 59–119, at 73–74, 98.

121. "Answers of the Commissioners of Trade and Plantations, c. 1699," Bodl., Locke MS C. 30, fol. 119; "Dr Coxe's Paper," 18 September 1699, Lambeth Palace Library, Fulham Papers, vol. 2, fols. 16–17; *CSP, 1699,* 184; William O'Reilly, "Working for the Crown: German Migrants and Britain's Commercial Success in the Early Eighteenth-Century American Colonies," *Journal of Modern European History* 15, no. 1 (January 2017): 130–152; Haefeli and Stanwood, "Jesuits, Huguenots," 98.

122. Jeremy Gregory, "The Later Stuart Church and America," in Grant Tapsell, ed., *The Later Stuart Church, 1660–1714* (Manchester: Manchester University Press, 2012), 238; William Kellaway, *The New England Company, 1649–1776* (London: Longmans, Green, 1961), 192.

123. Dunn and Dunn, *Papers of William Penn,* vol. 3, 492.

124. Minutes of Board meeting, 7 March 1699/1700, Lambeth Palace Library, Fulham Papers, vol. 11, fols. 103–104; Brewster, *Essays,* 91–92; Owen Stanwood, "Between Eden and Empire: Huguenot Refugees and the Promise of New Worlds," *American Historical Review* 118, no. 5 (December 2013): 1319–1344.

125. De Beer, *Locke Correspondence,* vol. 7, 225–226.

126. Gilbert Burnet, *Of the propagation of the gospel in foreign parts* (1704), 20.

Chapter 9. The Colonies and the Meaning of "Britain"

1. Nicholas Canny, ed., *The Oxford History of the British Empire,* vol. 1: *The Origins of Empire* (Oxford: Oxford University Press, 1998), 2.

2. James Howell, edition of Selden, *Mare Clausum* (1663), preface; Edward Chamberlayne, *The Fourth Part of the Present State of England* (1683), preface; *Honest, Loyal Merchant,* 4.

3. For the most comprehensive modern account, see Douglas Watt, *The Price of Scotland: Darien, Union and the Wealth of Nations* (Edinburgh: Luath Press, 2007).

4. See especially Allan MacInnes, *Union and Empire: The Making of the United Kingdom in 1707* (Cambridge: Cambridge University Press, 2007); David Armitage, "Making the Empire British: Scotland in the Atlantic World, 1542–1707," *Past and Present* 155, no. 1 (May 1997): 34–63; Jane Ohlmeyer, "Seventeenth-Century Ireland and the New British and Atlantic Histories," *American Historical Review* 104, no. 2 (April 1999): 446–462; L. M. Cullen, "Merchant Communities Overseas: The Navigation Acts and Irish and Scottish Responses," in Louis Cullen and T. C. Smout, eds., *Comparative Aspects of Scottish and Irish Social History, 1600–1900* (Edinburgh: John Donald, 1977), 165–176.

5. John Prebble, *The Darien Disaster: A Scots Colony in the New World, 1698–1700* (London: Penguin, 1968).

6. William O'Reilly, "Ireland in the Atlantic World: Migration and Cultural Transfer," in Jane Ohlmeyer, ed., *The Cambridge History of Ireland, vol. 2: 1550–1730* (Cambridge: Cambridge University Press, 2016), 393–394.

7. See especially David Beers Quinn, *The Elizabethans and the Irish* (Ithaca: Cornell University Press, 1966), 22–28; Nicholas Canny, "The Ideology of English Colonization: From Ireland to America," *W&MQ* 30, no. 4 (October 1973); K. R. Andrews, N. P. Canny, and P. E. H. Hair, *The Westward Enterprise: English Activities in Ireland, the Atlantic and America, 1480–1650* (Liverpool: Liverpool University Press, 1978); Andrew Hadfield, "Irish Colonies and America," in Robert Applebaum and John Wood Sweet, eds., *Envisioning an English Empire: Jamestown and the Making of the North Atlantic World* (Philadelphia: Pennsylvania University Press, 2005), 172–191.

8. Mary Maples Dunn and Richard S. Dunn, eds., *The Papers of William Penn*, 5 vols. (Philadelphia: University of Pennsylvania Press, 1981–1986), vol. 2, 46, 513, vol. 3, 205, 292, 337; Thomas Povey to Daniel Searle, 20 October 1659, BL Add MSS, 11411, fol. 93; Louise A. Breen, "Praying with the Enemy: Daniel Gookin, King Philip's War and the Dangers of Intercultural Mediatorship," in Martin Daunton and Rick Halpern, eds., *Empire and Others: British Encounters with Indigenous Peoples, 1600–1850* (Philadelphia: Pennsylvania University Press, 1999), 101–103; Nicholas Canny, "The Irish Background to Penn's Experiment," in R. S. Dunn and M. M. Dunn, eds., *The World of William Penn* (Philadelphia: Pennsylvania University Press, 1986), 139–156.

9. For trenchant critiques of the "Ireland first" model, see Alison Games, *The Web of Empire: English Cosmopolitans in an Age of Expansion, 1560–1660* (Oxford: Oxford University Press, 2008), 123–124; Audrey Horning, *Ireland in the Virginian Sea: Colonialism in the British Atlantic* (Chapel Hill: University of North Carolina Press, 2013).

10. Toby Barnard, *Improving Ireland? Projectors, Prophets, and Profiteers, 1641–1786* (Dublin: Four Courts Press, 2008), 41–85.

11. Report of the Lords of Trade to the King, 28 May 1679, BL Add MSS, 12429, fol. 90; Journal of the Lords of Trade, 16 September 1680, CO 391/3, fol. 99; Journal of the Lords of Trade, 14 October 1680, CO 391/3, fols. 108–109.

12. "Conferences with Sir Charles Wheeler, 7 and 10 December 1672," CO, 153/1/53; Anchitel Grey, *Debates of the House of Commons, from the year 1667 to the year 1694*, 10 vols. (London, 1763), vol. 1, 275–276.

13. Thomas Lynch to earl of Arlington, 27 December 1672, BL Add MSS, 11410, fol. 301; Jonathan Atkins to Joseph Williamson, 20 April 1675, CO 1/34/57.

14. Andrew Fletcher, *An account of a conversation concerning a right regulation of government for the common good of mankind* (1704), 46–47.

15. John Cary, Michael Pope, William Andrews, George Mason to Thomas Day, 16 December 1695, BL Add MSS, 5540, fol. 84; Aldermen of Bristol to Yate and Day, 21 December 1695, BL Add MSS, 5540, fol. 87.

16. Meeting of English commissioners, 16 February 1667, All Souls MSS, 229, fol. 81.

17. Journal of Sir Edward Dering, BL Add MSS, 22467, fol. 29; Thomas M. Truxes, *Irish-American Trade, 1660–1783* (Cambridge: Cambridge University Press, 1987), 24–25.

18. John Bergin, "Irish Catholics in Eighteenth-Century London and Their Networks," *Eighteenth-Century Life* 39, no. 1 (March 2015): 66–102.

19. John Cary and Edward Hackett to Sir Thomas Day, 1696; John Cary, Michael Pope, William Andrews, and George Mason to Day, 16 December 1695, both BL Add MSS, 5540, fols. 78, 84.

20. T. M. Devine, *Scotland's Empire, 1660–1815* (London: Penguin, 2003), ch. 1.

21. At the court at Hampton Court, August 1689, CO 5/1113, fol. 100; Dunn and Dunn, *Papers of William Penn*, vol. 3, 455; William Hamilton to earl of Arran, 8 July 1682, NRS, Hamilton papers, GD 406/1/3098; David Dobson, *Scottish Emigration to Colonial America, 1607–1785* (Athens: University of Georgia Press, 2004), 70.

22. Stock, *Proceedings and Debates*, vol. 1, 448.

23. William Seton, *A Short Speech Prepared to be Spoken by a Worthy Member in Parliament, concerning the Present State of the Nation* (1700), 5.

24. MacInnes, *Union and Empire*, 207–226; Esther Mijers, "Scotland, the Dutch Republic and the Union: Commerce and Cosmopolitanism," in Allan MacInnes and Douglas J. Hamilton, eds., *Jacobitism, Enlightenment, and Empire, 1680–1820* (London: Pickering and Chatto, 2014), 93–109.

25. Downing to Clarendon, 29 December/8 January 1664/5, Bodl., Clarendon MSS, 108, fols. 168–172; Sir James Couper, Petition to the King, NRS, Melville papers, GD 26/7, fol. 275; Devine, *Scotland's Empire*, 10–13.

26. John Clerk to James Galloway, 15 June 1700, NRS, GD 18/ 5218, fol. 28; James Foulis to Alexander Campbell, 22 June 1682, NRS, RH 15/14/37i.

27. *Commons Journal*, vol. 8, 504; George Clerk to Alexander Campbell, 27 May 1682, NRS, RH 15/14/37i; Dunn and Dunn, *Papers of William Penn*, vol. 3, 497; Mijers, "Scotland, the Dutch Republic, and the Union," 99–103.

28. Thomas Lynch to Archbishop Sheldon, 29 November 1671, BL Add MSS, 11410, fol. 199; Stuart M. Nisbet, "Clearing the Smokescreen of Early Scottish Mercantile Identity: From Leeward Sugar Plantations to the Scottish Country Estates

c. 1680–1730," in MacInnes and Hamilton, *Jacobitism, Enlightenment, and Empire*, 142–152; Sarah Barber, " 'Let Him Be an Englishman': Irish and Scottish Clergy in the Caribbean Church of England, 1610–1720," in MacInnes and Hamilton, *Jacobitism, Enlightenment, and Empire*, 99–108.

29. John Houghton, *Collection of Letters for the improvement of husbandry and trade*, 2 vols. (1681–1683), vol. 1, 38.

30. John Stewart to the duke of Hamilton, 1 February 1701/2, NRS, GD 406/11870, fols. 12, 24–25.

31. *Register of the Privy Council of Scotland*, vol. 7, 45, 97, 133; Plan for Scottish settlement in St Vincent, NRS, GD 103/2/4, fol. 42.

32. Stock, *Proceedings and Debates*, vol. 1, 449.

33. *Register of the Privy Council of Scotland*, vol. 7, 664–665, 671.

34. George Scot, *Model of the Government of the Province of East New Jersey* (1682), preface; MacInnes, *Union and Empire*, 205–206.

35. George Pratt Insh, *Scottish Colonial Schemes, 1620–1686* (Glasgow, 1922), 113–115, 162–207.

36. Lynch, "Accompt of the English Sugar Plantations," PRO 30/24/49, fol. 629; "Worsley's Discourse of the Privateers," BL Add MSS, 11410, fol. 328.

37. *Boyle Correspondence*, vol. 5, 309, 311–312.

38. Lyttleton, *Groans of the Plantations*, 32.

39. Edmund Bohun to John Cary, 18 January 1695/6, 15 February 1695/6, BL Add MSS, 5540, fols. 59–60, 65.

40. MacInnes, *Union and Empire*, 158–159.

41. Samuel Weller Singer, ed., *Correspondence of Henry Hyde, earl of Clarendon and of his brother, Laurence Hyde, earl of Rochester*, 2 vols. (London, 1828), vol. 1, 366.

42. Sir Robert Southwell to John Percival, 17 March 1683, BL Add MSS, 47022, fol. 108; Meeting of English commissioners, 16 February 1667, All Souls MSS, 229, fol. 80; Council of Trade to Charles II, n.d. [1661], Coventry MSS, 103, fol. 58.

43. Council of Trade to Charles II, n.d., 1661, CO 389/1, fol. 89; Response of Scots Commissioners, 25 March 1668, All Souls MSS, 229, fol. 90; "Concerning an union betwixt England & Scotland," 1670, BL Egerton, 3340, fols. 11–12; Robbins, *Milward Diary*, 127.

44. John Houghton, *Collection of Letters*, vol. 1, 39, 42–44; William Petty, "Of Uniting England and Ireland by a Common Parliament," and "An Experiment in Order to an Union of England, Ireland and Scotland," both in Marquis of Lansdowne, ed., *The Petty Papers*, 2 vols. (London: Reprints of Economic Classics, 1997), vol. 1, 13–14.

45. Commissioners of Trade to the Privy Council, 22 November 1661, PC 2/55, fols. 232–233.

46. Earl of Lauderdale to Marquis of Tweeddale, 9 November 1667, Edinburgh, NLS, Yester Papers, MS 7024, fol. 61.

47. Nicholas Plunkett, "A Light to the Blind," Bodl., Carte MSS 229, fols. 48–53, 56–57; Patrick Kelly, ed., "The Improvement of Ireland," *Analecta Hibernica* 35 (1992): 61.

48. Tweeddale to Yester, 5 January 1688/9, NLS, MS 7025, fol. 77; Alasdair Raffe, *Scotland in Revolution, 1685–1690* (Edinburgh: Edinburgh University Press, 2018), ch. 6.

49. Anonymous correspondent to Adam Colclough, 19 October 1692, Staffordshire CRO, D641/2/K/2/4, John Oldmixon, *Memoirs of Ireland from the Restoration to the present times* (London, 1716), 251; James Livesey, *Civil Society and Empire: Ireland and Scotland in the Eighteenth-Century Atlantic World* (New Haven: Yale University Press, 2009), 94–98.

50. Donald Akenson, *If the Irish Ran the World: Montserrat, 1630–1730* (Montreal: McGill-Queen's University Press, 1997), 137–151.

51. Thomas Bartlett, "This Famous Island Set in a Virginian Sea": Ireland in the British Empire, 1690–1801," in P. J. Marshall, ed., *Oxford History of the British Empire*, vol. 2 (Oxford: Oxford University Press, 1998), 255, 257.

52. John Cary, *A discourse concerning the trade of Ireland and Scotland, as they stand in competition with the trade of England* (1695); Edward Clarke, "On the Wool Trade," 1698, Clarke of Chipley MSS, DD/SF/13/2/32, fol. 65; Political working papers, Irish wool trade, n.d., Clarke of Chipley MSS, DD/SF/13/2/29.

53. "Answers of the Commissioners of Trade and Plantations . . . to the House of Commons," n.d. [1699], Bodl., MS Locke, c. 30, fol. 119; "Votes of the House of Commons," Clarke of Chipley MSS, DD/SF/13/2/29; D.W. Hayton, *Ruling Ireland, 1685–1742: Politics, Politicians and Parties* (Woodbridge, UK: Boydell & Brewer, 2004), 237–275.

54. Jacqueline Hill, "Ireland Without Union: Molyneux and His Legacy," in John Robertson, ed., *A Union for Empire: Political Thought and the British Union of 1707* (Cambridge: Cambridge University Press, 1996), 271–296; Charles Ivar McGrath, *The Making of the Eighteenth Century Irish Constitution, 1692–1714* (Dublin: Four Courts Press, 2000); Charles C. Ludington, "From Ancient Constitution to British Empire: William Atwood and the Imperial Crown of England," in Jane Ohlmeyer, ed., *Political Thought in Seventeenth-Century Ireland: Kingdom or Colony* (Cambridge: Cambridge University Press, 2000), 244–270.

55. William Molyneux, *The case of Ireland's being bound by Acts of Parliament in England, Stated* (1698), 103–105, 149–150, 173–174.

56. Sir Richard Cox, *Some thoughts on the bill . . . for prohibiting the exportation of the woollen manufactures of Ireland to foreign parts* (1698), 6, 8–9, 15.

57. Ludington, "From Ancient Constitution," 255–258; Clarke, "On the Wool Trade," fol. 65; William Atwood, *The history and reasons of the dependency of Ireland upon the imperial crown of the kingdom of England* (1698), 52–53, 197–198.

58. John Cary, *An answer to Mr. Molyneux* (1698), 13, 71–73, 108, 142–143; John Cary, *A vindication of the Parliament of England, in answer to a book written by William Molyneux* (1698), 95–96.

59. Simon Clement, *The interest of England, as it stands, with relation to the trade of Ireland* (1698), 23.

60. Molyneux, *The case of Ireland's being bound*, 56.

61. Jeffrey Stephen, *Defending the Revolution: The Church of Scotland, 1689–1716* (Farnham, UK: Ashgate, 2013), 83–92; Devine, *Scotland's Empire*, 28–41.

62. David Armitage, "The Scottish Vision of Empire: Intellectual Origins of the Darien Venture," in Robertson, *Union for Empire*, 97–101.

63. Stock, *Proceedings and Debates*, vol. 2, 133–134, 406; Aldermen of Bristol to Day and Yate, 4 January 1695/6, BL Add MSS, 5540, fol. 94.

64. *Commons Journal*, vol. 11, 401–406; Devine, *Scotland's Empire*, 41–42.

65. Annandale to Tweeddale, 9 December 1695, NLS, MS 7019, fols. 153–154; Stock, *Proceedings and Debates*, vol. 2, 400–401.

66. *The Darien Papers: Being a selection of original letters and official documents* (Edinburgh, 1849), 19–31; Tweeddale to Lord Yester, 28 February 1696, NLS MS 7030, fol. 69.

67. "An Act for preventing Frauds and regulating Abuses in the Plantation Trade, 1695–6," in John Raithby, ed., *Statutes of the Realm*, 9 vols. (London, 1810–1825), vol. 7, 103–107, https://www.british-history.ac.uk/statutes-realm/vol7; MacInnes, *Union and Empire*, 185–186.

68. Gilbert Burnet, *History of his own time*, 2 vols. (1724–1734), vol. 2, 217; Toppan and Goodrick, eds., *Randolph*, vol. 2, 133; Richard Johnson, *Adjustment to Empire: The New England Colonies, 1675–1715* (New Brunswick, NJ: Rutgers University Press, 1981), 225, 227.

69. Thomas Lynch to Sir Robert Moray, 2 March 1671/2, BL Add MSS, 11410, fol. 237; "The Present State of Jamaica," 1677, BL Add MSS, 12429, fols. 77–78; Peter Heylin, *Cosmographie* (1652), 1046.

70. "A Memoriall concerning the settling a colony on the Isthmus of Darien in America," 1697, Bodl., MS Locke c. 30, fols. 127–128; Philo-Caledon, *A Defence of the Scots Settlement at Darien* (1699), 2–4.

71. Directors to "Our General and Council of Suratt," 28 October 1685, BL, IOR, E/3/91, fols. 5–6.

72. William Paterson to the Court of Directors, 15 January 1700, NLS, Adv. MSS 83.7.5, fol. 56; *The Writings of William Paterson* (London, 1858), 158.

73. Philo-Caledon, *Defence of the Scots Settlement*, 6–7; "Memoriall concerning the settling a colony," fol. 127.

74. Company of Scotland, Address to the General Assembly, 4 December 1699, NLS, Adv. MSS 83.7.5, fol. 33; Robert Ferguson, *A Just and modest vindication of the Scots Design for having established a colony at Darien* (1699), 69; Paterson, "Brief View," fols. 51–52; Alexander Shields, *A proper project for Scotland to startle fools and frighten knaves* (1699).

75. "That it is the Interest of England to joyn with the Scots in the Colony of Caledonia," NLS, Dunlop Papers, MS 9255, fols. 218–220.

76. "Memoriall in behalf of the Scotish Company," 1697, NRS, GD 26/13/105, fol. 11; *Scotland's Right to Caledonia (formerly called Darien) and the legality of its settlement* (1700), 33.

77. Ferguson, *Just and modest vindication*, 203; New England Company bills and accounts, London Metropolitan Archives, "Bequests," MS 7948, fols. 9–10.

78. *Diary of Samuel Sewall*, 3 vols., Collections of the Massachusetts Historical Society, 5th ser. (1898), vol. 1, 437, 484–485, 488–490, 496.

79. *Diary of Cotton Mather*, 2 vols. (New York: F. Ungar, 1957), vol. 1, 284, 296.

80. Duke of Hamilton to Tweeddale, 3 June 1699, NLS, MS 7020, fols. 150–152; *A Perfect List of all the Several Persons Residenters in Scotland, Who Have Subscribed as Adventurers in the Joint-Stock of the Company of Scotland (1696)*; T. C. Smout, *Scottish Trade on the Eve of Union, 1660–1707* (Edinburgh: Oliver & Boyd, 1963), 150–151.

81. Joseph McCormick, ed., *State Papers and Letters Addressed to William Carstares* (Edinburgh, 1774), 405–406.

82. "Copy of a Representation relating to the Designes of the Scotch East India Company upon the Isthmus of Darien in America," 10 August 1697, Bodl., MS Locke c. 30, fols. 49–51.

83. Armitage, "Scottish Vision of Empire," 109.

84. [Walter Herries], *A Defence of the Scots abdicating Darien* (1699), 3.

85. "Copy of a Representation," fol. 50; Roderick Mackenzie to Tweeddale, 7 April 1699, NLS, MS 7020, fol. 144.

86. McCormick, *State Papers*, 480–481, 546–547; Christopher Storrs, "Disaster at Darien (1698–1700): The Persistence of Spanish Imperial Power on the Eve of the Demise of the Spanish Habsburgs," *European History Quarterly* 29, no. 1 (January 1999): 5–38.

87. McCormick, *State Papers*, 480–481, 514–515, 516; Seton, *Short Speech*, 8; Journal of Sir John Clerk, July 1699, 22 May 1700, NRS, Clerk of Penicuik papers, GD 18/2092 (2); Devine, *Scotland's Empire*, 46–47.

88. McCormick, *State Papers*, 527, 539; Ferguson, *Just and modest vindication*, 43–44, 196; Sketch of English interventions in Scottish affairs, NRS, GD 26/13/111.

89. McCormick, *State Papers*, 514–515, 516.

90. Hamilton to Sir Francis Scott of Thirlstane, 16 January 1700/1, GD 406/1/4671.

91. Belhaven to Hamilton, November 1700, GD 406/1/11774.

92. McCormick, *State Papers*, 527, 626–627; Commentary on Scottish politics, n.d., NRS, Melville papers, GD 26/13/125; Daniel Szechi, *Britain's Lost Revolution? Jacobite Scotland and French Grand Strategy, 1701–1708* (Manchester: Manchester University Press, 2015), ch. 4.

93. John Cary, *Essay on the State of England in relation to its Trade* (1695), 113.

94. Lord Basil Hamilton to Tweeddale, 11 January 1700, NLS, MS 7021, fol. 5.

95. Dunn and Dunn, *Papers of William Penn*, vol. 3, 605–606.

96. Hamilton to Scott, 16 January 1700/1, NRS, GD 406/1/4671.

97. Commentary on Scottish politics, n.d., NRS, Melville papers, GD 26/13/125; Melville to Seafield, 4 January 1700/1, GD 26/13/114.

98. Hamilton to Scott, 16 January 1700/1, NRS GD 406/1/4671.

99. George Mackenzie, Viscount Tarbat, *Parainesis Pacifica; or, A Perswasive to the Union of Britain* (1702).

100. McCormick, *State Papers*, 584; Armitage, "Intellectual Origins," 115–117.

101. MacInnes, *Union and Empire*, 94.
102. Fletcher, *Account of a conversation*, 46–47; John Robertson, "Empire and Union: Two Concepts of the Early Modern European Political Order," in Robertson, *Union for Empire*, 5, 14, 30–34; MacInnes, *Union and Empire*, 31–39.
103. David Armitage, "The Political Economy of Britain and Ireland after the Glorious Revolution," in Ohlmeyer, *Political Thought*, 241–243.

Conclusion

1. William Cobbett, ed., *The Parliamentary History of England*, 36 vols. (1806–1820), vol. 5, 1258–1259, 1276, 1286; L. F. Stock, ed., *Proceedings and Debates of the British Parliaments Respecting North America*, 5 vols. (Washington, DC, 1924), vol. 2, 358; William Blathwayt to George Stepney, 9 September 1701, Beinecke, OSB MSS/2, box 2, 33.
2. Blathwayt to Stepney, 13 June 1701, Beinecke, OSB MSS/2, box 2, fol. 32; Henry Ashurst to Benjamin Jackson, 27 April 1700, Bodl., MS Don c. 169, fol. 180; Ashurst to Council of Massachusetts, 10 July 1701, Bodl., MS Don c. 169, fol. 192.
3. *Commons Journal* 13 (1699–1702): 746–747, 818.
4. John Oldmixon, *The British Empire in America*, 2 vols. (1708), vol. 1, xxxvii.
5. Eric Hinderaker, "The Four Indian Kings and the Imaginative Construction of the British Empire," *W&MQ*, 3rd ser. 53 (July 1996): 487–526; Eric Hinderaker and Peter C. Mancall, *At the Edge of Empire: The Back Country in British North America* (Baltimore: Johns Hopkins University Press, 2003).
6. "Answer of the Commissioners of Trade," 12 March 1700, BL Add MSS, 46542, fols. 46–47; W. A. Speck, "The International and Imperial Context," in J. P. Greene and J. R. Pole, eds., *Colonial British America: Essays in the New History of the Early Modern Era* (Baltimore: Johns Hopkins University Press, 1984), 388–391.
7. Blathwayt to Stepney, 27 March 1701/2, Beinecke, OSB MSS 2, box 2, fol. 33.
8. Carla Gardina Pestana, *Protestant Empire: Religion and the Making of the British Atlantic World* (Philadelphia: University of Pennsylvania Press, 2009), 159–186.
9. Daniel Baugh, "Great Britain's 'Blue-Water' Policy, 1689–1815," *International History Review* 10, no. 1 (February 1988): 33–58.
10. See especially Daniel Defoe, *A Plan of the English Commerce* (1727), 71.
11. Steve Pincus, Tiraana Bains, and A. Zuercher Reichardt, "Thinking the Empire Whole," *History Australia* 16, no. 4 (December 2019): 616.
12. Kathleen Wilson, "Histories, Empires, Modernities," in Wilson, ed., *A New Imperial History* (Cambridge: Cambridge University Press, 2004), 1–26.
13. Philip D. Morgan, "Encounters Between British and 'Indigenous' Peoples, c. 1500–c. 1800," in Martin Daunton and Rick Halpern, eds., *Empire and Others: British Encounters with Indigenous Peoples, 1600–1850* (Philadelphia: Pennsylvania University Press, 1999), 62.

14. Brent S. Sirota, *The Christian Monitors: The Church of England and the Age of Benevolence, 1680–1730* (New Haven: Yale University Press, 2014), 230–233; H. V. Bowen, *Elites, Enterprise, and the Making of the British Overseas Empire, 1688–1775* (Basingstoke: Macmillan, 1996); S. D. Smith, *Slavery, Family, and Gentry Capitalism in the British Atlantic: The World of the Lascelles, 1648–1834* (Cambridge: Cambridge University Press, 2009), 226–259.

15. Daniel K. Richter, *Before the Revolution: America's Ancient Pasts* (Cambridge: Harvard University Press, 2011), 327–345.

16. Richard Beale Davis, ed., *William Fitzhugh and His Chesapeake World, 1676–1701* (Chapel Hill: University of North Carolina Press, 1963), 269–270.

17. *Diary of Cotton Mather*, 2 vols. (New York: F. Ungar, 1957), vol. 1, 215; *Diary of Samuel Sewall*, 3 vols., Collections of the Massachusetts Historical Society, 5th ser. (1898), vol. 1, 490–491, vol. 2, 65, 72–73; T. H. Breen, "An Empire of Goods: The Anglicisation of Colonial America, 1690–1776," *Journal of British Studies* 25, no. 4 (1986): 467–499.

18. Oldmixon, *British Empire*, vol. 1, iv, 62, 107–109.

19. "An American," *Essay upon the government of the English Plantations* (1701), 73; Lyttleton, *Groans of the Plantations*, 23; Cotton Mather, *The wonders of the invisible world* (1693), preface, 25, 65.

20. Mather, *Wonders of the invisible world*, preface, 25, 65.

21. Oldmixon, *British Empire*, vol. 1, xxxv–xxxvii; Paterson, "Brief View," 37–38.

22. Dalby Thomas, *An Historical Account of the rise and growth of the West-India Collonies* (1690), 2–3.

23. Davenant, *Discourses*, 61, 232–233.

24. Thomas, *Historical Account*, 1–3; Henry Martin, *Considerations upon the East-India Trade* (1701), 115.

25. Steve Pincus, "Rethinking Mercantilism: Political Economy, the British Empire, and the Atlantic World in the Seventeenth and Eighteenth Centuries," *W&MQ* 69, no. 1 (January 2012): 27–28; Defoe, *Plan of the English Commerce*, 348–349.

26. Paterson, "Brief View," fols. 39, 41.

27. Brendan Simms, *Three Victories and a Defeat: The Rise and Fall of the First British Empire* (London: Penguin, 2007), 44–76.

28. Oldmixon, *British Empire*, vol. 1, xxxiv–xxxv.

29. J. H. Elliott, *Empires of the Atlantic World: Britain and Spain in America, 1492–1830* (New Haven: Yale University Press, 2006), 136; Wilson, "Histories, Empires, Modernities," 8; Jack P. Greene, *Peripheries and Center: Constitutional Development in the Extended Polities of the British Empire and the United States, 1607–1788* (Athens: University of Georgia Press, 1986), 23–24.

30. James Muldoon, *Empire and Order: The Concept of Empire, 800–c. 1800* (Basingstoke: Macmillan, 1999), 139; Michael W. Doyle, *Empires* (Ithaca: Cornell University Press, 1986), 11.

31. Linda Colley, *Captives: Britain, Empire, and the World* (London: Jonathan Cape, 2002), 40.

32. George Mackenzie, Viscount Tarbat, *Parainesis Pacifica; or, A Perswasive to the Union of Britain* (1702), 7–8.

ACKNOWLEDGMENTS

IT IS AS MUCH A PLEASURE AS a duty to acknowledge the many debts incurred in the course of writing and researching this book. I am extremely grateful to Yale University Press, especially to my editor, Adina Berk, whose advice and support has been essential in steering the project forward. The vital contribution made by other members of the commissioning, production, and editorial teams, especially Ash Lago and Mary Pasti, has been very deeply appreciated, as has the work of Julie Carlson and Meridith Murray. Particular thanks, too, are owed to the anonymous reviewers selected by the press, whose comments and suggestions have significantly enhanced the quality of the finished product.

I have benefited very considerably from the kindness, support, and time given by academic colleagues. Toby Barnard, Steve Pincus, and Stephen Taylor offered crucial insight and generous enthusiasm as the project got under way. Many of the key ideas emerged during my time in Warwick University's History Department. As scholars and as people, my former colleagues Mark Knights and Peter Marshall have provided enduring inspiration for every aspect of my academic career. The ideas formed through the course of research have been enriched by conversation with other scholars and contemporaries. Grateful thanks go to Mark Williams, Richard Ansell, Leslie Theibert, Naomi Pullin, Bill Bulman, and Patrick McGhee. The writing of the book was vitally dependent on a Mid-Career Fellowship conferred by the British Academy. The postdoctoral fellowship previously awarded by the academy, and generously hosted by Hertford College, Oxford, offered an earlier, equally important, springboard.

More recently, the examples set by my current colleagues have made Cambridge University the perfect environment to bring the project to its completion. In the faculty of History, I am deeply thankful for the unstinting encouragement offered by Alex Walsham and Paul Cavill. Mark Goldie has been an indispensable influence on my career—as on those of so many colleagues—since my time as a student. I owe much to the stimulus created by a vibrant, dynamic community of historians at Fitzwilliam College, ably steered by its fellows, lecturers, and research fellows. In this setting, I am fortunate to have worked alongside Rosemary Horrox, Julia Guarneri, Matt Neal, Jean-Michel Johnston, Ben Wiedemann, Stuart Middleton, and Caitlin Harvey. The History students at Fitzwilliam have inspired me more than perhaps they know, while equal gratitude extends to the cohorts of undergraduates who have opted to take my course "Overseas Expansion and British Identities" and so provided an unwitting sounding board for many of the ideas brought to fruition here.

Other debts are more personal. My interest in the complex history and legacy of the British Empire, and its intertwinement with domestic politics, owes much to superb sixth-form history teaching by Howard Norton. My mother, father, and brother stand out among family members who have given endless encouragement and affection and who have been unfailingly tolerant of the demands engendered by life in academia. Above all, the writing of this book would have been impossible without the love, support, and forbearance of my wife, Tamara, and our son, Tobias. It is dedicated, without hesitation, to the two of them.